A–Z
of the
Catholic Church

by

Luke Connaughton

Kevin Mayhew
Publishers

First published in Great Britain in 1980 by
KEVIN MAYHEW LTD
55 Leigh Road
Leigh-on-Sea, Essex

© Copyright 1980 The Estate of Luke Connaughton

ISBN 0 905725 79 4

Printed and bound by E. T. Heron & Co. Ltd, Essex and London

FOREWORD

Luke Connaughton did not live long enough to see this book published; in fact, he submitted his last contribution (on Pope John Paul II) the very week of his untimely death.

Thus, his *A-Z of the Catholic Church*, on which he laboured so long, becomes his memorial and his final offering to the Church he loved and served so well.

The book reveals much that was Luke—his special interest in the Church's history, his preoccupation with theological orthodoxy, his abiding love of things liturgical—all are here, tributes to his piety, his learning and his affection for the Church.

He will be remembered for many things; for his artistry in wood and stone, for his patience as teacher and friend, for his love as husband and father.

For my part, I am grateful for the privilege and blessings of his friendship and collaboration over many years. Luke's was a great and varied talent matched by an even greater humility. I remember especially his unique contribution to Church music. His hymns, such as 'Love is his word', 'Bread from the earth' and 'This is the bread' have enriched the liturgy throughout the English-speaking world.

The one thing Luke left undone was an acknowledgement of the help he had received in writing this book. It would have included many people and his thanks would have been generous. The names which follow are those known to his beloved wife, Kath, and to his publishers. There are sure to be others of whom we are not aware, and to whom we offer our thanks and apologies.

Father Godfrey Anstruther, O.P., who read and advised on much of the early material.

Hugh McGinlay, who worked on the final draft with Luke and saw the book through the press.

Sister Angela, Canoness of the Lateran of the Holy Sepulchre, who was of special assistance when the book was first proposed. The Lady Abbess, Oulton Abbey, and Dom Anselm Richardson, O.S.B., for allowing the use of the library at Oulton Abbey, and their advice about the Benedictine Order.

The Very Rev. James McGettrick, Chancellor of the Archdiocese of Southwark, and Rev. Thomas Duffy, J.C.D., for their professional help regarding recent changes in Liturgy and Canon Law.

Father Matthew Rigley, O.P., for his insights as Dominican and Theologian.

The Staff of Bishop Bright School, Longton, and especially Father Walter Joret, for assistance and friendship over the years.

Kevin Mayhew
February, 1980

ABBREVIATIONS USED IN THIS BOOK

A.A.S.	Acta Apostolicae Sedis
Ar.	Aramaic
A.S.	Anglo-Saxon
A.V.	Authorised Version
Can.	Canon
C.I.C.	Codex Iuris Canonicis (Code of Canon Law)
C.O.D.	Concise Oxford Dictionary
F.	French
Ger.	German
Gk.	Greek
Heb.	Hebrew
Ir.	Irish
It.	Italian
J.B.	Jerusalem Bible
Lat.	Latin
LXX	Septuagint Version of O.T.
MS.	Manuscript
Med. Lat.	Mediaeval Latin
N.T.	New Testament
O.D.	Old Dutch
O.E.	Old English
O.T.	Old Testament
R.S.V.	Revised Standard Version

* beside a word or phrase refers the reader to a separate entry on this item.

Abba

(Syriac for Father.) From contemporary writings, it appears to have been a familiar form of address used by children. In the N.T., it occurs only with the translation (Mk.14:36, Rom.8:15, Gal.4:6), so that the pleonastic formula *Abba, Father,* passed into Christian prayers.

Abbé

(F. Originally the term was identical with *Abbot*). The Concordat* of 1516 authorised Francis I of France to appoint secular* priests as abbots *in commendam**, and the word was gradually applied to any member of the secular clergy. *Monsieur l'Abbé*, however, is now being replaced by *Père*.

Abbess

The superior of certain communities of nuns of the Benedictine rule, and of some Orders of Canonesses*. The earliest known use of the title (*abbatissa*) is in a Latin inscription of 514 in Rome. Certain mediaeval abbesses exercised wide powers e.g., the Abbess of Conversano, on her election, sat mitred to receive the homage of the local clergy. Innocent III* found it necessary to restrain the Abbesses of Palentia and Burgos from hearing the confessions of their nuns, while in England, abbesses would be present at Synods, as St. Hilda at Whitby* in 664. The Council of Trent cancelled most of the abbesses' prerogatives, appointing the local ordinary as general overseer. Nowadays, the abbess may not pass outside the enclosure* or allow her nuns to do so without the Bishop's permission; and every five years he conducts a visitation of the abbey.

Abbot

(Syriac *abba*—father.) Superior of one of the larger houses of the Benedictine group of Orders, and of some Orders of Canons Regular*. In the Rule of St. Benedict, the Abbot is to be the father of his monks. An Abbot Primate presides over the whole Order and there is an Abbot President for each congregation*. Elected normally for life by his community, the Abbot receives a solemn blessing (Can.625 of C.I.C.), regarded as a sacramental and bestowed as of right by the diocesan bishop. An *abbas regiminis* has the government of the monastery in his hands and is exempt from episcopal jurisdiction. A *titular abbot* has the title of an abbey no longer in existence (e.g., there is an Abbot of Westminster, usually a retired Abbot of Ampleforth). He exercises none of the functions of an abbot, while an *abbas nullius* (sc. *diocesis*) has full abbatical authority, including the power of orders. Since the early Middle Ages, abbots have used mitre, crozier and ring and, from the 8th Council of Toledo in 653, Abbots Primate and Abbots President have attended Councils of the Church.

Aberdeen, the Use of

A variant of the Sarum* Use, prevalent in the Diocese of Aberdeen and other Scottish dioceses until the Reformation.

Ablution

The ceremony of washing the chalice after the communion at Mass.

Absolution

(Lat. *absolvo*, I set free.) The canonical, sacramental remitting of sin by the Church's minister (in priest's orders at least); for which is required, in a conscious penitent, a clear sign of sorrow and of a firm purpose of amendment of life, and usually the oral confession of sin and readiness to accept the penance proposed by the confessor. The absolution is the only absolutely essential external of the Sacrament of Reconciliation.

Absolutions

After the funeral Mass, the Absolutions take place, with incense and holy water, round the body which is lying before the altar. These intercessions of the Christian community on behalf of the deceased person or persons have, in their new form, much more a cast of confident hope, and dwell less than the old form on the dread of judgement.

Abstinence

(Lat. *abstineo*, I refrain) sometimes confused with fasting, abstinence (from meat) has long been used by the Church as a penance and as a bodily mortification for spiritual health, e.g. total abstinence from meat is part of the Carthusian* way of life, and the faithful were formerly forbidden meat on every Friday of the year as well as on many other days. Now the only days of mandatory abstinence are Ash Wednesday and Good Friday.

Accident

The Scholastic philosophers and other followers of Aristotle used the word to designate any relationship of a contingent (i.e. non-essential) character between an attribute and the subject in which it inheres: thus redness, roundness, sweetness, etc, are *accidents*. 'Accident' is one of the five 'predicables', together with genus, difference, species, property. More recent theories are that what we call accidents are forms of motion or of energy; while Descartes denied all distinction between substance and accident. Catholic thinkers concerned themselves much with the problem of accidents in their philosophising over the Real Presence* and the operation whereby the accidents of bread persisted after their original subject of inherence had departed. This separability of accidents from substance, they maintained, while not supported by positive arguments from unaided reason, was not found by that same reason to be contradictory.
See also Transubstantiation.

Accidie or Acedia

(Gk. ακηδεια, sloth, carelessness, torpor.) In its theological dimension, this deadly* sin is spiritual sloth, the regret at the trouble involved in the gift of faith.

Acolyte

Originally, the title of 'cleric' in the highest of the Minor Orders. His duties, consisting of preparing the wine and water for Mass, lighting the altar candles and carrying candles in procession, are now performed by the ordinary faithful or by altar servers.*

Acta Apostolicae Sedis

(Lat., Acts of the Apostolic See.) Printed almost entirely in Latin, the publication carries official documents of the Vatican: decrees, decisions, announcements of various kinds, pronouncements of Roman Congregations, Tribunals and Commissions, a diary of the Roman Curia, and notices of ecclesiastical appointments and honours. The promulgation of Papal legislation dates officially from its appearance in the A.A.S.

Acta Sanctorum

See Bollandists

Active Life

By St. Gregory the Great, the active life is defined in these terms: 'To feed the hungry, to teach the ignorant, to correct the erring, to recall our neighbour to the path of humility when he becomes proud, to care for the sick, to dispense to all that which they need, to provide for those entrusted to our care.' As regards the active religious Orders and congregations, although the contemplation of the Divine Perfections is still held, with Aristotle, to be the 'noblest occupation of the mind of man', there is, in modern theology, very little of the traditional assumption of the superiority of the life of contemplation over that of activity (St. Thomas in fact teaches that contemplation itself can be perfect only when it overflows into good works). The Second Vatican* Council, in its Decree on the Appropriate Renewal of the Religious Life, says, '. . . by divine plan, a wonderful variety of religious communities has grown up. This variety has contributed mightily towards making the Church experienced in every good deed (cf. II Tim.3:17) . . . whatever the diversity of their spiritual endowments, all who are called by God to practise the evangelical counsels* and who do so faithfully, devote themselves in a special way to the Lord . . . a life consecrated by the profession of the Counsels is of surpassing value. Such a life has a necessary role to play in the circumstances of the present age.' (*Perfectae Caritatis* Art.1.) Speaking specifically of the active orders, the Decree continues, quoting St. Paul on the variety of gifts under the same Spirit (I Cor.12:4) '. . . in such communities, the very nature of the religious life requires apostolic action and services' and, to remind the active religious of their need for the deepest prayer, it adds, '... the entire religious life of the members of these communities should be penetrated with an apostolic spirit, as their apostolic activity should be animated with a religious spirit. Therefore, in order that the members may above all respond to their vocation of following Christ and may serve Christ Himself in his members, their apostolic activity should spring from an intimate union with him.' (Art.8.)

Acts of Paul

Apocryphal book written in the second half of the 2nd cent. It mentions the sign of the cross and prayers for the dead as current practice, and to some degree opens the ministry of the church to women, but it almost goes so far as to make virginity necessary for salvation.
See Apocrypha.

Acts of Pilate

An apocryphal 4th cent. compilation giving an account of the trial, death and resurrection of Our Lord, which is sometimes found with another work, the *Descent of Christ into Hades*, attached to it, the two together being known from the 13th cent. on as the *Gospel of Nicodemus*. This second section, the *Descent*, purporting to have as its authors Carinus and Leucius, sons of Simeon (of the infancy of Christ, Lk.2:25ff), gives detailed descriptions of the Lord's sojourn among the imprisoned souls, basing itself chiefly on 1 Pet.3:19; it appears with the *Acts* from the 5th cent. onward. There were circulated in the early 4th cent. (under Maximin) spurious accounts of Jesus' trial before Pilate, and it is probable that the Acts of Pilate was composed to counter this anti-Christian propaganda; it leans heavily on the four Gospels, evidently seeking to supplement them with fresh grounds for belief in the Resurrection.
See Apocrypha.

Acts of the Apostles

The second work of Luke the Evangelist (Acts 1:1), usually placed, in editions of the N.T., immediately after the Gospel of John. Its content is the narrative of the Church's growth, from the Ascension of Our Lord to the first Roman imprisonment of Paul, who figures very prominently in the book, and was accompanied in some of his ministry and journeying by the author. The volume can be described as demonstrating the way in which was fulfilled the prophetic command in 1:8. In recent years, there has been a steadily increasing respect for the author's accuracy as a historical writer.

Ad Clerum

(Lat., to the clergy.) The phrase used as a substantive for the occasional letter a bishop will circulate in print to the clergy of his diocese; distinct from a *Pastoral*, which is addressed to the whole diocese.

Ad Limina (Apostolorum)

(Lat., to the dwelling of the Apostles.) A visit must be paid every five years by all bishops-in-ordinary* and archbishops, to the Pope, the representative of the Apostles Peter and Paul. The visitor carries with him to Rome a detailed account of all the affairs of his diocese.

Adoration

The offering of such worship as is suited to God only, in recognition of his supreme perfection, his omnipotence, our total dependence on him, etc. The word sometimes follows its Latin original and carries what might seem a scandalous hint of idolatry: liturgical books are to be found speaking of the *Adoration of the Cross* on Good Fridays, whereas this and the *adoratio* offered to a newly-elected Pope are, in fact, forms of reverence, respect, devotion, homage, etc and should be so translated.
See Latria, Dulia, Hyperdulia.

Advent

The season of roughly four weeks preceding and preparing for Christmas. The Church's year begins on the First Sunday of Advent, which is the first day of this season. It is a penitential season, in which the *Gloria* is not said or sung at Mass, purple vestments are worn, flowers are not used on the altar and the organ is silent, unless as necessary to sustain the singing. Sometimes it was known as 'Little Lent'.

Ages of Faith
A description sometimes used of the Middle Ages, as a period during which a civilisation emerged and flourished which based itself explicitly on Christian principles, calling itself 'Christendom' and producing a system of law, philosophy, art and thought which reached its climax in the 13th cent.
See Dark Ages, Friars

Agnus Dei
i) (Lat., Lamb of God.) The triple invocation at Mass, shortly before the Communion, beginning with these words (cf. John 1:29).
ii) A small disc of wax stamped with a figure of a lamb representing Christ as Victim, blessed by the Pope in Holy Week of the first and seventh years of his pontificate and often worn round the neck.
iii) An image (painted, carved, embroidered, etc) of a lamb, sometimes haloed, *passant* or *couchant*, and holding a banner or pennon with a red cross: symbol of the Victory of the Lamb (Rev.14).

Alb
(Lat. *tunica alba,* white tunic.) The white linen ankle-length vestment, caught at the waist with the rope-like girdle* and worn under the chasuble*, dalmatic or cope*; probably derived from the Roman *tunica* worn under the toga. Immediately derived from the white garment given in Baptism, and originally worn until *Dominica in Albis*.

Albigensians
An heretical group named after the city of Albi in the département of Tarn, France, flourishing in the 12th and 13th cents; starting from Manichaeistic* dualism, they despised the flesh as evil, revived the Docetists* teaching that Christ had no true human body (thereby destroying belief in the Resurrection), discarded the Sacraments as dealing with the body, and objected particularly to Matrimony, which respects the body and reproduction. Their philosophy led naturally to suicide as the most 'perfect' action and was thus opposed not only to the Church's teachings but to the very idea of human society. Condemned by several Councils, the movement spread among the ignorant, partly because of the contrast between the austere lives of their own leaders and the laxity of many of the clergy. Innocent III sent the Cistercians* and then St. Dominic* to convert them by preaching, but when this effort failed, he declared a Crusade against them. This campaign, led by Simon de Montfort, involved much cruelty and was concluded in 1218. Continued fighting until 1229 was of a political nature, the issue then being the incorporation of Languedoc into the kingdom of France. One result of this particular heretical movement seems to have been the setting up of the Inquisition* to examine heresy. Until 1229, heresy had been dealt with by the secular power at the prompting of the bishops, but in that year, Pope Gregory IX instituted the Inquisition for the prevention and punishment of heresy.

Alcantara, Knights of
A military order* of Castile, founded in the 12th cent. to combat the Moors. Having grown wealthy and discredited itself, the Order was put down by Pope Alexander VI in 1494. Since the 16th cent. it has been an honorary lay order of Spain.

Alexander VI, Pope (1431–1503)
Rodrigo Borja, a Spaniard by birth, a generous patron of the arts and a man of unscrupulously immoral and ambitious life, is held to be a symbol of all that was undesirable in the Renaissance papacy. Created cardinal by his uncle, Pope Callistus III, in 1456, and appointed Chancellor of the Roman Church, he exercised his considerable talent for politics and organisation during that and the next two pontificates, and the election of Sixtus IV was largely of his contriving. At the time of his own election, to which he bribed his way in 1492, he had not only nephews to provide for, but four children of his own (including swaggering *condottiere* Cesare and the much-married, much-maligned Lucrezia). It was Alexander who divided up the New World between Spain and Portugal (1493–4); he pursued and had executed the Florentine reformer, Savonarola, in 1498 and declared a Jubilee

for the year 1500 and a crusade in 1499–1500. As the official Vatican list of Popes has it, he should be Alexander V, his predecessor of the title (1409–10) being an antipope.

Alma Redemptoris Mater

(Lat., Gracious Mother of the Saviour) The Antiphon of Our Lady that is recited or sung in the Divine Office from the first Sunday of Advent* to the Presentation* of Our Lord. It consists of six hexameter verses (the work of Hermann the Cripple +1054), a versicle and response and prayer. Many translations have been made. The Antiphon became very popular and is made the *casus belli* in the anti-Semitic tale of the miracle of 'yonge Hugh of Lyncoln', told by the Prioress in Chaucer's Canterbury Tales:

This litel child has litel boke lerninge
as he sat in the scole at his prymer,
he *Alma Redemptoris* herde singe
as children lerned thir antiphoner.

Alphonsus Liguori, St. (1696–1787)

Practising as a youthful and highly successful barrister, Alphonsus, son of a noble family of Naples, lost, by an oversight, a case in which a Neapolitan nobleman was suing the Grand Duke of Tuscany for a vast sum (it would now be accounted well over a quarter of a million sterling), and began to reflect along the lines of *sic transit gloria mundi:* he took Orders and founded first the Redemptoristines*, then the Redemptorists*. A reluctant bishop, he became famous for his theological and devotional writings. He was declared a Doctor* of the church by Pius IX, in 1871.

Altar

(Lat. *altare*.) The early Eucharistic service of Apostolic times took place—as did the Last Supper—at an ordinary domestic table, and it would appear that the use of stone altars arose from the later custom of celebrating on the tombs of the martyrs. The word 'table' was favoured by those 16th cent. reformers who challenged the sacrificial nature of the Mass (cf. Article XXXI of the Thirty-Nine Articles), though 'altar' has never been authoritatively disowned by the Church of England.

Even while wooden tables were still being used, Christians began quite early to speak of *altar* e.g., St. Ignatius at the end of the 1st cent. The word in Hebrews 13:10 refers presumably not to the Eucharist at all but, in a mystical sense, to the cross of Christ or to Christ himself in his Passion and death. Canon* Law has much to say about the material, adornment, consecration and care of altars while the Pontificale Romanum assumes that the High Altar will stand free of the east wall. '. . . let the (consecrating) bishop go seven times round the altar.' In the reforms consequent upon the Second Vatican Council, it was decreed that all new churches must have their high altar built away from the wall so that the priest may stand and face the people as he celebrates Mass, and in fact most existing churches have had an altar erected in such fashion towards the front of the sanctuary.

Altar Breads

Custom has long since standardised the shape, size, colour, etc., of this element of the Eucharist, presumably for easy packing of large numbers in the ciborium*. The product is flat, circular, white, impressed with a cross, crucifix, I.H.S. symbol, etc., large for display at Mass and for the monstrance*, small for the Communion of the faithful, and has little enough resemblance to bread in texture or taste. There is a small but growing inclination to the use of leavened bread.

Altar Rail

The barrier, often provided with a gate, which served the two purposes of separating the sanctuary from the laity's section of a church and later of giving the faithful something to lean on as they knelt to receive Holy Communion. In the light of recently changed attitudes in the Church, the altar rail as separation has been less emphasised (in contrast to the Eastern inconostasis or the former roodscreen), and many of the faithful now stand to receive the Sacrament.

Altar Stone

In Canon Law, if the 'table' of an altar is not consecrated (and for this it must be a single, unbroken piece of stone) and thus does not contain the statutory relics, there must be set in or on the table, before Mass may be offered, an altar-stone containing relics, which is the true altar. In modern conditions, it is not demanded that a stone be used on a portable or temporary altar. The custom, and the law of relics in the altar, arose from the primitive practice of offering Mass over the tombs of the martyrs, and is a symbol of the unity of the Church.

Ambo

(Gk. αμβων, ridge, raised place.) A small platform in early Christian basilicas, from the steps of which the readings and Gospel were delivered; later superseded by pulpit and lectern with many churches having one ambo on the north side for the Gospel and one on the south for the other Biblical readings. Of recent years, with the revival of explicit emphasis on the importance of the Word of God in the liturgy, some churches have an ordinary pulpit on either side, each of which is called an ambo.

Ambrosian Chant

The official chant of the Ambrosian Rite*, it was at first strictly syllabic and to a large extent remained so during its later development. One of the Roman Rite's borrowings from the Ambrosian is the *Veni Creator Spiritus*.

Ambrosian Rite

The ancient liturgy of the Church of Milan and its surrounding province. It is disputed how much it owes—or ever did owe—to St. Ambrose, and may now be regarded as a Use of the Roman Rite, though some scholars claim it is of Gallican origin.

Ambulatory

The extension of the aisles of the choir to meet behind the high altar and make a processional way, as in many cathedrals and large abbey churches. Also, a section of a cloister, or a covered walk: in this sense it has sometimes been strangely substituted by *ambulacrum*, a zoological term.

Amen

(Heb., firmly, indeed, 'verily'.) Used to express assent as in Deut.27 and, for the N.T., *passim* throughout the Letters and Revelation, particularly as a response to any mention of the glory or power of God (e.g: Rom.11:36, II Tim.4:18, II Cor.2:20, I Pet.4:11, Jude v.25, Rev.7:12)—it is from this sense that the liturgical use by the Christian Church arose, so that it is now the universal conclusion to all the Church's prayers, most notably as the *Great Amen*, the answer to the Doxology with which the *Anamnesis* in the Mass ends, the Amen whose effect is greatly diminished when the congregation joins with the celebrant in the *Anamnesis* itself. The other use of Amen in the N.T., confined to the Gospels, and found most frequently in Matthew, occurs when Jesus is recorded as prefacing a remark with *Amen* (in John always *Amen, Amen)*, to give it weight: the A.V. gives *Verily, verily I say unto you (thee)*, the Douay simply, *Amen (Amen, amen) I say* . . ., the Jerusalem renders *I tell you solemnly (most solemnly)* . . .

Amice

The first of the vestments put on for Mass or for any ceremony needing the alb*, the amice is a piece of linen about two and a half feet square, put on so as to appear above the alb and round the neck, and secured with two tapes. Probably it orginally served as a scarf in cold churches and could be pulled up to cover the head (monks and friars still wear an amice shaped to their hood). In the high Middle Ages, it would be ornamented with an *apparel*, a band of embroidery which stood up round the neck like a collar. This has beeen preserved in some rites (e.g., the Dominican) and in some places is being revived.

Anathema

(Gk., A thing set apart—for the service of God or as accursed.) The LXX use of the word is translated 'the devoted thing', 'the accursed thing', 'abomination' (A.V.), 'under ban', 'detestable' (J.B.); in the N.T., St. Paul applies the word—rendered 'accursed', 'anathema' (A.V.), and 'cursed', 'condemned' (J.B.)—to any who pervert the Good News of Christ, who will not love the Lord Jesus, who are separated from Christ. From this sense of being separated, it came to be used to signify 'cut off from the Church (the Body of Christ)' and therefore 'abandoned to evil'. Thus Canon Law, Papal Documents and the Councils of the Church have used it in definitions, e.g. in the classic phrasing *Si quis dixerit . . . anathema sit*—if any man asserts that . . . let him be anathema.

Angel

(Gk. αγγελος, messenger.) The name used in Judaeo-Christian tradition to describe any of the spirits who serve God in uncountable numbers and in any capacity, whether to be his courtiers and sing his praises (Job 1:6, Is.6), control the fate of nations (Dan.10:13), guard the purity of God's holiness (Gen.3:24), protect his chosen ones (Tobit 5:4ff), deliver his law to men (Acts 7:53, Gal.3:19) or bring messages to individuals, beginning with Abraham and stretching right through the Old and New Testaments. Jesus was attended by angels at important moments of his life, and John's Revelation is itself a study in angelology. The indications in the Bible of different functions and of their names (Raphael, one of the seven angels who stand ready to enter the presence of the glory of the Lord in Tobit 2:15, Michael 'the warrior', Dan.10:13 and 12:1, Gabriel 'the wise', Dan.8:17) were elaborated by theologians with the help of St. Paul's catalogues in Eph.1:21 and Col.1:16, into the Nine Choirs, 'Angels' being the lowest, under Seraphim, Cherubim, Thrones, Dominations, Virtues, Powers, Principalities, and Archangels. Writers have based their speculations on the sayings of Jesus to the effect that angels are spiritual beings (Mt.22:30) who enjoy the Beatific Vision permanently (Mt.18:10) and will accompany him as Judge at the Second Coming (Mt.16:27). All the great Schoolmen treated of angels, generally agreeing that they are each a person and so different as each to constitute a species. Angels have had a large share of representation in Christian art, which was in this sphere adversely influenced towards sentimentality by the decadent figures of the Winged Victory in late Hellenistic sculpture.

See also Guardian Angel

Angelicum

The pontifical University of St. Thomas Aquinas (the *Angelic Doctor*) was founded as a school by the Dominican Friars in the 13th cent. attached to their church in Rome, Santa Maria Sopra Minerva, the only true Gothic church in that city. In 1580, the institute was erected by Gregory XIII into a university for the conferring of a degree in theology, and in 1727, Benedict XIII opened it to others not of the Dominican Order. Since then, there have been added faculties of Philosophy, Canon Law and Social Studies.

Angelus

A prayer to commemorate the Incarnation, named after its first word in the Latin, *The angel of the Lord . . .* and consisting of three versicles and responsories, each followed by a Hail Mary; the whole being concluded by the prayer 'Pour forth, we beseech thee, O Lord . . .' It is usually recited three times daily, in the morning (6 a.m.), at noon and in the evening (6 p.m.), and in many places a bell is rung, three times for each Ave and nine for the prayer. In Italy, the evening Angelus bell is called the *Ave Maria*. The prayer can be traced back to the 14th cent.

Anno Domini

(Lat., 'In the year of the Lord'.) The system of dating years from the birth of Christ was initiated by Denis the Little, who died about 550. It is believed that the actual year of the Lord's birth was, by that reckoning, about 4, or perhaps 7, B.C., it having been established that the death of Herod the Great took place in 4 B.C. (cf. Mt.2:19). Some prefer 6 A.D., the year in which it is supposed the tax was imposed under Quirinus (Lk.2:1ff).

Annulment

See Nullity.

Annunciation (of the Blessed Virgin Mary)

'Lady Day', the feast of the message brought by the archangel Gabriel (Lk.1:26–38) and of the conception of Jesus, is kept on March 25th, the reckoning being made from the feast of the Nativity, Dec.25th, itself not fixed in early days. There is evidence to suggest that the

Annunciation was kept at Constantinople about 430, and, by the 8th cent., it was universal in the West also. The Spaniards for a long time observed it on Dec.18th, to avoid its occurance in Lent. In many countries, it was counted as New Year's Day, and is still a day for paying rents and other debts.

Anointing of the Sick

The Sacrament, formerly known as *Extreme Unction,* in which the sick person is anointed (with Oil of the Sick, blessed by the bishop on Maundy Thursday) on the forehead and the hands, while the accompanying prayers express the desire of the Church that God may not only give his grace but also restore health, if such be His will. Cf. the Apostles' anointing of the sick in Mk.6:13 and the direction given in Jas.5:14-15.

Anselm, St. (1033-1109)

A Lombard who succeeded Lanfranc first as abbot of Bec in Normandy, and again as archbishop of Canterbury. He suffered exile for the spiritual rights of the Church under both William Rufus and Henry I; from his final return in 1107 until his death, he introduced many reforms into the Church and abolished the slave trade. Described by modern writers as the most luminous and penetrating intellect between St. Augustine* and St. Thomas Aquinas*, Anselm stands foremost among the early Scholastics* as an exponent of the defence of the Faith by reasoning rather than by scriptural or authoritarian argument. God he equated with Plato's *Idea of the Good* (see Ontological Argument); faith is a pre-condition for the right use of reason—*credo ut intelligam*—but then we are bound also to exercise our minds on the apprehension of revealed truth. Perhaps his best-known work is *Cur Deus Homo?,* a deeply influential book on the Atonement.

Antipope

One who claims to be pope against the true pope. Some of these have been honestly mistaken, some have been ambitious rogues, one of them, the first, is a canonised saint (Hippolytus, 3rd cent.) The official Vatican list records 37 antipopes (and expresses a few doubts in footnotes), the last name being that of Felix V in the 15th cent; it will probably not take much notice of the excommunicated Spanish priest who in 1978 proclaimed himself Gregory XVII.

Apocrypha

(Gk. αποκρυφος, hidden.) Many books have been presented as part of the Canon of Scripture (i.e. the list of works accepted by the Church as of divine inspiration), but rejected as false or of uncertain authenticity. Some are Jewish, such as the Book of Enoch, the Fourth Book of Ezra, the Third Book of Maccabees and a sprinkling of prayers and psalms. Some are Jewish-Christian, like The Testament of the Patriarchs and the Ascension of Isaiah, while many are of Christian origin—the Gospels of James and Gamaliel, the Gospel according to the Hebrews, the Gospel according to the Egyptians, an Arabic Gospel of the Infancy, the Pilate literature, the Acts of Peter, of Peter and Paul, of Paul and Thecla, of Matthew, and many Apocalypses. The Reformed Churches, and some Greek and Russian Orthodox thinkers, also call *apocryphal* those books which, not being found in the Hebrew Bible of the Jews but in the Greek versions, particularly the LXX, are accepted by the Roman tradition and called Deutero-Canonical*: Tobit, Judith, Wisdom, Ecclesiasticus, Baruch, the two Books of the Maccabees, parts of Esther (those not found in the Hebrew), the so-called Additions to Daniel (the Song of the Three Children, the Story of Susanna and the Bel and Dragon incident).

Apollinarianism

The heretical theory of Apollinaris, Bishop of Alexandria (+ c.392), to the effect that there was such a unity in Christ that his flesh was of one substance with his divinity and was brought into the world by him; nor had he any human intellect; thus it was God the Son who died on the cross. The bishop's denial of any true Incarnation was a result of his efforts to ensure the unity of Godhead and humanity in our Lord, to teach his full divinity and to avoid the supposition of a moral development in his life. Much confusion was brought about in the ensuing controversies by the lack of definitions for the terms *person* and *nature,* and by uncertainty as to whether the human person was to be constituted of body and soul or of body, soul and spirit.

Apologia Pro Vita Sua

(Lat., Defence of His Life.) One of the greatest autobiographical works in the language, and certainly the most moving, the Apologia was wrung from Newman's* retiring, very private spirit by the puppy-like persistence of Charles Kingsley. The author of *The Water Babies* placed the Victorian age and all posterity in his debt with an alarming tour de force of insensitivity and impertinence: beginning with a gratuitous and anonymous insult to Newman conveyed in a book review published late in 1863—'*Truth for its own sake has never been a virtue with the Roman clergy. Father Newman informs us that it need not, and on the whole ought not to be*'—he continued through two months' correspondence, which he rounded off with a pamphlet extending his intemperate attack with naive bigotry to the whole system of the Roman Church, its moral theology, miracles, devotions and all. This he incautiously entitled *What, Then, Does Dr. Newman Mean?* and Newman, in making it monumentally clear what he meant, felt compelled, after dealing magisterially with his gadfly, to declare his whole thought and history: '*He asks about my Mind and its Beliefs and its Sentiments; and he shall be answered. . .*' To this he adds another, general, answer to Kingsley and, in an appendix, a further, detailed answer. The work appeared immediately on the publication of Kingsley's pamphlet and in weekly instalments; on reading it, one is aware that Charles Kingsley did not live in vain.

Apostleship of the Sea

Founded in Great Britain in 1890, this organisation is dedicated to the welfare of seamen, in collaboration with the Society of St. Vincent de Paul*. It works by means of establishing sailors' shore institutes, visiting ships, recruiting priests for chaplains' work, setting up libraries, etc. In 1920, there was started in Glasgow a centre for organising the Apostleship as an international body.

Apostolicity

One of the Marks* of the Church: the Church that Christ founded must be the Church of his Apostles. The quality of being apostolic has three spheres—*doctrine:* the Church teaches what the Apostles taught; *authority:* she derives her authority from them through an unbroken succession of pastors; *society:* the Church is the same historical body or society as that which the Apostles founded.

Aramaic

The semitic tongue of Babylonia and Syria, which superseded Hebrew as the language of the Jews during the Captivity. It was still spoken by them at the time of Christ, and would be used by Jesus himself as his daily language. Some words of it remain in the original in the N.T., such as *talitha cumi, eloi, eloi, lama sabachthani,* and a few others. The Christians of the Syriac rites use a dialect of Aramaic in their liturgy.

Archbishop

A bishop who has authority, closely defined by Canon* Law, over other bishops whose dioceses, together with his archdiocese, constitute a province*; these bishops (there need be only one) are *suffragans* and the archbishop is called *metropolitan;* he must call them to a provincial council every 20 years and his court appeals from theirs, but the law strictly limits his power of interfering in their dioceses. He may not undertake metropolitan duties until he has received the Pallium*. England has four metropolitan sees: Westminster*, Birmingham*, Liverpool*, Southwark*; Wales has one, Cardiff*; Ireland four: Armagh*, Cashel, Dublin and Tuam; Scotland two: St. Andrews and Edinburgh and Glasgow*.

Archangel

See Angel

Archdeacon

In the Middle Ages, when each diocese was divided into archdeaconries, the archdeacon held an important office. In Ireland and Australia, the title survives and carries the addition *The Venerable*. In England, the archdeacon's place, once one of great importance, has been subsumed into that of the *Vicar General*, and in the Western Church generally, the title means very little and is given to the first and sometimes the second dignitary of certain chapters.

Archdiocese
See Diocese

Arianism

The heresy of Arius, an Alexandrian priest, who maintained that the Son was not eternal nor the equal of the Father, but created by Him, granted sonship on account of his 'foreseen righteousness' and then used by the Father in his creative and redemption work. This teaching caused great division and turmoil among the faithful and prompted Constantine* to summon the Council which met at Nicaea* in 325 and, while condemning and banishing Arius, introduced in its creed the term *homoousion* (Gk. ομοου-σιον, of the same substance or nature) latinised as *consubstantialem (Patri)* to oust the Arian word *homoiousion* (ομοι-ουσιον, of like substance or nature). However, the heresy spread, largely through the support of emperors, and by 359, a group of orthodox bishops who had met at the Council of Ariminum (Rimini) to settle the dispute which had so devastated the Christian body, were persuaded under pressure from the Emperor Constantius to subscribe to an Arian Creed. It was this victory for the heresy that moved St. Jerome* later to write *ingemuit totus orbis et se Arianum esse miratus est*; the whole world groaned, astonished to find itself Arian. However, this triumph itself served to frighten a great many of the less enthusiastic Arians and of the Semi-Arians back to orthodoxy; its chief champion, Constantius, died, and in 362, St. Athansius* held a Council which reasserted Nicaea and reconciled many. The heresy still lingered in the East under the protection of the Arian Emperor Valens but in the West its demise was hastened by Valentinian who was Catholic. Final victory for the Nicene Creed was assured, after Athanasius' death, at the First Council of Constantinople* (381). Thereafter the heresy, exiled from the boundaries of the Empire, found followers among the remote Teutonic tribesmen, who after persecuting the Catholics in lands they occupied, began to relinquish their heresy on the conversion of the Franks to the Catholic faith in 496.

Ark
i) The Ark of Noah, in which he and his family escaped the Flood (Gen.6-9); its wood was claimed to be extant by a Babylonian historian in 300 B.C., and used for making bracelets and amulets.
ii) The Ark of the Covenant (Exod.25) first made to hold the Tables of the Law and to signify God's presence, so holy that to touch it, even with good intent, for a 'profane' person, meant death (Sam.6:6-7). The Ark disappeared at the siege and fall of Jerusalem (587-586 B.C.).
iii) The title *Ark of the Covenant* is found in the Litany of Loreto,* an inspiration due perhaps to a sermon attributed to St. Ambrose in which Mary bearing Christ in her womb is compared to the Ark containing the holy Law.

Armagh
(Ir. *Ard Macha*, the Height of Macha, Macha being a legendary queen of Ireland.) The primatial see of All Ireland was founded by St. Patrick*. The most renowned occupant of the see was Oliver Plunkett martyred in 1681 in the wake of the Titus Oates Plot*.

Ascension
Ascension Day or Ascension Thursday, the fortieth day after Easter, commemorates the departure of Christ from the world to his Father, his redeeming work being accomplished. This event is recorded in the 'long ending' to Mark's Gospel (Mk.16:19), in Lk.24:51 and in Acts 1:9; and it is referred to, explicitly or implicitly, elsewhere (Jn.20:17, Eph.4:8-10, Heb.4:14, I Tim.3:16, I Pet.3:22). Its theological emphasis is the enthroning in heaven of Christ's human nature at God's right hand (Eph.1:20-23, Phil.2:9-11).

Asceticism
(Gk. ασκησις, exercise.) Self-discipline, especially when practised for religious purposes and particularly when it includes voluntary physical hardship or mortification. Asceticism has played a part in all the major religious movements and its part in the Christian life is sanctioned by Our Lord's own example in the Gospels. Its end is the quest for the Kingdom of God. Austerity for its own sake or as a 'stunt' is condemned by the Church.

Ash Wednesday

The first day of Lent, which takes its name from the blessing and distribution on that day of ashes, the ancient traditional sign of mourning and sorrow, and, as sorrow for sin, of repentance. The Bible abounds (Es.4:1, Is.61:3, Job 42:6, Mt.11:21 etc.) in references to the custom, which the Jews shared with Egyptians, Chaldeans, Greeks and other ancient peoples, of strewing ashes on the head, formalised with use into a discreet sign of the cross smudged on to the forehead (for the clergy, on top of the scalp, on the site of the tonsure*).

Aspersion

Besides its ordinary meaning of sprinkling (sc. with holy water), the word is also used to describe a method of baptism by sprinkling, which is illicit, but which was anciently used by the Celtic* Church.

Association of the Holy Family

An unenclosed institute of sisters founded in 1820 in France, now consisting of four separate branches or sections. See Sisters of the Immaculate Conception.

Assumption

The Assumption of Our Lady (Aug 15th)—the fact that *the Immaculate Mother of God, Mary ever virgin, having run the course of her earthly life, was taken up body and soul into the glory of heaven*—was defined, in those words, by Pope Pius XII's Apostolic Constitution *Munificentissimus Deus* (1950), as of faith, for Catholics. The feast-day of the Assumption had been observed since the late 8th cent. on Aug. 15th (until that time, a general feast of Our Lady had been observed in Rome on Jan. 1st, to which the modern Solemnity of Mary, Mother of God, on the same date can be seen as a reversion), the earliest written mention of the belief being in certain N.T. apocrypha*, some of them tinged with Gnosticism*. These describe the death of the Blessed Virgin, attended with various miraculous circumstances, and assert that the body was taken up on the way to burial or after three days in the tomb, or at varying dates after the Ascension of her Son, such as three years or fifty. The first Western historian we find accepting the Assumption as fact is Gregory of Tours (+594), and it had currency in the Eastern Church from the 7th cent. According to St. John of Damascus, it was narrated at the Council of Chalcedon* in 451 that all the Apostles, having been present at the Virgin's death, later found her tomb empty: this story was credited with the authority of Dionysius the Areopagite of Acts 17:34, and, because of its antiquity and prestige, was adopted in the 16th cent. into the Lessons for the Octave of the Feast, in the Roman Breviary. Though expunged from the Book of Common Prayer in 1549, the feast was retained in the Calendar of Oxford University, and is at present observed by many in the Church of England.

Assumptionists

See Augustinians of the Assumption.

Assyrian Christians

The misnomer by which a group of Nestorian* Christians are known, now surviving in Iraq. They lived in isolation on the N.W. borders of Persia, and in the 19th cent., received some level of learning—at that time they were almost without it—from the Archbishop of Canterbury's *Assyrian Mission*. Their taking sides with Russia in the First World War put them in great political difficulties in the subsequent years, and they were eventually placed under Iraqi suzerainty. They still, as a Church, refuse the *Theotokos**, and they honour Nestorius as a saint.
See Nestorianism

Athanasius, St. (c. 296–373)

A native of Alexandria, he attended the Council of Nicaea*, as deacon and secretary to his bishop, whom he later succeeded. His determined opposition to Arianism* caused him to suffer exile on five different occasions, in the course of which he spent time at Trier and Rome (where he was supported by Pope St Julius I): he is said to be the first to bring to the Western Church the knowledge of the monastic life (he was a friend of Pachomius, who introduced community life among the monks of the Egyptian desert). After his last exile, he spent the rest of his life consolidating the Nicene party which, together with Athanasius' resolution and theological writings, assured the final defeat of Arianism at the Council of Constantinople*. His books form a great contribution to the theology of the Trinity and of the Incarnation. His feast-day is May 2nd.

Augustine, of Canterbury, St. (+ 604 or 605)

A Benedictine prior in Rome, he was chosen by Gregory* the Great to lead a missionary expedition to England, to restore the Church after the Saxon depredations. In mid-journey across Gaul, he gathered such tales of the savagery of his future flock as decided him to turn back, but, encouraged on by Gregory's letters, he persevered and in 597, reached the court of Ethelbert at Canterbury. There the Faith was quickly established, Queen Bertha being already a Christian. Augustine, having visited Arles to be consecrated archbishop, remained in his see of Canterbury the rest of his life, writing regularly to Gregory for advice, and attempting, without success, in 603, to reach agreement with the Celtic* Church on matters of discipline and practice. He established the sees of Rochester and London, probably in 604.

Augustine of Hippo, St. (354–430)

A Father* of the Church, one of the seminal influences of Christian thought, supreme and unchallenged until the 13th cent. and permantly moulding the theology of the West, Augustine abandoned in his youth the ideals he had received from his Christian mother: he followed Manichaeism* and took a mistress —rather, a common-law wife, since he remained faithful to her for 15 years; disillusioned with the Manichees after five years, and aware, as he tells us, that his mother St. Monica was praying for his conversion all this time, he left the University of Carthage and opened a school of rhetoric in Rome, where the behaviour of his pupils so disgusted him that he transferred to Milan, where, as a professor, he came into contact with the bishop St. Ambrose. Learning much from him, Augustine approached Christianity again, with a detour through Neo-Platonism, until, as he tells us, the final obstacle was no intellectual problem but his inability—or unwillingness—to live a chaste life: the prayer, 'Lord, give me chastity, but not yet' is not apocryphal, it is Augustine's. Brought safely home again through reading Rom.13:13, as a result, he says, of casually hearing a child's song, he asked for baptism and returned to Africa, where he lived a monastic life. This was interrupted once when by popular acclaim, he was offered to the bishop for ordination, and again—and finally—when, now very influential in the African Church, he was made a coadjutor bishop, succeeding to the see of Hippo in 395. He ruled until 430, when the Vandals were at the gates, and was so deeply convinced of the importance of Rome that, being told the City had fallen, he died in the belief that this was the end of the world. Augustine's immense effect on all subsequent theology is due mainly to his having had to formulate his Christian thought in defence of orthodoxy against three heresies in succession: Manichaeism, Donatism (a schism whose followers, to justify themselves, fell in to the heretical teaching that sacraments cannot be validly administered by a sinful minister and that sinners are not truly members of the Church) and Pelagianism*. Against the Manichees, he laid down the metaphysic on which later stood the structure of Scholasticism* (the uniqueness and goodness of God, the universal creator and sustainer, the essential goodness of created things, the concept of evil as the deprivation of some good quality due). His reaction to the Donatists produced a dramatic advance in the theology of the Church, the sacraments and Grace: the Church is one and she is holy—in her purposes—and contains good men and wicked (here he used the Parable of the Tares) and there are good men outside the Church; the civil power is part of God's plan, but must be founded on justice, which includes the worship of God—he accepts the aid of the State for the punishment of schism and heresy, but demurs at the death penalty. Pelagius' attack on a phrase of his, from the *Confessions*, the renowned *Da quod iubes et iube quod vis*, provoked, in the ensuing controversy, the Augustinian teaching on the Fall, Original Sin and Predestination: man, having lost through Adam his birthright of supernatural gifts, has inherited a moral sickness and the legal liability for that first sin, from all of which evils he can be delivered only by the grace of God. Augustine's extreme view of the helplessness and wickedness of man (*massa peccati*, the clod of sin), which strongly influenced e.g. Calvin, grew out of his own experience of sin and of the power of grace. The most renowned of his non-polemical works are the *Confessions* and the *City of God*: the former, not intended as autobiography but as thanksgiving, is a demonstration, from the life of the writer, of his phrase, 'You have made us for Yourself and our heart will not rest until it rests in You', an unrivalled account of the soul's experience of sin and grace. The *City of God*, inspired by the capture of Rome by Alaric in 410, rebuts the pagan charge that it was abolition of the worship of the gods that brought about the disaster, contrasts Christianity with the world and is in sum a masterpiece as a Christian philosophy of history.

Augustinian Canons
See Canons Regular

Augustinian Friars
See Hermits of St. Augustine

Augustinian Recollects
See Hermits of St. Augustine

Augustinians
The title is given to the Augustinian Canons*, the Augustinian Friars (Hermits of St. Augustine*), the Augustinian Recollects*, the Augustinians of the Assumption*, and to the nuns of the Order of Hermits of St. Augustine (above) and to other congregations of nuns, such as the Augustinian Sisters of Meaux, the Augustinian Sisters of Penance, the Sisters of St. Augustine, and others.

Augustinians of the Assumption
Founded in 1845 at Nîmes by the Abbé Emmanuel d'Alzon, the congregation has missions in Africa and the Middle East, with seminaries, colleges, schools and churches of Latin and Byzantine rite in Turkey and Eastern Europe, a hospice for pilgrims at Jerusalem, and a publishing house *La Bonne Presse*. It was suppressed in France in 1900, but has been re-established. The members recite the Divine Office in choir.

Ave Maria
(Lat., Hail, Mary.) The first words of the prayer, hence used for the prayer itself.

Ave Regina Coelorum
(Lat., Hail, Queen of the Heavens.) The title and first line of the Antiphon of Our Lady used in the Office* between the Feast of the Purification* and Maundy Thursday*.

Avignon
On the death of Pope Benedict XI in July, 1304, the conclave* of cardinals at Perugia split into factions of Italian and French prelates and it took 11 months to elect a successor, Clement V, a Frenchman. Intimidated by the anarchic condition to which the States of the Church had been reduced by political rivalry, he went to Lyons to be crowned in the presence of Philip the Fair of France, who was powerful enough to make Clement's policies subservient to his. After four years in various French cities, the Pope settled at Avignon (which was at the time a Neapolitan possession) and never returned to Italy: there ensued a line of French popes whose continued residence at Avignon and compliance to the French throne earned that seventy-year period the title of 'the Babylonian Captivity' in the writings of Petrarch and others (Dante in the *Inferno* compares Clement to the treacherous high priest Jason of II Maccabees, and has a letter to the Italian cardinals urging them to bring back the Pope to Rome, which in his absence is the city of Lamentations 'sitting solitary'). The subsequent Avignon popes were John XXII (in his pontificate, there was an antipope* Nicholas V), Benedict XII, Clement VI (who bought Avignon from Queen Joanna of Naples in 1348), Innocent VI, Urban V (later beatified), and Gregory XI, who was visited in 1376 by St. Catherine of Siena, coming to plead on behalf of Florence, then at war with him, and to persuade him back to Rome. He returned the following year, and died in March 1378. Later, in the Schism of the West, Avignon was inhabited by the antipopes Clement VII and Benedict XIII. See Schism of the West.

Avignon Popes
Those seven Popes, from Clement V (elected 1305) to Gregory XI (+ 1378) who resided during their pontificates at Avignon; all were Frenchmen. The name is also given, somewhat confusingly, to two claimants to the Papacy, living at Avignon and taking the names Clement VII (1378–94) and Benedict XIII, after the return from Avignon to Rome; they are also sometimes known as the Clementine Popes.
See Schism of the West, Urbanist Popes, and Antipope.

B

Babington Plot

A Catholic conspiracy uncovered in 1586, named after Anthony Babington, one of its prime movers, with the object of removing Queen Elizabeth I by assassination and replacing her with Mary Queen of Scots, at that time Elizabeth's prisoner. Walsingham, whose fixed intention of executing Mary had been resisted by the Queen, saw his opportunity: he sent in *agents provocateurs*, intercepted letters between Mary and the plotters, and, thus enabled to accuse her as accomplice in treason, brought her to the block at Fotheringhay. Babington and his accomplices were executed at Lincoln's Inn Fields.

Baldacchino

(It. *Baldacco*, Bagdad.) A canopy hung from the ceiling or the wall, so as to cover the altar, usually embroidered and fringed. If there is a *ciborium*★, the *Caeremoniale Episcoporum* does not demand the baldacchino.

Balm (Balsam)

After exorcism and blessing, balsam is mixed with olive oil at a special ceremony on Maundy Thursday★ by the bishop, to make chrism★. The mixing is taken as symbolical of the union of the divine and human natures in Jesus Christ.

Bambino

(It., baby.) The name used for the figure representing the Holy Child in a Christmas crib.

Bangor, the Use of

The mediaeval variant of the Roman liturgy prevalent in Bangor and other Welsh dioceses until the Reformation; cf. the Use of Aberdeen★ and the Sarum Rite★.

Baptism

Traditionally called the 'Gate of the Sacraments', Baptism is that sacrament which, bringing man to the new birth in Christ, makes him capable of the life of faith with its privileges and means of sustenance. The minister (who should in ordinary circumstances be the priest, though, in necessity, anyone may baptise) addresses the person by name and continues '. . . I baptise you in the name of the Father and of the Son and of the Holy Spirit'. The modern rubric recommends baptism by immersion, in harmony with the ideas of Rom.6:1–11, and emphasises the celebratory nature of the occasion—the Paschal candle, removed from the sanctuary after Pentecost Day, is kept next to the font and lit for baptism, which is the sacrament of resurrection; besides the prayers and special blessings, hymns and acclamations are provided; parents and godparents at the baptism of a child are reminded of their obligations and their privilege; there are separate blessings for mother and father, and all present are drawn in to make the baptism a joyful event shared by the Christian community. The water, moreover, is not left to stand in the font but consecrated fresh by the celebrant at each baptismal ceremony. The catechetical aspect of the sacrament is also strengthened by the provision of a variety of scriptural readings.

Baptism of Bells

See Bell

Baptism of Blood

The name given to the saving of one who, though not baptised with water, suffers martyrdom for the Faith or for some Christian virtue, and who is thereby justified before God and received into the community of the faithful at the moment of death.

Baptism of Desire

The Church has long taught that those who died unacquainted, through no fault of their own, with Revelation but adhering by a good life to their own hazy idea of God, were saved through their general good intention ('they would have asked for Baptism had they known about it'). This was known as Baptism of Desire and such persons were considered as 'Christians unaware'. Schillebeeckx, in *Christ the Sacrament*, calls them 'anonymous Christians'. In modern times, however, the question inevitably arises: 'What of those conscientious athiests who, honestly unable to accept Revelation as it is presented to them, die unbaptised after living a good life according to their lights?' Vatican II replies in its *Decree on Religious Liberty* that every man who follows his conscience will be saved, the grace of Christ being universal and conveyed not solely by the Sacraments and the Faith.

Baptismal Vows

Properly promises, not vows, the undertaking made by the person baptised or by the sponsor (Lat. *spondeo*, I promise) to reject Satan and all his works and false lures (formerly *pomps*) and to follow the Creed. These promises are renewed customarily at the end of a period of spiritual exercises, in the liturgy of the Easter Vigil, and in the ceremony of Confirmation.

Barnabas, Epistle of

A letter written in early Christian times and attributed by some to St. Barnabas, the companion of St. Paul. It is probably of the late 1st cent. A.D., contains virulent anti-Semitic sentiments, professing to find the whole O.T. worship erroneous and the Law of Moses useless, and could not therefore be the work of Barnabas.

Barnabas, Gospel of

A curious document, forged not earlier than the 15th cent. and thus probably the latest in date of all the 'apocrypha'*. It was the work of an Italian Christian who had turned Muslim.

Bartholomew, St.

The Apostle commemorated in the West on August 24th, found in all the N.T. lists of the Twelve, and usually taken to be the Nathanael of Jn.1:45. There are some unreliable traditions about his apostolic work; nothing of his life is known for certain.

Bartholomew's Day, Massacre of St.

In Paris and other French cities, between sunset of August 23rd 1572 and the night of the 25th, a vast number—between 5,000 and 10,000—of Huguenots were slaughtered, for which outrage, notable even in that period of the Wars of Religion in France, the Catholic Queen Catherine de Medici was evidently responsible. After using the Protestants to counterbalance the threat of the strong Catholic party, she later took very violent action in face of a rebellion on the part of the Protestants, action which culminated in the murder of their leader Coligny and the Massacre itself.

Basilica

(Βασιλιχα [οιχια], king's [house].) The earliest form of architecture used for Christian churches was derived directly from the Roman *basilica*, the building in which the Emperor would sit as judge or in which the commerce of the capital was conducted. The basilica's very simple plan consisted of a wide nave with two, or even four, aisles separated by columns having a raised platform at the east end, contained in a semicircular apse, with steps, the altar and the bishop's seat beyond it, roughly where the judge's seat had been. There was a porch—*narthex*—running the width of the building and outside usually a courtyard with a cloister. Another feature of the basilica was the *confessio**. The title basilica (i.e. Minor Basilica) has been latterly extended by popes to certain other important churches, regardless of architectural style.

Basle, Council of

(Seventeenth General Council.) Convoked by Pope Martin V just before his death in 1431, this Council met under the new Pope, Eugene IV. Among its other acts, it reconciled the less extreme of the Hussites by granting them Communion under both kinds, and other concessions. When Eugene, in 1438-9, transferred the Council to Ferrara (and later to Florence), some of the Council Fathers remained stubbornly at Basle and continued their deliberations there, including the election of an antipope, Felix V, who later submitted (1449) to Nicholas V. These events lead theologians to adjudge only the first part of Basle to be oecumenical, and not the events after Eugene's departure: *ubi Petrus, ibi ecclesia*: where Peter is—there is the Church.

Beards

The present discipline of the Western Church is that clerics shall be clean-shaven; the rule seems to have had its origin in the desire to distinguish clerics from laymen and also perhaps to avoid the inconvenience or danger of accident when drinking from the chalice. However, certain religious, e.g. Capuchin friars and Camaldolese monks wear the beard by rule, and there has been a bearded tradition among missionaries.

Beatification

The sancity of a deceased person being established by strict enquiry, that person can then be declared Blessed and referred to as the Blessed John, the Blessed Margaret, and so forth, this declaration being described as beatification (Lat. *beatus*, blessed, happy) and conveying permission to exhibit images of the person for public veneration and to offer Mass in his honour. The first inquiries into the sanctity of the life in question are made by the local ordinary, who then, with Rome's approval, hands over the cause* to the Sacred Congregation for the Causes of Saints; this body scrutinises most strictly the life, writings and alleged miracles of the candidate—an inquiry which usually lasts several years—after which the Pope, who is the final judge, proclaims the person Blessed in a high ceremonial at St. Peter's, with the unveiling of a picture of the new *beatus* and the chanting of the prayer from the Mass in his honour: no infallability is claimed for this declaration. See Canonisation.

Beda

The *Collegio Beda*, St Bede's College, founded in Rome in 1852, which in 1917, after half-a-century of association with the English College, Rome, became quite separate. Its purpose is the training of men who study for the priesthood late in life, including many convert ministers from other Christian Churches.

Bede

(O.E., prayer.) This Anglo-Saxon word for prayer, through its connection with various rosaries, gives us *bead;* and the *Bede-roll,* that is, the list of persons to be prayed for, becomes *bidding prayers.*

Bede, St. (c. 673-735)

The rare honorific of 'Venerable',. conferred on Bede within a century of his death, has been overtaken and diluted by history, being now only the first of three titles in the process of canonisation*—to which, in fact, Bede was never subjected. This holy and learned monk of Jarrow, precocious both in respect of Holy Order (he was deacon at 19 years of age) and of his writings, which he began in his early youth, gained himself a wide fame in his lifetime. His works, which were varied, include treatises on the reckoning of the date of Easter (in support of the Roman usage adopted at Whitby* in 664), which, with his historical writings, did much to popularise the custom of dating events from the Incarnation. He has a cosmography, *De Natura Rerum,* based on Isidore, Suetonius and Pliny the Younger. For his biblical homilies and expositions, immediately and immensely popular, he used the current Latin texts (Vulgate* and Old Latin) and the Greek. He produced historical works in the shape of lives of some English saints (his *Historia Abbatum* recounts the history of his monastery from its foundation to 716) and, his most valuable work in this field, the *Ecclesiastical History of the English People.* This is a prime source for the history of the period, trusted because Bede took trouble to inform himself from reliable persons, was careful to record his authorities, and knew how to distinguish assured fact from hearsay and legend; the *Historia Ecclesiastica Gentis Anglorum* is also worth reading for its vivid narrative style. Bede worked at his writings almost until his dying breath; in the 11th cent., his remains were removed from his modest monastic grave to the ante-chapel of Durham Cathedral, where the stone reads: *Hac sunt in fossa Baedae Venerabilis ossa,* In this tomb are the bones of Bede the Venerable.

Bell

i) The use of bells to summon the faithful to church has been general since the 8th cent. They are also sounded by immemorial custom for the dying and for funerals (*the passing-bell*), for the daily *Angelus*, for the *Gloria* on Holy Saturday:

in some places also for the *Gloria* of the Christmas Midnight Mass, for the *Magnificat* at Vespers of the Visitation and for the Consecration at the principal Sunday Mass. Church bells are also rung on public, non-religious occasions of rejoicing; during the Second World War, church bells in Britain were ordered to be silent during the period when there was a possibility of invasion by the enemy, in which event they would be rung as an alarm. The blessing of a church bell prescribed in the *Pontificale Romanum* is so elaborate and exotic as to have earned the popular title of the 'baptism' of bells: it includes the recitation of some psalms, the washing of the metal with holy water and anointing with chrism and Oil of the Sick; a smoking thurible is placed inside the bell and a Gospel passage (Lk.10:38–42) is read. The bell also given a name and 'god-parents'.

ii) The use of a hand-bell at Mass is of mediaeval origin and in the 'Tridentine Mass' was prescribed by the Rubrics at the *Sanctus* and at the elevation of the Host and of the chalice.

Bellarmine, St. Robert (1542–1621)

A Tuscan Jesuit of great learning and eloquence, professor of a theology not always and everywhere accepted, bishop and cardinal. He engaged in controversy with Protestant writers (among them James I of England) against whom he endeavoured to use reason and argument, while many contemporaries on both sides employed authority, assertion and abuse; he was one of many highly-placed ecclesiastics to show sympathy with Galileo*. He came to the rescue of Paul V against the Venetians and wrote another work—against W. Barclay of Glasgow, who denied the Pope any temporal authority—in which he describes the temporal power as only indirect, which view had earlier displeased Sixtus V, and was, apparently, long to delay his process of canonisation; he was declared Saint only in 1930. Robert was undoubtedly one of the greatest and holiest men of the Counter-Reformation.

'Bell, Book and Candle'

A traditional literary phrase to describe excommunication or cursing: for the greater excommunication *(anathema)*, the Book *(the Pontificale)* prescribed the presence of 12 priests with candles which, on the reading of the sentence, were flung down, to suggest the extinguishing of the light in the offender's soul; and the bell was tolled as for a death. R. H. Barham in *The Jackdaw of Rheims:* 'He called for his candle, his bell and his book'.

Belmont

A monastery of Benedictine monks of the English congregation, founded as a priory in 1858 near Hereford, and made an abbey in 1916. The monks have a school for boys.

Benedict, St. (c.480–c.550)

Born at Nursia, of senatorial rank, the 'Father of Western Monachism' went to Rome to be educated but, repulsed by the unbridled vice of the capital, retired to a cave at Subiaco, where he spent some years as a hermit. After the gradual growth of a community around him, he set up monasteries, until there were 12 houses of 12 monks each, with abbots of Benedict's appointing. About 525, he moved, apparently because of local jealousy, to Monte Cassino*, where, until his death, he worked at the reform of monastic life and the elaboration of his Rule*. There is no evidence that he ever was ordained or that he meant to found a clerical Order. He was buried at M. Cassino, in the same grave as his sister St. Scholastica.

Benedict, St., Rule of

Described by a modern lawyer as a 'monument of legislative art, remarkable alike for its completeness, its simplicity, and its adaptability', the Rule is based on earlier monastic tradition and writings, from the Desert Fathers onward, but moderation—excessive penances, for instance, are forbidden—and practicality, which of itself—and presumably without direct intention—became a deeply civilising influence; 'giving a world, worn out by slavery, the first example of work done by the hands of free men' as Michelet says, and later ensuring that Benedictine survivors should not only baptise the barbarians who settled in the devastated Roman lands, but also pass on skills and crafts, law and literacy. The Rule insists that the monks shall be a family, ruled by their father the abbot, and that amid all their occupations, the chief is to be the *opus Dei*, the worship of God in the Divine Office. Possessions are to be held in common and used for the corporal works of mercy (witness the status of mediaeval monasteries as charitable hotels for travellers). By vow, the monk is bound to *stabilitas*—residence in the one place,—obedience and monastic virtue; the Rule envisages the community as a group of laymen intent on serving God in community with self-discipline, prayer and good works: there would be a priest or two among them as required, the ordaining of choir-monks and the idea of the 'laybrother' being much later innovations.

Benedicite

(Lat. *Benedicite Domino*, bless the Lord.) The title given to the Song of the Three Children (Dan.3), which has been used liturgically since the earliest times: Rufinus, an early 5th cent. writer, claims that the *Benedicite* was sung all over the world; and the 4th Council of Toledo (633) ordered it to be said before the Epistle at Mass throughout Spain and Gaul. The 1549 Book of Common Prayer prescribed it in place of the *Te Deum* in Lent, and it remains as an alternative.

Benedictine

Contrary to popular belief, this exquisite liqueur is not "manufactured by monks": the only connection is that it is made on the site of the former monastery of Fécamp.

Benediction of the Blessed Sacrament

A post-medieval devotion in which the Sacred Host is set prominently in the monstrance* for the adoration of the faithful in prayers and hymns, with incense*, and which culminates with the celebrant lifting the monstrance and making the sign of the cross with it over the people, after which he replaces the Host in the tabernacle*.

Benemerenti Medal

(Lat., to one who has deserved well.) A Papal decoration instituted by Gregory XVI for the recognition of military valour and civil worthiness: as an ecclesiastical honour, it is extremely unusual in that it can be awarded also to women. It is received typically by sacristans and schoolmistresses.

Betting

Betting and gambling have never been condemned by the Church as wrong, though the expected warnings have naturally been issued and repeated against wrong intention, dishonesty, excess, etc, as the dangers attached to such pursuits. Pope Gregory XIV in 1590 saw fit to restrain the gambling instinct of the Romans by banning under excommunication all betting on the results of Papal elections, the length of time of conclaves* and the choice of new cardinals. The Church's tolerance of aleatory games is demonstrated and sealed by the use of Bingo to raise funds in so many parishes.

Beuron

From the Abbey of Beuron (Hohenzollern on the Danube) arose the Beuron Congregation of Benedictine monks, including the community at Maria Laach. The congregation did much work for liturgical reform and produced a school of art, characterised by work which is rather austere in general line but naturalistic and 'literary' in inspiration.

Beverley

A see was set up at Beverley in 1850 and dissolved in 1878, when the dioceses of Leeds* and Middlesbrough* were formed. While it lasted, it had St. George's at York as its pro-cathedral.

Bible

See Scripture

Bination

(Duplication.) The offering of Mass twice in the same day by a priest who is thus authorised, usually for reasons of distance or the smallness of the building and the absence of another priest. A priest is permitted by general law to offer Mass three times, out of devotion, on Christmas Day and All Souls' Day.

'Binding and Loosing'

The power conferred on Peter (Mt.16:19) and the Apostles (Mt.18:18) by Christ, and exercised clearly, though not only, in the Sacrament of Reconciliation. It is also referred to as the 'power of the keys'.

Birmingham

The see was established in 1850 and made an archdiocese* in 1911; it consists of Warwickshire, Oxon., Staffordshire, West Midlands, Worcestershire, and has Clifton and Shrewsbury as suffragans. It was a main centre of the expanding Catholic life of the country in the early and middle 19th cent., and has the first Catholic cathedral built after the Reformation. It also possesses the first publicly venerated statue of Our Lady, and the first Catholic public school (Sedgley Park*); the first three Synods of Westminster were held as Oscott*. Besides the church at Stonor which was consecrated in 1349, there are missions founded in penal times: at Radford (1613), Spetchley Park (1681), Worcester (1685), Birmingham (1689), and eight others of the 18th cent. The patron is Our Lady Immaculate, and the cathedral has relics of St. Chad, to whom it is dedicated.

Bishop

A bishop is the ruler of a diocese* and defined as one of the successors of the Apostles, in the sense that, from every bishop now alive, the 'chain of ordination' goes back through the ages to one of the Twelve (or to Paul). According to law, the bishop is responsible to the Pope, the chief bishop, for the affairs of his diocese, but is not the Pope's delegate: the bishop governs and teaches his flock in the name of God and as Christ's representative, exercising his powers by virtue of the Apostolic Succession, and is part of the Teaching Church.

Black Canons

See Canons Regular of St. Augustine

Black Friars

The Order of Preachers*, so named from their black cloak. In London, Blackfriars Bridge, Blackfriars Station Rd. etc. are named from the mediaeval Dominican house just by the Thames, south of St. Paul's, evacuated at the Dissolution. In 1596, Richard Burbage converted the remaining property, including the frater, for use as the second Blackfriars theatre.

Black Mass

i) The phrase sometimes used to describe a *Requiem Mass* by reason of the black vestments used.

ii) An insulting parody of the Mass used in devil-worship, with obscenities and contradictions such as the turning of a crucifix upside-down and the recitation of the Our Father backwards.

Black Monks

A name used in England since mediaeval times for Benedictine monks by reason of their black habit.

Black Pope

The Father General of the Jesuits* has been thus described. He was reputed to have immense influence, so as to be a kind of rival to the Pope, or his special counsellor. He resides in Rome and wears the Jesuit soutane (black).

Blaise, Blessing of St.

The legend, widely known, but of no historical value, recalls Blasius, bishop of Sebaste in Armenia and a martyr executed under Licinius in the early 4th cent. One of his miracles is said to be the saving of a young boy brought to him with a fishbone lodged in his throat; hence he was invoked for afflictions of the throat and voice, and a blessing is given on his feast-day, Feb 3rd, with two candles fastened together diagonally and held under the chin of the person being blessed.

Blessed

See Beatification.

Blessed Sacrament

See Eucharist, Real Presence.

Blue Nuns

See Sisters of the Temple.

Boat, incense

The small metal vessel used at liturgical functions for holding incense* in the form of powder or grains is usually shaped somewhat like a boat, but with a base.

Bollandists

A group of learned Jesuits, numbering usually about six, editors of the *Acta Sanctorum* (Lives of the Saints) and of *Analecta Bollandiana* and other scientific works. They have their headquarters in Brussels and are named after John van Bolland who began the *Acta* there about 1630.

Boniface VIII

Successor to St. Celestine V*, in whose abdication he played a major part, Boniface, who took as his two objectives the pacification of Europe and the liberation of the Holy Land from the Turks, found himself for the greater part of his pontificate (1294–1303) at odds with Philip the Fair of France: beginning with his prohibition of Philip's levying of special taxes on clerics without the Pope's consent, in the Bull *Clericis Laicos*, Boniface proceeded, in the Bull *Ausculta Fili*, to assert papal supremacy over kingdoms and princes and, a year later (1302), *Unam Sanctam** proclaimed the Pope's jurisdiction over all creatures, with many quotations from the Fathers*. The following year, Philip sought to put the Pope on trial and Boniface prepared a bull of excommunication against him, but before it could be published, Philip's man, William of Nogaret, brought mercenaries to capture him and hold him at Anagni, his native place. Though rescued after three days, Boniface succumbed to the ill-treatment he had suffered and, broken in spirit and health, he died a month later.

Book of Hours

A mediaeval prayer-book, the principal contents of which were the *Little Office of Our Lady* and the *Office of the Dead*. It was written (and in later times printed) in Latin, originating as it did in a day when those who could read at all could read Latin. It was also called a Primer.

Boston, Massachusetts

Named after Boston, Lincs, (*St Botolf's Stone or Town)*, the city in which was opened the first Catholic church in New England (1788), Boston became an episcopal see in 1808, the first bishop being John Louis Lefebvre. It became a metropolitan see in 1875.

Boy-Bishop

A mediaeval custom, commoner by far in England than on the Continent, which arose from the care of the Church to express in dramatic form the reverence shown by Christ in the Gospels for children. A boy was chosen in a monastry, school or country parish on Dec. 6th, the feast of St. Nicholas*, to carry out certain functions of a bishop until the day of the Holy Innocents. Thus, at Compline of the eve of that feast he would preside from a choir-stall and sing the blessing, in mitre and cope, attended by other boys in copes. The custom seems not to have any connection, in intent at least, with practices like the Lord of Misrule, with its echoes of the Roman custom, at Saturnalia, of putting a slave temporarily in charge of the household. The Boy Bishop was suppressed by Henry VIII, revived by Mary Tudor and finally abolished by Elizabeth I.

Brethren of the Lord

The words 'brothers' and 'sisters' are used in Mk.6:3, with names (James, Joseph—or Joset—Jude and Simon); Paul speaks of James, the Lord's brother, in Gal.1:19. See also Jn.7:3, Acts 1:14, I Cor.9:5. Catholic tradition has always stoutly denied that these could be children of Mary, the mother of Jesus, whose perpetual virginity has been insisted on as early as St. Jerome's* defence of it about 382; and she is nowhere described as their mother. There is no evidence that they are children of a previous marriage of St. Joseph. Modern scholarship inclines to the view that the mother in question is the Mary mentioned in Mk.15:40 and that she was the wife of Cleopas, whom some ancient writers believed to have been a brother of St. Joseph. One could compare the rather more extended and tribal Semitic use of such words as 'brother' and 'sister' to the preacher's *Dear brethren,* the Suffragettes' *sisters,* the trade unionists' *brother,* and *brother* and *sister* in religious community. It would, furthermore, be strange if Jesus handed over his mother to the care of the Apostle John (Jn.19:26) while she had sons to go to.

Breviary

(Lat. *breviarium.* compendium.) The volume or volumes containing the prayers, readings (biblical and other), hymns, antiphons, psalms, and whatever else is needed for the recitation of the daily Divine Office*, with the separate offices of various feasts throughout the year and of the dead. The Roman Breviary is that in common use in the Western Church, except for those religious Orders which have their own breviaries, notably Benedictines*. It is now commonly known as the *Prayer of the Church.*

Brief

A papal letter, signed by the Secretary for Briefs and stamped with an impression of the papal ring; a less formal and less weighty document than a Bull*.

British Church

See Celtic Church.

Brown Scapular

The most widely used of the scapulars, sometimes referred to merely as the Scapular, is worn by members of the Confraternity of Our Lady of Mount Carmel. Its origin is in the story of the vision of St. Simon Stock, wherein he received at the hands of Our Lady the scapular, which he then added to the Carmelite habit.

Buckfast

At Buckfast, in Devon, an abbey of the English Province of the Cassinese Benedictine monks of the Primitive Observance. Founded by monks of the French abbey of Pierre-Qui-Vire, banished in 1882, it was erected into an abbey in 1902. Its buildings occupy the site of former Benedictine and Cistercian monasteries. The church was built by the monks' own labour.

Bugia

The name formerly given to the candle held by an acolyte in ceremonies involving a bishop.

Bull

(Lat. *bulla*, seal.) The most formal kind of Papal letter, opening in the Roman style with the name of the Pope and his description as 'servant of the servants of God', and in previous ages sealed with a leaden seal.

Caeremoniale Episcoporum

(Lat., The Bishops' Ceremonial.) A liturgical book giving detailed instructions for pontifical functions, for the Mass and the ordering of a synod, directions for the ritual to be observed in the singing of Mass and the Office in cathedral and collegiate churches, for the ceremonies of Holy Week and of the death and election of a bishop, and for various extra-liturgical functions. It is also known as the *Pontificale*.

Caesaropapism

A historical and political term for a state of affairs in which the Church becomes, as it were, a department of state and is controlled by the civil power (*Caesar is also Pope*), as happened during the Byzantine Empire. This form of Erastianism has been a characteristic of over-centralised and totalitarian government, ancient, mediaeval and modern, Marxist and Right-Wing 'Catholic'.

Caldey

A very small island off Tenby on the coast of South Wales, inhabited by Celtic monks from about 550 and by Benedictines from the early 12th cent. to 1534. It became, in 1906, the home of a community of Benedictines of the Church of England, who became Catholic in 1913 and left the island in 1928, to be succeeded in that year by Cistercians, most of whom came from Belgium. This community remains.
See Prinknash.

Calendar

(or Kalendar.) The list of holydays, vigils, feasts etc with notes as to their relevance to the Mass and Office. The Calendar varies somewhat from year to year, being affected by the date of Easter; and each diocese, religious order and congregation has its own variant Calendar, published in its Ordo*, though in the West, all are based on the Roman Calendar.

Calvary

(Lat. *calvaria*, skull: 'Gologotha, that is the place of the skull,' Mt.27:33.) The one thing the Scriptures do not say about the place of Our Lord's crucifixion is that it was a hill or a raised place of any kind: nonetheless, it is easy to see how the Byzantine and later Western imagination placed the event on a dramatic height, silhouetted against the sky. We know that the Romans, having on the one hand made a law against execution within city walls, did on the other hand give their crucifixions the greatest possible publicity—they were meant as deterrents. The obvious place would be therefore just outside the city gate and John's account puts it 'hard by the city' (Jn.19:20). A legend, first found in Origen (2nd–3rd cent.)—and possibly invented by him, since, of his three ways of interpreting the Scriptures, literal, moral and allegorical, he preferred the last—supersedes the ancient Jewish tradition of Adam's burial at Hebron and inters him at Jerusalem, on the very spot of Calvary, thus neatly interpreting the name of the place (the Skull being Adam's) and balancing off the Old and New Testaments in the poetic justice of the blood of the Second Adam flowing on to the head of the first. It is not known precisely where Christ died, but tradition has it that St. Helena dug up the actual cross from its burial-place, which was supposed to be close to the place of execution. Her son, the Emperor Constantine, then undertook the restoration of the site (which had been used as a rubbish dump in Hadrian's time and planted with a grove in honour of Venus), erecting a basilica and other buildings to cover the spot. It is now sheltered by the Crusaders' church of the Resurrection. Other, more recent, excavators have claimed various other sitings for the true Calvary, none of them any more inherently likely than that of the Empress.

Calvinism

The system of religious thought identified with John Calvin (1509–64) of Picardy, a man of immense learning and single-mindedness, austere in life and utterly convinced that he was in the right, whose pen has had greater influence than that of any other of the Reformers. Breaking with Rome in the belief that he had a divine commission to restore the Church to its early purity, he developed his thought in his *Institutes* and his *Articles on Governing the Church* and attempted to apply it to the governing of the city of Geneva, until the citizens revolted against his severity and expelled him. He returned, however, and converted the city to a theocracy with himself as dictator. The theocracy used excommunication and torture, inflicted severe legal punishments even for purely religious offences, and banned such recreations as games and dancing. Calvin accepted the Bible as the only rule of faith (which includes the *testimonium Spiritus Sancti*, an interior light by which we can distinguish the canonical* books from others) and taught that since the Fall, which was willed by God, man has no free will, that all human deeds outside Christianity are sins, and even the good works of Christians are in themselves evil but 'covered' by the imputed merits of Christ; God, even before the Creation, had destined some of his creatures to glory and others to damnation: thus the sinner can never attain to salvation, nor the 'saved' ever fall from grace (the assurance sought for by the dying Oliver Cromwell). Calvin's teaching on the Eucharist was somewhat ambiguous, but appears not to countenance the Real Presence*; as for the Church, he sets it above the State, as he did in practice at Geneva. Calvinism was officially adopted by the French Protestants (Huguenots*) in 1559; it had some influence on the Church of England and a strong effect on the Nonconformist Churches, but in these islands is most evident in the mind and teachings of John Knox in Scotland. It has also penetrated many North American sects.

Camaldolese

An Order founded by St. Romuald, c. 1012, near Arezzo, with the ideal of a loosely united community of hermits, reminiscent to some degree of the Egyptian monks; the original severity was gradually mitigated and, in 1102, a monastery was founded on ordinary coenobitic lines. As the saint left no written rule, practice has varied and still varies somewhat in the different congregations*. There is also an order of Camaldolese nuns.

Camerlengo

See Chamberlain.

Candlemas

Known until recently as the Purification of Our Lady (Lk.2:22-39), now the Presentation of Our Lord Jesus Christ, Feb. 2nd involves the blessing of candles and the carrying of them in procession, in a symbolic remembrance of the offering made by the Mother of God on the occasion thus commemorated. Initiated in Jerusalem about 350, the feast changed its date from Feb. 14th to 2nd, was introduced into Constantinople by Justinian in 542, and spread thence throughout the East, being known as the Meeting (viz. of Christ and Simeon). Later it was brought into the Latin Church, the procession being introduced, it is believed, by Pope Sergius I (687-701).

Candles

There is a widespread and very ancient use of candles both in popular devotion and in the liturgy. Almost every Catholic church has a stand of candles or votive lamps for the use of the faithful, often set by an altar or shrine of the Sacred Heart or of the Blessed Virgin or some other saint. Candles in liturgical use on the altar itself cannot be traced before about 1175, when we read that the 'present custom' of the Papal chapel was to have one candle on either side of the altar cross; previously, the candles carried before the Pope in procession as a mark of honour were set down on the floor behind the altar. Later custom and legislation prescribed varying arrangements at Mass, according to the feast-day or the dignity of the altar or of the person officiating (see *bugia*): thus, one candle was frequently used to light the Missal, six became the norm for the high altar, and 12 at least for Exposition of the Blessed Sacrament. The Paschal* Candle, distributing its flame to the whole congregation at the Vigil Service, sums up the symbolism which had very early grown out of the use of candles as necessary

lighting, and which is elaborated in the *Exultet**, chanted before the candle. Candles are also required in the administration of certain Sacraments, e.g. Baptism, Communion of the Sick, Anointing of the Sick, Matrimony outside Mass. In certain Far Eastern countries, Christian converts adapted the custom of 'lighting a candle' by burning their traditional joss-sticks before Christian images.
See also Candlemas.

Canon

(Gk. χανων, rod, measure, norm, principle.) The word has acquired many ecclesiastical meanings. In early days, the Canons were the books received by the Church as the rule of faith and practice, the canonical scriptures. Later, the Canon was the collection of received books, and the earliest meaning of 'canonise' was 'to receive into the canon of scripture'. Eventually the word was used of the rules and institutions of the Church, then of the authentic catalogue of martyrs and saints. *Canon Law* became thus the accepted norm or rule of Church discipline and each particular item of the *Codex Iuris Canonici** is referred to as Canon, with its number quoted. Canon was also the name for that part of the Mass beginning at the Sanctus and containing the Consecration and now called the Eucharistic Prayer. Canon, as a person, is either Regular*, Cathedral* or Collegiate*.

Canon, Cathedral

A member of a cathedral chapter, appointed by the bishop. The canonry consists of the right to a stall in the choir, a voice in the chapter and a share of the chapter's income. Strictly, he is bound to residence in the Cathedral city, to the chanting of the Office and the assistance of the bishop in governing his diocese; but conditions vary from country to country and even from diocese to diocese. In England and Scotland, for instance, there being no revenues attached to the canonries, the canons are not bound to reside or to chant the Office. Canons appoint a vicar capitular* on the death of the bishop, and are allowed to submit to Rome three names in candidature for the see. Various dioceses have obtained varying privileges, chiefly of dress, for their canons; but the canons of Terni emulated

the Vestal Virgins of old by being permitted, on the feast of their patron St. Juvenal (May 3rd) to set free a condemned murderer: this prerogative, of great antiquity, renewed and confirmed by bulls of Paul IV in 1557 and Clement VIII in 1599, seems not to have found favour with modern Italian criminal law.

Canons, Collegiate

Members of the chapter of a collegiate church, i.e. a church served by a college of secular priests, called canons, because they form a chapter and in some instances live a common life. The rights and duties of such canons are similiar to those of cathedral canons, except that they refer to the college and not the diocese, and the chief occupation of such canons is the singing of the Divine Office. There have been no collegiate churches in England since the Reformation.

Canon Penitentiary

A kind of special confessor appointed in each diocese, with authority to absolve from sins and censures reserved to the bishop.

Canons Regular

Priests living in community according to a Rule and under the vows of religion. They sing the Divine Office and live like monks but are ready at any time to carry out the duties of the active life. Ordination, which to the monk is incidental, is of the essence for Canons Regular.

Canons Regular of Premontré

(Premonstratensians, also called *Norbertines,* after their founder St. Norbert, +1134.) A flourishing order of Canons Regular*, with houses in Europe and the New World. The Fathers engage in parish work, education and missions; the few nuns of the order are contemplative and strictly enclosed. A special characteristic of the order is devotion to the Blessed Sacrament.

Canons Regular of St. Augustine

Many groups of Canons Regular* adopted the Rule of St. Augustine and were known as Black Canons, by reason of their habit, as distinguished from the White

(Premonstratensian) Canons. They now survive mainly as the Canons Regular of the Lateran*, of the Immaculate Conception*, as the Crosier* Canons, as the Congregations of St. Maurice d'Agaune, and of the Great St. Bernard (the last being the monks of the Alpine hospices and of the St. Bernard dogs—the saint in question being St. Bernard of Menthon, who founded that congregation about 1000).

Canons Regular of the Holy Cross

(*Crosier Canons.*) Founded in 1211, now a small congregation best known for their faculty of blessing rosaries with the Crosier Indulgence.
See also Knights of the Cross.

Canons Regular of the Immaculate Conception

Founded in France in 1866 to restore primitive observance of the canonical life, with daily office, permanent abstinence, and strict fasting.

Canons Regular of the Lateran

The full title is the Sacred and Apostolic Order of Canons Regular of the Lateran of our Most Holy Redeemer. They were appointed for the service of the Lateran Basilica but were replaced in the 15th cent. by secular canons. They are now engaged chiefly in parochial work. Their English Province is governed by a titular abbot.

Canonesses Regular

Comparable to Canons Regular and roughly contemporaneous, the best-known being Canonesses Regular of St. Augustine*, of the Holy Sepulchre* and of the Lateran*. They are enclosed and have the Divine Office as their first duty; many of their communities keep schools.

Canonesses Regular of St. Augustine

There are a few houses in England, founded by Canonesses driven out of France by revolutionary laws; each of these communities maintains a school.

Canonesses Regular of the Holy Sepulchre

An ancient foundation, if not of precise date, their constitution was approved in 1631. They are bound to the Office in choir and to a life of penance; their English house near Chelmsford, founded by migration from Liège, has a school attached.

Canonesses Regular of the Lateran

(See Canons Regular of the Lateran.) The Canonesses have two houses of contemplative nuns in England, at Newton Abbot and Hoddesdon; other institutes, e.g. that at Haywards Heath, have schools.

Canonisation

The insertion of the name of a person (deceased) in the Canon* of the Saints entails the most rigorous and detailed scrutiny of the life, acts and writings of the candidate, to establish heroic virtue and the proof of miracles wrought at his or her intercession. All this was formerly the province of the Sacred Congregation of Rites*, but now has its own Sacred Congregation for the Causes of Saints and, since it is so painstaking and thorough and ends in lavish public ceremonial, it costs a great deal of money; hence the majority of canonisations have elevated priests and religious and such others as have become widely famous and have the corresponding resources of a large popular following or a religious order. The process of canonisation is no sort of comment on the sanctity of others whose cause is not publicly promoted: in fact many of the greatest saints were never formally canonised, as the process was first used as late as A.D. 993, when Pope John XV declared Ulrich of Augsburg a saint. A canonisation is publicly pronounced by the Pope in person at St. Peter's in the reading of a Bull* and the singing of a solemn Mass (a liturgy of the saint's feast having been already composed, for observation annually); prayer may now be offered publicly in his honour, churches and altars dedicated to him, statues and pictures displayed and his relics venerated. Canonisation is regarded as a public and infallible pronouncement of the Church.

Capuchins

The Friars Minor Capuchin (colloquial It. *scappuccini*, hermits) are the branch of the Franciscans set up in 1525 by Matteo da Bascio in an effort to restore the literal observance of the rule of the Saint; they wear the beard, their churches are very plain, and their life is strict. The first Capuchins came to England in 1599.

Cardiff

The Archdiocese of Cardiff, erected in 1916, was formerly the Diocese of Newport; it comprises Gwent, Hereford and Glamorganshire. In many places of the archdiocese, the Faith never died: Abergavenny, Monmouth, Hereford, Courtfield, Llanarth and Usk. The majority of the Catholics now are either Irish or English. The patron is Our Lady Immaculate, and the cathedral is dedicated to St. David.

Cardinal

(Lat. *cardo*, hinge.) The *presbyter cardinalis* was the priest permantly attached to a church, the term later being restricted to the Roman clergy, the natural assistants of the Bishop of Rome. Later on, there were added the *Cardinal Deacons*, who cared for the poor of the city (cf. Acts 6:2–6) and in the 8th cent., *Cardinal Bishops*, the Pope's neighbouring pontiffs, whom he sometimes called upon to represent him. This *College of Cardinals* became an advisory body to the Pope in Consistory*, growing steadily in public esteem, to become equals to princes of the blood. Cardinals in the modern Church have been nominees of the Pope and are either pastors of populous dioceses (it is now assumed that certain large sees, e.g. Paris, Westminster, New York, will have a Cardinal) or administrators domiciled in Rome and controlling Roman Congregations*, curial* offices or ecclesiastical commissions. The electing of a new Pope is done by all the Cardinals gathered in conclave*. Time was when Popes would create Cardinal anyone they chose, laymen and all. It appears that Mazarin, in the 17th cent., was the last lay cardinal, while in the 19th cent., Cardinals Consalvi and Antonelli had only deacon's orders—but modern Canon Law demands at least

priesthood. The Cardinal's title is *Eminence*; his robes include cassock and train in the 'sacred purple' (i.e. scarlet) and the Red Hat, wheel-shaped and broad-brimmed, set on his head for a moment by the Pope on reception of the cardinalate and then reserved unworn during life, to be suspended over his tomb until it falls to dust: *sic transit gloria mundi.*

Cardinal Virtues

The four *philosophers' virtues*—prudence, justice, fortitude, temperance—were taken over by Christian theologians as early as St. Ambrose and St. Augustine, and classified as contrasting with the Theological* Virtues.

Carmel

A house of the Carmelite* Order, usually of nuns.

Carmelites

These friars, the Brothers of the Order of the Most Blessed Mother of God and ever Virgin Mary of Mount Carmel, claim a living link with the O.T. hermits who lived on Mt. Carmel under Elijah and Elisha. Historically, we may take 1155 as their beginning, when a hermitage was founded there by St. Berthold; the community spread to Europe and a Kentishman, St. Simon Stock, modified their life and turned them into mendicant friars. In the 16th cent., the reforms of St. Teresa of Avila and St. John of the Cross resulted in two branches of the Order emerging, the Calced (shod) Carmelites 'of the Old Observance', who have somewhat tempered the severity of their rule, and the discalced (barefoot) or Teresian Carmelites, who follow the reform of St. Teresa, with night office, perpetual abstinence from meat and special fasts. Both branches engage in the ministry and foreign missions, the Calced also maintaining schools. There were in England, at the time of the Dissolution*, about 55 friaries of Carmelites. The nuns of the Order were founded in 1452, with the modified form of the rule then obtaining; from 1562, St. Teresa set up convents of the primitive, unmitigated observance, which later far outnumbered the others. These nuns live in strict poverty and enclosure, with limited numbers in community, perpetual abstinence, silence and manual work.

Carthusians

This order of monks whose contemplative regime combines Benedictine monachism and the asceticism of the solitary life, was founded by St. Bruno* in 1084 at La Grande Chartreuse in the Dauphiné Alps. There is total abstinence from meat, one meal a day, and night office for about three hours. Their chant, left without the polish achieved in certain other orders, has 'a certain *rusticitas*, which they treasure—and three Offices are recited daily, the Divine Office, that of the Blessed Virgin and that of the Dead: silence is suspended on Sundays and feast-days. The founder wrote no Rule, the record of their customs *(Consuetudines Carthusianae)* being compiled and approved in the 12th cent. and receiving occasional additions from General Chapters. The order was little affected by the general monastic decline at the end of the Middle Ages (it has been described as *Numquam reformata quia numquam deformata*, never recalled because never astray), its members suffering heroically in the English Reformation and in the French Revolution. The monks were put out of La Grande Chartreuse by the anti-clerical laws of 1901 and permitted to return only during the course of the Second World War. The celebrated green and yellow Chartreuse, the world's most expensive liquer, made for a long time in the monastry, is now produced at Tarragona under the supervision of laybrothers, the proceeds still being used to maintain the Order and its very substantial charities. The nuns of the Order live the same severe life as their brothers, except that they have a daily community meal; their houses, very few in number, are supervised by the monks.

Castel Gandolfo

The residence and grounds, in the Alban Hills near Rome, which are used by the Popes during the hot and unhealthy Roman summer. Papal tenure of this property was confirmed and guaranteed by the Lateran* Treaty.

Casuistry

'Person, especially a theologian, who lays down application of ethical rules to special cases' says the C.O.D. Casuistry is always needed, in simpler or more involved form, whenever moral issues are to be judged in particular cases, and it was the introduction of universal private penances which gave rise to formal casuistry in the Church; by the 7th cent., there were in use numerous *Guides to the Giving of Penances*, which were later gathered into *Compendia of Penance*, to constitute complete legal digests. Later theologians formed schools of casuistry in contention with each other, such as Probabilism, Probabiliorism, Equiprobabilism, the first of which, with the support of St. Alphonsus Liguori*, won the widest acceptance. The fault to which Probabilism is most liable is obviously laxism (which was deplored by the Jesuit General Aquaviva in 1604) and casuistry as such got tarred with the same brush, so that the C.O.D. can end its list of definitions quoted above with 'quibbler'. Casuistry in its derogatory sense is usually attributed only to Catholic theologians, though the Church of England has had notable casuists—such as Jeremy Taylor—and the system has been and is necessarily practised in courts of law everywhere.

Catechism

(Gk. κατηχησις, instruction by word of mouth, instruction of catechumens; cf. 1 Cor. 14:19.) The teaching of Christian doctrine by question and answer; a book of instruction so arranged. The use of such summaries of doctrine is of considerable antiquity, though the term seems to have been used—in 'modern' times—only since the 16th cent.; the Council of Lambeth (1281) issued such a document set out in groups of seven, explaining the seven petitions of the Our Father, seven Beatitudes, seven Gifts of the Holy Spirit, seven Capital Sins, seven principal Virtues, seven Works of Mercy. Later, J. Colet, Dean of St Paul's, put out a catechism, and in France, at the end of the 15th cent., Gerson's *ABC des simples gens* was much used. Of the great number of catechisms produced by the Reformers, the most famous was Luther's *Kleiner Katechismus* of 1529, still the standard text for Lutheran churches in many countries; the Book of Common Prayer includes a short catechism of questions and answers 'to be learned of every person before he be brought to be confirmed by the bishop'. The 'Catechism of the Council of Trent' or 'Roman Catechism' is not strictly a catechism but a manual of instruction compiled at the order of the Council of Trent. The catechism besι known and longest used in England and Wales has been the 'Penny Catechism' approved by the hierachy for use in all dioceses; of latter years, there has been much discontent over its adequacy and over the way it has come to be used. In the U.S., the staple has been the Baltimore Catechism of 1885, in Ireland, the Maynooth (1875). The two most important modern compilations are the Australian Catechism and the Dutch Catechism.

Catharism

(Gk. καθαρος pure.) The name given to a group of dualistic sects which arose about the year 1000, the most important Cathars of the West being the Albigensians*. According to Catharism, matter is evil, being either the creation of an evil principle which was God's rival, or a form of creation in rebellion. To extend matter in any way, e.g. by procreation, was sinful. The logic of Catharism is not only a warped denial of true religion but a demented attack on human society itself.

Cathedra

(Gk. Lat., seat.) The chair or throne of a bishop in his church, which is therefore called *cathedral church*, the church of the chair; also, symbolically, the chair of the supreme bishop as the teaching authority. See Ex cathedra.

Cathedral Church

The cathedral of a diocese is the church in which the bishop has set up permanently his episcopal seat (Lat. *cathedra*). It is usually situated in the town from which the diocese is named, and which is the residence of the bishop. The date of the cathedral's consecration and of its titular saint are kept as feasts in the diocese. A cathedral has a chapter of canons whose duties ordinarily include the chanting of the Divine Office and the remaining liturgical functions (this is not done in Great Britain, but at Westminster, there is a special college of chaplains appointed for the purpose). The cathedral is the central and mother church of the diocese. See Pro-Cathedral.

Catholic Apostolate, Society of the

See under Society of Catholic Apostolate.

Catholic Relief Acts

In 1778, Parliament passed the Acts 17 & 18 Geo. III, c.49 (Ireland), by which Catholics were permitted to own landed property provided they took an oath not involving denial of their religion; priests were no longer to be persecuted on the word of a common informer, the sentence of life-long imprisonment for keeping a Catholic school was abolished. This Act provoked the Gordon Riots. In 1791, Catholics who took the prescribed oath were freed from the Statutes of Recusancy and the Oath of Supremacy, toleration was extended to Catholic schools, and Catholic worship and certain posts in the law and in the armed forces were opened to Catholics. By the Act of 1793, Catholics in Ireland were admitted to the franchise, the professions and the universities. The most decisive of the series of Acts was 10 Geo. IV c.7, of 1829 (which became known as the 'Year of Catholic Emancipation'), when the Irish situation was critical: nearly all disabilities were taken away, Catholics being now admitted to most public offices, while some of the disabilities that remained were already a dead letter, e.g. the prohibition of public religious celebrations and the denial of validity to marriages before a Catholic priest; but Catholics were (quite unnecessarily) forbidden to take the names of ancient episcopal sees for their new dioceses (see Ecclesiastical Titles Act). The last Act passed was 16 & 17 Geo.V c.55, of 1926, by which all remaining disabilities were removed except that: a King or Queen may not be a Catholic nor marry a Catholic; a Catholic may not be Regent, Lord Chancellor, Keeper of the Great Seal, nor may he present or nominate to a benefice; nor may a Catholic priest sit as a Member in the House of Commons (a disability he shares with the clergy of the Established Church).

Catholic Truth Society (C.T.S.)

An organisation of members of the Catholic faith, men and women, clerical and lay, founded to promulgate the truths of the Catholic religion by means of the written word and otherwise. It was founded in 1868 by Herbert Vaughan (then Rector of St. Joseph's College, Mill Hill, later Cardinal Archbishop of Westminster) in collaboration with Fr. Bampfield and Lady Herbert of Lea. When Vaughan was consecrated Bishop of Salford in 1872, the Society seems to have been allowed to disappear. It was revived in 1884 by James Britten, a learned botanist, with the blessing and support of Vaughan. After early struggles, the C.T.S. gathered strength and has since been publishing vast quantities of information and devotion, chiefly in the form of pamphlets. It earned the praise of Pope Paul VI, who conferred on it the title 'publishers to the Holy See', because of its activity for the spread of Catholic culture. It defines its objects as: to disseminate amongst Catholics low-priced devotional works; to assist Catholics to a better knowledge of their religion; to spread among non-Catholics information about the Catholic faith; to assist the circulation of Catholic books.

Catholic Women's League

Founded in 1906 to help women put themselves at the service of the Church and of the community, the League takes, as its chief spiritual work, the help it can give in the religious education of children (under the title of Our Lady's Catechists); its other fields of endeavour include work for the aged, for deprived families and the handicapped and, where appropriate, international relief; the World Union of Catholic Women's Organisations (including autonomous Catholic Women's Leagues in nearly all the English-speaking countries) has consultative status with UNESCO.

Cause

The Cause of a Servant of God (the latter being the term first used of any deceased person considered a candidate for canonisation*) is the process of inquiry and subsequent promotion through the stages of being declared Venerable*, then Blessed* (at which point public veneration may be paid), then Saint*. These titles are bestowed only by the Roman Congregation* for the Causes of Discovery of Saints. Any prior public veneration brings the cause to a permanent halt.

Celebret

A document signed by his bishop, to be used by a priest as guarantee of his identity and of his ordinary's approval when, e.g., he requests permission to celebrate Mass in places where he is not known.

Celestine V, St. (c. 1215–96)

After the death of Pope Nicholas IV in 1292, there was a 'hung' conclave* for two years until, at the suggestion of one of the 12 cardinals*, a holy and aged hermit was chosen. Peter del Murrone, taking the name of Celestine, embarked on a pontificate remarkable for its brevity and its astonishing ineptitude. Totally ignorant of the 'world'—and the Curial Church at that time was highly political—his decisions went from disaster to naive disaster; for instance, in doubling the number of cardinals, he chose Frenchmen for six of the new red hats—a move which led indirectly to Avignon and the Schism of the West. Most of his acts are not known in detail, as they were all abrogated by his successor Boniface* VIII. After a few months, the necessity of a change was clear to all, including Celestine, who made further history by resigning on Dec. 13th of that same year 1294. He was kept in custody by Boniface until he died. The harsh verdict of Dante, calling the saintly octogenarian's 'great refusal' an act of cowardice (*Che fece per viltà lo gran rifiuto*, Inferno iii, 60) was soon countered by Clement V's canonisation of Celestine (1313).

Celtic Church

The name given to that form of Christianity which flowered in Britain proper until the end of the 6th cent., in Wales, Scotland, Ireland and Brittany until the 11th. The faith brought to the Province, the 'Roman Island', by soldiers and merchants (there being enough of such traffic to render not entirely absurd the legend of the merchant Joseph of Arimathaea's arrival in the Severn estuary, with or without the Holy Grail) spilled over into Hibernia, where it is known to have existed in the 4th cent. After the great revival and expansion due to Patrick*, there was great missionary activity from that country (e.g. Columba's foundation on Iona as a base). British migrants took their faith to Brittany, incidentally exterminating the natives in the western parts and integrating with those of the East. These Celtic communities used seven Sacraments and liturgies of Catholic origin; the rather meagre Celtic representation at the Synod of Arles (314) and the Council of Rimini (359) suggest a church not yet of great public influence, its spread to the army and the upper classes appearing later. Contact with Rome (with e.g. Leo the Great on such matters as the date of Easter) survived the Roman evacuation, but the Saxon invasions swept Celtic church and culture away to Wales, Cornwall and the North, and the next communication with Rome was through the Church founded by Augustine*. Whitby* (664) meant that the whole of the Church in England accepted the Roman discipline, and it was only in the 11th cent. that the Irish conformed (the Celtic organisation being very strongly monastic—so that a bishop could have an abbot as his superior—and not based on dioceses). The period beginning about the time of the Rescript of Honorius (410) was one of intense missionary and scholarly activity for the Irish Church: St. Brendan's fabled voyage in his leather boat is now proved possible, and monks carried their faith and learning into Europe (John Scotus Erigena and Sedulius Scotus illuminated among the Franks that Carolingian renaissance inspired by Alcuin of York) and numberless preachers, hermits and seafaring monks left their names—as our maps testify—scattered, by popular canonisation, over Brittany, Cornwall and Wales.

Chair of St. Peter, Feast of the

The commemoration of the (episcopal) Chair of Peter at Antioch, his first bishopric, was kept on Feb 22nd, and that of his Chair at Rome on the 18th of that month, which was and is the opening day of the Octave of Prayer for Christian Unity. Now there is one commemoration, on the 22nd, for both feasts.

Chalcedon, Council of

(Fourth Oecumenical.) Summoned in 451 to deal with heresies concerning the nature of Christ, this Council of 630 bishops, all Eastern apart from two Africans and the two legates of Pope Leo I,

accepted and acclaimed Leo's Tome* (Peter has spoken through Leo) as the classic statement of Catholic doctrine. It annulled the acts of the Latrocinium*, condemned Eutyches once again, and put out, together with a reaffirmation of Nicaea* and Constantinople*, a definition concerning the Incarnation which was accepted by all but the Monophysite churches: those are mistaken who deny the Virgin Mary the title of Theotokos*, thereby implying that the humanity of Christ is separable from his Divine Person; as are those who confuse the divine and human natures into one and hold thereby that the divine nature is passible. The condemnation is extended to the ideas of a duality of Sons, the possibility of the Godhead, the mixture or other confusion of the two natures in Christ, the heavenly essence of his human nature, the pre-existence of two natures which became one at the Incarnation; there exists, finally, the one Person in two natures which are united without confusion, without change, without division, without separation. Even after this defining of the limits of legitimate speculation, the Monophysite* and Monothelite* heresies continued to divide the Church until the end of the 7th cent., when they had shrunk to the limits of the Copts, the Armenians and the Syrian Jacobites, most of whom are still out of communion either with Rome or with the Orthodox Church. The 28th Canon of Chalcedon made Constantinople a patriarchate and gave it first place after Rome; Leo rejected this as impugning the status of the older Patriarchates of the East.

Challoner, Richard (1691–1781)

One of the most outstanding figures of the penal times, Challoner, born of Presbyterian parents, became a Catholic in his boyhood and went at the age of 14 to Douai* to study for the priesthood. It was only after he had held the vice-presidency of that college that he returned to England, in 1730, to leave again in 1738, a course he deemed wise in view of the irritatingly witty reply he had written to A Letter from Rome, Showing an Exact Conformity Between Papacy and Paganism by the irascible pamphleteer Conyers Middleton. Consecrated titular* bishop of Debra in 1741 and named coadjutor to Bishop Petre, Vicar Apostolic* of the London district, he succeeded in 1758. Besides his controversial writings, he left devotional books, chiefly the *Garden of the Soul** and *Meditations for Every Day of the Year* (used widely by non-Catholics also), and very carefully documented historical works, such as *Memoirs of Missionary Priests* and *Britannia Sancta* (lives of traditional native saints). In his scriptural work, the Bishop's purpose was to make the Douai* readable by modernising the language and correcting errors.

Challoner's Bible

The version of the Bible commonly known as the Douay (or Rheims) is in fact a revision made by Bishop Challoner, of the N.T. in 1749–52, of the O.T. in 1750. This severe recension (Newman wrote, '. . . almost amounted to a new translation' and Wiseman, 'It has been altered and modified until scarce any verse remains as it was originally printed',) took the form of approximating to the King James version and clearing up obscurities in the original.

Chamberlain

The Papal Chamberlain (*Chamberlain of the Holy Roman Church*) is always a Cardinal, his duty being to administer the Holy See's property and income. On the death of the Pope, he becomes temporary head of the Sacred College, administers the affairs of the Church, summons the conclave* and is in general command until a new Pope is chosen.

Chantry

The office or benefice kept up for the offering of Mass (often sung, 'chanted') for the soul of the donor: also the chantry chapel, the small chapel built for the offering of such Masses. Wealthy persons, among them some mediaeval English kings, left endowment for Mass to be sung in perpetuity for the repose of their souls. Such a chapel was frequently contained within a larger church—many cathedrals have chantry chapels—and enclosed within a screen of stone or wood, and sometimes it would be a small separate building erected by or attached to the church. The chantry priest, besides offering the prescribed Masses, usually had some other duty, e.g. as curate,

schoolmaster or chaplain; many chantry chapels became centres of education, a number of them evolving into the so-called 'Edwardian' grammar schools. To finance Henry VIII's French war, an Act was passed declaring the King proprietor of the Chantries and their possessions; but it was only in 1547, after his death, that the chantry and guild chapels were suppressed—to the number of 2,374. The new Act prescribed that the revenues should be used for public and charitable purposes, though Edward's advisers in fact pocketed a great deal; however, it laid down that pensions should be provided for the dispossessed chantry priests.

Chaplain

A priest appointed to serve an institution such as a school, convent, prison, or a certain class of persons such as members of the armed forces. In Great Britain, as in some other countries, chaplains are commissioned officers of the branch of the armed forces they serve, and here their superior is a titular bishop. At Westminster Cathedral, the canons not being resident, their choir duties are discharged by a college of chaplains equal in number to the canons.

See Confessor.

Charismatic Movement

(Gk. χαρισμα, free gift, gift of God's grace.) Observable in various forms from the earliest part of the century in groups known as the Pentecostal Churches, this movement spread to the Catholic Church after, and, it is claimed, as a result of, the Second Vatican* Council; Pope John XXIII* prayed at the opening of the latter for a second Pentecost. The first group to be publicly known was at Ann Arbor, Michigan, U.S.A. The groups experience the Baptism of the Holy Spirit ('Immersion with the power of God') and exercise the Gifts of Tongues (for praise), of Prophecy (for imparting the immediate message of God), of Healing (physical and inner), of the Word, of Wisdom, of Knowledge, and others. Membership effects a deep conversion and a commitment to Christ, with daily prayer; and there has been a renewal, through the groups, of daily Bible reading. The aim of the Charismatic Renewal is to transform the individual, the family, the Church and society.

Charles Borromeo, St. (1538–84)

An outstanding character of the Counter-Reformation*. Of a noble Italian family, he was made cardinal and archbishop of Milan by his uncle Pius IV, a great nepotist—this is one of the rare examples of the Church benefiting from this undesirable practice—and distinguished himself at the later sessions of the Council of Trent*, taking an important part in drafting the Catechism*. Returning to Milan, he instituted, against strong initial opposition, a radical reform of his diocese, encouraging the Jesuits, setting up seminaries for the training of the clergy, founding the Confraternity of Christian Doctrine for the instruction of children. He gave devoted personal service to the sick and poor of his diocese, particularly in the plague of 1576.
Feast-day Nov 4th.

Charterhouse

Anglicisation of *chartreuse**. The name in current English usage, attaches to the school built in 1611 on the site of the London Charterhouse at Aldersgate and later moved out to Surrey.
See Carthusians.

Chartreuse

Any house of Carthusians*. See Grande Chartreuse. Also the name of the renowned liqueur first concocted by the monks of La Grande Chartreuse and said to contain the essences of 137 different herbs.

Chasuble

The outermost vestment worn by the celebrant at Mass and in some processions of the Blessed Sacrament. The modern cut of the garment, much resembling the mediaeval, recaptures the original form (*chasuble* from Lat. *casula,* little house) which was the ancient Roman *paenula,* the voluminous mantle made of a single circle of material with a hole for the head, much like a large poncho. The chasuble is made in various colours for different feasts and seasons of the liturgical year.

Cherub

(pl. cherubim, *Heb.* k'rub, k'rubim.) What has sunk linguistically to a term of patronising endearment and visually to a severed baby-head floating on sub-auricular wings, began—and, in the Bible, remains—a menacing multiple creature, whose task is to guard the divine Presence from all that is defiled. (Gen.3:24, Ex.25;10–22). The cherub, like its probable original, the Assyrian *karibu,* embodies conjointly the wisdom of the man, the courage of the lion, the strength of the bull, the swiftness of the eagle, and is correspondingly represented both in Assyrian art and in Ezekiel's bewilderingly magnificent visions in chapters 1, 9, 10, 11. St John's borrowing from these in Rev.4:6–8 gives rise, through the interpretation of St Irenaeus, to the symbolic use of man, lion, bull and eagle for the four Evangelists.

Chi Rho

The name, approximated in English, for the sign composed of the two Greek letters χ (ch) and ρ (r), used by the early Christians as a sign for the name *Christos,* of which they are the first letters. The sign has persisted in Christian art and decoration into modern times.

Chrism

Olive oil into which a little balsam has been mixed. It is blessed on Maundy Thursday by the bishop and is used at the blessing of fonts, at Baptism, Confirmation, the consecration of a bishop and in consecrating churches, altars and the sacred vessels.
See Balm.

Christian Brothers

i) The Brothers of the Christian Schools, a congregation of laymen founded by St. John Baptist de la Salle in 1684 to bind themselves by the three vows of religion for the work of educating the poor.
ii) A similar congregation, the Christian Brothers of Ireland, founded by Edmund Ignatius Rice in 1822.
See Presentation Brothers.

Chrysostom, St John

(Gk. χρυσοστομος of golden mouth.) John undermined his health around the age of 30 by a too-austere monastic life under the Rule of St Pachomius*. Ordained priest in 386 by Flavian, bishop of Antioch, he established his unsurpassed reputation as *the* Christian orator with his homilies, mostly on the N.T. which he preached in an effort to restore the failing

Christian life of that city. His works demonstrate both a clear perception of the biblical passage's spiritual meaning and a direct practical application. Made Patriarch of Constantinople against his will, he undertook to combat the corruption of court, clergy and faithful. Here, however, he was thwarted by his own blend of honesty, asceticism and tactlessness, and the deadly combination against him of the hatred of Theophilus, who had hoped to be Patriarch, and the malevolence of the Empress Eudoxia, who took all John's denunciations personally: he was removed from the see by the Council of the Oak, an assembly packed with Theophilus' followers. Recalled by the court, he once more offended the sensitive Empress, and in 404, he was banished, despite the clear support of the people of Constantinople, of Pope Innocent I and of all the Western Church. His first place of exile not proving harsh enough for his persecutors, he was removed to Pontus and there done to death by being made to travel extensively on foot in the severest weather. Perhaps the most influential of his multifarious writings is still his early work 'On the Priesthood'. The Liturgy named after him, and still in general use in the Orthodox Churches though later than his time, owes much to the liturgical reforms he instituted at Constantinople.

Church

The earliest known use of κυριακον, the Lord's (house), is early 4th cent., while the political word εχχλησια is borrowed by LXX to express *qahal*, the Hebrew religious assembly, and taken over in the N.T. for the Christian community. It is not easily understood how the remote Northern tribes assimilated the former word into their Germanic speech—to make *kirihha, kirke, church*—instead of the more accessible Romanised *ecclesia*, which had already come to carry also the meaning of *church* as building. Apart from the architectural meaning, the word is used for a) the Church of Christ, the visible society in union with the Pope, b) the Christians of a particular Patriarchate or other large grouping e.g. the Church of the West, the Orthodox Churches, c) a local community such as the Church of Westminster, the Church of Salford—an ancient concept of Church recurring frequently in the documents of the Second Vatican Council, d) the pastors or authorities of the Church (Mt.18:17), e) the clergy (as e.g. 'That young man is entering the Church') a form of thought and speech not much encouraged nowadays, f) those communities of the Eastern rite not in communion with Rome: it is an interesting item of progress that, though in 1949 a Catholic work of reference could note that the title 'Church' is extended 'to Protestant religious organisations only by courtesy', the Second Vatican Council, while reserving the phrase 'the Church' *tout court* to the Roman Communion, does nevertheless speak several times of the 'different Churches and Communities' in reference to oecumenical work (Decree on Oecumenism, Art. 3,4).

Church Militant, the

A designation of the condition of Christians in this world, who are still 'fighting' against evil on their way to the Vision of God, to join the Church Triumphant*: the *pilgrim Church*. See also Church Suffering.

Church Suffering, the

In popular Catholic parlance, the 'Holy Souls': those Christians who have departed this life not yet fit for the Vision of God and who are therefore undergoing the cleansing process of Purgatory*, with full understanding and loving acceptance (as portrayed e.g., in the Dream of Gerontius*). The Church has always encouraged the faithful, as an exercise of charity, to help the souls of the departed by prayer and by assisting at Mass. Many indulgences* have attached to the practice of praying for the souls of the dead.
See Purgatory.

Church Triumphant, the

The description used of those followers of Christ, including the angels and led by the Holy Mother of God, who have overcome in their time of trial and won through to their reward, which is to rejoice for ever in the Vision of God.

Church Unity Octave

See Octave of Prayer for Christian Unity.

Ciborium

i) (Lat. *cibus*, food.) The lidded cup, usually of precious metal (gilt is prescribed for the inside if it is not gold) used for keeping the Sacred Hosts in the tabernacle and for distributing Holy Communion at Mass. The Ciborium has been in use since the early Middle Ages.

ii) Architecturally, the word is sometimes used of the four-pillared canopy (*baldacchino*) constructed over the high altar in churches of the basilica type: an extension, presumably, of the honorific canopy borrowed from the East (see *ombrellino*), for examples of which, visit Westminster Cathedral or Bernini's renowned Ciborium with its 'barley-sugar' pillars in St. Peter's, Rome.

Cistercians

In 1098, St. Robert of Molesme, intending to establish a form of Benedictine life more strict and primitive than any then existing, set up a monastery at Cîteaux. The Order spread rapidly into almost all of western Europe, its most famous member in the ensuing period being St. Bernard of Clairvaux. Within a century, there were 530 abbeys, the first notable house in England being at Waverley in Surrey and the next at Rievaulx, Yorks, and there were very many in Ireland. The ideals of the Order were seclusion, strict community life and intercessory prayer: there are severe rules on diet and silence (this is the 'Silent Order' *par excellence)* with an insistence on simplicity in building and ornament, manual labour being emphasised, to restore it to its primitive Benedictine dignity—one result of which is that the Cistercians became notable farmers. The 'Charter of Love', drawn up in 1119 by St. Stephen Harding, an Englishman who became abbot of Cîteaux, contains the constitution: the houses regulate their own affairs in accordance with the decrees of the annual General Chapter. The Cistercian way of life powerfully influenced other mediaeval foundations, particularly those of Canons Regular, and their custom of the annual General Chapter was adopted by other monastic orders after 1215. In the 17th cent., La Trappe became famous as a centre of reform in the Cistercian Order (in common parlance today, 'Trappist' is used for the severest form of austere monastic life). There are houses of the 'White Monks', as they are called, in Leicestershire (St. Bernard's Abbey, Coalville) and on the Isle of Caldey off the south coast of Wales, several in Ireland, and many in the U.S., of which the best-known is the Abbey of Gethsemani in Kentucky, the home of Thomas Merton, whose writings did so much to enlighten Catholics and the general public about the facts of monastic life.

Clandestinity

(Lat. *clandestinus*, secret.) A clandestine mårriage is one rendered null and void by the lack of prescribed form, viz. the attendance of the parish priest (or his delegate) and two other witnesses, as these constitute the publicity required by the Church. Such a marriage can be validated by the repetition of the ceremony with the required witnesses, or by *sanatio in radice*⋆.

Clare, St. (1194–1253)

Attracted by the life and teachings of St. Francis⋆, this noblewoman of Assisi left all she had and joined him at the Porziuncula⋆. He at first sent her to a Benedictine convent but later yielded to the persuasion of Clare and other women to be allowed to live the Franciscan life. As abbess⋆ of the community, she superintended the establishment of several daughter houses both in Italy and abroad. When some of the other communities received dispensation from the original Rule's ban on even communal property, her house and two others obtained leave from Gregory IX to continue in their state of primitive poverty; the rule went further in austerity than any women's rule before. Her feast is Aug 11th.

Cleric

In modern practice, as opposed to the previous definition as 'one who has received the tonsure'⋆, a cleric is a man who has received the Order of Deacon.

Clericis Laicos

See Boniface VIII.

Code of Canon Law

Codex Iuris Canonici, the collection of the common law of the Latin Church, last codified in 1918 and at present, i.e. since Vatican II, undergoing revision, is binding only on members of the Roman

Church except where matters arise which in the nature of things affect others also. All local law must be so framed as to conform to the *Codex*.

Collegiality

There has been a revival of thought on the subject of the bishops of the world *qua* college, a development summed up in its time by the Second Vatican Council. In its Dogmatic Constitution on the Church, the Council declared, 'The collegial nature and meaning of the episcopal order found expression in the very ancient practice by which bishops appointed the world over were linked with one another and with the Bishop of Rome by the bonds of unity, charity and peace; also in the conciliar assemblies which made common judgements about more profound matters in decisions reflecting the views of many . . . also, it is suggested in the practice, introduced in ancient times, of summoning several bishops to take part in the elevation of someone newly elected to the high-priesthood . . . the order of bishops is the successor to the college of the Apostles in teaching authority and pastoral rule . . . this college, insofar as it is composed of many, expresses the variety and universality of the People of God, but insofar as it is assembled under one head, it expresses the unity of the flock of Christ' (22). It also emphasised the responsibility of a bishop for the church outside his own diocese (an echo of a passage in the encyclical *Fidei Donum* of Pius XII), a responsibility to be exercised not by way of jurisdiction but by solicitude. Bishops should also 'extend their fraternal aid to other churches, especially to neighbouring and more needy dioceses . . .' (23). Missionary activity is likewise brought under this head, in the Decree on Bishops, in which it is said that 'they should also arrange for some of their own priests to go to such missions or dioceses' (6), and there is a strong desire expressed that members of the Roman Curia* 'be drawn more widely from various geographical areas of the Church' (10). And the Synod of Bishops*, announced during the Council by Paul VI (motu proprio *Apostolica Sollicitudo*, Sept 15th 1965), is an immediate, permanent and practical instrument of collegiality.

Commendatory Abbot
See In Commendam.

Commission for the Communications Media

As a result of the Decree of the Second Vatican Council entitled *Inter Mirifica*, there was an expansion of what had begun as the Pontifical Commission for the Educational and Religious Use of the Cinema, under Pius XII in 1948, into the *Pontifical Commission for the Communications Media*, which has as its scope 'all that concerns the Catholic religion in connection with the cinema, radio, television and the press' (Paul VI, Motu Proprio *In Fructibus Multis*, 1964).

Commissions

Commissions, set up and entrusted by a bishop or by the Holy See with some special work or inquiry, were formerly composed entirely of clerics. There are Pontifical Commissions at present for the Laity, for Justice and Peace, for the Revision of the Code of Canon Law (Roman and Eastern), for the Interpretation of the Decrees of the Second Vatican Council, for Social Communications, for Latin America, and for the Pastoral Care of Migrant Workers and Tourists.
See Roman Curia.

Companation

A Lutheran error concerning the Eucharist: after the consecration, says Osiander, a 16th cent. theologian, the substances of both the bread and of the Body of Christ co-exist in the species.
See Impanation, Real Presence, Transubstantiation.

Company of Jesus

The earliest name for the Society* of Jesus.

Company of Mary

See Montfort Fathers.

Conciliar Theory

The theory that a Pope is subject to the authority of a General Council made its first appearance in connection with the Great Schism of the West* (in a decree of the Council of Constance, the 16th Oecumenical, 1414–18, but that decree was not among those confirmed by the Papacy) and reappeared as a tenet of Gallicanism*. It was finally disposed of at the First Vatican Council in 1870.

Conclave

(Lat. *cum clavi*, with the key.) The locked apartment in the Vatican in which the Cardinals* are shut up while they elect a new Pope; also the body of cardinals so shut up. The custom of locking their Eminences in to hasten the election was initiated in 1271 to break a deadlock of three years' standing, and has been continued for Papal elections ever since. The conclave is concluded when one candidate receives two-thirds of the votes plus one and accepts the office of Pope. By tradition, the conclave passes news to the outside world by smoke signal: wet straw is burned to put forth black smoke through a famous tin chimney, signifying an inconclusive vote while dry straw is used to make white smoke for a decisive result—*Habemus Papam!* The conclave that elected John Paul I in 1978 used chemical substitutes to give more definite black and white smoke than straw, but the waiting multitudes were as puzzled as ever over the ambiguous grey vapour which emerged.

Concordat

A treaty drawn up between the Holy See and a sovereign secular state concerning matters of religion, the purpose of the treaty being the welfare of the faithful. Far from indicating warmth or friendship towards the state in question, a Concordat usually suggests friction or distrust, and thus the necessity of safeguarding the interests of the Church in a particular country. Analogy would perhaps help to explain the recent borrowing of the term by governments in affairs of industrial relations.

Confessio

(Lat., testimony.) The name originally used of the tomb of any martyr*, and later limited to the shrine or crypt under the high altar in which the martyr's bones were kept and reverenced. The most renowned is the *Confessio* in St. Peter's in Rome.

Confessor

A Conféssor is a male saint who was not a martyr. A Cónfessor is a priest chosen as spiritual guide for a pope, bishop, king, religious community or other group or indeed for any individual. In the 18th cent., the King's confessor in Catholic countries (usually a Jesuit*) was also a powerful political figure.

Confitor

(Lat., I confess.) The confession of sin which was used as preparation for Mass, originally as private prayer of the celebrant. In the early Eastern liturgies, Mass began with this Confession, though it was still said privately in the Roman Church, where the public rite began with the Introit*. Later, the Western Church fell in with the Eastern practice. An 11th cent. Latin formula runs: 'I confess to Almighty God, to these Saints (i.e. those whose bones were in or under the altar), to all the Saints and to you, my brother, that I have sinned in thought, word and deed, to the defilement of mind and body; therefore I beseech you, pray for me'. Since the Counter-Reformation, the formula of Pius V has been universal in the Roman Rite, with a few minor variants permitted to some of the older Orders; the current shape of the prayer, since the reform of Vatican II, abbreviates it by leaving out the 'litany' of Saints invoked in the first half and telescoping it in the second to 'Blessed Mary ever virgin, all the angels and saints'.

Congregation

Besides the use of the word to describe the gathering of the faithful in a place of worship, there are several kinds of Congregation: a) Diocesan—a religious institute set up by a bishop without having yet received the approval of the Holy See (the *decretum laudis,* decree of praise) for extra-diocesan expansion. b) Religious—an institute whose members seek Christian perfection bound by simple* vows (commonly referred to as 'order', from which they are canonically distinct), which vows are public, i.e. received by the superior in the name of the Church. c) Monastic—a group of monasteries under one head, whose only superior is the Pope, each house being independent as regards its internal administration and having its own novitiate. d) The Benedictine Order is made up of Congregations: Cassinese (of Monte Cassino*), English, Swiss, Bavarian, Hungarian, Brazilian, Solesmes (or French), American Cassinese, Beuron* Cassinese of the Primitive Observance, Swiss-American, Congregation of Subiaco, Austrian, Slavonic, Olivetan, Vallombrosan, Camaldolese, Dutch, Sylvestrine, the Congregation of the Annunciation, the Congregation of St Ottilia (or Odile) and the Panamerican Benedictine Federation. Of these, the English is the oldest Congregation, having been founded in 1336. e) Finally, there are the Roman* Congregations.

Consistory

A meeting of cardinals summoned by the Pope for a particular purpose; a private consistory includes only cardinals, semi-public cardinals and bishops, and at a public consistory, the laity are present also. It is essentially an audience gathered to hear an announcement, thus a private consistory is the occasion for the naming of new cardinals by the Pope and for the formalities connected therewith, for the appointing or translation of bishops, or for the pontiff to address his colleagues on some matter of public importance, while at a public consistory, the red hat is conferred on new cardinals, and the formalities connected with canonisation and beatification take place at any of the three kinds of consistory.

Constance, Council of (1414-18)

This Council put an end to the Schism of the West*, and is known as the 16th Oecumenical Council, though it was oecumenical only in respect of those of its decrees which were confirmed by the Pope it elected, Martin V. It condemned the teachings of Wyclif and Hus.

Constantinople, Councils of

The First (2nd Oecumenical), in 381, defended the faith against Arianism*, Apollinarianism* and the heresy of one Macedonius, who denied the perfect divinity of the Holy Spirit; it was to this last point that the Council inserted into the Creed 'and in the Holy Spirit, the Lord, the Giver of Life, who proceeds from the Father; with the Father and the Son, he is worshipped and glorified. He has spoken through the Prophets'. The Second (5th Oecumenical, 553) condemned certain Nestorian* writings known as the Three Chapters. The Third (6th Oecumenical, 680-81) defined the two wills of Christ, the divine and the human, and condemned Pope Honorius*. The fourth (reckoned as 8th Oecumenical 869-870,) repeated the excommunication of Photius* issued in 869 by a Council at Rome, and confirmed the Formula of Hormisdas*. This Fourth Council was repudiated by the Orthodox Churches (no general Council having since been held in the East), and recent Catholic scholars have doubted its oecumenicity: at a Council of 879-80, papal legates appear to have reinstated Photius' reputation and annulled the decision of the Council of 869-870 in his regard.

Contemplative Life

The Church's permanent attitude to the life of contemplation is expressed in the Second Vatican Council's Decree on the Religious Life: 'Members of those communities which are totally dedicated to contemplation give themselves to God alone in solitude and silence, and through constant prayer and ready penance. No matter how urgent may be the needs of the active apostolate, such communities will always have a distinguished part to play in Christ's Mystical Body, in which 'all members have not the same function'. For they offer God a choice sacrifice of praise. They brighten God's people with richest splendours of sanctity ...' (7). Those families recognised by the Church as devoting themselves to the worship of God, aiming at the prayer of contemplation and accepting the attendant austerity, are the Carthusians, Camaldolese and Cistercian* orders of monks, and, of nuns, the Carthusians, Carmelites, Poor Clares, Dominicans (of the Second Order) and some others. Over and above these, many communities of monks—and most of the nuns—of the Order of St. Benedict are to be called contemplatives.

Convent

Historically, the word was used for a house of religious*, whether of men or women, and is now restricted in English to houses of women.

Conventuals

The Friars Minor Conventual are that branch of the Franciscan Order which obtained in 1317 the approbation of Pope John XXII for their policy of holding property in common (which St. Francis had forbidden), and for which Urban VIII, in the early 17th cent., modified the Rule. They have charge of the basilicas of St. Francis at Assisi and of St. Anthony at Padua, wherein the two saints are buried.

Conversion of St. Paul, Feast of the

A feast of Gallican, not Roman origin, Jan. 25th is now also the last day of the Octave of Prayer for Christian Unity*.
See Chair of St. Peter.

Cope

A mantle, semi-circular in shape and commonly having on the back a smaller half-circle (the relic of the hood), which was originally the Roman outdoor garment for rainy weather (its Latin name is *pluviale*); worn, with a clasp in front, by the assistant priest at Pontifical Mass, by the ministers at Solemn Vespers and Lauds, by the celebrant in processions, and at nearly all solemn offices except the Mass.

Cornelia Connelly (1809–79)

The name at the centre of a most unusual case which, after being exposed to the fiercest publicity, was then for a long time wrapped in an almost conspiratorial silence until interest began to be renewed in the earlier years of this century. Cornelia Peacock, of Philadelphia, Pa, was brought up an Episcopalian and married a clergyman of that persuasion, Pierce Connelly. His later interest in the Catholic Church brought him and his wife to conversion; four years later, in 1840, Connelly being convinced that he had a vocation to the priesthood, he and Cornelia canonically separated, she leaving her four children in good hands and taking up residence in a convent of the Sacred Heart nuns in Rome. Pierce was ordained in 1845. The following year, Cardinal Wiseman* asked Cornelia to come to England and found an Order for the education of girls, the result of this being the establishing of a school and of the Society of the Holy Child Jesus*, with Cornelia as superior. Connelly then began to attempt to take part in the conduct of the new society and when she would have no such interference, he demanded that she return to him as his wife. This demand for the restoration of conjugal rights he took to the highest English courts, which to their credit, found in favour of Cornelia and the previous agreement to separate. For the rest of his life, Connelly persisted in harassing her and denigrating her character, leaving the Catholic Church in the process; Cornelia bore all with admirable patience and unflinching resolve. Her cause* for beatification has been introduced.

Corporal Works of Mercy

See Seven Corporal Works of Mercy

Corpus Christi

(Lat., the body of Christ.) The feast, now known as the Feast of the Body and Blood of Christ and held on the Thursday after Trinity Sunday, was ordered first by Urban IV in 1264, in response to the spreading devotion which itself owed much of its impetus to the activity of Blessed Juliana, a nun of Liège, who claimed to have had a vision in 1230. Maundy* Thursday, the obvious choice of date, being already bespoken for the commemoration of the Last Supper in the context of the Passion, the first free Thursday after Paschaltide was designated for the Feast, the liturgy of which was drawn up by St. Thomas Aquinas* and contains some gems of mediaeval Latinity, including the renowned Sequence *Lauda Sion*.

Cosmological Argument

See Five Ways.

Cotton College

See Sedgley Park.

Council for the Public Affairs of the Church

Part of the Roman Curia*, the Council, established in 1967 by Paul VI* as a new form of the Sacred Congregation for Extraordinary Ecclesiastical Affairs (itself an expansion, in 1814, of the Congregation for the Extraordinary Affairs of the Kingdom of France erected in 1793), deals with matters which concern civil governments and civil law, working closely with the Papal Secretariate of State*, with the duty also of overseeing the Commission for the Communications Media*.

Counter-Reformation

The movement of reform and purification within the Roman Church, usually dated from the middle of the 16th cent. to the end of the Thirty Years' War. It is an error to think of the Counter-Reformation merely as a reaction to the outbreak of Protestantism: well before the Council of Trent or the Jesuits, there were perceptions and efforts by individuals and groups in many countries, towards rectifying the state of the Church.We have the strictures of St. Thomas More and Erasmus on abuses and the protests of satirists such as Skelton. It could be said that the organised reform of the church began in Spain, before the end of the 15th cent., when the Franciscan Ximénes cleansed the church in that country, beginning with his own Order, so successfully that it has been said 'had Ximénes done his work in Germany instead of Spain, Luther might never have been heard of.' In Italy, quite apart from Savonarola, many genuinely sought reform, several of their efforts (including those of the scandalous Alexander VI) being frustrated by political events—though, strangely enough, the Fifth Lateran Council (1512–17) busied itself with matters other than reform. The Capuchins*, initiated in 1525, had for their aim the return to the primitive observance and became later a powerful instrument of the Counter-Reformation; the Barnabites were founded in 1530 'to regenerate and revive love of divine worship and a properly Christian way of life . . .', while the Theatines, founded in 1524 by St. Cajetan and Gian Pietro Carafa (afterwards Pope Paul IV), took as their object the reform of the Church from the grave abuses and scandals then corrupting it. As the movement gathered momentum, the Jesuits, approved in 1540, became its spearhead and their theologians were prominent at Trent*. This Council saw the codification of the reforms so long fought for by so many holy and determined Catholics; and in the later decades of the 16th cent., while the Popes (particularly Paul IV,

Pius V, Sixtus V) stiffened the discipline and efficiency of the Roman Curia* and of the entire episcopate, Philip II appointed himself the secular arm of the Counter-Reformation for the whole of Europe. On the purely spiritual plane, this period is made remarkable also by such heroic figures as Francis de Sales*, Charles Borromeo* and the Spanish mystics, Teresa of Avila* and John of the Cross*. Intellectually and artistically, the Counter-Reformation manifested itself in the Baroque culture, which dominated the first half of the 17th cent. Through the whole revitalising process of that time, the Church not only turned back the floodtide of Protestantism (Southern Germany, Poland and Austria were recovered), but re-established itself as a dynamic force in the affairs of the new Europe that had been born; its missionary activity was renewed in an endless stream of apostolic travellers to very many parts of the world, and the Papacy recovered its credibility in the eyes of men.

Creed

A concise and convenient formula of profession of faith, a catalogue of revealed truths, e.g. Apostles' Creed, Nicene Creed (the reciting of which at Mass was introduced in the Eastern Church in the 5th cent. and spread therefrom), the Athanasian Creed (also called *Quicumque Vult*), associated with St. Athanasius and apparently composed in his lifetime, but probably not by him; there are also Creeds promulgated by Pius IV and Paul VI. No Christian Creed is to be considered a final and complete expression of the Faith, nor was intended as such by those who composed it.

Cremation

The disposal of the body by fire was, until recently, forbidden by the Church except in urgent cases of public danger to health. The reason for this strict prohibition was connected with the contemporary idea of the reverence due to the temple of the Holy Spirit (I Cor.6:19), though in more recent centuries, cremation was associated with anti-religious propaganda and the use of this method to 'disprove' immortality and the resurrecton of the body. The general public no longer associates such ideas with cremation.

Crib

In the phrase *Christmas Crib*, the word includes not only the manger (the Church of St. Mary Major in Rome claims to have relics of the actual wooden crib in which the Christ child was laid), the Bambino* and figures of Mary and Joseph, but the representation, often large and elaborate in scale, detail and colour, of the entire environment of the birth constructed round the manger. This can include figures of shepherds, angels, kings, travellers, passers-by with their beasts of burden—besides the ox and ass suggested by Is.1:3—and, often enough, landscapes, cities and starscapes. The theme afforded scope for some extremely populous canvases by late mediaeval and Renaissance artists; and, correspondingly, in modern shopping centres, one often finds sumptuous window displays of the Crib which, in view of the many customers they attract, are possibly not a symbol of disinterested piety on the part of the proprietors. The popular, non-liturgical custom of having the Bambino carried to the Crib by the ministers at Midnight Mass was adopted by St. Francis* at Christmas, 1223, and rapidly spread, though it seems to have existed earlier.

Croagh Patrick

A mountain in the present archdiocese of Tuam where St. Patrick is said to have spent the 40 days of Lent in 441. It has been a place of pilgrimage and penitential hardship ever since; the chapel, destroyed in penal times, was rebuilt in 1905.

Crosier

A bishop's staff: not the episcopal cross borne before him but the *shepherd's crook* he carries himself, symbolising the power of correction and the shepherd's care. For reasons unknown, the Popes, chief bishops, have not used the crosier since the 11th cent. Others beside bishops are entitled to the crosier: cardinals, abbots and many abbesses. Many crosiers were wrought by fine artists out of precious metals and opulently decorated. In the official English translation of the new *Pontificale**, it is called the 'Pastoral Staff'.

Crosier Canons

See Canons Regular of the Holy Cross.

Cross

The N.T., indeed the Bible as a whole, supplies very little information about the use of the cross as punishment; we learn of it chiefly from Josephus and other ancient secular writers. The instrument, imported from Persia, was little used by the Greeks, but extensively by the Carthaginians and Romans. The kinds of cross employed by the latter were the *crux immissa* or *capitata* (sword-shaped) and the *crux commissa* (T-shaped, the *Tau* cross); the greater likelihood of the *immissa* being used in the case of Jesus is suggested in Mt.27:37, *over his head*. There is no evidence in antiquity for the *St. Andrew's cross*. In the Roman custom, the criminal carried the bar of the cross to the place of execution (outside the city, according to law) where the upright stood permanently in the ground; he was fastened to the bar, which was hauled into place on the post; to the latter his feet were then secured. If nails were used, as in the case of Christ—a fact we gather almost incidentally from Jn.20:25ff and indirectly from Lk.24:39, none of the Evangelists mentioning nails in his narrative of Christ's death—there were four, and they were supplemented by ropes about the torso, arms and legs, the body being left naked while the clothing was given to the executioners, a gratuity which was to survive many centuries. There is no reason to suppose that the Romans would waste timber by making crosses very high (as they are sometimes painted in Renaissance masterpieces): the criminal and the 'title' of his misdeed were easily perceived by his being placed by the side of the road or the city-gate. The offering of a pain-killing drug (Mt.27:34) was a Jewish custom, not Roman; but the 'vinegar' (Mt.27:48) must be in fact *posca*, the legionary's ordinary drink of vinegar and water, from his flask, and therefore a kindness (the passage about vinegar in the Good Friday Reproaches was a misconception). As with later systems of government, the body of the executed man was legally the property of the state, necessitating permission for private burial. Crucifixion was abolished under Constantine. The Cross is taken by Our Lord as a symbol of suffering and of the life of self-renunciation (Mt.10:38, Mk.8:34, Lk.9:23), by Paul for the saving power of God exercised through Christ

(I Cor.1:18, Eph.2:16, Col.12:14) and in both senses by the entire Church, by preachers, writers, artists, liturgists, ever since. The cross reputed to be the cross of Christ and discovered at Jerusalem by the Empress St. Helena*, was captured by the Persians in 614 and brought back in 629 by the Christian Emperor Heraclius, who then set it up in the Holy City. From this event originates the Feast of the Exaltation of the Holy Cross (Sept 14th, though it was in the spring of 629 that the above-mentioned veneration took place). It is not known how much of the actual wood had survived to that date, for within 50 years of the discovery by Helena, pieces of the timber had been sent as precious relics to distant parts of the Empire. However, the Lady Etheria*, writing about 385, assures us that the main part of the Cross was in Jerusalem to be venerated on Good Friday and that she took part. Its subsequent history is obscure. Many tiny slivers were distributed as relics, though very many of them can still be traced. The question of the authenticity of Helena's cross was in no way affected—nor was the trustwor-thiness of its custodians—by the smear in anti-Catholic polemic that by putting together all these relics, one could build a ship: it has been reckoned that all the minute fragments which can be located, together with those lost but recorded, would not make a cross 12 ft by 8. There is a relic kept at Downside Abbey and one is enclosed in the cross which surmounts the campanile of Westminster Cathedral. The Feast of the Exaltation of the Cross is now known as the 'Triumph of the Cross'. See Sign of the Cross.

Cross, Altar

Central on the altar there must be a crucifix 'as often as Mass is celebrated' (Constitution *Accepimus* of Benedict XIV, 1746), unless a crucifix is the principal feature of the altarpiece or of the wall behind it or hanging prominently above.

Crucifix

The representation of the figure of Christ on the cross, in painting, carving, glass, or in any other manner. In Catholic liturgy, the word *cross* always means crucifix. The crucifix was not in general use before the 6th cent. and even then, the Christ was not represented as dead or even suffering,

but as crowned and in priestly robes, reigning from the cross, not hanging on it. The suffering figure was not widely used until the 12th cent.

Crusades

Marred as they were by brutality, aggres-sion, ruthless acquisitiveness and cynical exploitation, and failing as they did of their lofty objectives, these 'holy wars' nonetheless represent the highest in mediaeval society. The movement was made possible by the organising of the ex-isting religious passion which underlay the still crude and unregenerate warrior ethos of the unformed national groups of Christendom. It was Urban II who, like other great Popes, wrought his achieve-ment out of a seemingly desperate situa-tion, whose shrewdness and enthusiasm combined to inspire the thousands of nobles and knights at Clermont in 1093 to their famous response *Deus lo volt*. For the individual, this was a way of salvation, to gain pardon for sin by seeking Jerusalem; to the whole of Christendom, though pro-bably this was perceived at the time only by Urban, it offered a transcendent com-mon cause to unite feudal society across the boundaries of the local particularisms in a venture for God under the leadership of the Church. The scale and strangeness of this vast, inspired march is described by an eye-witness, the Byzantine historian Anna Comnena: ... *the whole of the West and all the barbarian tribes which dwell bet-ween the further side of the Atlantic and the Pillars of Hercules, had all migrated into Asia ... with all their household ... For these Frankish soldiers were accompanied by an unarmed host more numerous than the stars or the sand, carrying palms and crosses on their shoulders ... (Alexiad XV)* This enterprise can be described as a watershed in the history of the West, quite apart from the military achievement of the defeat of the Turkish and Egyptian hosts and the setting up of the Kingdom of Jerusalem and the chain of other Christian states along the Syrian coast and inland: it brought Western Christianity out of its long isolation and inferiority into contact again with the unbroken culture of the Eastern Mediterranean. This essentially papal initiative, launched when the Emperor and the Kings of England and France were excommunicated, when

Europe lay under threat of Turkish invasion and the Byzantine Empire seemed ready to succumb to its encompassing enemies, could not but add immensely to the respect and authority accorded to the Papacy—a respect which in time declined as dissension broke out between pontiff and Emperor, robbing the crusading armies of the necessary unity of command. Then, too, the Italian maritime powers had begun to think of the Crusades as means to their own commercial and political advantage; and by the close of the Middle Ages, when the idea of the Christian monarchy had evaporated, the Crusade survived as an ideal and a theoretical obligation but also an embarrassment which kings gladly commuted to gifts of money or the founding of religious houses. Yet the ideal lingered: in 1492, Charles VIII, invading Italy, planned to take Naples and then to march for Constantinople and the East; even Leo X, the first Medici Pope, made strenuous efforts in 1517 to reconcile the European princes so as to organise them for a Crusade; Vasco da Gama, Columbus and other explorers wore the cross on the voyages which they hoped would bring them, by rounding Africa or approaching Asia from the East, to take the Muslim in the rear; and the Conquistadores thought of themselves as auxiliary Crusaders. The last Crusade, the expedition led by Don Juan of Austria, in response to Pius V's appeal, to trounce the Turks at Lepanto, was a kind of anomaly, for at that date the idea of the struggle for Christendom was almost totally obscured by the preoccupation of the Christian Mediterranean states with maintaining their sea-power and thus their prosperity. In the end, the access of pilgrims to the Holy Places was secured by means of the *Capitulations* made with the Ottoman power in 1536, 1673 and 1740.

Cujus Regio Ejus Religio

(Lat., Whoever owns the land, [let] his religion [prevail].) The political principle, intended to secure peaceful sway for the ruler and social unity in the realm, which was the basis of e.g. the attempts of Elizabeth I to wipe out nonconformity of any kind. It was first enunciated as a concession to the Protestant princes at the Peace of Augsburg in 1555 and confirmed

by the Treaty of Westphalia almost a century later, against the sternest Papal opposition. It can be said that thereby slaughter and chaos were at least postponed for the German states until the Thirty Years' War, which was concluded at Westphalia. In theory, the system would still hold in the case—if one envisages such—of one of the Swiss cantons changing its religion by majority.
See also Freedom of Conscience.

Curate

(Lat. *curatus*, one having a charge; cf. Fr. *curé*.) Strictly, one with the cure of souls*, in Eng. usage a priest appointed by the ordinary to assist a parish priest in his cure of souls*. When the parish becomes vacant, the curate (or senior curate) takes charge until another parish priest is appointed. There is a general tendency now to use the phrase *assistant priest* instead of *curate*.

Cure of Souls

The phrase used (Lat. *cura*, care, solicitude) for the pastoral responsibility for the faithful which falls primarily on bishops (chiefly and universally on the Pope) and rectors of parishes (parish priests) and then on those to whom they delegate it. It comprises the offering of Mass with and for the people, the administration of the Sacraments, the ministry of the word by preaching and instruction, the care of the sick, the needy and of children. It requires residence in the territory in which it is exercised.

Curia

The *Court* of a bishop, the body of officials who assist him in the government of his diocese, such as the vicar general, chancellor, ecclesiastical judges and others. The *Curia Romana,* the Papal curia, consists of the groups of officials which have grown, since the Middle Ages or earlier, around the Pope as Universal Bishop, for the administration of the entire Church: The Roman Congregations*, the Tribunals* and various curial Offices* and Commissions*.

Curial Offices

The departments of the Roman Curia* so named are: the Apostolic Chamber, which has judicial functions with regard to fiscal, penal and civil affairs of Vatican City and has as president the Cardinal Chamberlain (Camerlengo*); the Prefecture of the Economic Affairs of the Holy See; the Administration of the Patrimony of the Apostolic See; the Prefecture of the Pontifical Household which, created in 1967, combines the functions of the Congregation of Ceremonies, the office of the Majordomo and of the *Maestro di Camera*, and comprises the Pontifical Chapel, the Pontifical Family, Ecclesiastical and Lay, the Office of Pontifical Ceremonies, the Pontifical Musical Chapel, the Corps of Swiss Guard, the Papal Welfare Service, led by the Almoner to His Holiness, the Office of Vatican Industrial Relations, the Central Office of Ecclesiastical Statistics.

Cyril of Alexandria, St.
(+444)

An outstanding theologian, whose years as Patriarch (from 412 onwards) were tempestuously pugnacious: he warred vigorously with various heretics, with the Jews, with Orestes, Prefect of Valentinian III and most notably with the opponents of the *Theotokos*, dominating the Council of Ephesus* which condemned them by formally approving the title.

Cyril of Jerusalem, St.
(c. 315–86)

Being three times banished from the Holy City, his see, for his sturdy opposition to Arianism* and finally reinstated, he came under some suspicion from the orthodox for his dislike of *homoousios*, which he considered a philosopher's concoction. However, at the First Council of Constantinople*, he vindicated his acceptance of the Nicene Creed. His *Catecheses*, instructions delivered in 347 or thereabouts, are very informative on the subject of the preparation for baptism then obtaining, and for the contemporary Palestinian liturgy; they stress the efficacy of Baptism and insist on the Real Presence*.

Dames of St. Maur
See Holy Child Jesus, Congregation of the

Dance of Death
A morality play pointing out the inevitability of death and the impartiality of judgement. Also used to describe any work of art (e.g. Holbein's series of engravings) on this theme.

Dark Ages
The period in European history between the fall of the Roman Empire and the beginning of the Middle Ages; the time of the invasion by the barbarian tribes and their settling into the nations of Europe. The term is sometimes used, by the uninstructed or by those hostile to mediaeval culture, to cover the Middle Ages also.

Dark Night of the Senses
The name given in the writing of St. John of the Cross* to the time of transition between meditation and contemplation, marked by an aversion to thought, prayer and self-scrutiny, by temptation and other trials; the soul is being deprived of the comfort even of the interior senses and has to seek God by faith alone.

Dark Night of the Soul
After passing through the dark Night of the Senses*, the soul has a further purifying to undergo before its ultimate union with God: it comes after several years of contemplation and can continue for several years. In this form of contemplation, the soul experiences deep sterility and feels totally abandoned by God without losing its intense longing for him; it is as if the divine brilliance served both to blind the soul from the enjoyment of God and to shed a relentless glare on personal defects, misery and helplessness.
See St. John of the Cross.

Daughters of Our Lady Help of Christians
The Salesian Sisters, as they are also called, were founded in 1872 by St. John Bosco* and St. Maria Mazzarello to do similiar work to that of the Salesians and had a similar period of phenomenal growth, which advanced their apostolate into very many countries.

Daughters of the Cross
A congregation founded by Mother Marie-Thérèse at Liège in 1832 for work in hospitals, schools, prisons etc. Other congregations of this name do similar work in education and nursing.

Deacon
(Gk. διακονος, servant, minister.) The institution, though not the name, is recorded in Acts 6:1–6, where the seven deacons were ordained for the service of the poor; in other parts of the N.T. (e.g. Phil 1:1), the name is used and they are clearly ministers who serve under the presbyter-bishops. Later acquiring liturgical functions such as chanting the Epistle and Gospel, distributing the Eucharist and directing the prayers, they grew in importance (the archdeacon being the bishop's chief administrative officer), particularly in Rome through their association with the Pope, who always had seven deacons. Nicaea* checked their powers, and the Council of Toledo in 633 emphasised the inferiority of the deacon's office to the priesthood. Later in the Middle Ages, the order was reduced to a preliminary stage on the way to the priesthood, carrying with it certain liturgical obligations and the bond of celibacy; the deacon's liturgical functions were largely absorbed into those of the priesthood and his ministry to the poor practically disappeared. It was not until the Second Vatican Council* that the anomaly was tackled; it was decreed that the diaconate should be revived, not merely as a step towards the priesthood, but as an order in its own right, as a witness to the Christ the Servant. The Dogmatic Constitution on the Church quotes St Polycarp: 'Be merciful, diligent, walking according to the truth of the Lord, who became the servant of all.' The document lists the duties of deacons as being, under competent

authority, 'to administer Baptism solemnly, to be custodian and dispenser of the Eucharist, to assist at and bless marriages in the name of the Church, to bring Viaticum to the dying, to read the sacred Scripture to the faithful, to instruct and exhort the people, to preside at the worship and prayer of the faithful, to administer sacramentals and to officiate at funeral and burial services.' (Art.29) It proceeds then to permit the diaconate to be restored as a permanent and proper rank of the hierarchy. . . with the consent of the Roman Pontiff, this diaconate will be able to be conferred upon men of more mature age, even upon those living in the married state. It may also be conferred upon suitable younger men. For them, however, the law of celibacy must remain intact' (ib.) It is also forbidden for a deacon who has become a widower to remarry. In many dioceses, bishops have ordained men to this new diaconate, to the great profit of the faithful and of the rest of the clergy; it is claimed among bishops that the married deacon has an invaluable contribution to make in the ministry to married people, and can be of immense help to the celibate priest. One English bishop writes, 'At ordination, a deacon enters permanently into the clerical state. He receives the grace of the sacrament of Order as the seal of the gift of the Holy Spirit, which cannot be lost. This reality configures him to Christ, consecrates him and gives him a special share in Christ's mission.' Such deacons are distinguished from those clerics who spend a short time as deacons before being ordained priest by being known as Permanent Deacons; they carry the title Reverend.*

Deaconess

In the early Church, a woman entrusted with certain functions, the office, though not the title, being of Apostolic antiquity. *Deaconess* in 'Phoebe, a deaconess of the Church at Cenchreae' (Rom.16:1) translates διακονος, which is used in the Epistles as of common gender. διακονιοσα is not found before the 4th cent., when its equivalent is *diaconissa*, though earlier Latin documents have *diacona*, besides *virgo* and *vidua canonica*, the distinction between this last and Deaconess being obscure. The office expanded greatly in the 3rd and 4th cents., according to the

Apostolic Constitutions and the Didascalia, the latter of which reduced the age of entry from 60, as decided by St. Paul, to 50, which the Council of Chalcedon* brought down to 40. The deaconess served women who were poor or sick, assisted women at interviews with the clergy, instructed female catechumens, kept order in the women's part of the church and—her most important function—assisted at the baptism of women, propriety forbidding the deacon from performing certain of the ceremonies. With the decrease in adult baptism, there was a decline in the importance of the office of deaconess; furthermore, abuses had crept in, when deaconesses in e.g. Monophysite and Nestorian communities, administered Holy Communion to women and read the Scriptures in public. The office was abolished by the Councils of Epaon (517) and Orléans (533), but it appears to have survived elsewhere as late as the 11th cent. Among the Eastern churches, where the prerogatives of the deaconess had been more evident, including investiture with the stole and the distribution of the chalice, the disappearance was proportionately slower. Perhaps the reception of the stole and maniple by the Carthusian nun at her profession is a relic of the ancient office.

Deadly Sins, the Seven

Popular name for the Seven Capital Sins: pride, covetousness, lust, anger, gluttony, envy, sloth. They can be analysed as the root of all sin, since excessive attachment to any temporal good may lead to inordinate ways of pursuing or enjoying it.

Dean

(Lat. *decanus*, one in authority over 10.) i) The chief dignitary of a diocesan or collegiate chapter, appointed by the Holy See, as in Ireland and France, but sometimes ranking below the Provost. In certain German dioceses, he has powers beyond those of the other canons, but not elsewhere; he presides at chapter meetings, with a casting vote, enjoys precedence and has certain liturgical responsibilities. In some monasteries, the prior is called Dean. ii) Rural Dean is a senior priest who oversees a group of parishes; his duties and rights are determined in each case by

the bishop, but will include the summoning of and presiding over the meeting (usually monthly) of the deanery.
iii) The senior member of certain bodies is called Dean, e.g. of diplomatic representatives or of a university faculty.

Decade
(Lat., a group of 10.) One 'mystery' of the Rosary, that is the recitation of the *Our Father* once, the *Hail Mary* 10 times and the *Glory Be* once.

Decalogue
(Gk. δεκα, ten, λογος, word.) The Ten Commandments.

Defender of the Bond
(i.e. the Bond of Marriage.) A theologian is appointed for each diocese, whose duty it is to plead for the validity of the marriage when a case is brought wherein the validity is questioned. His task is to ensure that nullity is declared only for the weightiest of reasons: so that if nullity is granted by the first court, he must appeal to the higher court and, nullity being found there too, he may appeal further, but is not bound to do so. However, where facts are clearly proved from the start which make nullity obvious, he may consent to the declaration without appealing.

Defender of the Faith
On the publication by Henry VIII of the book *Assertio Septem Sacramentorum,* a defence of the Sacraments and of Papal supremacy against Luther's attacks, and overseen—if not written—by St. Thomas More, Leo X awarded the monarch the title *Fidei Defensor*; and later Pope Paul III bestowed the same title on James V of Scotland. The English title was made hereditary to future monarchs by Act of Parliament in 1543, and Elizabeth I so prized it as to set it down before *Supreme Governor* . . . according to Our just Title, Defender of the Faith, and Supreme Governor of the Church, within these our Dominions . . .' (Declaration preceding the Thirty-Nine Articles). It still appears on the coins of the realm, shrunk now to F.D.

Definition of Dogma
Defining is the process of setting forth in formal terms some teaching which is thereby offered to the whole Church with the full authority of the magisterium, to be accepted without argument or contradiction. Such pronouncements, made by the Pope or by an oecumenical council in union with him, state clearly the full and unreserved acceptance they demand of the faithful. To define is not to invent but to delimit: a dogma is not something new or recent, it is something newly formulated but which has been contained in the Deposit of Faith* and, in being defined, is made explicit because this is the time when it becomes necessary or opportune to make it so: thus the definition of Christ's divinity in 325 against heretical teaching to the contrary, or of the Immaculate Conception* in the 19th cent., when it was found opportune for the good of the faithful to formalise what had been held by so many for so long.

Degradation
An ecclesiastical penalty formerly prescribed in Canon Law, whereby a cleric judged guilty of certain crimes was deprived for ever of the exercise of his orders. There was a solemn ceremonial form laid down in the *Pontificale* *Romanum,* last used in 1853 when a Polish priest was publicly degraded on a charge of murder and handed over to the secular power, which sent him to Siberia. After his death, it turned out that, far from being guilty, he had suffered in place of the real murderer, whose crime he knew under the seal* of confession.

De Haeretico Comburendo
(Lat., concerning the burning of a heretic.) The law passed by Henry IV against Lollardry*: Whereas diverse false and perverse persons . . . do perversely and maliciously . . . preach and teach these days openly and privily new doctrines and wicked heretical and erroneous opinions . . . if any person upon the said wicked preachings etc be before the bishop convicted and do refuse duly to abjure . . . then the sheriff, or mayor or other, shall receive the same persons and cause them to be burnt before the people in a high place, that such punishment may strike fear to the minds of others'. Dangerous though the Lollards may have been to the peace of the realm, and the Lollard leader Oldcastle (perhaps the original of Falstaff)

was certainly a rebel leader after being convicted of heresy, it appears, nonetheless, that this legislation occurred very conveniently for King Henry's attempts to ingratiate himself with the ecclesiastical authorities and to help them to forget his usurpation of the throne. Its provisions were not altogether new: they already had force in the common law of some other European countries, and, before it, the civil power in England could be compelled by the Church authorities to burn those found guilty of heresy in the bishop's court (cf. the hasty execution of William Sawtre, the Lollard*, before the Act was passed.) It was repealed under Edward VI, reintroduced by Mary Tudor and repealed finally by Elizabeth I.

Deism

A system of thought which accepts the existence of a Deity but denies that he cares for the human race in any particular way or that he has revealed himself to it. Deism is a product mainly of 18th cent. rationalism.

Delegate, Apostolic

A representative of the Holy See in a country which has no regular diplomatic relations with it (Great Britain has an Apostolic Delegate). His duties consist in watching over the state of the Church in such a country and keeping Rome informed; he takes precedence over all ordinaries except such as are cardinals and can give final decisions in appeals from diocesan and metropolitan courts, always safeguarding the right of appeal direct to Rome first. An Apostolic Delegate is also sometimes appointed temporarily for a special purpose.
See Nuncio.

Deo Gratias

(Lat., Thanks be to God.) A common expression in either language, not only in the liturgy. Some people are in the habit of writing it in letters, etc., abbreviated to D.G. or T.G.

Deo Volente

(Lat., God willing.) A familiar phrase used by the faithful, now usually in English, and frequently abbreviated in writing to D.V.

Deposing of Monarchs

Like the social consequences of excommunication*, the Papal claim to the power of deposing a prince and releasing his subjects from their allegiance could be maintained only in the context of a certain widely accepted concept of the Church and her relations with the State. Significantly, it was Pius IX who said in 1871, the year after Victor Emmanuel had seized Rome, and the Papal States* had been absorbed into the new Italy, '. . . The reverence of the Christian nations for the Pope as the supreme judge for Christ extended to his passing even civil judgement on princes and nations. But the present state of affairs is entirely different . . . No one now thinks any more of the right of deposing princes which the Holy See formerly exercised . . .' It is not difficult to see how the idea was born: in the tumult of the few centuries after the collapse of the Roman Empire, the only prominent institution of any stability was the Church. The Papacy became an enduring symbol which pre-dated all the new barbarian dynasties and was confident of outlasting them. Thus, the newly-baptised warrior kings were grateful for the political *cachet* bestowed on them by tokens of approval from the Church; St. Boniface anointed Pepin III King of the Franks, the champion of the Catholic cause against heathen and Arian, a ritual repeated two years later (754) by Pope Stephen II; and in 800, Pepin's son, Charlemagne, was crowned King of the Romans by Leo III. These precedents and the custom of ecclesiastical anointing of the Visigothic kings of Spain could well have encouraged the idea that 'Peter has raised up, Peter can put down', an idea in no way discounted by the mediaeval Papacy as it grew in power and prestige; and the custom of anointing monarchs spread further over Europe. The climax of the theory was the Bull *Unam Sanctam**, and the last attempt at deposing by a Pope was Pius V's *Regnans in Excelsis**, directed at Elizabeth of England.

Deposit of Faith

The entire revelation, comprising truths to be believed and rules of conduct to be followed, given to the Apostles by Christ and transmitted by them through their successors for the benefit of the Church; it includes what is explicitly contained in Scripture and what is implicit; its two elements are Scripture and Tradition*, both of which are entrusted to the infallible *magisterium* for preservation and interpretation. The word deposit is taken from I Tim.6:20 and the theological technical term *deposit of faith* has been in use since the 16th cent. The first Vatican Council uses the phrase 'the divine deposit delivered by Christ to his spouse to be by her faithfully guarded and infallibly declared'.

Descent into Hell

'He descended into Hell', the phrase in the Creed being sometimes interpreted as describing the visit of the soul of Christ, after his death, to the Hebrew Sheol, not the Hell of the Lost (though this also is enacted in an early, un-theological mystery-play) but as liberator to the souls of the just who were awaiting his redemption. A more likely interpretation of the phrase is that it is a Hebrew way of stating that Christ 'really died' on the Cross, against those who say that he only seemed to die. Hence, 'he descended into Hell' means 'he went into the Land of the Dead (Sheol)'.
See Docetism.

Design, Argument from

The last of St. Thomas* Aquinas' *Quinque Viae*, his Five Roads (that lead us to accept the existence of God): since all things in the universe act for a common purpose, which is the good, unity and beauty of that universe, and since this tendency is evidently not due to chance but to intention, and since these things are clearly incapable of intention, being irrational and without knowledge, therefore, they being thus unable to direct themselves to any purpose, such direction as they have must be imparted to them by some intelligence outside themselves: this we call God.

Desire, Baptism of

See Baptism of Desire.

Deutero-canonical Books

Those O.T. books which are not included in the Hebrew Bible but which were admitted into the Canon of Scripture, and are called Deutero-Canonical because they were authenticated only by the second Canon, the Christian one, the rest of the O.T. books being already proclaimed by the Jews to be inspired works (the first Canon). The 16th cent. Reformers, rejecting the competence of the Church to authenticate such books, threw them out and adhered only to the Jewish canon. (See Tradition.) The passages in question are: Tobit, Judith, Esther 10:5-onward, both Books of Maccabees, Wisdom, Ecclesiasticus, Baruch, Daniel 3:24-4:3, and 13 and 14 entire. They are known in non-Catholic circles as the *Apocrypha*.

Development of Doctrine

The Church holds and has held that the complete revelation from the Father was given to Christ and his Apostles, that after the death of the last Apostle there can be no further revelation, and that she possesses, from that time on, the faith which, according to Jude 3, '*has been once and for all entrusted to the saints*' ('Private revelation' is not at issue here, and can have at most only the approval of the Church, provided it contains nothing against faith or morals and holds sufficient of evident truth to allow us to accept it without falling into superstition or imprudence: it is never part of the Church's message). Thus, in questions of definition, the only point of debate has been, 'Is this doctrine found in Scripture or in the apostolic tradition*?' The First Vatican Council* lays down that the meaning of the Church's dogmas does not change as human knowledge increases, but recognises that there is a legitimate mode of development, quoting St. Vincent* of Lérins: 'As regards the Church's doctrine, let understanding and knowledge progress . . . but in its own order, keeping the same dogma, the same sense, the same import'. The clearest and most comprehensive exposition of this idea is Newman's* first publication on becoming a Catholic, his *Essay on the Development of Christian Doctrine*. In this, he rebuts at length the charge that the Church of Rome had corrupted primitive teachings by adding to them. He examines the difference between corruption and development: a true and fertile idea, he claims, has its own vital and assimilative energy, whereby, without substantive change, it attains to more and more complete expression as it is brought into contact with new aspects of truth or into collision with new errors. He compares the life of an idea to an organic development (it is of interest to note that the evolutionary writings of Lamarck, Buffon and Erasmus Darwin were already widely known, and Charles Darwin's work on the Origin of Species was in gestation). By the tests he applies, including preservation of type and continuity of principles he established to his satisfaction that Roman teaching carries the mark, not of corruption, but of true development. His conclusion, that the whole teaching, in later as in earlier forms, was thus contained in the original revelation given by Our Lord and the Apostles, was taken seriously enough for some later writers, condemned as Modernists, to attempt to justify their views on dogma as analogous to Newman's theory of development. Of recent times, there is an explicit intention to develop set forth in one of the documents of the Second Vatican Council: '. . . this Sacred Synod intends to develop the doctrine of recent Popes on the inviolable rights of the human person and on the constitutional order of society . . .' (Declaration on Religious Freedom, Art1).

Devil's Advocate

Officially entitled *Promoter of the Faith*, a theologian is appointed, in processes of beatification and canonisation, to examine with the greatest hostility the evidence submitted for the virtue and miracles of the subject candidate, so as to ensure that none who is in the least way unworthy shall receive the seal of the Church's highest accolade.

Diaspora

(Gk., scattering.) The dispersal of the Jews from their country, chiefly in the deportations to Assyria (722 B.C.) Babylon (597 B.C.)—and then at the fall of Jerusalem to the Romans in A.D. 70. These exiles held tenaciously to their religion and culture, which they have kept vigorously alive right up to the return to Israel in modern times. The word *diaspora* was well chosen, being itself an agricultural term—the scattering of seed—and they regarded themselves as carrying the knowledge of the true God to the nations, though their missionary activities were severely hampered by their persistent exclusiveness and were later overtaken and almost extinguished by the growth of Christianity. The word is also used by some modern theologians to express their concept of the Church's destiny. See Diaspora—Church.

Diaspora, Church of the

A new understanding of the Church has emerged out of Vatican II and the movements which preceded and produced it, a view which exchanges the traditional concept of the Christian community as steadily and triumphally expanding and possessing the world until all men are Christian, for—what is more in keeping with the signs of the times, e.g. the shrinking Christian Church not only in relation to other resurgent religions riding high on a new pride in national and racial cultures, but also in the heartlands of the former 'Christendom'—a vision of a kind of pre-Constantinian community without pomp or prestige, uncorrupted by power, which shall give hidden and humble service to the world, co-operating with all men of good will, to sustain them, not to dominate them, pursuing its primary task of helping the human race to work together in love, recognising that wherever there is true love, there is the Holy Spirit. It will thus be by the existence of this community of grace, in which Christ is vitally and sacramentally present, that the work of the world and the saving of the world are to be accomplished. The chief proponents of this 'anti-triumphalist' view of the Church have been Yves Congar and Karl Rahner.

Didache, the

(Gk. Διδαχη κυριου δια των δωδεκα αποστολων, the Teaching of the Lord through the Twelve Apostles.) A brief document used by some early Christians as a guide to morals and ecclesiastical practice. Its composition, by an unknown author, is dated very early, to the first century by some, and it appears to have arisen in, and to describe the life of, a Christian community in Syria. The book quotes from the Sermon on the Mount, gives the Lord's Prayer in full, mentions fasting on Wednesdays and Fridays, allows baptism by threefold pouring if the triple immersion is not feasible, gives two Eucharistic Prayers, foretells the Antichrist and the Second Coming, shows acquaintance with the Gospels of Matthew and Luke and perhaps John also, gives instructions on how to treat bishops, deacons (priests are not mentioned) and travelling prophets; these last 'are your chief priests' and may celebrate the Eucharist.

Dies Irae

(Lat., the Day of Wrath.) A 13th cent. poem, named from its opening words, the work of a Franciscan friar, though probably not, as had been thought, of Thomas of Celano. Apparently not meant for liturgical use (it is written in the first person singular), it did achieve that status, originally, it has been suggested, for the First Sunday of Advent (when stress is laid on preparation for Judgement). It was first printed in the Venetian Missal of 1493 as Sequence for the Requiem Mass, and as such it continued, being recited or sung (to incomparable chant of immense power and melancholy) until recently it was excluded in the liturgical reforms consequent on Vatican II as dwelling too much on the fear of judgement and not enough on the mercy of God: a hell-fire sermon in music. The lean vividness and finality of the Latin are a supreme example of 'untranslatability'; of all the innumerable attempts at Englishing it, only Swinburne's seems worth considering.

Difference of Worship (Difference of Religion)

The technical term used by ecclesiastical lawyers in reference to marriage, signifying that one of the persons involved is a baptised Catholic and the other not baptised. It is a diriment* impediment to matrimony and may be dispensed for a suitably grave cause, and with due precaution taken for the faith of the Catholic party and of any children of the marriage. See Mixed Religion.

Dimissorials, Letters Dimissorial

Written authorisation by an ecclesiastical superior to permit his subject to receive Orders at a place outside the superior's jurisdiction; usually granted by a bishop for one of his own subjects, and sometimes by the Pope, for any candidate, to any bishop, sometimes also by the abbot or other superior of exempt religious, usually to the bishop of the diocese.

Diocese

(Gk. διοίκησις, district—to describe some of the smaller Provinces of the Roman Empire.) The geographical unit on which the Church is based, viz. the territory of a Bishop, over which he has jurisdiction as ordinary*, and which is divided into parishes*. The earliest word for a local group of Christians was εκκλησια (as the Athenian democracy described its parliamentary assembly); diocese was used as early as the 4th cent. in Africa and was paralleled for a long time by its continued imperial administrative usage. The diocese originally consisted of a city, and later extended its bounds to include the surrounding rural tracts also, while keeping the name of the city as its title. An archdiocese is the diocese of an archbishop*.

Diriment Impediment

See Impediments to Marriage.

Disabilities of Catholics

Such disabilities as Catholics still laboured under after the Roman Catholic Relief Acts of 1781, 1791 and 1829 and the abolition in 1871 of the oath (without taking which they could not legally inherit or purchase land), were removed by the 1926 Act, except for the following: no Catholic may be king or queen of the realm (this disability also affects any who marries a Catholic), nor Regent, nor (but this is not certain) Lord Chancellor and Keeper of the Privy Seal, nor High Commissioner of the Church of England nor of the Presbyterian Church of Scotland; nor hold a post in an ecclesiastical court of those Churches nor a professorship of Divinity at Oxford, Cambridge, or Durham, nor certain Anglican scholastic posts; nor may he present to an Anglican living. After the removal in mid-19th cent. of the compulsory oath of allegiance, acceptance of the Act of Supremacy and membership of the Church of England (until then conditions mandatory on candidates for the Bachelor's degree at the old Universities), Catholics petitioned the Congregation of Propaganda* for permission to enter these universities. It was not until the 1890's that they were there in any notable numbers. A Catholic priest may not sit as a member in the House of Commons—but then, neither may his opposite number of the Established Church.

Discalced Religious

Discalced (unshod) religious are those who wear sandals as a sign of austerity of life; they are usually friars* or nuns of strict orders or of reformed branches of orders, e.g. Friars Minor, Discalced Carmelites.

Dissolution of the Monasteries

In the later Middle Ages, many of the English monasteries had grown wealthy and powerful, and the consequent laxity in their observance had drawn much criticism, not merely from such tolerant observers as Chaucer; monasteries, like the Church in general, were in need of reform. However, it is nowhere maintained that the motives of Henry VIII in this matter were virtuously detached or that he was bent on doing good to the Church. After a hasty 'token' visitation of a risibly small number of religious houses, a report denounced the abuses of the monastic life therein lived and Parliament was prompted to beseech the King to confiscate the property of all monasteries whose income was less than £200, 'that it should be converted to better uses and the unthrifty persons so spending the same be compelled to reform their lives' (Act for the Dissolution of Smaller Monasteries, 1536). Thus were suppressed some 200 houses; later, the Pilgrimage of Grace* having meanwhile been dealt with, the greed of the King and of his agents pressed on to the richer prizes, and the second Act was passed in 1539 whereby the greater monasteries were dissolved and their goods confiscated: plate and jewels were kept for the King, saleable goods realised, lands and buildings distributed to the monarch's friends or sold off. In all this, the King's chief agent, who drew most of the odium on himself, was Thomas Cromwell, Henry's Vicar General. Of the dispossessed religious, about 6,000 men and 2,000 nuns, most received pensions and many of the priests eventually obtained beneficed posts (though such were not available to the women, who were not allowed to marry either, until the next reign), but vast numbers of lay dependents were turned out of home and occupation. Eight hundred and fifteen religious foundations thus disappeared, and to this smooth and ruthless operation there was hardly any opposition. The major part of the spoils found its way in time into the hands of the new class that had risen on the backs of the Tudor monarchs; part of the royal acquisition was put to the founding of six new sees, at Bristol, Chester, Gloucester, Oxford, Peterborough and Westminster (the last was shortly suppressed).

Divine Office

In the West, there is an obligation of certain vocal prayer (preferably as a common exercise, though frequently, through necessity, solitary), laid chiefly on monks, priests and certain religious of monastic and non-monastic life. This 'Office' (Lat. officium, duty), consisting of psalms, lessons, hymns and formularies of prayer, is an attempt to fulfil man's primary duty to praise God. There was among the Jews a daily practice of offering the prayer of praise at certain fixed hours, and the first Christians, as Jews, continued the custom (hints of this in Acts 2:46, 10:9, 16:25). There was probably a development in connection with the preparation for the Eucharist on great feasts (cf. Vigil); by the beginning of the 6th cent., the monks of the West already had their Office arranged into Night Office (Matins) and Day Hours (Lauds, Prime, Terce, Sext, None, Vespers, Compline), St. Benedict being evidently responsible for this ordering of what he termed Opus Dei, God's Work, his arrangement being based on the then current Roman usage. Besides the obligation on those mentioned above, the Office is recited publicly in cathedral churches (though not usually in England or U.S.A—where there are no resident canons—Westminster being an exception). The obligation on secular clergy to recite the Office was reduced some time after the Second Vatican Council, to Morning Prayer (Lauds), one of the Small Hours and Evening Prayer (Vespers).

Divine Right of Kings

A political theory defensive of the position of monarchs, elaborated through the Biblical idea of consecration by anointing (I Sam.10:1, II Sam.2:4, 5:3. I Kg.1:39, etc. In II Sam.1:16, David executes the young Amalekite because '. . . you said, "I killed the Lord's anointed" ' and even Jehu says, after slaying Jezebel, '. . . give her burial; after all, she was a king's daughter.'—II Kg.9:34). The theory was enhanced by Byzantine splendour, the mediaeval mystique of kingship, and Renaissance and Tudor absolutism (in Richard II, the king is

'... God's substitute,
His deputy anointed in His sight'

and '... the figure of God's majesty,
His captain, steward, deputy elect,
Anointed, crowned ...'

Richard further asserts

'The breath of wordly men cannot depose
The deputy elected by the Lord'

and challenges his enemies

'... show us the hand of God
That hath dismist us from our stewardship').

The theory, pushed to extreme logical conclusion in the proposition that 'the King can do no wrong', never had any theological sanction (see Rebellion); it was used in the later Middle Ages by monarchs against both their princely enemies and the Papal teaching on the supremacy of the spiritual over the temporal, which led Pontiffs to claim the power of deposing* monarchs, a power formulated by Boniface VIII in 1302 (see *Unam Sanctam)* and used for the last time by Pius V against Elizabeth I in 1570 (see *Regnans in Excelsis)*. The Divine Right has not been heard of since Charles I lost his head.

Divine Saviour, Society of the
See Salvatorians.

Divine Word, Society of the
Fr Arnold Janssen founded this missionary society at Steyl, Holland in 1875; it established many missionary posts in China and in 1933 was given charge of the Catholic University of Pekin, transferred in 1961 to Taiwan.

Divini Redemptoris
An encyclical published in 1937 by Pope Pius XI on the subject of Communism, condemning its atheism, its materialism, its advocacy of class-war, its denial of human rights; the pontiff concludes that atheistic Communism is intrinsically evil and that therefore a Catholic may in no circumstances collaborate with it.

Divinity of Christ
The Church takes the words literally and stands immovable with the Apostles Peter (Mt.16:17) and Paul (Rom.9:5) and with the earliest traditions of orthodoxy (see Homoousion) against the recurring intellectual fashion of reducing him to a demiurge, a prophet, a hero, an outstanding leader of men, an indefatigable social worker, a superstar.

Divino Afflante Spiritu
See Pius XII (Pope).

Docetism
(Gk. δοκεω, I seem) A tendency or movement rather than a formulated doctrine, which under-emphasised or even denied the humanity and the sufferings of Christ (cf. II Jn. 7), though these ideas grew to their main strength later, especially with the Gnostics*. Some docetists claimed e.g. that Jesus did not suffer on the cross, his place being taken by some phantom, or even by Judas Iscariot or by Simon of Cyrene.

Doctors of the Church
(Lat. *doctor,* teacher.) The title was coined in the Middle Ages for theological writers whose saintly lives and outstanding thought had greatly benefitted the Church, whose works also are accorded very great respect. The four original Great Doctors of the Western church are Gregory*, Ambrose, Augustine*, Jerome*, of the East, Basil the Great, Gregory* of Nazianzen (*the Theologian)* and John Chrysostom*. After the Reformation, the Roman Church added Athanasius*, Hilary*, Ephrem* of Syria, Cyril of Jerusalem*, Cyril of Alexandria*, Peter Chrysologus, Leo the Great, Isidore, Bede* the Venerable, John of Damascus*, Peter Damian, Anselm*, Bernard of Clairvaux, Antony of Padua, Thomas Aquinas*, Bonaventure, Albert the Great, Peter Canisius, John of the Cross*, Francis* de Sales, Robert Bellarmine*, Alphonsus* de Liguori.

Dogma
(Gk. δογμα, opinion, what is worth holding.) Like *propaganda*,* this word, wrested from its context, has acquired a strange parallel meaning: for the

uninstructed and the hostile, it signifies an opinion foisted or imposed on the unwilling or the gullible by arrogant and irresponsible authority. Very early in its history, it evolved to something stronger than mere 'opinion': in Greece, in the 5th cent. B.C., it already meant a decision firmly taken, a decree, that which had 'appeared (good)' to a legislator; likewise in the Roman Republic, laws were published with the tag *visum est Patribus,* it has seemed (good) to the Senate. This is precisely the phraseology of the famous letter sent by the Apostles from Jerusalem (Acts 15:28)—'it has seemed good to the Holy Spirit and to us' concerning their delegation of Paul, Barnabas and others to carry the letter (Acts 15:22). As a technical term, *dogma* means a statement directly proposed by the teaching Church as part of divine Revelation* and thus to be accepted as assured truth.

Dolours
See Sorrows.

Domicile
Canonically, the term carries its ordinary legal meaning: the place in which a person has permanent residence, which is established either by actual residence for 10 years, or by the intention of living there permanently. *Domicile* decides which is one's diocese and parish.

Dominations
See Angels.

Dominic Barberi, Blessed (1792–1849)
A Passionist* priest who for many years longed to work in England for the conversion of that country, but was appointed to lecture in theology in various Italian colleges of his order and was then made Provincial to S. Italy. Posted eventually to Tournai, Belgium, he met some English friends, through whose assistance he came to Staffordshire in 1841. Settling near Stone, he soon overcame the active hostility and scorn of the local people (he was sworn at and stoned and his command of the English language aroused amusement to the end of his life) and endeared himself not only to Catholics but even to those who first held him to be an emissary of

Antichrist (the Pope). It was to Dominic that J. H. Newman* made his submission in 1845, prostrating himself before the simple missionary and begging him to hear his confession and receive him into the Church. Dominic Barberi died at Reading in 1849 and was beatified in 1963.

Dominic, St.
The founder of the Order of Preachers* was born in Castile in 1170; at the age of 21, for the relief of the poor in a famine he sold everything, books and all; he joined the canons of the Cathedral of Osma, who lived the Rule of St. Augustine* and was soon involved in preaching against the Albigensians*. Having the castle of Casseneuil put at his disposal, he began to execute his plan for an Order which would work for the heretics' conversion. In 1216, he obtained formal papal approval for his Order of Friars* and travelled about Italy and Spain founding houses, until his attendance at the first General Chapter in 1220. A year later, having set out to preach to the heathen in Hungary, he took ill and was brought back to Bologna, where the Chapter had been held, and there died, on August 6th, 1221. A less appealing figure than Francis*, his contemporary, he had, in his austere sanctity, the humility thrice to refuse a bishopric. Dominic, despite popular belief, was not the originator of the Rosary.

Dominica in Albis
The Latin name for Low Sunday*, the day on which those baptised at Easter put off their white garments: the full title was *Dominica in albis deponendis,* The Sunday for laying aside the white robes.

Dominican
See Order of Preachers.

Donation of Constantine
The *Donatio Constantini* or *Constitutum Constantini* was a forged document, probably of the 8th or 9th cent. and of the Frankish Empire, purporting to be a deed wherein the Emperor Constantine granted to Pope Sylvester I (314–335) primacy of all Patriarchs wherever in the world and sovereignty over Rome and Italy and all the cities 'of the Western parts (of the Empire)'. The Pope is declared supreme

judge of the clergy, whose leaders are granted the rank of Senators, and is offered the Imperial crown. The document, put out presumably to support the Pope's primacy and his temporal power—both, by that time, established facts in any case—was universally accepted until its refutation in the 15th cent. by the Italian scholar Valla, the Welshman Reginald Pecock, Bishop of Winchester, and the German scholar Nicholas of Cusa.
See also False Decretals.

Doom

(A.S. *dóm*, judgement, sentence at law.) Representation of the Last Judgement painted or carved, usually over the chancel-arch or over the West door of a mediaeval church, with Christ sitting as judge, with angels, demons, the saints, and the damned.

Door, Holy

There are four Holy Doors, each at one of the Major Basilicas in Rome: St. Peter's, St. John Lateran, St. Mary Major, St. Paul Outside the Walls. These doors are usually bricked up inside and out and opened traditionally (i.e. since 1450) only for Holy Year*, to symbolise the re-opening of Paradise (by penance) and the offering of sanctuary.

Douay

i) (Also Douai, Doway.) At Douai, in Flanders, in 1568, William Cardinal Allen founded the English College, the first seminary to be set up according to the decrees of the Council of Trent*; it migrated to Rheims in 1578, and returned to Douay in 1593. Founded to provide for England a learned clergy when the Faith should be re-established, it immediately became a missionary centre, sending a continuous stream of men to minister, in the face of the death penalty, to the isolated faithful of the country, men who remain one of the great glories of the English clergy. One of the tasks undertaken by the College was the translation of the Bible known as the Douay or Douay-Rheims Version*. The French Revolution suppressed the College, which continued at Crook Hall, Ushaw* and at St. Edmund's, Ware*. The Benedictine monks founded a house at Douay in 1605, which also had to move in the revolutionary upheaval; arriving in England in 1795, it has been established as Downside* Abbey since 1814.
ii) Douai Abbey: the Benedictine abbey of Our Lady and St. Edmund, Woolhampton, Berks, the descendant of the royal abbey at Bury St. Edmunds, one of the Greater Abbeys, suppressed in 1539 and restored in Paris in 1615. Later assisted by both James II and Louis XIV, after the Revolution, it re-emerged at Douai in 1818; in 1903, driven out by French anti-religious laws, it removed to Woolhampton, where the monks maintain a large school and engage in parochial work.

Douay Bible (Douay-Rheims Bible)

Undertaken to provide a translation free from the heretical renderings of earlier English versions, the Douay remained—in its later modified form—the standard work for English Catholics until mid-20th cent. (its main equivalent in the U.S. being a revision by Mgr F. P. Kenrick, Archbishop of Baltimore, published in 1859.) The Douay was the work, in the main, of the Oxford scholars William Allen, Gregory Martin, Thomas Worthington, and Richard Bristowe. The New Testament, published at Rheims in 1582, had a strong influence on the language of the Authorised Version, which was begun in 1607, an influence due largely to the Puritan scholar W. Fulke, who, the better to attack the Rheims N.T., printed it parallel to the text of the Bishops' Bible of 1571, thereby giving it wide publicity. The O.T. did not appear until 1609, at Douay. This version was made, not from the Hebrew and Greek of the Bible, but from the Latin Vulgate* and was itself much 'Latinised' in language. Editions more recently in use are based on the revisions made by Challoner* in mid-18th cent.

Dove

The dove, much used in Christian art, has a varied symbolism: from the story of Noah (Gen.8), it is a sign of peace and reconciliation; in the Song of Songs, it is used to signify love (as in the classical writers of the pagan world,) which sorts well enough with the symbolism (from the baptism of Jesus in Mt.3:16) of the dove as manifestation of the Holy Spirit, who, the theologians say, is the substantive love existing between the Father and the Son, and who activates the Father's love for each human being through the Son; the Fathers applied the term from the Song of Songs to the Church—and to the individual soul—as object of love (Song of Songs, 2:14, 5:2). As symbol of the Spirit, the dove also represents divine inspiration (St. Gregory is depicted as composing music with the dove on his shoulder) and guidance, also as purity and simplicity.

The Hebrew word for dove is *Jonah*, hence the Book of Jonah is the Book of the Dove—a story of reconciliation and peace.

The 'Eucharistic Dove' was a metal receptacle, suspended over the sanctuary of some mediaeval churches for the reservation of the Blessed Sacrament, a kind of hanging tabernacle. This use is still to be found in Amiens Cathedral and in the Greek College in Rome.

Downside

A community of Benedictine monks, founded in 1605 at Douay*, and expelled in 1795, took refuge for a time at Acton Burnell in Shropshire, and moved to Downside near Bath in 1814, being erected into an Abbey in 1899. Downside is the senior house of the English Congregation. The Abbey church is a superb example of modern Gothic; the community maintains a well-known school and many parishes, and edits a quarterly, the Downside Review.

Dowry of Mary (Our Lady's Dowry)

A name bestowed abroad on mediaeval England for its devotion to the Blessed Virgin. Arundell, Archbishop of Canterbury, wrote in 1399, 'We, the English, being the servants of her special inheritance, and her dowry, as we are commonly called, ought to surpass others . . .'

Doxology

(Gk. δοξα, glory.) The giving of praise in its highest form, to God alone. The Greater Doxology is the hymn used at Mass, the *Glory to God in the Highest*, the Lesser Doxology is the *Glory be to the Father;* Doxology is also used of the metrical praise of the triple name of God which forms the last stanza of almost every Catholic hymn. An important doxology is found at the conclusion of the Eucharistic Prayer at Mass.

Dream of Gerontius, the

Published first in 1865, this poem of Newman's* was set later to music by Elgar, to rank very highly in the list of English oratorio; it describes the death of a Christian and the passage of the soul from the body to Purgatory, and is remarkable as an exposition, fine in language and sound in theology, of Catholic teaching on Purgatory, repentance and the holiness of God. Two pieces from it—*Praise to the Holiest in the Height* and *Firmly I believe and truly* became very popular hymns.

Dulia

(Gk. δουλεια, service.) The homage which may fittingly be paid to saints and angels. See Hyperdulia and Latria.

Duns Scotus (c. 1262–1308)

Called, because of his teachings, *Doctor Subtilis* and *Doctor Marianus,* this mediaeval philosopher, native of Roxburgh and Franciscan* friar, taught at Oxford, Paris and Cologne. His system, adopted by the Franciscans, was at one with that of Thomas* Aquinas in maintaining that reason and revelation cannot contradict each other, but differed in giving the psychological primacy to will and love (the Thomists gave it to reason and knowledge) and in its explanation of Matter and Form, superimposing a separate principle of individuation (*Haecceitas,* 'thisness', which so strongly influenced Gerard Manley Hopkins); Scotus has the distinction also of being the first major theologian to support the doctrine of the Immaculate* Conception, against Aquinas and most of the great Schoolmen*.

Durham, the Use of

A variant of the Roman Liturgy in use at the Cathedral of Durham until the Reformation, closely resembling the Use of York and of the North of England generally.

Easter

The greatest solemnity of the Church's year, the commemoration of Christ's rising from the dead. The derivation of the name is uncertain, the only constructive suggestion being that of St. Bede, who offers the name *Eostre*, an ancient goddess of dawn or of spring; and it appears that, in Northern climes at least, Easter supplanted ancient spring festivals which involved the exchange of gifts of eggs (symbol of fertility and of immortality) and the lighting of fires symbolic of the renewal of life. The date is fixed as the first Sunday after the full moon which occurs on or next after March 21st; which sets its limits between that date and April 25th inclusive. Some Eastern churches, while following this rule of the Council of Nicaea★, hold also to that Council's regulation that Passover must always precede Easter; and some also follow their own outmoded calendars: hence much confusion. The Easter Vigil Service of the Roman Rite had, in the course of time, been advanced to an earlier and ever earlier hour until clergy and faithful found themselves kindling a Holy Fire which the sun rendered well-nigh invisible and celebrating the sacred night of Christ's rising on the cold clear daylight of Holy Saturday morning, thus stultifying the entire symbolism and draining the liturgy of its riches. Pope Pius XII approved in 1951—and made compulsory in 1956—the reform by which the service was restored to a Vigil for Easter, so timed that, as the directive has it, its final stage, the Mass of Easter, shall begin about midnight between Saturday and Sunday; yet, in places with less liturgical perceptivity, there is already a tendency to start early; and perhaps the drift towards Saturday morning has set in again.

Easter Candle

See Paschal Candle.

Easter Controversy

The name is given to two historical disputes: the disagreement about when Easter should be kept, which arose in the late 2nd cent. (see *Quartodeciman)* and the later differences between the native British Churches and the discipline introduced from Rome by Augustine★. These were that the British were using a different cycle of years for the dating of Easter (an 84-year cycle, complicated by some indigenous errors, while Rome had by this time adopted the 19-year cycle decided on at Nicaea★ in 325). There were other controversial practices: the British or Celtic tonsure differed from the Roman, and there was some obscure feature of the native rite of Baptism which was criticised by the Romans. Augustine himself was unwilling to impose Roman practice and uniformity was brought in only at the Synod of Whitby★.

Easter Duty

A Catholic is bound to receive Holy Communion annually at least, 'Easter' being the time from Ash Wednesday to Trinity Sunday; the Sacrament should preferably be received in one's own parish church.

Eastern Churches

These groups of Churches are either Catholic (see Eastern Rites★) or dissident: the latter being those groupings of Eastern Christians who, while following their own distinctive Rites, refuse the authority of the Pope, although they have valid Orders (there is apparently some doubt about Copts and Ethiopians) and are differentiated from Protestantism by holding to the Real Presence, the Eucharistic Sacrifice, auricular confession, veneration of the Mother of God and of the Saints, prayers for the dead and other things characteristically Catholic.

Eastertide

(Or Paschal Time.) The season from Easter Day to Whit★ Sunday.

Ecce Homo

The representation, sometimes in sculpture but most frequently in painting, of the Saviour (usually half-figure or head and shoulders) as he is imagined to have appeared when Pilate presented him to the people (Jn.19:5—where the Roman's phrase, usually rendered 'Here is the man', probably carried more of the tone of 'Look at the poor devil!').

Ecclesiastical Titles Acts

By the Ecclesiastical Titles Act of 1851, it was made illegal for any Roman Catholic bishop to take as his title the name of any place in Great Britain; any act performed under such title was null and void and any bequest to a person using such title was forfeit to the Crown. The Act, passed as a hasty reaction to Papal Aggression*, was never taken seriously, and Bishop Hogarth was soon signing public documents as 'William, Bishop of Hexham'. He, along with the rest of the new hierarchy, thought it sufficient to obey the clause in the Catholic Relief Act* of 1829 which forbade them the use of existing Anglican diocesan titles (and which was faithfully observed: though, unexpectedly enough, the Church of England later duplicated Catholic diocesan titles, e.g. Birmingham, Liverpool, Southwark). The Ecclesiastical Titles Act of 1851, after 20-years of ineffectual existence, was repealed by the Ecclesiastical Titles Act (34 and 35 Vict. c. 53) of 1871.

Ecstasy

(Gk. εχσταοις., the state of being outside of oneself, being 'beside oneself': the N.T. versions say things like 'amazement seized them', 'they were astounded', in Lk.5:26, and 'a great astonishment' in Mk.5:42) Theologically, one of the normal stages of the mystical life, when power of the divine activity in the soul causes the alienation of the senses, usually for only a short time. It is not miraculous, nor is the alienation of sense considered to be necessary for the *possession* of the soul by God which is the essence of ecstatic prayer.

Edict of Milan

See Milan, Edict of

Edict of Nantes

See Nantes, Edict of

Ejaculatory Prayer

(Lat. *jaculum*, dart.) Prayer consisting of a short form of words, or even of only one word, which can be often and easily used; e.g. 'My Lord and my God!' 'Jesus, Mary and Joseph!' 'Jesus!'

Elevation of the Host

The raising of the Host for adoration immediately after the words of consecration was first done in Paris at the end of the 12th cent., against the opinion, then gaining ground, that the Body of Christ was not present until the chalice was consecrated. The elevation of the chalice was not prescribed until the end of the 16th cent.

Eleven Bishops, the

The bishops who were put out of their English sees by Elizabeth I and died either in prison or in some kind of restraint between 1559 and 1578: Tunstall of Durham, Boyle of Lichfield, Oglethorpe of Carlisle, White of Winchester, Pate of Worcester, Poole of Peterborough, Bonner of London, Bourne of Bath and Wells, Thirlby of Ely, Turberville of Exeter, and Heath of York. The last survivor of the Catholic hierarchy was Goldwell*, who died in Rome in 1585.

Emancipation, Catholic

The liberation of Catholicism in Great Britain—a minority group of about 500,000—and Ireland from most of the handicaps imposed during penal times was brought about in four stages: in 1778, *18 George III c. 60* removed the punishment of life imprisonment for keeping a school, allowed Catholics, on taking the oath of loyalty, to buy and inherit land, and no longer permitted priests to be prosecuted through common informers; then *31 George III c. 32* in 1791 made Catholic schools legal, permitted those who took the oath to hear or offer Mass, to become priests or religious, to join the army or the legal profession but not to be officers, judges or King's Counsel; later, by *33 George III* (1793) Irish Catholics got the vote and access to the universities, the bar, the army and navy; and *10 George IV c. 7* in 1829, which became known as the year of Catholic Emancipation, renewed the obnoxious oath (removed in 1871) but reinstated Catholics as almost equal citizens. They now had the franchise and could sit in Parliament, though there remained the invalidity of marriage before a priest (some priests have of recent years become Registrars) and the prohibition in public of religious dress and religious celebration (both of these dead letters, though there were certain protests at the Eucharistic Congress of 1908); no-one took seriously the injunction on resident religious (Jesuits being named) to be registered or the description of the entry of religious from abroad as a misdemeanour.

See also Disabilities of Catholics.

Embassy Chapel

Being extra-territorial, the chapels of foreign embassies in London were immune from the penal laws operative in England from 1559 to 1829 and much frequented by Catholics in the 17th and 18th cent., particularly the chapels of the Bavarian, Sardinian and Spanish embassies.

Embolism

(Gk. εμβολος, a stopgap.) A prayer 'thrust in' between the Our Father of the Mass and the Breaking of the Bread: it begins 'Deliver us, Lord', and is an extension of the last phrase of the Our Father.

Eminence

The title given to Cardinals*; more widely used until 1630, when Pope Urban VIII restricted it to cardinals, the Grand Master of the Knights of St. John of Jerusalem* and the Imperial Electors. The previous style of cardinals was 'Most Illustrious' or 'Most Reverend'.

Enclosure

That part of a monastic property which is canonically enclosed and reserved for the religious. The extent of the enclosure will vary according to requirements; the choir, e.g. of a monastic church is usually enclosed, though not the nave. The limits of the enclosure are to be clearly indicated. A male religious is bound by enclosure to the extent of having to ask his superior's permission to leave it, a permission freely given when reasonably requested; men may be invited within the enclosure of a house of men, but women are forbidden, though an exception is made for queens and such persons and their retinues, and some great benefactresses have received papal permission. For houses of women, the rule has been stricter: a religious in solemn vows was forbidden to leave the enclosure, apart from danger of death, without permission from Rome or at least from the bishop; now the superior herself is empowered to give permission as she thinks fit. In the matter of entry, the bishop or religious superior comes in for visitation*, the chaplain or confessor to minister to the religious, reigning sovereigns with consort and retinue, cardinals and their court, workers, male or female, on their lawful occasions; for visitors, there is a room set aside, a 'parlour' where they sit and speak to the religious across a kind of counter or bar, an arrangement which has recently, in most places, replaced the former system of two separate rooms, one for the visitor and one for the religious, who sat, often with face veiled, beyond a steel grill which in some cases was defended by suitable spikes in horizontal *chevaux de frise*. There has been much legislation on the subject of the *clausura;* as early as 362, the Synod of Alexandria bound monks and religious celibates to avoid meeting women, speaking to them and, if possible, seeing them. Boniface VIII imposed the enclosure on all *moniales** and Trent* tightened the rules for women in both solemn and simple vows. Now, in houses of simple vows (with, therefore, no papal enclosure) the rules are made in conjunction with the ordinary*.

Encyclical (letter)

Etymologically, the name is the same as *circular;* used in earlier times of a letter sent by any bishop to his flock, it is now restricted to a 'universal' letter addressed by the Pope as chief bishop to the whole Church or to a substantial part thereof (e.g. *Mit Brennender Sorge** written by Pius XI to the German Catholics in 1937). The custom is to refer to an Encyclical by its initial phrase: *Clericis Laicos*, Providentissimus Deus, Rerum Novarum**. Encyclicals addressed to the universal Church are still written in Latin.

Encyclopaedists

The group of contributors, under the editorship of Diderot and d'Alembert, to the *Encyclopédie,* published between 1751 and 1780, and including Rousseau, Voltaire, Condorcet, Buffon and others who, having to conform in their major articles to the rules of Church and State censorship, contrived to insert into the lesser pieces a great amount of strong anti-aristocratic and anti-Catholic writing. These writers, who gained the name of *les philosophes,* were a main part of the intellectual disruption which prepared for the irreligious character of the Revolution of 1789.

English College, the Venerable

The seminary founded in Rome in 1579—on the site of a pilgrims' hospice of 1362—to train missionaries for work in Elizabethan England; in those times, 42 of its ex-students died as martyrs and six in prison. It is the third oldest of the national seminaries in the Eternal City. Today the students pursue most of their studies at the Gregorian* University and are in general supported by their dioceses and by bursaries. The college is known in Rome and among the clergy as the *Venerabile.* See also Beda, Douay, Lisbon, Valladolid.

English Ladies

See the Institute of Mary

English Mystics

See under Mysticism

Enthroning

A bishop's solemn taking possession of his church and diocese is signified by the ceremony in which he first sits on his episcopal chair and receives the homage of his clergy (see Cathedral). Pope John Paul I, however, set a new example of modesty on his election in 1978 by declining to be enthroned and crowned, breaking an age-old Papal tradition which was redolent of power and of ecclesiastical imperialism.

Entrance Song

The name now used for *Introit;* the hymn is said or sung by the celebrant and people as the former proceeds to the sanctuary for Mass. It differs from the *Introit* also in not being, as a rule, written specifically for that Mass.

Epact

The age of the moon (the number of days' difference between the length of the solar year and that of the lunar), which is a necessary part of the calculation of the date of Easter.

Ephesus, Council of

(Third Oecumenical.) Summoned by Theodosius II in 431 and guided largely by St. Cyril of Alexandria, this Council passed eight canons, seven of them directed to doctrinal matters, and firmly rejecting Nestorian* dualism by reasserting the title *Theotokos*—to the great public rejoicing of that city, whose populace, long before, had chanted the praise of their pagan goddess (Acts 19:28–34).

Ephraem, St. (c. 306–373)

Called the Syrian (born at Nisibis), he may possibly have attended the Council of Nicaea*. The miraculous deliverance of the city of Nisibis from the Persians in 338 was attributed to his prayers; but on its cession to them 25 years later, he withdrew across the Roman frontier and lived at Edessa. This loquacious deacon then wrote voluminously, mostly in verse and in his native Syriac, producing hymns, exegesis, controversy, dogma and ascetical works. He wrote luridly of the Last Judgement (one of his favourite themes) and tenderly of the Mother of God—his strenuous assertion of her perfect sinlessness has led many to adduce him as an early witness to belief in the Immaculate* Conception. He was declared a Doctor of the Church in 1920. Feast-day June 9th.

Episcopacy

Either the bishops of the Church as a body (see Collegiality) or the doctrine of the Church concerning bishops, viz that there is an order of bishops who are not merely priests but have office and powers over and above those of the priests, etc—as defined by the Council of Trent* in Section 23; the Second Vatican Council also has a decree on the bishops' Pastorial Office in the Church (Christus Dominus 1965).

Episcopate

The office of a bishop, or the bishops of a province, a country or the whole Church.

Epistle side

The end of the altar or the side of the sanctuary opposite to the Gospel* side.

Eschatology

(Gk. εσχατα, the last things.) The word—apparently not in English use before the 19th cent.—for the theology of the 'last things', viz death, the end of the world, the destiny of the human being, the Second Coming*. Many of our Lord's parables are eschatological, as are the warnings in e.g. Mk.13 and Mt.24; St. Paul likewise treats of such matters in I and II Thess., as do many of the more dramatic sections of Revelation. The caution of theologians in dealing with these matters has not always been followed by writers and preachers; and modern advances in astronomical physics have opened wide, if entertaining, vistas of fresh speculation on such questions as the destruction of the world.

Establishment

The status of the established church of a political group such as a nation (the Church of England is the Established Church, the official religion of the country). Though it can assist in the proper relationship between Church and State, it is regarded warily by theologians on account of the danger of a church becoming in some measure a dependency of the State and, by being under obligation to it, losing independence.

Etheria

A 4th-cent. pilgrim, a nun, perhaps an abbess, travelling probably from Spain, whose account of her journeyings to Asia Minor, Constantinople, Edessa, the Holy Land, and Egypt displays remarkable intelligence and observation. Besides making such interesting identifications as the capital city of Melchisedeck and the spot where the Golden Calf was cast, she adds to our genuine information on the liturgical life of Jerusalem in her day. She records her participation in the liturgy of the Epiphany, in the ceremonies of Holy Week and Easter (including the procession with palms* to the Mount of Olives and the Veneration of the Cross*) and of Pentecost*. We find in her book, first known erroneously as *Peregrinatio Silviae*, and written in very idiosyncratic Latin, the earliest mention of the Feast of the Purification (which she places on Feb 14th) and we learn that in Jerusalem and Egypt at that time, the Nativity of Christ was kept on Jan 6th. Her name is found also in the variants Egeria and Aitheria.

Eucharist

(Gk. ευχαριστια, thanksgiving: I Cor.11:24, Mt.26:27, etc: the enacting of the Eucharist has always been the central act of Christian thanksgiving). The word is used both for the sacred elements which we receive and adore and for the act itself, the service, the Mass: traditionally, 'the Sacrament of the Holy Eucharist is the true Body and Blood of Jesus Christ, together with his soul and divinity, under the appearances of bread and wine' (Catechism, Q.266). As regards its sacramental status, the Eucharist is the food of the faithful, its matter being bread and wine, its form the words of consecration; while the consecration itself may be performed only by a priest or bishop, the administering of the Sacrament, long confined to bishop, priest and deacon, is now being extended to the laity. The nature, mode and effects of the Eucharist have been the subject of centuries of speculation, discussion, controversy and heresy. See Companation, Impanation, Real Presence, Transubstantiation, Lauda Sion.

Eucharistic Congress

An international meeting, usually on a very large scale and presided over by a papal delegate, the purpose of which is to give and encourage honour to the Blessed Sacrament by means of the liturgy, devotions of various kinds, discussions and addresses. The first was at Lille in 1881, and they are usually held in large cities, from country to country in turn. Pope Paul VI travelled to Colombia to attend the Eucharistic Congress at Bogotá, and to India for the Congress in Bombay.

Eucharistic Fast

The present discipline of the Church requires a fast of one hour (to the time of Communion, not to the beginning of Mass); water is not forbidden during this hour, and the sick may take non-alcoholic drink and any medicine, even solid, which is recommended to them.

Euthanasia

(Gk., An easy, happy death.) A euphemism for the killing—usually out of misplaced kindness—of one who on account of great pain, the impossibility of a cure or general 'uselessness', is considered better off dead. The Church still stoutly condemns this as murder and opposed to the sole sovereignty of God over the disposition of human life. Amid the strong advocacy of the legalisation of euthanasia, confusion is being introduced by the extension of the term 'euthanasia' to cover the permitting of persons to die, i.e. letting nature take its course, not having recourse to extraordinary means simply to prolong life; this course the Church has always countenanced, that one is not bound *officiously* to keep alive', when modern medicine can preserve life without movement, or even consciousness.

Evangelical Counsels

The Evangelical Counsels—Voluntary Poverty, Perpetual Chastity and Entire Obedience—are counsels of perfection, not necessary means of salvation, and are embodied in the vows* of religion, as aids for those thus called, in the quest for the highest love of God and of neighbour.

Evangelisation of Peoples, Sacred Congregation for

See Roman Congregations.

Evangelist

The word is used in the N.T. in three contexts to mean an itinerant preacher of the Gospel (Acts 21:8, Eph.4:11, II Tim.4:5), probably not as the title of a specific office; in modern times, certain Protestant groups call their travelling preachers *Evangelists*. As a historic title of identification, the word is used of the traditional writers of the four Gospels, Matthew, Mark, Luke, John.

Evening Prayer

In the Divine Office*, that hour which used to be called *Vespers*.

Evensong

The translation of the Latin word *Vesperae*, evening (prayers); one of the Hours* of the Divine Office: the word was in use in all England until at least 1812:

about that time, the Catholics replaced it with *Vespers*, and Evensong now means only the Anglican evening service.

Evesham, Our Lady of

Evesham (Worcs) is the only town in England founded as a result of an appearance of Our Lady: Eoves, a swineherd, saw the Mother of God, who later appeared to St. Egwin, Abbot of Worcester; the abbey was founded in 714 and the town of Evesham was later built. The Abbey became a very popular centre of pilgrimage until the Dissolution*. The pilgrimages have only recently been revived, under the encouragement of the Archdiocese of Birmingham.

Exaltation of the Cross

See Cross.

Excardination

The permanent transfer of a man in Holy Orders from the jurisdiction of one bishop to that of another.

Ex Cathedra

(Lat., From the throne.) The phrase to describe a certain manner of pronouncement by the Pope: he is speaking *ex cathedra* when, exercising his office as shepherd and teacher of the whole Church, he defines, with full apostolic authority, a truth concerning faith or morals which is expressly to be held by the whole Church.
See Cathedra and Infallibility.

Excommunication

The ecclesiastical penalty which separates the subject of it from the community of the faithful (cf. Mt.18:17): in earlier ages, there was a 'greater' excommunication, cutting off the offender from all contact of any kind with other Christians, apart from allowing him the last rites in his time of need, and a 'lesser', depriving him only of the ordinary reception of the Sacraments. Excommunication in the 1917 Code* renders a person either *vitandus* (to be avoided—one who lays violent hands on the Pope, or is named as *vitandus* by the Holy See, and whose exercise of ecclesiastical functions is not only forbidden but, if performed, void) or *toleratus* (tolerated—debarred likewise from Sacraments and liturgy, except sermons, whose forbidden exercise of ecclesiastical rights, e.g. of election, would not be void). Excommunication says nothing about the state of grace of the person penalised: the union of the soul with God depends on His grace alone and is unaffected by any ecclesiastical censure; and though the ex-communicate is precluded from benefit-ing by indulgences* or public Mass or prayers, the faithful should pray privately for him and priests may offer Mass for him, likewise privately. In accordance with the changes in society, the social and psychological effects of excommunication have dwindled since the Middle Ages, and it is now purely a spiritual penalty; it is understood that the new Code of Canon Law at present being prepared will make a fresh approach to the whole question of excommunication.

See also Interdict, *Regnans in Excelsis*.

Exeat

The document or letter of Excardination* necessary for the transfer of a priest from one diocese to another.

Exegesis

The science of explaining the true mean-ings of the Sacred Scriptures; the one who practices this is an *exegete*.

Exequatur

(Lat., He may perform.) The legal term for the recognition of a counsel by the govern-ment to which he is accredited, was used —interchangeably with *Regium Placet* —for the right claimed by certain sovereigns to control the publication in their territories of Papal documents (see *Mit Brennender Sorge*). Edward III in 1351 declared invalid all appointments made to English sees made without regard to the existing rights of patron or chapter. This decree was provoked, though not justified, by abuse of power by some popes, particularly by John XXII. The bishops of England protested against the Act which, though enforced by *Praemunire**, was frequently disregarded. The Council of Trent* and Pius IX's Syllabus* both vindicated the Pope's rights in these matters.

Exposition of the Blessed Sacrament

The custom grew, apparently from the early 14th cent., of setting out the Sacred Host on or above the altar after Mass for the veneration of the faithful. This probably led to the invention of the monstance* and is certainly connected with the rise of Benediction of the Blessed Sacrament*. The devotion was given a further impetus in the 16th cent. as a counterblast to the Lutheran teaching that Christ was present in the Sacrament only at the moment of Communion.

Exsultet

Also *Praeconium Paschale*, the Proclama-tion of Easter, the Easter Song of Praise, it is a magnificant prose composition, to music which makes it one of the richest gems in the liturgy of the Latin Church. This song of praise (named after its open-ing *Exsultet jam angelica turba coelorum*, Now let the angel host of heaven rejoice) is chanted at the Vigil Liturgy by the deacon*, who stands beside the Paschal Candle* and celebrates it as a symbol of Christ the Light, illuminating the world by His Resurrection. Left originally to the free composition of the deacon, the Ex-sultet took, in the 7th cent, its present form, which, by the 9th, had superseded all others. The words are renowned for their consistently lyrical quality and for their inclusion of such daring paradoxes as, *Truly necessary was that sin of Adam's, which was wiped out by Christ's death! How fortunate that fault, which earned for us so glorious a Redeemer!*

Extern Sister

In certain strictly enclosed Orders, a member of the community who lives out-side the Enclosure* and acts as link with the world outside, answering the door, go-ing to shops, etc; different from the lay sister, who lives within the enclosure, the extern is sometimes known as *la tourière*, one of her duties being to attend to the revolving wooden drum *(tour)* by which parcels etc. are passed into the enclosure.

Extra Ecclesiam Nulla Salus

Latin phrase, outside the church there is no salvation, based on the final proposition of the Athanasian Creed, summing up all the previous articles: this is the Catholic Faith, which except a man believe faithfully he cannot be saved.
But see Salvation Outside the Church.

Extraordinary Ecclesiastical Affairs, the Sacred Congregation of

See Council for the Public Affairs of the Church.

Extreme Unction

See Anointing of the Sick.

Exultate Deo

See Pro Armenis.

Faith, Sacred Congregation for the Teaching of the

See Roman Congregations.

Faithful Companions of Jesus

A congregation founded by the Comtesse de Bonnault d'Houet in 1820 at Amiens; the Sisters are not enclosed, and conduct many schools of different kinds. Their Rule is based on that of the Society of Jesus.

Faldstool

A kind of stool, having arms and used as seat and *prie-dieu* by a bishop when he officiates outside his diocese or inside it but not using the throne.

Falk Laws

The May Laws*, named after the Minister of Worship who drafted them. Gerard Manley Hopkins' *Wreck of the Deutschland* is dedicated 'To the happy memory of five Franciscan nuns exiled by the Falk Laws drowned between midnight and morning of Dec 7th, 1875'.

Falling Asleep, the

(Dormition; Lat. *dormitio*.) The name used by Eastern Churches for the Assumption* of the Mother of God. Also the translation of the title (*Transitus Mariae*) of an apocryphal work of the 4th–5th cent., which, beneath its rich layers of fantasy and marvel, bears witness to the status of the Blessed Virgin in the Church of that time (she is Our Lady and Mother of God, without sin, unspotted in body or soul; she intercedes with her Son, is venerated by angels and men and obtains miracles) and to the use of incense in the liturgy, as well as the terms 'altar' and 'sacrifice'.

False Decretals

A collection of documents published about the middle of the 9th cent. by one Isidore Mercator (presumably a *nom-de-plume* and presumably taken to suggest St. Isidore of Seville, to whom the writings were long attributed) containing a number of letters purporting to be written by pre-Nicene popes, all of them forged: a compilation of canons of Councils, most of them genuine: many letters of popes between 335 and 731, 35 of which are forgeries. This astonishing and ingenious collection was produced somewhere in the Frankish kingdom, its main trend being the defence of diocesan bishops against metropolitans and, to a lesser degree, the claiming of early support for papal supremacy; perhaps its acceptance was assisted by the fact that it contained no ideas that were not already familiar; the canons it quotes were largely used as sources for mediaeval Canon Law. The genuineness of much of the document being under suspicion by mid-15th cent., it was soon repudiated by all scholars.

Fathers

The Fathers of the Church are those writers (Greek Fathers and Latin Fathers, according to their language) who, early in the history of the Church, were given weighty respect for their holiness and orthodox wisdom: some prominent names among them are these saints: Clement of Rome, Ignatius of Antioch, Justin, Irenaeus, Polycarp, Cyprian, Dionysius, Optatus, Epiphanius, Basil, Gregory of Nazianzen, Vincent of Lerins, Caesarius of Arles. Newman was a great patristic scholar and his thought was profoundly influenced by the Fathers.

Fathers of the Desert

The Desert Fathers were the Hermits and monks who inhabited the wilderness, chiefly in Egypt, in the 4th cent. and from whom derives all Christian monasticism. The scale of the exodus to the desert prompted the contemporary Alexandrian poet, Palladas, a cynic with faith neither in this world nor the next, to exclaim that these solitaries

By multitude their name belie.
If solitaries, who so many?
If many, solitaries why?

At one period, there were 5,000 monks presided over by St Antony. There was no strict organisation, most of the devotees living either alone or in groups of two or three, younger men being 'apprenticed' to experienced monks, and sometimes meeting for worship (very few being priests); they practised astonishing austerities, besides praying and working: in Southern Egypt, under St. Pachomius, there developed eventually a community life, with a rule, fixed hours of common prayer and the practice of agriculture, joinery, tanning, where the earlier custom had been restricted to the making of mats and basket-work. Other names of renown are those of Paul, Hilarion, Epiphanius and their historian Palladius.

Fatima

A place of pilgrimage in Portugal: in 1917, three children are said to have had a vision of the Mother of God, who announced herself as 'Our Lady of the Rosary*', told them to recite the Rosary daily and to have a chapel built in her honour. Two of the children died soon after, the third, Lucia Santos, became a Carmelite and wrote accounts of the visions, emphasising the threefold message of the necessity of the practice of penance, the recitation of the Rosary and the devotion to the Immaculate Heart of Mary. Many miracles are reported from Fatima, and Lucia's other manuscript, the Secret of Fatima, not to be unsealed until after 1960, was lodged in the Vatican, where it is presumed still to be kept.

Febronianism

An extreme form of Gallicanism* preached by a German bishop, von Hontheim (1701–90) who used the name Febronius. The power of the keys, he said, was deposited with the entire body of the faithful, though to be used only by the clergy; the bishop had unlimited authority; the Holy See was not superior to a Council or the body of bishops but should in fact be restrained by them. Febronianism was condemned by Clement XIII and Pius VI but was understandably popular with certain Catholic princes. See Josephinism.

Fête-Dieu

The common French term for the feast of Corpus Christi.

Fidei Defensor

See Defender of the Faith

Filioque

(Lat., And from the Son.) The phrase, signifying the double Procession of the Holy Spirit, became a touchstone, not to say shibboleth, of orthodoxy between West and East: introduced into the Latin creed—so that it now read *Who proceeds from the Father and the Son*—in 589 at the Third Council of Toledo, it became general in the West from about 800, when the Creed began to be chanted at Mass throughout the Frankish Empire. When Frankish monks introduced it into their monastery in Jerusalem, it gave offence to the Eastern monks. The matter being referred to Leo III, he took the tactful course of disapproving the use of the formula while accepting the doctrine. However, the *Filioque* soon after 1000 spread to Rome itself, having been a bone of contention between East and West since the time of Photius (and not yet resolved: discussions on the point between Anglicans, Old Catholics and the Eastern Church in the 1870s and between Anglicans and Russian Orthodox in 1912 bore no fruit). It is clear, however, that there is more at stake than pure theology, since divines on both sides admit that the theological point is not beyond solution—as witness the agreement reached at the Council of Florence*.

Finding of the Christians

In 1865, eight years after Commander Perry's expedition, a missionary, Fr. Petitjean, discovered numbers of Catholics in Japan, descendants of those who survived the massacres of 1638—the 'death' of the Japanese Church—living without clergy but baptising their children and passing on the Faith as best they could.

Fire

Fire-worship was a prominent part of many pagan cults and its use as a symbol, a god and a means of healing long persisted: we find a bishop of the 12th cent. condemning, to his Slavonic flock, the worship of fire and other elements of nature; as late as the 19th cent., certain Russian country-folk, in the event of an epidemic, would put out all fires, go outside the village and strike new fire, which they would then bring in as an instrument of cleansing and healing. The Church seems to have taken the ritual of the New Fire of Easter from an ancient worship of the Celtic races, transferring the symbolism of newness, light, power, protection, to the Risen Christ. The other Christian use of fire is in art, as symbol of the Holy Spirit (Acts 2:3).

First Fridays
See Nine Fridays.

Fish
In Christian symbolism, the fish occurred very early as a representation of i) Christ, ii) the newly baptised, iii) the Eucharist. It came into use in the 2nd cent., but its origins and full significance are still uncertain: it is thought that there may have been Babylonian or Indian influence, and there is speculation as to whether the commonly accepted acrostic making the Greek word for *fish* (ΙΧΘΥΣ=Ιησους Χριστος Θεου Υιος Σωτερ, Jesus Christ, Son of God, Saviour) could have been concocted to account for the already existing sign. The fish was frequently used in the 4th and 5th cents. for the Eucharist, and is found in the art of the catacombs juxtaposed with bread and wine.

Five Ways, the
St. Thomas Aquinas sets down five methods (the *Quinque Viae)*—at philosophical length in the *Summa contra Gentiles*, then more crisply in the *Summa Theologica*—of indicating the existence of God *a posteriori*, i.e. from observation of the world; these five 'roads' to God are: the Argument from Motion—movement implies a First Mover; the Argument from Causality—the series of efficient causes we notice in the world, together with their effects, postulates finally an uncaused Cause; the Argument from Contingency—things which exist but whose existence is not self-explanatory or necessary, demand some necessary Being; the Argument from the Degrees of Being—the fact that we make comparisons (nobler, better, more true, etc) calls for a Standard by which comparisons can be made and which must itself be the perfection of all these qualities; the Argument from Finality or Design—the carrying out by inanimate or unintelligent creatures of an evident purpose (Aristotle's *Nature does nothing in vain*) indicates an Intelligence beyond them and planning for them. The first four of these arguments are often grouped together under the title of the Cosmological Argument and treated separately from the fifth, or Teleological, Argument.

Five Wounds, the
The wounds of Christ received in his Passion became the object of devotion in the Middle Ages, and five particular wounds were chosen, that in the side (Jn.19:34) and the nail-wounds (Lk.24:39–40, Jn.20:20 & 27), as symbols of his sufferings and his love for mankind. This devotion flourished very early in the literature of England, e.g. in *The Dream of the Rood* (about 750).

The corners of the earth
Gleamed with fair jewels,
Just as there were five
Upon the cross-beam . . .
of the glorious tree of victory—
and was encouraged particularly by the writings of St. Bernard and the Stigmatization* of St. Francis*. Liturgically, the Five Wounds were represented by the five grains of incense in the Paschal Candle,* by the five crosses of consecration on an altar-stone and, according to some, by the five signs of the Cross made by the celebrant over the Host and chalice in the *Unde et memores* in the Tridentine Mass. The emblem of the Wounds was adopted by Portugal on her flag, was worn by the rebels on the Pilgrimage of Grace* and was engraved on many rings in 15th-cent. England. This idea of the Wounds as 'wells of grace', the source of life, was condensed into the one Wound of the Side:

Water and blood from the wound so wide:
The blood brought us from the bane of hell,
And stopped our second death being died,
The water is baptism, truth to tell,
as *The Pearl* has it, and led directly to the devotion to the Sacred Heart*.

'Flaminian Gate, Out of the'

The title of the pastoral letter written by Cardinal Wiseman* to the English Catholics on his appointment as archbishop of the new see of Westminster at the Restoration* of the Hierarchy in 1850. The ringing title was in fact a slight breach of etiquette, as only the Pope had the right of dating letters from Rome; but the real trouble arose from its being sent at all and from its tone of triumphant rejoicing, which convinced many in high places in England that Papal Aggression* had begun.

Florence, Council of

(Seventeenth Oecumenical, 1438–45.) A continuation of the Council of Basle*, which is not recognised as Oecumenical, for lack of universal representation and of Papal recognition of its acts: at Florence, re-union was effected with the Orthodox, the Armenians, the Copts and some Syrian Jacobites, but this was not of long duration, political considerations having played a large part in its achieving, and it never being popular with the Orthodox. The Orthodox patriarch of Constantinople repudiated it within 40 years, though the union seems to have lingered with the patriarchates of Alexandria, Antioch and Jerusalem until the early 16th cent., and in the province of Kiev considerably longer.

Fordham

The Catholic university of New York, which originated as a college founded in 1841 by Bishop Hughes. The Jesuits were given charge of it in 1846. It is now the largest Catholic institution of higher education in the U.S. and can boast of very many alumni who have distinguished themselves in ecclesiastical and civil life.

Fort Augustus

An abbey of the English congregation of the Benedictines in Inverness-shire which, when founded in 1876, incorporated the few surviving monks of two German monasteries earlier suppressed. It became an abbey in 1888 and maintains a school for boys; two American foundations, at Washington and at Portsmouth, R.I., have been made from Fort Augustus.

Forty Hours

The devotion of 40 hours of prayer before the Blessed Sacrament exposed, reckoned at that number as a rough calculation of the time the body of Christ was in the tomb: originally a service for the obtaining or preserving of peace (a Mass for peace being prescribed for the second day) it became regarded later as a reparation for the sins of the world. The devotion begins and ends with Mass and should include processions with the Host, according to regulations of Clement XII in 1736. It is now allowable to break the sequence so that all the acts of devotion take place in the hours of daylight.

Four Basilicas

The Great Basilicas* of Rome, St. John Lateran, the Church of the Patriarch* of the West, St. Peter's, that of the Patriarch of Constantinople, St. Paul-Without-the-Walls, of the Patriarch of Alexandria, St. Mary Major, of the Patriarch of Antioch.

Francis, St. (1181–1226)

The son of a rich cloth merchant of Assisi, the wordly young man of 20 had a change of heart which directed him to prayer and the service of the poor. On a pilgrimage to Rome, he changed clothes with a beggar at the doors of St. Peter's* and spent a day as a beggar himself, thus discovering, as he said, the hardships and the joys of poverty. His return to Assisi was quickly followed by a period of ministering to lepers, and trying to rebuild the ruined church of San Damiano; then, disowned by his father, he took literally the words he heard read at the Porziuncula* from Mt.10:7–19, and withdrew to live on the absolute necessities of food and clothing. Disciples joining him in his new life, he drew up a simple rule, the *Regula Primitiva*, for which he obtained the approval of Innocent III in 1209. His followers, now calling themselves Friars Minor*, went further and further afield to preach the Gospel, and in 1212, a local noblewoman, Clare*, founded a similar group of women at the church of San Damiano. The Friars were numerous enough by 1217 to organise themselves into Provinces. Francis, in keeping with the Friars' ideal of mobility for the Gospel's sake, travelled as far as Spain, intending to convert the Moors in Africa, but was prevented by illness; he went preaching with 11 companions through Eastern Europe and Egypt, and was in the Holy Land in 1219, being present at the siege and capture of Damietta in the Fifth Crusade*. On his return, he confessed himself incapable of administering the vast organisation of his Order, and allowed it to rest in the hands of other Friars. He himself later set up the Franciscan Tertiaries, men and women who wished to follow the Franciscan ideal in their ordinary occupations. Two further versions of the Rule were approved, the *Regula Prima* in 1221 and the *Regula Bullata* in 1223. Francis' friendship with Cardinal Ugolino of Ostia was of benefit to his Order when the Cardinal was made Pope in 1227. The Saint, a layman all his life, received the Stigmata* on Mt. Alvernia in 1224; he died in 1226, and was canonised by Gregory IX (Ugolino) in 1228. By reason of his pure faith, charm and simplicity, Francis became, and remains, perhaps the most popular of all the canonised; the popularity itself, however, has become in large measure a hedge against the realities of sanctity—there must be a thousand persons in the English-speaking countries who know Francis as the 'patron saint of animals' for one who appreciates his zeal and his sufferings.

Franciscan Order

The Friars Minor, founded by St. Francis in 1209 at Assisi, are divided into three independent branches, known as the Friars Minor*, the Friars Minor Conventual* and the Friars Minor Capuchin*, the latter two being among the most populous Orders of the Church; they had, e.g. in England, where they were known as the Grey Friars, 64 houses at the time of the Reformation. Francis, as a person, was one of the most outstanding and remarkable in the history of the Church, and one of the most endearing (if greatly sentimentalised in later times by the uncomprehending); and his Order has had a proportionate influence. The Friars have gone to the furthest parts of the earth to carry the good news of Christ and fostered faith and devotion 'at home' in the Western Church. It is chiefly to them that is due the spread of such devotions as the Stations of the Cross and the Christmas Crib. The nuns of the Order are called Poor Clares*; there are also several congregations of Sisters of the Third Order Regular, and many other congregations which follow the rule of the Franciscan Third Order, without having any other connection with the Order itself.

Franciscans

See Friars Minor.

Francis De Sales, St. (1567–1622)

A Savoyard, who gave up the prospect of a brilliant career to take Holy Orders, Francis became one of the most influential figures of the Counter-Reformation*. After a most difficult and dangerous mission, in which he re-converted the Chablais from Calvinism in the space of four or five years, he was made bishop, succeeding to the see of Geneva in 1602. With St. Jane Françoise de Chantal, to whom he was, for many years, confessor and friend, he founded the Order of the Visitation* in 1610. Francis, in great demand as confessor and preacher, addressed himself to the question of lay spirituality, and his teachings, advice and writings all demonstrate a spirit of patience and gentle understanding, his most famous books being the *Introduction to the Devout Life* and his *Treatise on the Love of God*. He was declared a Doctor of the Church in 1877, and Patron of the Catholic Press in 1923.

See also John Bosco and Salesians.

Francis Xavier, St. (1506–52)

Known as the Apostle of the Indies and the Apostle of Japan, Francis, the son of a noble Basque family, met St. Ignatius* of Loyola at the University of Paris, and was one of the six who took vows with Ignatius in 1534, thus forming the Society* of Jesus. Ordained in 1537, Francis set out four years later for the East, and established a mission at Goa, which he made his headquarters and went on to evangelise the peoples of Travancore, Sri Lanka, Malacca and Maluku (Moluccas). He reached Japan in 1549, learning the language and establishing a church that endured until the early 17th cent. (see the Finding of the Christians); his ambition to preach in China was never realised: he died *en route* on a lonely island, Chang-Chuen-Shan. In all his voyagings, Francis suffered incessantly from seasickness. According to Jesuit reports, he was responsible for over 700,000 baptisms; against him, it has been alleged that his zeal led him to ride rough-shod over the native religions he encountered, and to approve of the Inquisition and of the persecution of Nestorian★ Christians. He is apparently not the author of the hymn *O Deus Ego Amo Te*, commonly attributed to him. He was declared by Pope Pius X 'Patron of Foreign Missions'.

Frater

Name, no longer in use, for the dining-hall or refectory of a monastic community.

Freedom of Conscience

In the Church's eyes, the freedom of a man to follow his conscience has always been qualified, in the first place, by the fallibility of that conscience (it is not the voice of God, but a man's own conviction, presumed honest, about what is right and wrong: thus a mentally deranged person who honestly believes its his duty to kill the postman must be restrained from following his perverted conscience—that would be a freedom he has no right to) and again by the consideration, often recurring in her teaching, that we have a concomitant duty that goes with the right of freedom—the duty to see that at all times and in all matters, our conscience is as well and carefully formed as we can ensure. Thus, not even Luther's renowned phrase at Worms, '..since it is neither right nor safe to act against conscience, God help me, Amen' can be taken as an absolute, implying, as it must, the previous earnest effort to ensure that the conscience in question is meticulously formed and informed. Not that the age of the Reformation was a sudden dawning of respect by all for the freedom of others' conscience: the persecution went on, from both sides of the Christian divide, and it was the time of the invention of the pragmatic principle *Cujus regio ejus religio★*, your prince decides your religion for you. The Inquisition★ proceeded in

practice on the assumption that rejection of orthodoxy could only be insincere and perverse—had not the dissenter had the truth of God offered for his assent by learned theologians? There was invented likewise the saying *Error has no rights*, which derogated from a man's dignity by equating him with his mistakes or shortcomings. It was only in the Second Vatican★ Council that the Church explicitly dealt with the question of Freedom of Religion: freedom, that is, for all men from all authoritarian interference in the practice of their religion—or their refusal to practise; a late approach to a principle long conceded in the constitutional law of civilised countries and offered lip-service even among the Marxist-Leninists (one can find, in a Catholic work carrying an *imprimatur★* of 1946, Freedom of Worship defined as 'The inalienable right of all men to worship God according to the teaching of the Catholic Church'). In its Declaration on Religious Freedom, the Council bases itself on what it incorporates into the title, *Dignitatis Humanœ*, speaks in praise of the modern world's respect for the dignity of man and hastens to assert that 'all men are to be immune from coercion on the part of individuals or of social groups or of any human power, in such wise that, in matters religious, no one is to be forced to act in a manner contrary to his beliefs.' (Art.2.)

Friar

(Fr. *Frère*, brother.) A member of a Mendicant Order. A common misconception prompts many to label any man in a habit a 'monk'; friars are to be clearly distinguished: they use their house as a base from which to operate, sometimes at great distances, while the monk normally lives his entire life within the walls of his monastery, since his work is prayer, and the friar's is the active ministry; the friar's allegiance is to the central authority of his Order, while the monk's is to the abbot of his monastery; the friars still live by a variant of the original rule (modified by the Council of Trent) which forbade them to own property even in common, whereas there is no prohibition on a monastery's ownership. There are four 'Mendicant Orders of the common law', Dominicans★, Franciscans★, Carmelites★,

Augustinians*. The lesser friars are the Servites*, Trinitarians*, Mercedarians*, Minims*, Brothers of St. John of God* and the Order of Penitence*.

Friars Minor

The largest of the three divisions of the Franciscan* order; its members observe the original rule of St. Francis* and engage particularly in preaching and in the sacred ministry, holding themselves to be specially bound to the poor and to those in missionary areas. The English Province has its headquarters at Forest Gate, London; there is one province for Ireland and five for the U.S. They have been established in Jerusalem since the 13th cent., and a Friar Minor is Custodian of the Holy Land, which meant, until the last century, that he governed—with episcopal authority, though not a bishop—the Latin Catholics of what was then Palestine (a scope now limited by the existence of a Latin Patriarch in Jerusalem) and that he was superior of all the Minors in the Levant; his full title is the Most Reverend Father Custodian of the Holy Land and Guardian of Mount Zion.

Friars Preacher

See Order of Preachers.

Friday

The day of the week which is, in the Christian mind if not in liturgy, the commemoration of the Passion of Christ Our Lord and in former times was observed with some form of mortification (fasting, abstaining from meat), laid down by the Church.

Friday, First

See Nine Fridays.

Fridays, the Nine

See Nine Fridays.

Fruits of the Holy Spirit, Twelve

See Twelve Fruits of the Holy Spirit.

Galileo

The case of Galileo Galilei has been used by many to demonstrate either that the Church is opposed to science or that Papal infallibility is illusion, or both. Neither is relevant to the events as they happened. In the first place, the Church put up no opposition at all to Copernicus' theory ('Earth round sun, not sun round earth')—indeed, his *Commentariolus*, the brief outline of his theory, had the approbation of Pope Clement VII in 1531, and the astronomer dedicated the completed treatise *De Revolutionibus Orbium Coelestium* (1543) to Paul III. It was into this volume that a preface was inserted, without Copernicus' knowledge, warning the reader against accepting its conclusions, since they were only hypothetical: this was the work of the Lutheran theologian Osiander. Neither was infallibility in question: Galileo, coming to prominence as a scientist more than half a century after these events, was promoter and victim of a personal quarrel in which both the principals, he and Urban VIII, behaved very badly. His savagely satirical writings made that Pope out to be timid, stupid and reactionary, and Urban took his revenge by abusing his spiritual power to contrive his enemy's downfall. He used the Inquisition* to force Galileo's 'recantation' and punishment. The whole disgraceful episode probably afforded much satisfaction to resentful churchmen at the 'lesson' thus taught to presumptuous intellectuals, and put stones in many hands to cast at the Papacy; but infallibility has never been held to attach to any Roman Congregation or to the private grudges of a Pope. F. Sherwood Taylor came to the Faith through the researches he made into the case of Galileo for an anti-Catholic book he had been commissioned to write.

Gallican Rites

i) The rite used in Gaul and the Kingdom of the Franks until roughly the time of Charlemagne, who introduced the Roman Rite.

ii) A variant of the Roman Rite used by the Normans in Sicily and Southern Italy.
iii) Certain French uses which were adhered to in some dioceses, e.g. Bayeux.

Gallicanism

(From the phrase, first appearing in the 13th cent., *les libertés de l'Eglise Gallicane*, the liberties of the Church of Gaul.) The sentiment, and the theory arising therefrom, that the local church, especially the French, ought to have more or less complete ecclesiastical independence of the Papacy. This spirit informed the teaching at the Sorbonne* almost from its foundation in 1257, the supposed *libertés* being based on imaginary prerogatives of the French Crown. In the 16th cent., the French King was conceded the right to nominate bishops in his territories, the constitutional decrees of the Council of Trent were not accepted in France, and writers of that country advocated a style of Church government which would reduce the authority of the Pope over national churches and individual bishops. In 1663, the Sorbonne put forth a declaration which was substantially confirmed by the Assembly of French clergy in 1682 in their Four Gallican Articles. The first of these propositions asserted that God had given Peter and his successors no temporal power over princes and therefore no right of deposing them; the second, that an Oecumenical Council was superior to the Pope; the third confirmed the validity of the laws of Gallican and other local Churches; the fourth dealt with the position of the Pope as arbiter in matters of faith, declaring that his judgement is not irreformable unless it has the consent of the Church. Gallicanism continued strong in France and Flanders for the 17th and 18th cents., and had its brief day in Ireland too. It was checked at the Revolution and effectively destroyed by the condemnation by the First Vatican Council of the second, third and fourth of its Four Articles; it lingers on among the Old Catholics.

Garden of the Soul

A well-tried and most popular volume of prayers, devotion and instruction, compiled by Challoner* in 1740 and only in recent years largely discarded; it went through numerous reprintings and was in the process somewhat modified by additions. The author described it as 'A Manual of Spiritual Exercises and Instructions for Christians who, living in the World, aspire to Devotion'.

Gate of Heaven

One of the titles of Our Lady in the Litany of Loreto*: she is the gate whereby the Son of God opened heaven again to mankind. Its use is first found in the writings of St. Peter Damian (11th cent.) and in the antiphon *Alma Redemptoris Mater,* attributed to Hermann the Cripple, who died in 1054.

Gates of Hell

Phrase to describe the power of evil or of death (Heb. *sheol).* To a walled city, the gates were of prime importance, so the metaphor became very early accepted for 'armed might', that upon which safety and prosperity depended. This dependence was emphasised in some cultures of the Middle East by the ritual sacrifice frequently offered by the founder or restorer of a city: he would slaughter one of his children and pour the blood into the foundations of the walls or gate-posts, or mix it into the cement of the footings. (e.g. 1 Kings 16:34, where the A.V. has the clearest translation: '. . . he laid the foundation thereof in Abiram his first-born and set up the gates thereof in his youngest son Segub. . .').

Gaudete Sunday

See Mid-Lent Sunday.

Genuflection

The bow, still customary with certain religious orders (e.g. Carthusians), was generally superseded from the 16th cent. by genuflection as the usual mark of worship for the Blessed Sacrament, of reverence for such phrases as 'and was made man' in the Creed at Mass, for the bishop enthroned and for the altar-cross. In many cultures, prostration was the accepted form of reverence for kings and nobility (Est.3:2); it is said that for a courtier passing through the empty throne-room of Elizabeth I, etiquette demanded a genuflection to the throne. The double genuflection (both knees and a bow) is used before the Blessed Sacrament exposed.

German Christians

(Ger. *Deutsche Christen.*) During Hitler's struggle to subdue Christianity to his own ends, there arose a large group of Protestants who, to produce a partnership between Nazism and Christianity, claimed to find the Holy Land in Germany and their Prophet in the Führer, excising the O.T., St. Paul (the 'Rabbi'), St. Augustine (with his 'Jewish' sense of sin) and everything in the Gospels which was 'Hebrew' or 'servile'. They asserted that they were completing Luther's reformation; the movement disappeared after the Second World War.

Gesta

(Lat., Deeds, performance.) A word used frequently from the 5th cent. onward as equivalent to *acta (Acta Apostolorum,* the Acts of the Apostles): it is used rather quaintly in *Gesta Romanorum,* a mediaeval collection of stories with an imagined historical connection with Rome, and surprisingly in *Gesta Dei Per Francos* (God's Achievements through the French).

Gethsamani

The Abbey of Our Lady of Gethsamani in Kentucky is the senior Cistercian* house of the United States; it was founded in 1848 by monks from the monastery of Melleray in Brittany. There had been Cistercians in the U.S.A. since 1802 when French monks settled near Baltimore.

Gifts of the Holy Spirit

Traditionally identified as Wisdom, Understanding, Counsel, Fortitude, Knowledge, Piety, Fear of the Lord, these are derived from Is.11:2. Piety is not found in the Hebrew but seems to have been inserted in the Septuagint*, being in fact a duplication of the Fear of the Lord.

Girdle

(Or Cincture.) The linen rope, tasselled at the ends and usually white in colour, used to confine the alb*.

Glasgow

The see founded by St. Kentigern—who is also called Mungo—about 543, was made metropolitan in 1492; it remained vacant from 1603 until 1878, being in that year re-established as an archdiocese without suffragans; then, in 1947, it was made metropolitan again, with Motherwell and Paisley as suffragans. It includes the county of Dunbarton and parts of Stirling and Lanark.

Glastonbury

Supposed to be built on the site of a prehistoric lake village (with the present road from the east, A361, laid on an ancient causeway), the town became famous as the place where Joseph of Arimathea, according to legend, brought the Holy Grail* and buried it, some say, under Glastonbury Tor; besides thrusting into the ground of Weary-All Hill his staff, which miraculously flowered into the Glastonbury Thorn*, he built a church. On the site of this shrine, King Ine of Wessex established in 688 a monastery, round which the town grew up and which, having become very powerful and wealthy, was one of the chief targets at the Dissolution* of 1539-40, its abbot, Whiting, being executed on the authority of a document from Henry stating that 'the abbot of Glaston shall be taken, tried and hanged'. A later legend claims that King Arthur's bones lie in the Abbey Church and there is a spot so marked to be seen in the ruins.

Glastonbury Thorns

The original Thorn, from which cuttings were taken by the faithful before the Roundheads cut it down, was said to be the tree into which Joseph of Arimathea's staff blossomed by miracle. It is in fact *crataegus praecox*, a variety of the common thorn which, given mild weather in October and November, will produce a second flowering about the end of December—hence the 'miraculous' Christmas blossom, which still persists in the present plants, descendants of the cuttings taken in 1653. Some relish is added to the legend by the detail that the soldier who cut down the original Thorn brought such enthusiasm to the task as to sever his own leg also. When the Thorns did not blossom on Dec 25th, 1752, some took this as a sign that God was against the New Style date and still operated by the old, Julian calendar.

Gloria

The hymn used in the Mass, 'Glory to God in the highest' (Lk.2:14) from its Latin version *Gloria in excelsis Deo*. It is not known when or by whom the hymn was composed, but it was used as part of morning prayer in the 4th cent.

Glorified Body

The body after resurrection, the Church teaches, will resemble the glorified body of Jesus at his rising from the dead, in that the body of the just man, identical with the body he had in this world, will be somehow 'spiritualised' into being incorruptible, immortal and, according to the Scholastic philosophers, endowed with impassibility, agility, clarity, and subtlety.

Glorious Mysteries of the Rosary

The Glorious Mysteries are: The Resurrection, the Ascension, the Coming of the Holy Spirit, the Assumption of Our Lady into Heaven, her Coronation and the Glory of all the Saints.

Gnosticism

A system of thought, of pre-Christian origins, whose several schools held in common that salvation is for the few, being wrought through knowledge (Gk. γνωσις). In the first three centuries of our era, the Gnostics, with their magic, their invention of *aeons* as God's intermediaries and governors of the created world (among whom they numbered Christ, thus denying him divinity), their description of matter as a corruption of the divine and of existence as an evil from which knowledge would liberate, were condemned as heretical.

Godfrey of Bouillon

See Crusades.

Golden Legend

(Lat. *Legenda aurea.*) Also called *Lombardica Historia;* a collection of lives of saints and treatises on the Christian festivals, written or compiled by James de Voragine O.P., between 1255 and 1266, and called by him the Legends of the Saints. It is arranged in 177 (or according to another reckoning 182) chapters, which follow the liturgical year; the work achieved extraordinary popularity in the Middle Ages and, though almost worthless as history, constitutes what has been described as the most readable book of devotion in the world. After being widely translated, it tended to be submerged in the 16th cent., when strict scholars censured it as not sufficiently factual.

Golden Number

The number of any year (1–19) in the Metonic Cycle—devised by the Athenian astronomer Meton in 432 B.C.—based on the reckoning that 235 lunar months (iunations) correspond to 19 years of the sun. The system was adopted by the Church in the 2nd–3rd cent. as being useful in calculating the date of Easter (it is this that gave the number its title, not the fact that it used to be printed in gold in calendars); the moon's phases recur on the same days of the month every nineteenth year. The Golden Number is found by adding 1 to the year's A.D. number and dividing by 19; the remainder is the Golden Number, or if there is no remainder, the Golden Number is 19.

Goldwell, Thomas

The last to die of the old Catholic hierarchy of England, Thomas Goldwell, on leaving Oxford, attached himself to Cardinal Pole, becoming his chaplain. Made Bishop of St Asaph, he revived the ancient custom of pilgrimage to Holywell*; in 1558, on the accession of Elizabeth, he fled to the Continent, attended the Council of Trent* where he was received as a hero, the only English bishop present, and in 1585 died in Rome, of which Gregory XIII had made him Viceregent*.

Gospel Side

The side of the altar and sanctuary which is to the right hand of the priest as he stands for Mass, with his face to the people; the north side, if the church is properly orientated. The custom arose very early for the one proclaiming the Gospel at Mass (priest or deacon) to stand facing a point about half-way to north; one explanation of this is that the Good News was being symbolically spoken to those who had not yet heard it, viz. from the point of view of Rome, the northern barbarians.
See Epistle Side.

Grace

(Lat. *gratis,* free.) Defined as a gratuitous gift of God to an intelligent creature, imparted with a view to eternal life, it can be described as the presence and aid of God in the soul in token of his love for his creatures. The theologians divide grace into various classes and kinds according to the immediate purpose or direction of the aid afforded. Pope Clement XI in 1713 condemned by means of the bull *Unigenitus* the Jansenist* proposition that no grace is given to those outside the Church.
See also Indwelling of the Holy Spirit.

Grail, the

A movement of women who are trained over a period of three years at least to take a lead in Catholic life, religious and cultural; they work also among non-Catholics and in missionary areas; the founder was Fr van Ginneken, SJ (+1945) and the movement has spread from Holland to Great Britain, Germany, the U.S., Australia and New Zealand.

Grail, the Holy

(Perhaps from Lat. *gradalis,* dish.) The fabled vessel, a dish from the table of the Last Supper or the cup used and consecrated by Christ; said to have been brought to England by Joseph of Arimathea, it became central to the Arthurian legend. In the Cathedral of Valencia is the Holy Chalice, its bowl cut from a single onyx; Genoa treasures the Holy Dish, a hexagon of green glass—stolen from Caesarea in 1101—with the cachet not only of use at the Last Supper, but also of having been a gift of the Queen of Sheba to Solomon. Apart from these places, the Grail, the talisman of the Knights of the Round Table, is also to be found at Monserrat and under Glastonbury* Tor.

Grande Chartreuse, la

The headquarters of the Carthusian* Order. St. Bruno's building and several of its successors were destroyed by fire; the present edifice dates from 1679. The Prior of this house, elected by its monks, is *ex officio* Prior General, the only General of an order who resides outside Rome.

Great Schism

The name given either to the Schism* between Eastern and Western Churches or—more frequently—to the Schism of the West, this being not really a schism at all but a conflict between two parties each of which claimed to support the true Pope. The essence of this quarrel, which split Europe in two, was a deep French nationalist feeling against Rome; the French were supported in general by Spain, Provence, Naples and Scotland, the claim of the 'Roman' Popes by Portugal, Flanders, Hungary, Germany, Scandinavia, England, Ireland and Wales. The beginning of this lamentable affair was the declaration by the French party of Cardinals in August 1378 that their election of Urban VI three months earlier was invalid because, they said, they had been intimidated by the Roman mob clamouring for an Italian Pope; they then chose Robert of Geneva who took the name Clement VII and went to live in Papal state at Avignon. Urban settled in the Vatican and replaced the rebel cardinals with 28 of his own naming. On the two sides, men bearing the title of Pope died and were succeeded by others, the Church torn meanwhile, with wise, learned and holy persons on both sides, until the Council of Constance in 1417 set aside the competing claimants (there were at that time three) and elected in a three-day conclave Odo Colonna as Martin V, to the great relief of Christendom. It is accepted now that Urban and his successors were the true Popes: the official Vatican list has it so, and the numbers of the rival claimants have been used in later ages, e.g. the official Clement VII was Pope at the time of the Sack of Rome in 1527, and John XXIII assembled the Second Vatican Council in 1962.

Greek

Greek was used liturgically by the Roman Church while it was the vernacular of the city, and was replaced by Latin about the middle of the 3rd cent. The *Kyrie* of the Mass and litanies may be a relic of this usage; the *Trisagion* of the Good Friday liturgy seems to have been introduced by Greeks arriving in Rome about the 8th cent., and in the Papal Mass, the Gospel is still read in Latin and in Greek, symbolising the universality of the Church.

Gregorian Calendar

In 1582, Pope Gregory XIII adjusted the existing (Julian) calendar; he corrected the ten-day error into which it had drifted over the centuries by subtracting ten days from that year, providing against a repetition of the error by altering the rules governing leap years (the leap year was now to be ignored at the beginning of each century, starting with the year 1700—except once in four hundred years); this further example of 'Papal interference' was stoutly ignored by the Elizabethan Protestants. When England caught up with the rest of Europe in 1752 by recognising the new Calendar in an Act of Parliament, people made a great pother, demanding to be given back their lost days.

Gregorian University

(Also called the Roman College.) The Pontifical Gregorian University: a foundation was made in Rome by St. Ignatius Loyola* and St. Francis Borgia in 1553, which was established as a University by Pope Paul IV in 1556 and extended by Gregory XIII, after whom it was named in 1582; to it were united in 1928 the Pontifical Biblical Institute and the Pontifical Institute for Oriental Studies, the former of which was founded in 1909, the latter in 1917. The University is under the direction of the Society of Jesus*.

Gregory of Nazianzus, St. (329–389)

Son of a bishop also called Gregory, he entered the monastic life, and was made a bishop of a small village in Cappadocia; in 379, he was called to Constantinople, where his preaching was instrumental in restoring the Nicene* faith and in establishing it finally at the Council of Constantinople (381). He resigned the See of that city and retired to his native place. Gregory ranks among the Fathers of the Church, famous in his own time as preacher and writer (particularly on the doctrine of the Holy Spirit), controversialist and poet.

Gregory the Great, Pope St.

Gregory I, Pope from 590–604, was the son of a Roman senator. Having served as Prefect of the City of Rome, he gave up his enormous wealth to relieve the poor and built seven monasteries, six in Sicily and the last in Rome, St. Andrew's which he entered himself in 574. Ordered by the Pope, after a short time, to leave his strict monastic life, he worked as one of the seven Deacons* of Rome, then for seven years as a Papal representative at the Byzantine court. It is to the next period of his life, as abbot of St. Andrew's, that we should assign the story, told by St. Bede*, of Gregory's observation of the Saxon slaves as *Non Angli, sed angeli.* His accession to the Papacy took place in a time of immense trouble for Italy; there were floods, famine and pestilence, the Lombards had the run of most of the country except the south, which was occupied by the imperial troops of Byzantium; and Gregory's frail health was a poor promise for such a daunting task. But by means of strongly independent action executed with gentleness, unfailing charity and dogged stubbornness, he succeeded in his great enterprises of taming and baptising the barbarians and maintaining the independence of the Western Church. Appointing governors to Italian cities (thus establishing the temporal power of the Papacy), and coolly negating the authority of the Exarch at Ravenna, spending lavishly of the Church's possessions to aid the poor, opposing a humble tenacity to the extravagant claims of the Patriarch of Constantinople ('Servant of the servants of God'* as against 'Oecumenical Patriarch'), taking on the improbable venture of a mission to the English, writing indefatigably (letters, 854 of them extant, including advice and reproof to bishops and kings, homilies, biographies, exegesis and the *Liber Regulae Pastoralis* which became a textbook of pastoral life for mediaeval bishops), Gregory was a late flowering of all that was best in the tradition of the Roman senator, and one of the makers of Europe. In liturgy, his great achievement is the establishment of the chant named after him; in theology, not a great originator, but an admirer of Augustine, he developed the doctrine of Purgatory and taught that the offering of Mass could help the souls of the departed.

He promoted Benedictinism by granting the monks privileges and exemptions which reduced the control of local ordinaries over them, and put them under direct papal jurisdiction. By his personality and his policies, he did much to establish Rome as the supreme authority of the Church. Gregory was canonised by popular acclamation immediately on his death in 604.

Gregory VII, Pope St. (c. 1021–1085.)

This Pope, known also by his own name of Hildebrand, was educated in the monastery of Santa Maria in Rome, but apparently did not become a monk; appointed to the Curia* by Gregory VI, to whom and to the four succeeding Popes he was a trusted and almost sole advisor, he was the chief influence in the legislation, under Victor II, which placed the election of a Pope in the hands of the cardinals. Elected Pope by unanimous vote in 1073, he set about a programme of wide reform, which he accomplished almost completely. He had to deal with simony and the immoral lives of many of the clergy, and—bound closely with these abuses—the vast problem of lay investiture*: the promoting by princes of simoniacal and loose-living clerics not only saddled very many dioceses with undesirables, it also assured the subjugation of the Church to the secular power and its reduction to a mere element of the feudal system. Gregory's measures were naturally greeted with violent opposition from kings and their episcopal toadies: in England, the Conqueror, perhaps through his meticulous observance of the Pope's other reforming decrees, escaped excommunication for his refusal on the point of investiture and thus prolonged the abuse into the reigns of his successors; in the teeth of the opposition of Philippe I, almost the entire French hierarchy was replaced; when Henry IV of Germany went so far as to summon two Councils to declare the Pope deposed, Gregory excommunicated the Emperor until in the following year, he submitted and did penance at Canossa. Excommunicated again for not keeping his promises there made, Henry put up an antipope* (Wibert, Archbishop of Ravenna, also excommunicated), laid siege to Rome for two years, and took the city. The Pope was rescued by Robert Guiscard, whose troops, unfortunately, behaved so badly that the Roman people turned against Gregory and hunted him from the city. He took refuge first at Monte Cassino*, then at Salerno, where he soon died. Hildebrand's long struggle with Henry impeded many enterprises he would have undertaken, including a more intense effort at reconciling the Eastern and Western Churches and a response to the appeal of the Byzantine Emperor Michael VII for a crusade against the newly-arrived Turks. He received back into orthodoxy Berengar of Tours, who had denied the doctrine of the Eucharist; but his great achievements were the reform of the Church and the conclusion of the investiture question: the Concordat of Worms (1122) which produced a settlement, may well be regarded as the direct product of his efforts. Historians no longer regard him as a man dominated by personal ambition but credit him with pure and unselfish motives, whether or not they recognise his dedication as sanctity, or accept as historical the words which tradition puts on the lips of the dying Pope, 'I have loved justice and I have hated iniquity—therefore I die in exile'.

Guardian Angel

The belief that God appoints a guardian spirit to every human being is found in pagan writings (as in Plato, *Phaedo, 108*) and in Jewish thinking, though not clearly set down in the O.T. (the Book of Enoch says that the just have protecting spirits). In the N.T., we have Christ's reference to the children's angels in Mt.18:10 and the remark of the company in the house of John-Mark's mother (Acts 12:15). Christian thinkers vary in their teaching: Hermas (c.150) says that each man has an angel to guide him; St. Ambrose believed that the just were deprived of guardian spirits so that, their struggle against evil being thus the harder, their glory might be the greater; St. Basil and St. Jerome* both claim that the guardian spirit departs in the face of sin. It was Honorius of Autun in the 12th cent. who first clearly enunciated the teaching which became common to most later theologians, that each soul, at the moment of its introduction into the body, is set under the protection of a spirit (who, according to St. Thomas*, is an angel* proper, i.e. a spirit of the lowest order, but who, according to Duns Scotus*, can be of any rank in the celestial hierarchy). The Church has frequently approved of this belief and encouraged the faithful in their custom of trusting to their Guardian Angels for protection against spiritual and bodily harm (cf. Hamlet's 'Angels and ministers of grace defend us!' I,4) and for aid in the practice of virtue, but has not defined it as of faith. There is a Feast of the Guardian Angels on Oct. 2nd.

Guild

In modern Catholic usage, a fraternity or devotional fellowship, as *Guild of the Blessed Sacrament*.

Gunpowder Plot

Besides the ringleaders, such as Catesby and his seven accomplices, and the renowned Guy Fawkes, it was asserted that certain Jesuits were privy to the plot. Fr Henry Garnet in particular, of whom it was claimed in his defence that he knew nothing outside the confessional and then only in vague terms of an 'attempt for the relief of the Catholic cause'; he was executed, though no complicity was ever proved. On the other hand, much serious writing of later times makes out the Plot to have been, in whole or in part, a trap laid by the Government *pour encourager les autres*.

Hail Mary

There was a custom, as old as the 5th cent., of using as a prayer the salutations to Mary of the Angel Gabriel and Elizabeth (Lk.1:28 & 42); to which in later centuries was added the petition now forming the 'second half' of the Ave. In the 1490s, a translation of a French work reads '. . . Holy Mary, mother of God, praye for us synneres. Amen', and the entire prayer is printed in its modern form (in Latin) in a Camaldolese breviary. The accepted English version apparently ran '. . . Our Lord is with thee', and Cardinal Wiseman criticised the change to 'the Lord' as 'stiff, cantish, and destructive of the unction which the prayer breathes'. It was until about the same time that in Ireland the prayer was held to finish at the name of Jesus and penitents, being given Aves for penance, would often inquire, 'Will I say the Holy Marys, too, Father?'

Halo

(Gk. αλως, disc—sc. of the sun or moon, and then the halo seen round it—also *Nimbus*.) Pre-Christian cultures used to represent goodness and majesty as light emanating from the person, and particularly from the head and face, so portraying gods and sometimes kings in art with a circle or disc of light behind the head. Christian art adopted the halo as a mark of holiness only slowly; in the 3rd and 4th centuries, it was restricted to images of Christ and of his symbol, the Lamb, and later extended to the Mother of God, the angels and saints. The halo with a cross or the Alpha and Omega is reserved for Our Lord (or the Lamb), the Father and the Holy Spirit; in the Middle Ages, a rectangular 'halo' was sometimes used in representations of important persons such as Popes and bishops. Until the 5th cent., the halo seems always to have been blue, but later gold, yellow and other colours were permitted. It is not allowed to decorate with the halo images of persons not beatified.

Hearth-Penny

An old name for Peter's Pence*.

Hedge-School

In Ireland during the 18th and 19th centuries, numerous schools were carried on in cabins by the side of the road or on the edges of fields, in ditches and under hedges, in which children and adults were instructed in Latin, English, Irish, reading and writing, arithmetic. The usual fee was three Irish shillings and three pence per quarter. The schools, being illegal, were suppressed in hundreds, but continued to be renewed.

Helena, St. (c.255–330.)

See Exaltation of the Cross. The mother of Constantine the Great has been made an honorary daughter of the British Isles through being confused with another Helena, the wife of Magnus Clemens Maximus, who held Britain, Gaul and Spain as Emperor from 383 to 388, who also named one of her sons Constantine; from Geoffrey of Monmouth onward, legend makes this conflated empress-saint the daughter of King Coel (Old King Cole) of Colchester. The mother of Constantine the Emperor was born at Drepanum in Bythinia, which town was later renamed Helenopolis.

Help of Christians

A title of the Blessed Virgin added to the litany of Loreto* by Pope St Pius V after the victory of the Christian fleet over the Turks at Lepanto in 1571; the Pope instituted a feast for the anniversary of the battle (Oct 7th) which is the feast of the Holy Rosary. Pius VII introduced the feast of Our Lady Help of Christians for May 24th in thanksgiving for his release from captivity on the fall of Napoleon.

Helpers of the Holy Souls

Founded in 1856, this institute of women (unenclosed) has for its primary purpose, prayer, suffering and work on behalf of the souls in Purgatory; they visit the sick and the poor and maintain orphanages and foreign missions.

Henri IV of France (1553-1610.)

Brought up a Protestant, he became King of Navarre in 1572 and, on the assassination of Henri III in 1589, King of France; but he was not recognised as king until his conversion to Catholicism in 1593. About this conversion, modern scholars accord the King much greater sincerity than he was formerly allowed in view of his widely-quoted remark, 'Paris is worth a Mass', placing more emphasis on his declaration that 'religion is not to be changed as easily as a shirt' and his prolonged discussions with theologians. His Edict of Nantes ended the religious wars of France and restored peace, prosperity and unity. He was assassinated in 1610.

Hereford, the Use of

A version of the Roman liturgy used in the mediaeval diocese of Hereford, and resembling the Use of Sarum.

Heresy

(Gk. αιρεσις, party, sect) The formal denial of a revealed and defined truth of the Faith, involving excommunication* *ipso facto*. The name *material heresy* is used to describe the state of mind of those who sincerely hold such beliefs as deny revealed truths of the Faith.

Hermits of St. Augustine

In 1256, Pope Alexander IV united several congregations of hermits under the Augustinian Rule with the title Hermits of St. Augustine, though some time later, most of the members took to the active life and the Hermits became an order of friars. There are now three independent sections: the *Calced Augustinians*, the largest group, with 18 provinces, one in the U.S. and one in Ireland (containing three English priories), the *Discalced*, in Italy and Germany, living an austere life, and the *Recollects*, a reformed branch conducting missions in Latin America and the Philippines, with one small house in the West Country. All the members of the order are employed in the cure* of souls, study, teaching or missionary work. The nuns of the Order live an enclosed, contemplative life.

Hilary, St.

A convert from Neo-Platonism and Bishop of Poitiers; his defence of orthodoxy against Arianism earned him the title 'Athanasius of the West'. Some of his works, besides their theological content, contain also valuable historical information about his times. He is a Doctor* of the Church.

Hildebrand

The name of St. Gregory VII before he was made Pope, and by which he is still frequently known.

Holy Blood of Bruges

A relic claimed to be drops of the blood of Christ collected by Joseph of Arimathea; given by Baldwin King of Jerusalem to the Count of Alsace, who passed it on to the city of Bruges in 1150. A feast was instituted in 1303 to celebrate the delivery of the city from the French, the origin of the annual procession in May in which the relic is carried. There are other alleged relics of the Precious Blood at Weingarten Abbey (Würtemburg) and at the cathedrals of Sarzana, Mantua and Mentone.

Holy Child Jesus, Congregation of the

('Holy Child Nuns') Founded by a priest, Nicholas Barré, in 1678, to provide trained teachers for schools in Europe and in missionary countries; not strictly enclosed, they are bound to the Little Office of Our Lady in choir.

Holy Cross Day

September 14th, the feast of the Exaltation or Triumph of the Cross*.

Holy Door

The description used of four doors in Rome, one in each of the Four Basilicas*, which are opened at the beginning of a Holy Year (i.e. on Christmas Eve of the preceeding year) and closed at the end thereof, not to be opened until the next Jubilee; each door is enclosed, inside and out, in a curtain wall of brick, and in the cavity are placed medals and a parchment to commemorate the Holy Year. The Door in St. Peter's is opened and shut by the Pope and the other three by cardinals appointed by him. The ceremony can be traced as far back as 1450.

Holy Ghost Fathers

The result of an amalgamation in 1848 of two congregations, one founded in Paris in 1703 by Abbé F.C. Poullart and one by François Paul Liebermann at Amiens in 1844, this society has many missions, most of them in African countries.

Holy Hand, the

A major relic, the hand of St. Edmund Arrowsmith SJ, executed for the Faith in 1628, is kept and venerated at Ashton-in-Makerfield, in the Church of St Oswald.

Holy Hour, the

A devotion in which the Blessed Sacrament is exposed for the space of one hour as object of prayers, meditation, hymns, etc on the themes of the Real Presence* and the Passion.

Holy Name, the

Jesus is the Greek and Latin form given to the Hebrew name *Jehoshua* (Joshua)— Ar. *Yeshu*—which means 'Jahweh is salvation', and was by no means an uncommon name at the time of Christ. The devotion to the Name, beginning from the use of it by the disciples for the glorifying of God (as in Rom.16:27) and the working of wonders (e.g. Acts 3:6) crystallised, in the Middle Ages, into local practices, such as that of giving the newly-baptised a medal inscribed IHS* and, fostered by the Franciscans, was eventually prescribed for the universal Church in 1721 by Innocent XIII who fixed the feast for the second Sunday after Epiphany. There was also for long a custom of bowing the head at the mention of the Name (cf. Phil. 2:9-11); there is a Litany of the Name of Jesus and the Jesus Psalter is still in use, though the feast has been recently suppressed.

Holy Office

See Inquisition. Faith, Sacred Congregation for.

Holy Oils

The collective name given to Oil of the Sick*, Oil of Catechumens* and Chrism*.

Holy Order(s)

The office and authority required for the service of the faithful by the administration of the Sacraments, the offering of Mass and the preaching of the word, which are passed on by the bishop to make a man deacon, priest or bishop, go by the name of Holy Order; of which the Council of Trent declares that it is 'truly a sacrament instituted by Christ the Lord' and not 'merely a kind of rite for choosing ministers', that moreover it imparts something permanent to the ordained '. . . if anyone say that . . . he who has once been made a priest can again become a layman, let him be anathema*' (Sess.33, cann. 3 and 4). For many centuries in the Western Church until about the time of the Second Vatican Council, it was held that there were Major Orders—Subdeacon, Deacon, Priest (the bishopric being the 'fullness of the priesthood')— and Minor Orders—Door-Keeper, Lector, Exorcist, Acolyte—these last four, originally independent functions in the Church, being gradually reserved to candidates for the priesthood and eventually considered simply as non-functional stepping-stones on the cleric's* way.
See also Deacon, Tonsure

Holy See

The see of Rome; in its common usage, the term denotes the Papacy with reference to its jurisdiction, authority and governing functions in general.

Holy Sepulchre, Church of the

Properly called the Church of the Resurrection, the present building has been described by one authority as 'structurally weak and aesthetically unsatisfying' and by another as 'an exceedingly ugly little building'; it was erected by the Orthodox Church after the fire of 1808 and incorporates the remains of the Crusaders' church, which covered the supposed sites of both Calvary and the Tomb. The roof of the latter and much of the rock walls were smashed in 1009 by the Khalif Hakim Bin Amr Illah. The first building on the spot was the Anastasis, a circular church put up by Constantine the Great. The Church of the Anastasis is now the Orthodox cathedral, with portions used by the Friars Minor*, Copts, Syrians and Armenians.

Holy Sepulchre, Guardians of the

A group of Friars Minor* has the duty of officiating in the Church of the Holy Sepulchre*, caring for the sanctuary and ministering to pilgrims; they belong to the community of the friary of St. Saviour close by.

Holy Souls, the

The familiar title used of the souls in Purgatory*.

Holy Thursday

See Maundy Thursday

Holy Week

The week preceding Easter Day, during which ceremonies are carried out to commemorate the events of Christ's sufferings and resurrection, and also to speak of these matters in terms of their fundamental theology; in this re-enacting and teaching, Holy Week is the centre of the liturgical year. Passion Sunday (Palm Sunday) with its procession of palms re-creates the entry of the Lord in triumph into Jerusalem, as recorded in all four Gospels, then, with the reading of the Passion from one of the Synoptics, looks into the darker days to come; Holy Thursday, the first day of the *Sacred Triduum*, commemorates gratefully and joyfully the institution of the Eucharist 'the night before he suffered', emphasising Christ's chosen role of servant by incorporating into the liturgy the *Mandatum*, the ceremony of foot-washing (Jn.13:1-15) from which Maundy* Thursday is named. Good Friday is given over to the pains and death of the Lord, without the offering of Mass: O.T. readings precede the Passion of John, and there are General Intercessions, the day itself rendering most poignantly relevant the phrasing '. . . through Christ our Lord'. The second part of the liturgy is the Veneration of the Cross, and the third is the Communion Service, the Sacred Species having been reserved in a place apart since the Mass of the previous day. During Saturday, the altar is left bare, to signify the absence of Christ from his orphaned Church, until the Vigil Service, which, it is prescribed, should not begin

before dark, and which is in four parts: the Service of Light, involving the eloquent symbolism of the Paschal Candle* and the Exsultet*, a special Liturgy of the Word, inviting the people to meditate on God's wonderful works, the Liturgy of Baptism, the sign of rebirth—and if none are baptised, those present renew their baptismal promises—and the Liturgy of the Eucharist. These rites, in their original forms, seem to have begun at Jerusalem in the 4th cent. when, in the Peace of the Church, it became possible for pilgrims to visit the Holy Places.
See Etheria

Holywell

St. Winifred's* Well, in Flintshire, a place of pilgrimage so renowned that the Reformers did not succeed in turning away the crowds that continued to frequent it; over 1,000 went there on the Saint's feast-day in 1629, and King James II visited it. The Bishop of St. Asaph in 1713 grumbled that 'great resort is had to Holywell by pilgrims, as they call them, from all the different quarters of the kingdom, and even from Ireland.' Dr Johnson observed pilgrims bathing in the waters in 1774. The well is now the property of the Duke of Westminster; the town has it on lease from him and sub-lets it to the Catholic authorities.

Holy Year

Boniface VIII declared the year 1300 a Holy Year, that is a time when, to celebrate the Redemption of the human race, the Pope proclaimed a Jubilee, as a special occasion when the faithful might obtain remission of sin by gaining the Jubilee Indulgence* (cf. Leviticus 25:10ff) on visiting the tombs of the Apostles at Rome. The Jubilee was meant by Boniface to be observed every 100 years; in 1343, however, Clement VI changed the period to 50 years, while Urban VI, in 1389, reduced it to 33, in honour, he said, of the years of Our Lord's life. The present span of 25 years was introduced by Paul II in 1470: the next celebration will be in the year 2000. The Jubilee and its conditions (usually the worthy reception of the Sacraments* and visits to the Four Basilicas*) and the benefits (notably a

Plenary* Indulgence), are announced in a Bull* issued on Ascension Day of the previous year. The Indulgence was extended in 1500 to all churches in the world and for six months after the closing of the Jubilee in Rome. The ceremonies of the Holy Year involve the opening and closing of the Holy Door*.

Homily

The informal discourse aimed at revealing the lessons contained in a passage of Scripture is the oldest form of preaching, used e.g. at Mass; and the Homilies of the Fathers of the Church formed a staple of the readings of the Office of Matins for the Sundays and feast-days.

Homoousion

(Gk. ομοουσιον, of one substance or being.) The word, used at the Council of Nicaea* in 325, to demonstrate the orthodox belief that the Son was, in the words of the modern translation, 'of one being with the Father' (the Semi-Arians* described Him as ομοιουσιον—of similar substance or being): a case of an iota of difference making all the difference in the world. The word was rejected at the Council of Antioch (255–272) as signifying 'of one person with the Father', but after clarification, it was accepted as the technical term for identity of substance or of being, and has been so used ever since.

Honorius, Pope

Honorius I (625–638) used to be celebrated by anti-Catholic controversialists as 'the pope who disproves papal infallibility'. Receiving an appeal from Sergius, Patriarch of Constantinople, for support for a formula 'one mode of activity' in reconciling the Monophysites*, the Pope, unfortunately in his approving reply substituted for 'one mode of activity' in Christ, 'one will'. This teaching was the heresy of Monothelitism*, and Honorius was condemned for it by his three successors. Apart from the rather remote possibility that by his phrase he meant a complete accord of the divine and human wills, his pronouncement does not involve infallibility: this epistolary statement was not ex cathedra*, not being issued as from the supreme teaching authority to the whole Church; in fact, Honorius wrote, 'It is not for us to twist what they say into dogmas of the Church.'

Hormisdas, Formula of

St. Hormisdas, Pope from 514 to 523, healed the schism of Acacius, which had split East and West since 484, on the Monophysite question, by offering for signature his Formula, which proclaimed the authority of Rome. The Catholic religion, it said, is preserved in its purity by the Apostolic See of Rome, only in communion with that See can it be perfect and complete, and those who disagree with that See are out of communion. The Formula was confirmed at the 'reunion' Councils of Lyons* and Florence*, and much quoted at the First Vatican* Council, with reference to Papal Infallibility.

Hortus Conclusus

(Lat., a garden enclosed.) The phrase from the Song of Songs 4:12, reminiscent as it is of the many uses of the simile of a new garden, a freshly cultivated land, a flower in bloom, a spreading tree, the garden of God, to describe the New Israel which shall have accepted God's merciful love, is found applied to Our Lady in the Benedictine Office of the Blessed Virgin Mary (Antiphon in the Third Nocturn of Matins: Hortus conclusus, fons signatus . . . a garden enclosed, a fountain sealed up . . .), and by St. Bernard (in his aqueduct sermon for the Nativity of Our Lady: 'This pure Virgin is a garden enclosed, a fountain sealed up, the Temple of the Holy Spirit. . .')

Hospitality

A bishop at his consecration undertakes to show kindness and compassion to the poor, to strangers and to all in want, and the Council of Trent* imposed the duty of hospitality on bishops and beneficed clergy; the monks and friars and religious in general have been noteworthy in the practice of this Christian duty, and the Rule of St. Benedict lays down, 'At the arrival and departure of guests, let Christ—who indeed is received in their persons—be worshipped in them by bowing the head or even prostrating on the ground. Let the Abbot pour water on the hands of guests . . .'.

Hospitallers of St. John of God

A nursing order founded by this Saint in Granada in 1540, the members being for the most part laymen (Brothers) with a few priests as required by the members and their patients. They take a fourth vow, to serve the sick all their lives; they follow the Rule of St. Augustine*, with daily recitation of the Little Office of Our Lady.

Hospitallers, the Knights

See Knights of St. John.

Host

(Lat. *hostia*, sacrificial victim) The name given to the 'altar bread', incorrectly before and correctly after Consecration, as it is then the Body of Christ 'who offered himself as the perfect sacrifice to God through the eternal Spirit.' (Heb.9:14)

Hot Cross Buns

These cannot be found to have a Catholic origin, being traceable only to two or three centuries ago, not to the Middle Ages, as is sometimes thought.

Hotel Dieu

(Or *Maison Dieu*.) The name still used for the museum at Faversham, Kent, by reason of its having been in the Middle Ages a hospital conducted by religious; the name is applied also to such hospitals in Paris and Quebec.

Hours

The name given to the divisions of the Divine Office, from their being roughly connected with certain times of day or night; the Hours are Matins, Lauds, Prime, Terce, Sext, None (the last four being known as Little Hours), Vespers and Compline.
See Book of Hours.

House Mass

Of recent years, permission has been given for the celebration of Mass in a private house, apart from cases of sickness. The practice, dependent on the permission of the bishop, has been much used in some places where groups of families or neighbours gather for a more intimate and lively Eucharistic occasion.

House of Gold

One of the titles of Our Lady in the Litany of Loreto*, first known to be used in 1463 by Isidore of Kiev.

Huguenots

French Protestants originated in Calvinism* in the 15th cent. and soon, most of their number being rich and influential, became a formidable force within the French nation. For over 30 years (1562–94), they were involved in a grim civil war which was hideously illuminated by the Massacre of St. Bartholomew*, then given freedom of worship by the Edict of Nantes*, on the revocation of which, in 1685, they suffered persecution and forced conversion, hundreds of thousands fleeing to England, Holland, Prussia, Switzerland, and America. Since 1802, the legal standing of the Huguenots *(les Prétendus Réformés)* has been guaranteed, but in 1872, there was a split into Traditional and Liberal groups, occasioning the creation of the National Union of Reformed Churches of France, which itself has combined with non-Calvinist churches to form the Protestant Federation of France.

Humani Generis

This encyclical of Pius XII* (1950), dealing with several questions concerning intellectual movements, including Existentialism, attitudes to Scholastic* philosophy, the Church's authority, Biblical studies, is remarkable in respect of this last matter, in that it declares plainly 'the teaching of the Church leaves the doctrine of evolution an open question, as long as it confines its speculations to the development, from other living matter already in existence, of the human body . . .' although the encyclical still insists on the descent from a single pair of ancestors. This pronouncement was most welcome, since, for more than half a century before, the ordinary teaching authority of the Church had been suspicious and grudging towards any theory of evolution—indeed, for a few years after the First World War, it was spoken of as a serious possibility that the Holy See would condemn all evolutionary theory—which would have awarded the Church the dunce's cap so well earned for the State of Tennessee by its prosecution of the teacher, Scopes, in the renowned 'Monkey Trial' of 1925.

Humeral Veil

A long, shawl-like vestment worn across the shoulders and draped so as to cover the hands, used thus by the celebrant who lifts or carries the Blessed Sacrament* at Benediction* or in procession (and formerly by the subdeacon holding the paten at High Mass).

Hussites

The followers of John Hus, a Bohemian (1369–1415) who imported Wyclifism into the University of Prague, was burned as a heretic and became a national hero. Adopting the Englishman's communism and predestination, they fell into sects among themselves, some demanding the abolition of the liturgy or the Anointing of the Sick, others demanding complete sexual license as of right. In the matter of Utraquism (the heresy that Communion in both kinds is essential for salvation), the less extreme Hussites were granted the chalice on the understanding that this was a disposition of the ecclesiastical authority and not a necessity.

Hyperdulia

(from *Dulia*) The special kind of reverence paid to Mary the Mother of God by reason of her relationship, unique among all creatures, to the Godhead.

Hypostatic Union

The union of the two distinct natures, divine and human, in the one person *(hypostasis)*, Jesus Christ; the doctrine proclaimed in the Creed* ... one Lord, Jesus Christ... true God from true God, begotten ... he became incarnate from the Virgin Mary and was made man. In the early centuries, there was some confusion over the use of the word υποστασις, that which stands under, hence Lat. *substantia,* hence substance, which was used for objective reality, basis, foundation, and sometimes made almost identical with ουσια, being, substantial reality (as in the anathemas* attached to the Nicene* Creed), and then, in the 4th cent. took on the meaning, in Greek Christian writing, of individual reality, hence of *person.* The terminology, once clarified, was accepted by both Eastern and Western Churches, and the First Council of Constantinople* (381) used the formula of 'three hypostases in one essence' to describe the Trinity.

Iconoclasm

The name given to a movement and a heresy; in 726, the Byzantine Emperor Leo the Isaurian, issued a decree which resulted in an outbreak of image-breaking and the persecution of their defenders. This was halted by the pronouncement of the Second Council of Nicaea (7th Oecumenical) in 787, that 'both the figure of the sacred and life-giving Cross and also the venerable and holy images' are to be set up in churches for proper reverence; which formulation embodies the attitude and teaching of the Catholic and Orthodox Churches to this day. The major Iconoclast attack broke out in 814, instigated by Leo the Armenian, and lasted until 842. One of the stoutest defenders of orthodox practice and belief was St John of Damascus★. It would appear that the Iconoclast mentality lingers somewhat in the Eastern custom of using flat or relief images, not sculpture in the round, and in the forbidding distrust of art characterising some of the sterner forms of Western Christianity. The name Iconoclasm is also applied historically to such incidents as the destruction of religious images in England in the 16th and 17th centuries and during the French Revolution.

Ignatius Loyola, St.

(c. 1493–1556.) The founder of the Society of Jesus★; born to a noble family in the Basque country, being wounded in battle and reading during convalescence the life of Christ and books of the saints, hung up his sword at our Lady's altar and spent a year in solitary prayer at Manresa near Barcelona. His mystical experiences there produced the *Spiritual Exercises★;* he went to Rome and Jerusalem, living on alms. Having studied at other universities, he founded at Paris, in 1534, the Company of Jesus (later the Society of Jesus, which was sanctioned in 1540). Ordained priest in 1537, and made first General of the Society, he spent the rest of his life promoting, through its activities, his great objec-

tives—the reform of the Church by education and the Sacraments, the carrying of the Gospel to the newly-discovered lands and the combating of heresy. Feast, July 31st.

IHS

Generally spoken and referred to as the English letters i h s, (which gave rise to varying interpretations of these 'initials', e.g. *Jesus Hominum Salvator,* Jesus, Saviour of Mankind, or—among the Jesuits—*Jesum Habemus Socium,* We have Jesus for our Companion, and to the mediaeval spelling *Jhesus),* this sign is in fact the first three letters, in Greek capitals, of the Holy Name: ΙΗΣΟΥΣ. Failure to distinguish between Greek and Latin script led to the confusion above mentioned. Used widely in the Middle Ages by the Dominicans, the sign later became identified as the mark of the Jesuits.

Illicit

Distinction must be made between what is invalid and what is illicit, i.e. unlawful, since an act can be illicit and yet have the full force and effect to be expected of it; e.g. a marriage between a Catholic and a baptised non-Catholic contracted without dispensation is illicit but a true marriage.

Illuminative Way, the

The second or middle stage of the spiritual life, in which, according to St. Thomas, 'man aims principally at progressing in good, this endeavour belonging chiefly to the proficient, who attempt to strengthen charity by increasing it.' It has been described as spiritual adolescence, in which a person earnestly follows Jesus Christ in holiness, being no longer weak in the love of God. The Illuminative Way is marked by affective prayer. See Purgative Way, Unitive Way.

Imitation of Christ

This book of spirituality, written in 1441 by a Canon Regular*, Thomas à Kempis, has had a very great influence ever since not only in monastic circles but among the laity, and not only among Catholics—Dr Johnson, John Wesley and General Gordon were among its devotees. The work combines genuine devotion with scholarship and bases itself on true and reasoned loyalty to the teachings of Jesus Christ and the practice of traditional Christianity as interpreted by the Church— one quarter of the 'Imitation', Bk IV, is given over to the Blessed Sacrament.

Immaculate Conception

Pius IX, in the Bull *'Ineffabilis Deus'* of 1854, declared that 'from the first moment of her conception, the Blessed Virgin Mary was, by a singular grace and privilege of Almighty God, and in view of the merits of Jesus Christ, Saviour of mankind, kept free from all stain of original sin' and that this 'is a doctrine revealed by God and therefore must be believed firmly and constantly by all the faithful.' The feast of the Conception of the Mother of God had been kept in the East from early times, St. John of Damascus* maintaining that perfect sinlessness was implicit in the title *Theotokos*—and spread westward, to Ireland in the 9th cent., to England early in the 11th, and to France in the 12th where the theory of the Immaculate Conception was opposed by St. Bernard. Later, the chief Schoolmen also argued against it, including St. Thomas, who was followed by most of the Dominicans, while at Oxford, and later at Paris, Duns Scotus* supported it, as did the Franciscans generally. The Council of Basle (1439) declared the doctrine not against Catholic belief, tradition or Scripture, the Sorbonne in 1449 demanded of its candidate an oath to defend it, in 1476 Sixtus IV approved the feast (Dec 8th), while the Council of Trent* declared the Mother of God an exception to its decree on original sin. From the 16th cent., there was a general acceptance of the belief, many even of the Dominicans being converted. Clement XI extended the feast to the whole Church and made it a day of obligation (1708). To these developments the definition of 1854 appeared the logical conclusion.

Immersion

A method of Baptism* (such as is used by the Baptists and in most Eastern rites) allowed by the *Rituale Romanum*.

Immuring

See Walling-Up.

Impanation

First used by Guitmund of Aversa in the 11th cent., the word suggests that at the Eucharist the Body and Blood are contained in bread and wine, these latter maintaining their separate substantial existence. Later, certain heretics are recorded as explaining their use of the word *impanari* by claiming that 'as God was in person incarnated in human flesh, so here is Christ in person imbreaded'. The idea survived and was held by certain of Luther's followers.

Impassibility

The freedom of God from suffering, from emotion and from the ability to be influenced from without has been held by the Church, which takes the references in the Bible to God's anger, sadness etc as figures and analogies. The Council of Chalcedon (Fourth Oecumenical) in 451 defined the divine nature of Christ as impassible, the human as passible. Impassibility is considered by theologians to have been an attribute of Adam and Eve before the Fall, of the humanity of the risen Christ, and of the bodies of the just after their resurrection.

Impeccability

Frequently confused with Infallibility* but demonstrated historically not to have been a Papal prerogative, impeccability or the inability to sin belongs only to God (also therefore to God Incarnate), the Blessed Virgin being without sin through divine privilege, not through being by nature impeccable.

Impediments to Marriage

These are of two kinds: a) diriment (Lat. *dirimo*, I destroy), which make the attempted marriage null and void; such are insufficient age, already existing marriage, consanguinity, affinity, spiritual relationship, public honesty, solemn vows, holy orders, difference* of worship, certain kinds of crime, error in grave matter, impotence, imbecility, violence and fear, abduction, clandestinity*. Only the Church has authority to decide what is and is not a diriment impediment, and only the Pope and those he delegates may dispense therefrom; impediments of natural law can never be dispensed; b) prohibiting, which make a marriage illegal but not invalid; e.g. betrothal already existing, forbidden seasons, simple vows, mixed* religion; dispensation is readily given for good cause.

Impotence

Sexual impotence is an impediment of natural law to marriage if it precedes the marriage and is of its nature permanent (in cases of doubt, the marriage is not to be impeded), and a claim of nullity can be based on it.

Imprimatur

(Lat., Let it be printed.) The official permission, represented by this word, granted by a bishop for the publication of a book; now required only for works of scripture and theology.

Imprimi Potest

(Lat., It may be printed.) The official phrase for the approval granted by a major religious superior for the printing of a work by a member of his Order.
See Imprimatur and Nihil Obstat.

Improperia

The Reproaches, in the Liturgy of Good Friday, are addressed by the crucified Lord to his ungrateful people; they consist of 12 utterances, based on O.T. passages, the first three, which are longer, followed by the Trisagion*, formerly sung in Greek and Latin, the rest by the formula, 'My people . . .' Probably of French origin in the 10th cent., the Reproaches were part of the Roman liturgy by the 12th cent.

In Articulo Mortis

(Lat.) At the point of death.

In commendam

The Latin phrase *beneficium in commendam depositum,* a benefice placed in trust, was used to describe a benefice or office which, being unoccupied, was placed in temporary care of an ecclesiastic who also drew its revenues. This custom has been unknown of recent times except in the cases of certain curial cardinals*. The commoner historical use of the phrase *in commendam* is for an abbey or other religious house, the revenues of which were granted to a person not of its community, nor necessarily a cleric, he being then abbot *in commendam* or commendatory abbot while a religious was appointed acting superior. This abuse, in existence as early as the 8th cent., contributed more than any other single cause to the decline of monastic life, reducing abbeys to fiefs in the feudal system. It reached its worst depth in the 13th and 14th centuries, bishops, nobles and even kings being commendatory abbots, and in France it endured until the Revolution—Richelieu held 20 abbeys *in commendam.* The only known example of a commendatory abbot in England was Cardinal Wolsey, who held St. Albans *in commendam* from 1521 until his death in 1530.

In fieri

A term used in Scholastic* philosophy for the transition from potency to act, and opposed to *in facto esse,* i.e. being, or the goal of transition.

In Partibus Infideium

(Lat., In the territories of the unbelievers.) Since the office of bishop has always been of its nature geographical, and since on the other hand there are a great number of assistant or auxiliary bishops to prelates of named dioceses, each of the auxiliaries was given the title of a diocese no longer functional, usually one of the ancient cities taken over in the capture by the Arab nations of southern and eastern parts of the former Roman Empire. Still sometimes used colloquially—and abbreviated to 'in partibus'—the designation was officially replaced by 'titular*' (Leo XIII, 1882). English auxiliary bishops are now given the titles of ancient British sees.

In Petto

(It., In the bosom.) The private appointment of a cardinal is thus described, when for various reasons a Pope makes such appointments and reserves the announcement of them to the Sacred College to a later date. John Lingard the historian and joint founder of Ushaw*, is said to have been thus honoured by Leo XII, whose death prevented the publication.

Incense

(Lat. *Incensum,* that which is burnt.) The burning of aromatic gums in the form of grains or powder probably dates from the earliest closed and roofed temples, being a protection against the stench of carcases cut open either during or after sacrifice. In both pagan and Jewish usage, it came to signify worship or reverence, the Hebrews taking it explicitly as a symbol of prayer (e.g. Ps.141:2). The passage in Rev. 8:3–5 is held not to indicate the actual use of incense in the early Church, and there is no other evidence of it until c.500; incense-burners appear first to have been fixed on a stand or to a wall, then censers were carried about in imitation of those borne before high Roman officials. The liturgical incensing of the altar, the church, the congregation, etc, appears not to predate the 9th cent., since when it has been used consistently to add solemnity to a liturgical act. Incense, sternly objurgated by most of the Reformers, began to make itself noticed in certain parts of the Church of England as part of the ceremonial revival provoked by the Oxford Movement*.

Inclusus

(or Inclusa): a monk (or a nun) who, for stricter penitential life and with permission of the superior, lived in a cell whose doorway was walled in, with aperture enough for the passing in of food and other necessities.

Indefectibility

The continuance of the Church through the entire history of the human race, as promised in Mt. 28:20, is witnessed by her survival of so many perils both from without and from within.

Indulgences

The temporal punishment still due for sins whose guilt is forgiven can be remitted by the performance of certain acts prescribed by the Church which acts therein as dispenser of the treasury of satisfaction gained by the merits of Christ. This remission is known as an indulgence, and the theology involved is based on the ideas that this 'treasury' is infinite (and that it subsumes the merits which Christ allowed his Mother and the saints and the entire Church to amass) and that the Church is entrusted with the dispensing and application thereof. It implies, naturally, the Communion of Saints—as St. Paulinus wrote, *'Aliud est quando tu solus oras pro te, et aliud quando multitudo pro te ad Deum trepidat'.* It is one thing when you have none but yourself to pray for you, quite another when the prayers of the multitude go beating up to God for you.' The theory of indulgences can be said to have taken shape in those early days (3rd cent. or before) when it was decided to allow the intercession of those awaiting martyrdom to mediate the merits of Christ for the less worthy and thus to shorten the penances laid on public sinners. It must then have seemed quite logical to extend this application of the vicarious merits of Christ and his saints to the temporal punishment due to be paid in Purgatory. After the centuries in which indulgences were accepted as an ordinary means in the Church's hands—and during which they were sometimes blasphemously ill-used as merchandise to be bought and sold and all the time accumulated embarrassment by being forced into a mathematical mould ('a cardinal may grant 200 days' indulgence, an archbishop 100', etc) or a geographical ('the indulgence that can be gained only by visiting a certain shrine'), Paul VI reformed and simplified the whole practice. Taking as his principles the notions that the Church's intention in this matter is to encourage the faithful to expiate their sins and to do works which increase faith and charity and contribute to the common good, and that the gaining of indulgences, which demands the love of God and hatred of sin, is accomplished by what the faithful do, not where they do it or through what instrument (crucifix, medal, etc), he laid down new norms in the Apostolic Constitution *Indulgentiarum Doctrina* (1967). These allow the customary application of indulgences to the dead, remove the numerical factor altogether—anything less than a plenary indulgence is now known as a 'partial indulgence' (plenary being an indulgence that takes away all the temporal punishment due)—reduce the number of plenary indulgencies and forbid the gaining of more than one plenary indulgence on the same day (except by those on the point of death), permitting this single one under the usual* conditions, take away the classification of personal, local and real (i.e. attached to objects of devotion, as above), revise—and reduce—the lists of indulgences published for the whole Church and for religious and for other groups; they also extend the plenary indulgence which used to attach to the Porziuncula* to every parish church, and grant partial indulgence on the devout use of any object of piety if blessed by a priest, and plenary if by the Pope or a bishop (this latter only on the Feast of St. Peter and Paul and with an approved profession of faith).

Indwelling of the Holy Spirit

That aspect of the Divine activity which is concerned with the work of sanctification in the soul of man, which is effected by the presence and work of God (Jn. 14:23, 26;15:4) as Sanctifier and Paraclete; without him, man can do nothing for his salvation or to please God (Jn. 15:2, 4, 6 and, from the *Veni Creator Spiritus,*

God whose mighty indwelling is life, how can man be whole or sound?— No health in him if you are not within).

Infallibility

The inability to teach what is false in matters of the essence of Christ's message of salvation is inherent in the idea of the Church as derived from the N.T. The First Vatican Council defines the divine protection of the Church from such error: 'the doctrine of faith that God has revealed has not been proposed by a philosophical discovery, to be improved by human talent, but has been committed as a divine deposit to the Bride of Christ to be faithfully guarded and infallibly interpreted by her.' This infallibility was defined as residing in the Pope personally, in an oecumenical council subject to the Pope's confirmation and in the bishops throughout the world teaching definitively in union with the Pope. Of the Pontiff's personal infallibility, the Council declared it a dogma of faith that 'when the Roman Pontiff speaks *ex cathedra*, that is, when, using his office as shepherd and teacher of all Christians and in virtue of his apostolic authority, he defines a doctrine of faith or morals to be held by the whole Church, then, by the divine assistance promised him in the blessed Peter, he possesses that infallibility with which the Divine Redeemer was pleased to invest his Church in the definition of doctrine on faith and morals, and that therefore such definitions of the Roman Pontiff are irreformable in their own nature, and not because of the consent of the Church.' The intention of binding all members of the Church must be manifest—if not necessarily expressed—in such pronouncements; and there is no question of impeccability or of inspiration; it is the guidance that is divine, not the method of acquiring knowledge, nor does the Pope's infallibility depend on his personal holiness. It appears, however, that even this strictly limited gift of infallibility took some prelates by surprise; there was in very popular use in Ireland and Scotland, and bearing the *imprimatur** of the Scottish bishops, a manual, Keenan's Catechism, which had to have one Question and Answer deleted on publication of the Council's definition—Q. Must not Catholics believe the Pope in himself to be infallible? A. This is a Protestant invention; it is no article of the Catholic faith: no decision of his can oblige under pain of heresy, unless it be received and enforced by the teaching body, that is, by the bishops of the Church.

Infulae

The Latin name for the two lappets which hang from the back of the mitre.

Infusion

In baptism, the method of pouring the water (usual in the Latin and other churches) as distinct from Immersion* and Aspersion*.

Innocent III, Pope

His occupation of the papacy (1198–1216), to which he was elected when cardinal but not yet priest, marks the brief and remarkable climax of the temporal power of the popes. With his business-like and legal mind, his gifts of sincerity, of immense energy and of penetrating judgement, he realised, for a few year, his vision of himself as Melchizedek, priest-king and creator of a Christendom whose power-centre would be the throne of Peter; this throne he spoke of as 'set between God and man, below God but higher than man'. 'No king can rightly reign,' he claimed, 'who does not devoutly serve Christ's vicar' (a title first used by Innocent). In the Bull *Venerabilem*, he lays down that, though the electing of an Emperor rests with the Imperial electors, the Pope still has the right to examine the person elected, and he supports his assertion that the appointing of the Emperor comes within the papal sphere of authority by appealing to the tradition of the blessing, crowning and investiture of Emperors by the Pope (see Deposing of Monarchs). The Imperial throne becoming vacant, the Pope supported, one after another, three rivals, the last of whom, Frederick II, was elected on condition of doing homage to the Pope for his overlordship of Sicily, from whence Innocent had driven the German mercenaries. He compelled the reconciliation of Philippe Auguste with his wife Ingeborg of Denmark; John of England, in the affair of Stephen Langton's appointment to Canterbury, capitulated and acknowledged Innocent as his feudal overlord. The papal authority was felt as far afield as Scandinavia, the Iberian peninsula, the Balkans, Cyprus, Armenia, and—by means of the fourth Crusade*—Constantinople itself. Innocent's judgement displayed itself in masterly fashion in his approbation of the new orders of Friars (Minor* and Preachers*). One triumph of his pontificate was the Fourth Lateran* Council (1215), which condemned the Albigensians*, formulated doctrine and initiated reforms.

Inquisition

The first form of punishment for heresy* was excommunication*, a purely spiritual penalty, but, though the Fathers in general condemned physical punishment, once the Empire had become Christian, the heretic began to regarded by the princes as guilty of treason (since his crime tore apart the body politic, which was co-terminus with the Body of Christ, the Church). Penalties such as confiscation of goods and even death began to be inflicted, though the Church held to her original attitudes, and as late as the 12th cent., St. Bernard was writing *'Fides suadenda non imponenda.'* It was in the crisis of the Catharist* movement, which was seen as threatening not only the Faith but the very institutions of society, that the Church's judgement changed, and she began to seek the help of the secular power. The Inquisition as such came into being when the Emperor Frederick II appointed officials ('inquisitors') to investigate heresy throughout the Empire. Gregory IX, suspicious of Frederick's political ambitions, declared such investigations to be in the realm of the Church, and chose Papal inquisitors instead. These, usually Franciscan or Dominican friars, went about persuading heretics to return to the Faith and deciding whether in fact they were in heresy or not. Such heretics as refused to return were handed over to the secular power for punishment, which, according to the custom of the day, was severe by our standards; in 1252, Innocent IV further conformed to contemporary practice by permitting torture for the obtaining of evidence. In extreme cases, the penalty was the handing over of the heretic to the secular arm; this meant death at the stake. As a final court of appeal in cases of heresy, the Sacred Congregation of the Universal Inquisition was set up by Paul III in 1542, and was referred to likewise as the Holy Office; which title was used officially from 1908, when Pius X deleted the word Inquisition, until Paul VI changed the title in 1965 to Sacred Congregation for the Teaching of the Faith, remarking in the process 'The best defence of the Faith is the teaching of the Faith.' A melancholy contrast to the general leniency of the Roman Inquisition is provided by the ferocity of the Inquisition of Southern France, which dealt with the Albigensians* and of the Spanish Inquisition, which was set up and used largely as a political tool of the monarchy, beginning with Ferdinand and Isabella. This was the Inquisition which made the word a bugbear in the English language; it was in fact briefly revived in the early 19th cent. (after being abolished by Joseph Buonaparte) to buttress the royal power, its last victim being a village schoolmaster, hanged in 1826.

INRI
The initial letters of the Latin inscription on the Cross (Jn.19:19) *'Iesus Nazarenus Rex Iudaeorum'*, much used as a Christian sign.

Inspiration
The Church teaches that the authors of the books of Scripture were inspired by God, that is, that by his influence their will was moved to write, their mind conceived and shaped the matter, so that the work produced in fact carries the truth that God intends to be expressed, though, naturally, in the style, and with other human characteristics, of the writers themselves. Chapter 3 of the Dogmatic Constitution 'Verbum Dei' issued by the Second Vatican Council sets forth contemporary Catholic thinking on the matter.

Institute of Charity
A congregation of religious founded in 1828 by Antonio Rosmini-Serbati to undertake all works of charity; it includes priests, clerics and lay brothers and has parishes, colleges and schools. The English province, founded in 1835, has a school for boys at Ratcliffe near Leicester, and has charge of the Church of St. Etheldreda at Ely Place, London. There are also houses in Ireland. See Sisters of Providence.

Institute of Mary
(Institute of the Blessed Virgin Mary *Dames Anglaises, Englische Fraulein, Loreto Nuns.)* Founded in 1609 by Mary Ward*, without enclosure and meant for the education of and apostolate among women, the Institute was suppressed in 1630, though kept alive illegally in Germany, and restored in 1633. It was set up in London in 1639 and at Fountains in 1642, this latter community transferring to York in 1686 and being known still as the Bar Convent, from its address in Micklegate Bar. For a century and a half, there were no other convents in Gt. Britain apart from these two houses; and this was the first institute of women to be founded without enclosure or choir duties and with simple vows.

Instruments of the Passion
The cross and other articles used in the crucifying of Our Lord—hammer, nails, lance, sometimes the crown of thorns—have been represented frequently in devotional art.

Interdict
An ecclesiastical censure under which members of the Church, while still remaining in communion with it, are debarred, individually or collectively, from certain sacred functions and from the reception of certain sacraments, e.g. the Eucharist, or from ecclesiastical burial if they die under interdict. Interdict was known as early as the 6th cent. In the Middle Ages, when the Church was an all-pervading spiritual and social power (see also Excommunication) it was used by the Papacy as a weapon against monarchs, by which the entire population of a country could suffer deprivation of the sacraments for the offences of their king: France was laid under interdict by Innocent III in his struggle with Philippe Auguste and England by the same pope in the reign of King John. With the decline of papal influence, interdict lost most of its force, and modern Canon Law does not mention *cessatio a divinis,* the suspension of all liturgical activity in an area. Interdict on a parish or a community of religious, which can be imposed by the bishop, means the cessation of the administration of Sacraments and of all solemn services (exception may be made for reception of the Last Sacraments, for clerics not personally responsible for the interdict to perform all religious rites in private and in a low voice, and for one Mass in the cathedral or parish church and for certain great feasts): the convent of Marienthal near Strasbourg was put under interdict in 1921, as was the parish of Barbentane in Provence in 1929, and, in recent years, an American bishop laid interdict on a parish of his diocese which refused the black pastor he had appointed them.

Interpretation, Private
See Private Interpretation.

Introit

The name previously used for the Entrance Hymn★, its suppression is regretted by many who consider it more liturgical than the substitutes.

Investiture

(Lat. *Investire,* to clothe, invest with authority.) The mediaeval term for the privilege, claimed by the Emperor and other princes, of investing a bishop-elect or abbot-elect with ring and staff, and of receiving his homage before consecration. From this actual investiture grew the custom for the temporal ruler actually to appoint the prelate, consenting to invest only his own candidate. This practice was condemned by Pope Nicholas II in 1059 and absolutely forbidden by Gregory VII★ in 1075, the prohibition being frequently repeated by Gregory and by subsequent popes. The controversy thus aroused went on bitterly and long: Hildebrand and some of his successors suffered greatly for their stand against lay investiture, and in England, Anselm★ refused homage to Henry I, refused to consecrate bishops who had accepted lay investiture, and solved his problem by allowing the King to invest the temporalities in return for a solemn undertaking not to interfere with elections. The dispute between Pope and Emperor was settled by the Concordat of Worms (1122) which, however, left the secular ruler with some influence in the election of bishops. The modern Church is suitably wary of any such interference: Canon Law★ states that there shall not even be permitted to arise in future any patronage (the privilege of the founder of a church, chapel or benefice to present a cleric thereto) and the Second Vatican Council's Decree on Bishops says '. . . this most holy Council desires that in the future no rights or privileges of election, nomination, presentation or designation for the office of bishop be any longer granted to civil authorities. Such civil authorities, whose favourable attitude toward the Church this most sacred Synod gratefully acknowledges and very warmly appreciates, are most kindly requested to make a voluntary renunciation of the above-mentioned rights and privileges which they enjoy by reason of a treaty or custom' *(Art 20).*

Invocation of Saints

The fears of many non-Catholics about idolatry or detracting from the worship due to God alone would be lulled by a perusal of the Catechism of the Council of Trent★ '. . . to God we say properly, "Have mercy on us, hear us"; to the saints, "Pray for us". . . the greatest care must be taken not to attribute to any other what belongs to God.' Neither is the Catholic bound to pray to the Mother of God or to the saints: Trent (Session 25) asks him merely to acknowledge that it is useful and good so to do. Theologically speaking, one does not 'pray' to saints: we pray only to God, and ask the saints to pray to him for and with us.

Iron Virgin, the

Disappointingly perhaps, it has to be acknowledged that this fascinating instrument of torture, reputed to have been in use in mediaeval Germany in the hands of the Inquisition and of the Jesuits, was in fact first constructed in the 19th cent. The Inquisition was in any case never established in Germany and the Jesuits were not founded until the 16th cent.

Itala Vetus

The original Latin version of the Bible used by the Western Church until the adoption of the Vulgate★. St. Jerome★ first revised the Psalms in 383, later completing the rest of the Scriptures, with the exception of Wisdom, Ecclesiasticus, Baruch and Maccabees, which he left almost or completely untouched. The *Itala Vetus* is a literal translation of the Greek without literary claims; its detailed history is not known.

'Italian Mission', the

An offensive title bestowed on the Catholic Church in England by Archbishop Benson (Canterbury, +1896) implying that since the Reformation, English Roman Catholics were an enclave intruded by an Italian prince, the Pope, into the English branch of the Catholic Church. Thus has spoken narrow nationalism in every age.

Itinerary

(Lat. *itinerarium.*) The form of blessing before undertaking a journey, which is contained in the Breviary; the general form is the *Benedictus* with an antiphon, the Lord's Prayer, versicles and collects.

Jansenism

Cornelius Jansen, Bishop of Ypres, who died in 1638, published a work named Augustinus, which claimed to offer the doctrine of St. Augustine; in it he denied free will and the possibility of resisting the grace of God and the doctrine that Christ died for all men, and taught that some of God's commandments are impossible for man to observe. The book was condemned by Urban VIII in 1642, and in 1653, Innocent X condemned as heretical five propositions which contained Jansen's errors. The heresy became very popular in France and was later identified with the nuns of Port Royal*; it gave a puritanical tone to much theological teaching and writing for the next century.

Januarius, St.

(It. *San Gennaro*.) All that is known for certain is that he was bishop of Beneventum, was martyred under Diocletian near Naples, and is now patron of that city. What has brought him fame is the phial of the Blood of St. Januarius, kept in the Cathedral, which is believed to liquefy 18 times a year, including the Saint's feast day, Sept 19th. Privileged places are reserved on these occasions for a group of poor and aged women known as the *zie di S. Gennaro*, 'aunts of St. Januarius'.

Jerome, St.

Eusebius Ieronymus (c. 342–420); born at Aquileia at the head of the Adriatic, he was baptised at Rome where he had done his studies; he passed some years in asceticism, in his native place and in Palestine; as a hermit in the Syrian desert, he learned the Hebrew language. Ordained priest, he was made secretary to Pope Damasus, at whose prompting he undertook his great work, the Vulgate*. He also wrote profusely in the fields of history, biography and controversy; the early Church has no rival to Jerome in scholarship. The last 34 years of his life were spent in study and writing while he ruled the monastery at Bethlehem. Jerome is frequently depicted in art with the red hat, the tradition being that Damasus created him cardinal, and with a lion, symbolising the desert, and thus his ascetic life. Feast-day, Sept 30th.

Jesse Window

A window, found in many a cathedral, abbey and parish church, designed as a pictorial genealogy of Our Lord progressing upward (unlike printed genealogies) from a recumbent figure of David's father Jesse, intermediate generations being depicted in the glass or stone as branches of a tree which culminates with the adult Christ or the Virgin and Child. See Is. 11:1.

Jesuits

See Society of Jesus.

J.O.C.

(Fr. *Jeunesse Ouvrière Chrétienne.*) See Young Christian Workers.

Jociste

(Fr., A member of J.O.C.) See Young Christian Workers.

John Bosco, St. (1815–88)

Born of a peasant family in Piedmont, from an early age he was granted visions of the Blessed Virgin, whom he took, under the title of Help of Christians, as patroness of all his works; ordained priest—and known henceforth as Don Bosco—he gave himself to the rescue of poor and abandoned boys from destitution, and to their Christian education. The helpers who joined him in this work became, later, the Society of St. Francis de Sales (Salesians* of Don Bosco). Don Bosco's influence over his boys rested on an all-embracing concern and continuous physical presence among them, an attractive presentation of the truths and practice of the Faith, and a minimum of discipline. Associated regularly with miraculous happenings, in enormous demand as confessor and spiritual director, adviser to Pio Nono*, he kept up an indefatigable interest in foreign missions, which he promoted zealously through his Society. This he had contrived to found at a time when the anti-clericals in government were expelling religious, such politicians as Cavour making an exception for the sake of the public good they saw accruing from Don Bosco's activities.

John of Damascus, St.

Also known as John Damascene, this Greek theologian and Doctor (so declared in 1890 by Leo XIII) lived from about 675 to about 749. Deprived of public office at the Caliph's court by reason of his faith, he became a monk and was ordained priest. Basing his philosophical ideas on Aristotle and Plato, and greatly admiring the works of St. Gregory of Nazianzus, he wrote voluminously on philosophy, heresies and the articles of orthodox faith, including the Hypostatic Union* and the Real Presence*. His Mariology embraced the divine maternity of Mary, the Immaculate Conception* and the Assumption. There are also commentaries, homilies and poetry, some of which is still used as hymns. John's influence has been very great in both Eastern and Western churches.

John of God, Order of St.

See Hospitallers of St. John of God.

John of the Cross, St. (1542–91)

A Doctor of the Church. His mystical teachings are transmitted in his cycle of books *The Ascent of Mount Carmel, The Dark Night of the Soul, The Spiritual Canticle* and *The Living Flame of Love.* His poems (outstanding enough to gain him a place in almost every collection of Spanish verse) express the rare depth of his experience, and his prose works are commentaries on them. His works rank as classics of mysticism. Entering the Carmelite Order* in 1563 and ordained priest in 1567, he was disillusioned by the prevailing laxity, and considered leaving for the Carthusians*. From this he was dissuaded by St. Teresa* of Avila, who proceeded with his help to institute her reform of the Order, setting up the Discalced Carmelites. John was persecuted by the friars who opposed the reform, and imprisoned by them for most of a year. Even after the two branches of

the Order were canonically separated, he had trouble with his superiors, who still distrusting him, sent him finally to one of their poorest houses, where he contracted his last illness and died. His works, addressed chiefly to contemplatives and spiritual directors, reflect his own experiences, his knowledge of the Scriptures and acquaintance with Thomistic* philosophy, his austerity, his psychological insight and his powerful poetic gift.

John Paul I, Pope

(1978, Aug 26–Sept 28) Patriarch of Venice, elected in a very short Conclave to succeed Paul VI, he captured the public imagination as the 'smiling Pope'; he took the names of his two predecessors as a sign of his intention to pursue their policies, but in the following month was found dead in his room: one of the shortest pontificates and one which drew from all manner of men expressions of regret and sympathy.

John Paul II, Pope

(Oct. 16th, 1978–) The first non-Italian Pope since the Dutchman, Hadrian VI (1522–23)—four and a half centuries and 46 Italians away—quickly endeared himself to the Roman people both by his personal qualities and his easy mastery of the Italian language. Formerly Cardinal Archbishop of Cracow, he arrived with a reputation as liturgist, scholar, poet, stout opponent of Communism, and forced labourer in quarries under the Nazi occupation. His election itself being a sign of a new confidence and openness in Rome, he proceeded promptly to exploit this by announcing his intention to visit Poland again, not having visited his country since the conclave*. This journey, considered by many a delicate venture, he managed superbly, and was received by the Communist authorities with distant formality, by the people with rapturous enthusiasm.

John XXIII, Pope (1881–1963)

On the death of Pius XII in October 1958, the cardinals, it was said, sensed the proximity, and the necessity, of important changes for the Church, and in this frame of mind elected Angelo Guiseppe Roncalli, then within a month of his 77th birthday, to be a stop-gap, a 'caretaker'

Pope. If this was so, he turned out to be a caretaker who took very good care. Three months after his election, John XXIII, who had talked of opening windows to let fresh air into the Church, and was not a man of the Roman Curia but who had wide diplomatic and pastoral experience—he treated the city of Rome as his parish—announced his intention of calling a General Council. This, the Second Vatican* Council, opened in October 1962 and the Pope died in the following June. In his short pontificate, this corpulent old gentleman had somehow shown the world the smile behind the remote formality of the Vatican, demonstrating what he had earlier preached as the ideal for the bishop: the seeking after the truth and the teaching of it, and the 'charity which begins with those forms of respect and courtesy which are the charm of human society and which aspire magnificently to the prodigious and heroic demonstration of pastoral service'.

Josephinism
The principle, named after its chief practitioner, the Emperor Joseph II (1765–90), that the Church is completely subordinate to the State, which is to rule it for what are judged to be the best interests of the nation.
See Gallicanism.

Joy
This gift, according to Thomas Aquinas, is not distinct from charity but an act or effect thereof. It was demanded in Benedict XIV's list for candidates for canonisation; and St. Francis de Sales says '*Un saint triste est un triste saint.*'
See Gifts of the Holy Spirit.

Joyful Mysteries
The five Joyful Mysteries of the Rosary of the Blessed Virgin are: the Annnunciation, the Visitation, the Nativity, the Presentation of the Child Jesus, and the Finding of the Child Jesus in the Temple.

Joys of Mary
Incidents in the life of the Blessed Virgin chosen as focus of devotion vary in number from five to more than 12. Those usually accepted are the Annunciation, the Visitation, the Nativity, the Epiphany, the Finding of the Child Jesus in the Temple, and the Resurrection. The Franciscans observe the Feast of the Joys of Mary on Aug 22nd, and it is kept in some countries (e.g. Brazil, Portugal) on the Monday after Low Sunday.

Jubilee
A Jubilee Year is proclaimed by the Pope, either to mark some particular, single event—and is called a Lesser or extraordinary Jubilee (e.g. the 50th anniversary of a pope's ordination to the priesthood)—or to celebrate the regularly recurring Holy Year*; this is a Greater Jubilee. The most prominent feature of a year of Jubilee is the plenary indulgence* to be gained by praying at the four Major Basilicas* in Rome or, for those unable to travel there, by fulfilling obligations laid down by their ordinaries*.

Judge, Ecclesiastical
In the Church, judicial power resides in the Pope universally and in the Bishop locally. The local ordinary* is the judge in causes of the first instance, and the metropolitan* in appeals. The Bishop usually delegates to a cleric, who is called the Officialis or to synodal judges or examiners; or he may appoint a collegiate tribunal of three or five judges. There is no jury system in ecclesiastical courts, but judges must follow the procedure defined by Canon Law.

Justification by faith
The Lutheran proposition that faith alone 'justifies unto salvation' was condemned as heresy by the Council of Trent, which in Session vi, can. 9 *De Justificatione*, rejects the opinion that 'the wicked man is justified by faith alone, meaning that no other thing is needed . . . and that it is not necessary for him to be prepared and disposed by the movement of his will'.

Kells, Synod of

Several synods of the Irish Church were held here, the principal one being the plenary Council of 1152 under the presidency of the Papal Legate, which confirmed the primacy of Armagh, conferred the pallium on Dublin, Cashel and Tuam, and suppressed several small dioceses; the present diocesan system dates from that synod.

Kiss of Peace

See Sign of Peace.

Knights of St. John

(The Sovereign, Sacred and Military Order of St. John of Jerusalem; Knights of Malta.) The descendant of the Knights Hospitallers*, this is the only Order of Chivalry to keep into modern times a number of members in the vows of religion; these Knights of Justice are vowed to the defence of the faith and the service of the poor. There are also Knights of Honour and Devotion, who must be of noble birth, and Knights of Magistral Grace. The Grand Cross of the Order is sometimes granted to princes who are not Catholic (as it was to Edward VII). The Knights work with various hospitals (e.g. Ss John and Elizabeth in London) and have diplomatic representation at the Vatican.

Knights of the Cross

The Sacred Military Order of Cross-bearers with the Red Star was founded in 1237 at Prague, as hospitallers*. The Knights were reconstituted in 1694 and are now known as the Crosier* Canons of the Red Star: few in number, they are engaged in education and parochial work.

Knights of the Hospital of St. John of Jerusalem

In England, a charitable organisation, to be distinguished from the Knights of St. John*, whose previous headquarters it occupies at Clerkenwell.

Knock

(Cnoc Mhuire.) A village in the eastern part of the County Mayo, where, in 1879, the Mother of God is said to have appeared to 15 persons. Since that time, the place has become a centre of devotion, miraculous happenings have been reported, and pilgrims from many countries visit the village, from May until October every year, the high point of the season being August 15th, the feast of the Assumption*. The ambulance corps of the Irish Association of the Sovereign Order of Malta cares for invalid pilgrims to Knock. Pope John Paul II declared the principal church a Basilica* with the title Our Lady, Queen of Ireland when he visited the shrine in September, 1979.

Kulturkampf

A campaign mounted against the Church in the 1870s by Bismarck, lest the influence of Catholicism should loosen the unity of the German Empire. He abolished the Catholic department of the Prussian Ministry of Public Worship in 1871 and appointed to the Ministry the following year P.L.A. Falk, who expelled the Jesuits, brought education under State control and framed the infamous May* Laws. In the surge of opposition to the Laws, several bishops were imprisoned; in retaliation to Pio Nono*'s encyclical *Quod numquam* of Feb. 1875, all financial assistance was withdrawn from the Church and the religious were driven out. In spite of these savage measures and of efforts to intrude official clergy who would woo the faithful away from Rome, and although at one time all the bishops of Prussia were either in prison or in exile, the Iron Chancellor towards the end of the decade realised the strength of his enemy and conceded, abrogating the anti-Catholic legislation—but not yet permitting the Jesuits to return—and made a Concordat with Leo XIII. One chief effect of the years of struggle was to strengthen the loyalty of the Catholics to their hierarchy and to Rome.

Labarum

The military standard used by the Emperor Constantine; it appears to have been the Roman cavalry standard with the Christian monogram, the Chi Rho⋆ replacing the eagle or other pagan symbol. After 324, it was used throughout the whole Empire, West and East. The name is probably a misspelling of *laureum* (the laurel symbolised victory), the troopers' colloquial term for standard.

Lady Day

See Annunciation.

Laetare Medal

On Laetare⋆ Sunday every year the University of Notre Dame, Indiana, presents a gold medal to a chosen Catholic American lay person.

Laetare Sunday

See Mid-Lent.

Laicisation

The return, by ecclesiastical process, of a person in Holy Orders to the lay condition, either at his own request or as a punishment, without removing his Orders; or the handing over of objects, such as buildings, to a secular purpose; or the removal, by law or by force, of ecclesiastical control of institutions or property, as happened in many revolutions. See Secularisation.

Lamb

In repeating at Mass the description of Jesus by John the Baptist as the 'lamb of God', the Church (Jn.1:29,36) extends his hearers' acceptance of the 'lamb' as the 'sacrifice of reparation' of Lev.14:12 and confirms the Baptist's phrase as prophetic both of his kinsman's death and of the sacrificial nature of that death. Hence the frequent use of the lamb in art as a symbol of Christ the victim, reflecting also the frequent mention in Revelation of the glory to be accorded in his victory to the 'Lamb that was slain' and with his blood redeemed men for God (e.g. Rev.5:9).

Lammas Day

The ancient name (O.E. *hlafmaesse*, loaf-Mass) for the former feast of St. Peter's Chains, Aug 1st, which was kept as a thanksgiving for the early harvest; loaves of bread from the new corn were blessed at Mass.

Lamps

Lamps, usually of glass with oil and wick or solid wax, are used—like candles—as marks of honour and as symbols of prayer. Since the 16th cent., it has been prescribed that a lamp shall hang or stand before the Blessed Sacrament.

Lance, Holy

There are several relics, the best known at St. Peter's in Rome, with the title of the spear used in Jn.19:34; none of them has any supporting evidence. See Longinus.

Language

See Vernacular and Latin.

La Salette

A place of pilgrimage near Grenoble; in Sept. 1846, a peasant boy and girl had a vision of Our Lady who urged 'all her people' to do penance and promised them, on this condition, the divine mercy. She also gave the children a secret message which was later sent to the Pope, Pius IX. Pilgrims have been visiting the place since the first reports of miraculous cures, and in 1852 the building of the present church was begun.

Last Sacraments

The term used collectively describes the Last Anointing (Anointing of the Sick), the Eucharist as Viaticum, sacramental absolution and other services to the dying.

Lateran

i) The Church of our Most Holy Saviour, at the Lateran in Rome, commonly known as St. John Lateran, is the cathedral church of the Bishop of Rome, whose primacy is signified in the inscription over the entrance *Omnium Urbis et Orbis ecclesiarum mater et caput*, Mother and Head of all churches, in the City and in the world. Above the high altar is a shrine said to hold the heads of Ss. Peter and Paul. During the era of the 'Prisoner of the Vatican'*, from 1870 to 1929, the Popes were unable to officiate in their cathedral. ii) Adjoining the church is the Palace of the Lateran, the original building on the site, the palace of the Laterani family, being given to the Church by Constantine and used as a papal residence from that time until the 14th cent.; the present Palace is the Pontifical Museum of Christian Antiquities.

Lateran, Councils of the

The First Lateran Council (9th Oecumenical, 1123), the first oecumenical council held in the West, ratified the Concordat of Worms and declared null the marriages of clerics and of persons closely related to each other.
The Second (10th Oecumenical, 1139) condemned Arnold of Brescia and dealt with morals and discipline, including simony and usury.
The Third (11th Oecumenical, 1179) condemned the Albigensians* and Waldensians and passed important decrees governing the election of a Pope—such as that only cardinals should vote, and that a majority of two-thirds be needed—and legislated against the ordination of clerics with no proper means of support, the demanding of money for burial or the administration of the sacraments or for admission to a monastery.
The Fourth (12th Oecumenical, 1215) convoked by Innocent III, was the greatest of mediaeval Councils and is sometimes referred to as the 'Lateran Council'; it condemned errors regarding the Holy Trinity, defined the doctrine of the Holy Eucharist, using the term *transubstantiation*, forbade pluralism and the establishing of any new religious orders and laid down the Easter Duty*; it also made rules about preaching in cathedral churches and reminded bishops of their duty of teaching.
The Fifth (18th Oecumenical, 1512-17) defined the Pope's authority over Councils, imposed the *imprimatur*, instituted ecclesiastical supervision of pawnshops, condemned the belief that one intellectual soul is shared by all men or that it is mortal.

Lateran, Treaty of the

Signed in 1928 between the Holy See and Italy (Pius XI and Mussolini representing Victor Emmanuel III), this pact settled the 'Roman Question' by establishing on the one side the liberty and independence of the Holy See in its sovereign state of Vatican City with certain buildings in Rome, including the Colosseum, and on the other the 'recognition of the Kingdom of Italy under the dynasty of the House of Savoy and with Rome as its capital', and offering the Holy See a large financial compensation for the loss of the States of the Church*.

Latin

Ecclesiastical Latin grew less out of the classical tradition of Roman literature than out of the living language of popular speech, somewhat resembling in this respect the κοινη, the Greek of the N.T. Latin replaced Greek as the language of the Western Church in the 3rd cent., beginning in Africa and gaining great prestige from the monumental work of St. Jerome, the Vulgate*. A great tradition of Latin writing developed in the following centuries, in secular works as well as in liturgical, devotional, philosophical and theological. At the Renaissance, attempts were made by purist classical scholars to amend some sections of liturgical Latin, sometimes with unhappy results; and more recently the search for 'correctness' robbed Jerome's Latin of much of its life and sonority, in the revised version of the Psalter, of which monastic complaints were made that it does not chant. Latin, from being the universal language of the learned European throughout the centuries (scholarly works on all subjects being published therein until at least the age of Newton's *Principia*), is still used by the Church for most papal documents and in much of the matter of the *Acta* *Apostolicae Sedis*, and though the official

language of Vatican II, it is giving way to modern languages in face of an increasing facility between the nations and the very widespread use of English; however, it is still used to preserve the official versions of liturgical texts, and in some places there is a manifest zeal for the continuance of Latin in the Mass.
See Latin Mass Society.

Latin Church

Also Roman Church, Latin Rite, Western Church, Western Patriarchate: that part of the Universal Church which has used the Latin liturgy (including, until recently, the Latin language in all liturgical functions) and accepts the Bishop of Rome as its patriarch and as supreme pontiff.

Latin Mass Society, the

Founded in 1965 to campaign for the retention of Latin in the liturgy, the Society, an association of clergy and laity, seeks to preserve the Tridentine* liturgy and contends that 'the liturgical tradition which since the Council of Trent has held the Western Church in a single bond of spiritual unity and which has existed substantially since the earliest centuries of Christianity should remain to us and be preserved for future generations'. Its constitution defines its aims as the upholding of the teaching and practice of the Church as defined by the Council of Trent* in matters of liturgy and religious observance, to promote regular and public celebration of Mass in the Tridentine rite and in Latin, to encourage the traditional music of the Church, especially the Gregorian chant, to work for the wider ecclesiastical use of Latin, to provide means for the laity to communicate their needs and desires in these matters to the Hierarchy. The Society has run into some opposition, not so much for its love of the Latin language and its desire to hear its continued use in the liturgy (this is ensured by the Constitution on the Liturgy of Vatican II, by an Instructio of the Sacred Congregation for Divine Worship in 1969, and by a papal indult granted to England and Wales in 1971) as for its noisy condemnation of the reforms of Vatican II, of which it speaks as almost a kind of heresy, quoting the bull Quo Primum of Pius V, in which the Counter-Reformation pope insists that his discipline in these matters is to last in perpetuity and can never be legally revoked or amended at a future date—which, if we accept at its face value, strips all later Pontiffs and Councils of their ordinary magisterium, and reduces the Church to an ever out-of-date museum piece of liturgical antiquities; to say nothing of Pius' commination of the wrath of God on those who amended his orders, viz, Popes John XXIII and Paul VI and the bishops of the world.

Latin Rite

See Rite.

La Trappe, Notre Dame de

Near Soligny, Normandy; an abbey founded in 1122. It adopted the Cistercian* reform in 1148 but deteriorated from the early 16th cent., mainly through the system of commendatory* abbots. It was one of these abbots in commendam, de Rancé, who introduced a severe and celebrated reform in 1664, after which the community flourished until its dispersal in the Revolution in 1790. It was re-founded in 1817, and in 1892, it was absorbed into the Cistercians of the Strict Observance, thus losing its distinctive character, though the name Trappists is still—mistakenly—used of Cistercians in general.

Latria

(Gk. λατρεια, service of the gods.) Adoration proper, that worship and honour to be paid to God alone.

Latrocinium

See Robber Council.

Lauda Sion

The title, taken from its opening words, of the Sequence* of the Mass of Corpus Christi, attributed, like the entire liturgy of that feast, to St. Thomas Aquinas*. It has long been considered a masterpiece of theological poetry, and the latter section, beginning Ecce panis angelorum, has been frequently used as a hymn in its own right.

Lauds

(Lat. *laudes*, praises.) The second office of the day which follows Matins*, and in monasteries is often sung immediately after; it is intended as the dawn office, its ancient hymns speaking, for instance, of cockcrow, of the return of daylight, of the rising sun as symbol of the Resurrection.

Lavabo

The symbolic washing of the celebrant's hands after the offering of the bread and wine at Mass, named from the first word of the Latin extract from Psalm 26 (vv 6–12) with which he formerly accompanied the action (*Lavabo inter innocentes manus meas*, I will wash my hands in innocence).

Law, Canon

The collection of Church laws with the title *Codex Juris Canonici* (Gk. κανων, straight line, rule) proclaims in the very first Canon that it proposes to be binding only on Catholics of the Latin Church, apart from such points as by their own nature affect the Eastern Churches. Canon Law is of two kinds, common, binding universally, and particular, or local. Before the promulgation of the *Codex* in 1917, the chief collection of canon law in the Western Church was the *Corpus Juris Canonici*, which consisted of the renowned *Decretum* (canons of Councils and decrees of Popes) compiled by Gratian in the 12th cent., and further collections of law later legislated or compiled by various Popes. This huge mass of law, first called *Corpus Juris Canonici* in 1580, had become so unwieldy that in 1904 Pius X* appointed a commission to reshape and reduce Canon Law, and in 1917 the new *Codex* appeared. At the time of the Second Vatican Council*, a further revision of Canon Law was set in motion.

Law of Guarantees

The device used by the new Government of Italy in 1871, after its seizure of the Papal States, to regularise the position of the Papacy. The law, offering the Holy See certain securities, including the inviolability of the Pope's person and his possession of the Vatican* and Lateran* Palaces and of Castel Gandolfo*, and the grant of certain monies, was rejected by Pius IX on the grounds that it implied that the status of the Holy See thereby established was a gift or privilege of the Italian State granted as to a subject—and therefore capable of being in future withdrawn. The Pope's repudiation led to the impasse in which he was known as the *Prisoner of the Vatican**. The Law of Guarantees was abrogated by the Lateran* Treaty of 1929.

Lazarists

See Vincentians.

Lectionary

(Lat. *lectionarium*, the book of lections, or lessons, i.e., readings.) The book of readings for Matins; also the book used at Mass and containing the cycle of Readings, the Responsorial Psalms, Alleluia verses and Acclamations for the liturgical year.

Leeds, Diocese of

Established in 1878 (with Middlesbrough*) on the suppression of the See of Beverley*, it consists of West Yorkshire and the city of York south of the Ouse, embracing in its area such ancient missions as Hazlewood, Carlton and Broughton Hall. It is suffragan to Liverpool*.

Legate

See Legatus a Latere and Legatus Natus.

Legatus a Latere

(Lat., legate from the side.) A cardinal chosen by the Pope for some mission of great delicacy and confidentiality and given special powers for the occasion.

Legatus Natus

(Lat., born legate.) A person who is legate of the Pope by virtue of the office he holds; such offices used to include the archbishopric of Canterbury. Since the 12th cent., the legateship has been only honorary and, still attached to Reims, Salzburg and some other sees, involves only privileges of dress and precedence.

Legion of Mary

An association, using the names of the divisions of the Roman legion, founded in Dublin in 1921 as a grouping of lay people with the object of assisting the clergy in the work of sanctification of the faithful; the members undertake any task approved by the clergy except the collecting of money and the provision of material relief. It spread rapidly into Gt. Britain, the U.S., India and other countries.

Leonine City

That part of the city of Rome, on the right bank of the Tiber, and including the Vatican and the Castle of Sant'Angelo, round which Pope Leo IV in the 9th cent. set up a defensive wall against the possibility of Saracen attacks.

Liber Pontificalis

(Lat., the Book of the Popes.) A collection of lives of the Popes from St. Peter to Stephen V (891); the earlier ones, up to Boniface II (530-2) were written about the time of that Pope and contain much that must be apocryphal, the rest being written Pope by Pope and more trustworthy. Similar biographies are included of Popes from Victor II (+1055) to Eugene IV (+1447).

Liber Usualis

(*Liber usualis Missae et Officii pro Dominicis et Festis*, Handbook of the Mass and Office for Sundays and Feast-Days.) A monumental compilation of these liturgies, accompanied by the appropriate Gregorian chants edited by the monks of Solemnes*, long issued in Latin, later translated.

Liberius, Pope

Much has been made in polemics of the case of Pope Liberius as disproving Papal infallibility*. This Pope, who died in 366, approved, it is said, the condemnation of St. Athanasius* by Arian bishops and accepted a semi-Arian profession of faith, thereby falling into error on a matter of faith and shattering the theory of Papal infallibility. Liberius, in fact, ordered by the Arian Emperor Constantius to assent to the condemnation of Athanasius as a rebel and refusing, was banished from Rome, to submit two years later (357): he then signed an Arian formula and was allowed in 358 to re-occupy the see of Rome. The nature of the document he signed is doubt-ful, but however heretical it may have been, we have the word of both Athanasius* and Jerome* that the assent was forced from him while he was exiled by the Emperor; thus he could not possibly have been speaking as chief teacher of the Church to the whole Church, with the intention of binding the Church to a doctrinal definition.

Light of Christ

At the Easter Vigil liturgy, the deacon walking into the darkened church cries out three times 'The light of Christ!' as other candles are lit from the Paschal Candle which he is carrying (See Jn.8:12).

Lisbon

The College of Ss. Peter and Paul at Lisbon was founded in 1622 for the training of priests to go back to England during penal times. It was closed in 1972. A similar Irish college in the city closed much earlier.

Lisbon, Patriarch of

See Patriarch.

Litany of Our Lady

(Litany of Loreto.) A catalogue of invocations to the Mother of God, first used at the sanctuary of Loreto in Italy, where its use is mentioned in 1558—there is also a theory that the Litany began among the Dominican confraternities of the Rosary* and was brought thus to Loreto. It appears to be a simplified version of litanies which went back to the 12th cent., and most of the earlier titles used, some of which have been criticised as extravagant, are to be found in one form or another in the writings of the Fathers of the first six centuries.

Litany of the Saints

There have been various forms of litany in Western usage, the earliest of them composed in Rome at the time of Pope St. Gelasius (492-6) the *Deprecatio Gelasii*, and extant until the 8th cent. It was then being superseded by the Litany of the Saints more or less as we know it; this diversified much in length with the inclusion of local saints, until, in 1570, it was made mandatory to use only the Roman formula except with Papal license. There are three versions: the Greater Litanies, used processionally, 'greater' only as regards greater antiquity than other litanies; the Lesser Litanies, referring in fact to occasions of lesser liturgical importance on which the same litanies are recited; and a shortened version used in the prayers for the dying.

Lithostrotos
(Gk., paved with stone.) The inner court of Pilate's praetorium (Jn.19:13), the floor of which was the actual *lithostrotos*, probably mosaic or at least tesselated.

Little Company of Mary
A congregation founded in 1877 in Nottingham to care for the dying and for the bodies of the dead and to pray continually for the dying and the dead.

Little Flower of Jesus
The popular name by which St. Thérèse* of the Child Jesus has been known since her canonisation in 1925: she describes herself thus frequently in her Autobiography.

Little House of Divine Providence
Founded in 1828 in Turin by St. Joseph Cottolengo, for corporal works of mercy of all kinds, this institute has hospitals, schools, workshops, orphanages, and almshouses. It incorporates the work of several religious institutes and has spread to other countries.

Little Oratory, Brotherhood of the
Attached to each house and church of the Congregation of the Oratory* is a grouping of laymen (Brothers) organised for spiritual exercises and for works of charity, especially among the sick and poor.

Little Sisters of the Poor
A congregation founded in Brittany in 1840 with the object of caring for the homeless poor over the age of 60; the Sisters make daily collections and have the name of being the world's most persuasive beggars.

Little Way Association, the
An enterprise, based in London and of lay foundation, for the support of missions overseas, with St. Teresa of Lisieux* as its particular patron.

Little Way, the
A phrase used by St. Teresa of Lisieux* to describe her unassuming form of spirituality.

Liturgical Movement
A steadily growing reaction to the obscurity and inaccessibility of much of the liturgy, this movement in the Western Church began in the 19th cent., owing a great deal to the activities and writings of Dom Guéranger, abbot of Solesmes* from 1837 to 1853, and to Pius* X's encouragement of Eucharistic piety and frequent Communion, as well as to his reform of the Breviary and his decrees on sacred music. In England, Cardinal Wiseman was prominent among its early supporters, as was Abbot Cabrol. The granting of permission for the Dialogue Mass (*Missa Dialogata*) by Pius XII* marked perhaps one of the most important milestones for the movement, in the restoration to the faithful of their vocal share in the Mass—delegated for centuries to altar servers who were theoretically in Minor Orders of Acolyte, in practice 'altar boys' for the most part; this appeared to crystallise certain aspects of the difficulty and incongruity of the language barrier and of the traditional posture of the celebrant, which was necessarily isolated and exclusive of the Christian community. There was, in addition, much agitation for the use of modern languages in the most impregnable areas of the liturgy (e.g. the Epistle and Gospel were read or chanted in Latin and then, to be 'understood of the people', read over again in the language of the country). Thus, those who were still battling manfully for this point of language (a change put to the Council of Trent but rejected as 'inopportune') were justly rewarded by the concessions and suggestions of Vatican II, with the insistence on simplification of rites, intelligibility and the opportunity for the faithful to take their proper part.

Liverpool

The See was created in 1850 and made an archdiocese in 1911. It comprises the western parts of Lancashire south of the Ribble, parts of Merseyside, Cheshire and Greater Manchester, the Isle of Man; suffragans are Hexham and Newcastle, Lancaster, Leeds, Middlesbrough, Salford. It has the largest Catholic population of any district in Gt. Britain, several parts where the Faith never died, and parishes which began as missions in the 16th and 17th cent., e.g. Little Crosby and Standish; the former seminary buildings at Up Holland now houses the Northern Institute, for pastoral training of clergy and laity. Patrons of the Archdiocese are Our Lady Immaculate, St. Joseph and St. Kentigern; the cathedral is dedicated to Christ the King.

Lollards

The name comes from O.D. *lollen*, to sing, thus a Lollard would be a 'chanter', a 'mumbler of prayers', or possibly from Lat. *lollium*, darnel, thus perhaps 'weed', 'emcumbrance' would be the intention of Wm. Courtenay, Archbishop of Canterbury (1342–96), the first to use it officially. It was used originally of the followers of Wyclif*, then of ecclesiastical malcontents in general: knights yearning for Church property, tenants oppressed by an abbey, tithe evaders, false mystics. Lollardry had two periods: the former, mainly academic, was terminated at the end of the 14th cent. when William Sawtrey was burned, the first victim of *De Heretico Comburendo**; in the second period, starting about 1400, the movement turned more directly to social questions and became more popular, drawing support from the poor and inclining towards revolutionary methods. It continued thus through persecution until it declined after half a century; it had a decisive influence on the Hussites* of Bohemia.

Longinus, St.

The name applied in different versions of the *Acts of Pilate** to the soldier who pierced the side of the dead Christ (which prompts scholars to derive the name from the Gk. λογχη, lance) and also to the centurion who spoke out (Mt.27:54, Mk.15:39, Lk.23:47) in appreciation of the Victim. The two thus amalgamated in legend were celebrated as a martyr, who suffered, according to many mediaeval authors, including Bede*, at Caesarea in A.D. 58, figuring in some ancient martyrologies on Mar. 15th.

Lord of Misrule

(Abbot of Misrule, Master of Misrule.) A mediaeval custom—a relic, perhaps, of the Roman practice at Saturnalia of making a slave master of the house—of selecting someone to preside over the exuberance and foolery of the Christmas revelry; connected with the Feast of Fools (on or about Jan. 1st), a mock-religious festival which led to broad buffoonery and blasphemous performances, rousing the condemnation of bishops and Councils.
See also Boy Bishop.

Loreto, Litany of

See Litany of Our Lady.

Loreto Nuns

The name used in Ireland for the Institute* of Mary.

Loreto, the Holy House of

Inside the Basilica of Loreto near Ancona, is a building of about 30 by 13ft, to which is attached the legend, originating in the 15th cent., that it is the house of the Blessed Virgin at Nazareth and that it was brought hither by the hands of angels in 1294, after a three-year stage at Tersatz in Dalmatia on the way. From the story of the flying house arose the naming of Our Lady of Loreto as patroness of airmen. Miracles have nonetheless been recorded in fair numbers, an indication that these favours are granted to faith and devotion, without regard to historical accuracy.

Lottery

See Betting.

Lourdes

A town in the diocese of Tarbes (Hautes Pyrénées). An illiterate peasant girl, now canonised as St Bernadette Soubirous, had, in 1858, repeated visions of Our Lady, who identified herself as 'the Immaculate Conception*'. Of the hundreds of cases of cures which the Medical Bureau* claims cannot be explained by science, some few have been described by bishops as miracles. Apart from such cures, the place has become a powerful centre of spiritual renewal for hundreds of thousands who annually travel thither for religious, not medical, reasons.

Lourdes Medical Bureau, the

The *Bureau des Constatations Médicales* is a permanent board set up to examine any claims of cures at the shrine. Its only permanent member is the President, appointed by the Bishop of Tarbes and Lourdes, his task being to oversee the examinations and the discussions which follow. The other members are doctors, unpaid and independent, who happen to be in Lourdes at any given time, e.g. accompanying pilgrims, or who have come for the purpose of joining the Bureau, which invites any doctor, of any nation or faith, or of no faith, to be present at the stringent examination of those who claim to be cured, to scrutinise all the documents, to challenge and question as he wishes. In its official publication dealing with these matters, the Bureau does not pronounce any cure to be miraculous; it leaves such statements to the ecclesiastical authorities and confines itself to stating the ascertainable medical facts.

Low Sunday

The Sunday after Easter (Second Sunday of Easter), so named possibly in contrast with the 'high' feast of Easter. The week following is Low Week.

Lucifer

(Lat., light-bringer.) Translation, through the Gk, of the Hebrew *Helel*, the Shining One, the name of Venus the morning (or evening) star, used in Christian tradition chiefly as a title of Satan, by analogy with Is.14:12 in conjunction with Lk.10:18. Its direct application, in the Isaiah passage, is the King of Babylon, in irony—J.B. and R.S.V. give *Daystar*, which A.V. has as an alternative—but the title is given to Christ in II Pet.1:19, in Rev.22:16 ("morning star") and in the prayers with which the *Exultet*★ concludes; the last, in fact, a 7th-cent. composition, uses a deliberate play on words to distinguish Christ the true Light-Bringer from the 'other'.

Lucius

The first Christian king of Britain, according to the story (based apparently on a statement in the *Liber Pontificalis*★) which has it that Lucius obtained from Pope Eleutherius (174–189) a mission from Rome, which resulted in the baptism of many of his subjects, the turning of pagan temples into churches and the ordination of converted heathen priests; the legendary king himself, dying at Gloucester, was subsequently magnified into a son of Simon of Cyrene, baptised by St. Timothy, and travelling as a missionary to Rhaetia, where he suffered martyrdom at Chur. Whatever else may be said of this conflation of legend (there was an independent set of stories about a Lucius of Chur, who could well have been an actual person), it was probably, in its general intention, an attempt to explain the very early arrival of Christianity in Britain.

Lunette or lunula

(Lat. *luna*, moon.) A slotted holder, consisting of a double crescent shape or a double circle, of gold or gilt metal, in which the Host rests upright in the monstrance.

Lyons, Councils of

The First (13th Oecumenical, 1245) occupied itself with the excommunication★ of the Emperor Frederick II and other semi-political affairs, raised a three-year levy on all benefices to finance a new Crusade and originated the wearing of the Red Hat by cardinals.

The Second (14th Oecumenical, 1274) arranged re-union with the Orthodox Church (this was repudiated by Constantinople within eight years) and passed legislation some of which still holds in Canon Law and is of importance for the governing of conclaves★.

Madonna

(It., My lady.) A title used of the Mother of God, and more generally of a picture or statue of her, as e.g. a Madonna and Child, the Bruges Madonna, Madonna With a Violet. The Madonna Lily is often found in art as a symbol of purity.

Magisterium

(Lat. *magister*, master, person in authority.) The Church has a divinely authorised power (a "mastership") to teach the truth in religion, consequent on Christ's granting of his own authority to the Apostles (Mt.28:19-20): "Go, therefore, make disciples of all the nations; baptise them in the name of the Father and of the Son and of the Holy Spirit, and teach them to observe all the commands I gave you." The *solemn magisterium* is exercised rarely, in dogmatic definitions of Oecumenical Councils or of Popes speaking *ex cathedra* or the decrees of other Councils which are formally ratified by a Pope; the *ordinary magisterium* is exercised "from day to day" in the universal practice of the Church in regard to faith and conduct, in the unanimous consent of the Fathers★ and of theologians, in the decrees of Roman Congregations on these matters, in the *sensus communis* of the faithful and in various historical documents; the teaching herein contained is, as a whole, infallible, but this is not to say that each or any individual item is infallible.

Magnificat

The title (from its opening word in the Latin, *Magnificat anima mea Dominum*, My soul proclaims the greatness of the Lord) of the Blessed Virgin's song of praise on being greeted as Mother of the Messiah by her cousin Elizabeth (Lk.1:46ff). Thoroughly Hebrew in tone, the song reflects and echoes many similar utterances found in the O.T. e.g. the Song of Hannah (I Sam.1); it has, from ancient times, had an honoured place in the Divine Office, chiefly at Vespers, and has been set to memorable music by many composers.

Major Basilica

See Four Basilicas.

Major Order

See Holy Order.

Malines Conversations

An early ecumenical effort, the initiative of Lord Halifax, this series of meetings between Anglican and Roman theologians went on, with the approval of the Holy See and of Canterbury, from 1921 to 1925, under the presidency of Cardinal Mercier, Archbishop of Malines. Certain points were agreed: that the Pope should be given primacy of honour, that the Body and Blood of Christ are truly received in the Eucharist, that the Eucharist is a true sacrifice but in a mystical manner, that episcopacy is of divine institution, and that Communion under both kinds is a matter of discipline not of dogma. Halifax published the Report of the meetings in 1928, having so long delayed it out of fear of antagonism by the more Protestant sections of the C. of E. In that year also, Pius XI sent out the encyclical *Mortalium Animos*★, which seemed to damp further progress; yet, though it brought no very tangible result, the venture stimulated the movement for co-operation.

Mandatum

(Lat., commandment: Jn.13:34.) That part of the Liturgy of Holy Thursday in which the celebrant washes the feet of 12 persons, in imitation of the humility of Jesus at the Last Supper, to renew in his and everyone's mind the idea that Christian authority is primarily service. See Maundy Thursday.

Manichaeism

Manichaeos was the hellenised form of the name of Manes, a 3rd-cent. teacher from Ctesiphon, the capital of the Persian Empire. Lacking any written records from Manes or from his immediate disciples, we gather our knowledge from later sources (including the works of St Augustine of Hippo, who was a Manichee for some time until his conversion); the system appears to be a conflation of many ancient heresies and fallacies, among them that of the Mandaeans, a Gnostic* sect which held that frequent Baptism is necessary and that the soul is held prisoner in the body until it is freed by the Redeemer. Manichaeism supposed a primaeval conflict between Good and Evil (light and darkness) and that the purpose of religion was to release the particles of light which Satan, the evil one, had stolen from the world of Light and hidden in man's brain; it was for this that Buddha, the prophets, Jesus, and, of course, Manes himself had been sent; the struggle entailed strict asceticism, including vegetarianism. The Manichees were accused of many objectionable practices, but St. Augustine, who was better acquainted with them than most, never criticises their morals. Much of their theory and practice puts one in mind of the later Albigensians* and other mediaeval sects, though it is difficult to establish a direct influence. Manichaeism is recorded as surviving in parts of Turkestan until the 13th cent.

Manning, Henry Edward Cardinal (1808-92)

Fellow of Merton College, Oxford, and later Archdeacon of Chichester, Manning was regarded, after Newmans's conversion to Rome, as the leading figure of the Oxford Movement. He nonetheless continued to disapprove of Tract* 90 and was deeply anti-Papal until, late in the 1840's, he became disgusted with the internal politics of the Church of England. He was received into the Roman communion in 1851, ordained priest in two months' time and soon made provost of the Chapter of Westminster Cathedral. Succeeding Wiseman as Archbishop in 1865, he attended the First Vatican Council four years later, fortifying his advocacy of Papal infallibility with a vow to see it defined. He was totally alienated from Newman not only by the *Rambler* affair (see Newman), but by temperament and by other factors, among them his dedicated opposition to the entry of Catholics into the Universities. Made Cardinal in 1875, he laboured incessantly in social work and mediated in the London

dock strike of 1889. Buried first at Kensal Green, his body was later translated to Westminster Cathedral, which he had founded.

Manresa

It was at Manresa, near Monserrat in Spain, that St Ignatius* lived for a time as a hermit and wrote his Spiritual Exercises. The place is now a centre of pilgrimage, and the name has been taken by many Jesuit houses, particularly novitiates.

Mantelletta

(It.) A knee-length cape or cloak, open in front but fastening at the throat, and with holes for the arms; worn by cardinals, bishops, abbots and certain prelates of the Papal court.

Maranos

The Spanish word for the Jews of that country who, having received Baptism, abandoned Christianity for their earlier faith. The punishment of the Maranos by the Inquisition blackened that institution's name still further with the charge of anti-Semitism.

Margaret Mary, St.

See Sacred Heart; see Nine Fridays.

Maria Monk

A book was published in 1835, advertised as the memoirs of a woman who had spent some time as a nun in Montreal and who was in fact a person of very doubtful morals and determined to make money out of anti-Catholic prejudice. 'Maria Monk's Awful Disclosures', setting forth such curious tales as the murder of a nun by the Bishop of Montreal (with the aid of five priests) proved to be entertaining, vastly popular and totally false. The volume survived repeated refutations in the United States and in England and the imprisonment of its author for picking pockets—which suggest that she herself was hoodwinked or defrauded of the substantial royalties which accrued; she died in prison in 1849.

Marian priests

Those priests at the time of Elizabeth I who had been ordained in England, most of them in the reign of Mary Tudor. They were exempted from the law aimed at the 'seminary priests', ordained abroad, which made it high treason for a priest to enter the country or remain in it; but they were ordered by the Act of 1559 to take the anti-Papal Oath of Supremacy; those who refused were deprived. The majority seem to have anticipated the 'wrath to come' and disappeared without waiting to be removed by law. In 1593, there were more than forty Marian priests working among the faithful in secret.

Mariolatry

(Mary and Gk. λατρεια, worship.) Strictly, the offering of divine honours to the Virgin Mary. Certain heretics of the 4th cent. were condemned by St Epiphanius for sacrificial worship in her honour. The word is used more recently by some less ecumenically-inclined of the 'separated brethren' to condemn what they consider the excess of honour paid to Mary by Catholics; and indeed, in certain small communities—usually rustic—in some Latin countries, popular devotion has been led into the appearance of according her more devotion than that locally given her Son.

Marists

The Society of Mary; missionary priests, who also maintain boys' schools. There is an Anglo-Irish province and provinces in the U.S. and New Zealand. The Society was founded at Lyons in 1816 by John Claude Colin. Another society, the Sisters of the Holy Name of Mary, was also founded by Père Colin to teach girls and to work with the Fathers on the missions. A congregation of teaching brothers has schools in very many countries, including Scotland, and in some places, works together with the Marist Fathers.

Marks of the Church

In the Creed, 'we believe in one, holy, Catholic and apostolic Church'—the Nicene* formula. Quoted by Boniface VIII* as the opening phrase of his Bull *Unam Sanctam*, these marks or characteristics of the Church were not widely written about until the controversies of the Reformation, when they were used by Catholic polemicists against the new, separatist groups. The argument is

that, if Christ did found a church and if that church is still extant, it must be one not many, it must be holy, to fulfil his purpose, it must be catholic, that is, universal, for all men, and it must be apostolic, that is, it must be a historical continuum from Christ's Apostles, without a break.

Marriage, prohibition of

Marriage may be forbidden either a) by a general ecclesiastical prohibition, e.g. mixed religion, failure to announce publicly, etc. b) by an explicit ban by the bishop in a certain particular case, on account e.g. of scandal or of a suspected impediment; such prohibition does not induce invalidity, c) by parents: Canon Law* recommends, but does not require, parental consent for the marriage of those under 21 years of age and no priest may assist, without the bishop's permission, at such a marriage in opposition to the parents' wishes.

Martyr

(Gk. μαρτυρ, μαρτυς, witness.) One who suffers martyrdom, i.e. voluntary death, for the Faith or for any article thereof or for the preserving of some Christian virtue or for some other act of virtue related to God. (See Baptism of Blood.) According to Benedict XIV, a person inculpably in heresy or schism who dies for an article of the true faith is a martyr in the eyes of God though not to be so called by the Church; and the Pope admitted the possibility of the same being true of such a one dying for what he held, erroneously, to be of faith. By the *Age of the Martyrs* is meant the first three centuries of our era, the Martyrs being those huge numbers of victims of the Roman persecution, which was terminated only by Constantine* on his accession. Until about the middle of the 3rd cent. the title *martyr* was given to any who suffered for the faith or who notably professed it.

Martyrology

A daily record of the commemorations of martyrs and other saints, usually with a brief note on each. Such record may be local or proper to, e.g. a religious order; and there were added thereto feasts of Our Lord and the Blessed Virgin and of important events, e.g. the coming of the Holy Spirit (Pentecost), the institution of the Holy Eucharist (Corpus Christi) etc.

Martyrology, the Roman

A liturgical book (a revision of the Martyrology compiled by Usuard in the 9th cent.) from which readings were made in choir as early as the 9th cent., a practice later prescribed for religious houses. Some of its many marvellous tales convey more edification than history.

Martyrs of Compiègne

From the Carmel of Compiègne, 16 nuns were sent to the guillotine in Paris in 1794, charged with leading the religious life, which was contrary to the laws of the Revolution.

Martyrs of the Commune

In 1871, Archbishop Darboy of Paris and a number of priests and laymen were murdered by soldiers of the Commune. On discovering the prelate's unburied corpse, the troops of Thiers shot 147 Communards in retaliation.

Martyrs of Damascus

During the massacre in the Lebanon in 1860, eight Friars Minor* and three Maronites were executed by the Muslims.

Martyrs of Japan

Fairly soon after St Francis Xavier* brought the Faith to Japan, Christians of that country began to suffer, from the first martyrs (by crucifixion) at Nagasaki (26 persons in the persecution of 1596-98) to those put to death in thousands, both natives and foreigners, between 1613 and 1640, after which date Christianity was forbidden in the country until the treaty with France in 1859.
See Finding of the Christians.

Martyrs of North America

The six Jesuits and two laymen slaughtered by the North American Indians at various times between 1642 and 1649, and canonised in 1930, the best-known of their names being John Brébeuf and Isaac Jogues.

Martyrs of Oxford University

Those students and graduates of Oxford who suffered under Henry VIII and Elizabeth I (including e.g. St Cuthbert Mayne and St Edmund Campion).

Martyrs of Persia

Very many Christians suffered in Persia in the period 339-628, and are mentioned in the Roman Martyrology* (April 22nd).

Martyrs of September

(*Martyres des Carmes.*) In the French Revolution, in Sept. 1792, three bishops and 188 other clerics, secular and regular, were put to death for their faith at the Carmelite church and in other parts of Paris.

Martyrs of Uganda

About a hundred Ugandans died in 1886 in the persecution instigated by King Mwanga when certain Christian youths refused to accommodate his unnatural appetites.

Mary Major, St.

See Basilica.

Mass-Priest

An ancient term for a man who had been ordained priest, from the times when those in other inferior, orders were also called priests. It was also used to distinguish a diocesan priest from a religious; and from the 16th cent., it began to be used (with its variant 'massing-priest') by some Reformers as a contemptuous description of a priest.

Master General

The title of the head of the Order of Preachers*. He is elected for twelve years and, a mendicant by profession, is *ex officio* a grandee of Spain with the right to remain covered in the presence of his Catholic Majesty.

Matins

The most ancient and the longest section of the Divine Office, deriving from the Vigil* service of primitive times. It is usually followed, in monastic recitation, by Lauds*, either overnight or in the early morning.

Maundy Thursday

(Maundy from Lat. *mandatum*, commandment—the 'new commandment' of Jn.13:34, and the opening words in this day's liturgy of the washing of feet.) The commemoration, on the Thursday of

Holy Week, of the institution of the Eucharist 'the day before he suffered' and of the lesson of love he left in that Sacrament, in his discourse at the supper table and in his washing of the Apostles' feet. This last is in many places re-enacted on the sanctuary, the celebrant kneeling to wash the feet of twelve 'Apostles' chosen for the occasion (for the Established Church, the Sovereign of England traditionally distributes 'Maundy money', specially minted in silver). At the end of the evening Mass, the Blessed Sacrament is removed in solemn procession to a place of reservation for Communion at the liturgy of Good Friday. On Maundy Thursday likewise, the Holy Oils* are blessed in cathedral churches.

May Devotions

The custom of practising certain devotions in honour of our Blessed Lady during the month of May, including the holding of processions, the daily recitation of prayers, the setting up and venerating of shrines, was introduced into England in about 1840 by Don Luigi Gentili. May Devotions had the approval of Pius VII, and were said by some to have originated in Rome in 1815, by others at the Franciscan church of St. Clare in Naples towards the end of the 16th cent. There is no very clear reason why May was chosen as the Month of Mary: the name derives from *Maia* the Roman goddess, and the origins of *Maypole* and *May Queen* are not connected with the Blessed Virgin.

May Laws

The Landtag of Prussia in May 1873, passed, at Bismarck's bidding, legislation aimed at bringing the church in Germany under control of the State, by subjecting to it all ecclesiastical appointments and discipline, secularising marriage, binding the clergy to a written undertaking to observe these laws, suppressing all religious who were not engaged in nursing and taking over the administration of vacant sees and all church property. These laws were a main part of the Kulturkampf*.

Maynooth

The 'Royal Catholic College'—St. Patrick's Seminary, Maynooth, Co. Kildare—was established in 1795 by the Irish Parliament, with the royal approval

(George III), for the education of the Catholic clergy; a reversal of previous official attitudes to 'seminary priests'. An annual grant of £8,000 was voted, which, having risen to £9,500 by 1845, was in that year raised to £26,000 by Sir Robert Peel; and on the disestablishment of the Church of Ireland in 1869, this was compounded for a capital sum. St. Patrick's is the chief seminary of Ireland and founded in 1916 its own missionary Society of St. Columbanus (the 'Maynooth Missions'), which resulted in widespread and arduous evangelism in China. The buildings now in use were erected to the design of Augustus Welby Pugin, the funds being raised by Parliament in 1846. A curious item of treasure in the College is the gift of Queen Victoria Eugénie of Battenberg, consort of Alfonso XIII, whose innocence—or surprising ignorance of history and politics—prompted her to offer a silver statuette of St. George, which has since been kept out of sight under lock and key.

Maynooth Missions

See Maynooth

Mediator Dei

See Pius XII, Pope

Memento of the Dead

(Lat. *memento*, remember.) That part of the Eucharistic Prayer in which commemoration is made of the faithful departed which the celebrant or others choose to pray for, the dead 'who have died in the peace of Christ' and all the dead 'whose faith is known to You alone'.

Memento of the Living

(See Memento of the Dead.) In the Eucharistic Prayer, mention is made by name of those living persons for whom the Mass is being offered and in general of 'all of us gathered here before you'.

Memorare

(Lat., remember.) A prayer found in many Catholic manuals of devotion, asking the Mother of God for her intercession. There are various translations of this very popular prayer, which is also known as the Prayer of St. Bernard, an attribution due probably to the zealous spreading of the prayer by Claude Bernard (1588-1641), the 'Poor Priest'; its author is unknown, the earliest text being a 15th cent. MS of which the Memorare is a shortened version.

Mendicant Orders

(Lat. *mendicus*, beggar.) Those Orders of friars (Franciscan, Dominican, Carmelite, Augustinian) which had to live by begging, being barred by their constitution from owning property, not merely as persons but even in common. Changing times caused the Council of Trent★ to modify this rule (except in the cases of the Friars Minor★ and Capuchins★), but religious poverty is still taken seriously by the Mendicants (the title now includes also Servites★, Minims★, Mercedarians★, Trinitarians★, Order of Penitence★ and Order of St. John of God).

Menevia

(Med. Lat. form of Welsh *Mynyw*.) The See, founded in the 6th cent., was suspended in 1559, the title being revived in 1850 and the diocese in 1898; it comprises the whole of Wales but for Gwent and the Glamorgans, and is suffragan to Cardiff★. This is the only Catholic diocese in England and Wales which holds an ancient mediaeval title. The bishop's home and the pro-cathedral are at Wrexham.

Menology

(Gk. μηνολογιον, monthly account.) A name given to various kinds of unofficial martyrology★, such as lists of local saints or even of important persons of a religious order or an ecclesiastical calendar arranged in months and days.

Mercedarians

The Glorious, Royal and Military Order of Our Lady of Ransom (or Mercy), founded by St. Peter Nolasco in the 13th cent. for the ransoming of captives from the Moors, is now a mendicant Order working chiefly in hospitals and evangelisation, and still taking the fourth vow, to become hostage among the infidel if necessary. It also has nuns, both contemplative and active, most of them in Spain and S. American countries.

Meridian

The midday rest of about an hour taken in some monasteries, especially in hot countries or when the night's sleep is broken by the Office.

Metempsychosis

The 'transmigration of souls', a pre-Christian doctrine which influenced some early ecclesiastical writers and was vigorously attacked by e.g. St. Augustine. Later it was implicitly condemned in the decrees of the Councils of Lyons★ (1274) and Florence★ (1439) affirming that souls depart immediately to heaven, hell or purgatory. It has been held by Manichaeans★ and Albigensians★ and has recently become prominent again through Spiritualism and Theosophy; it is quite at variance with the Christian doctrines of the Redemption and the Resurrection of the Body.

Metropolitan

The style attributed to an archbishop who has a province, i.e. at least one suffragan★ see.

Michael

(Heb., God is without equal.) St. Michael the warrior (Jude 9, Rev.12:7–9) has been taken as patron by all Christians fighting the Devil, particularly at the moment of death, when he was to be the guide of the Christian soul on its journey back to the Creator dwelling in eternal light; cf. the Offertory of the former Requiem Mass ... *signifer Sanctus Michael repraesentet eas in lucem sanctam.*

Middlesbrough, Diocese of

The See of Middlesbrough was formed, together with that of Leeds★, on the suppression in 1878 of the short-lived diocese of Beverley★; it comprises Cleveland, North Yorkshire, Humberside and the city of York north of the Ouse, and is suffragan to Liverpool★. In several places, e.g. at Everingham, the Faith survived throughout the Reformation period, and close on twenty parishes were set up in the 16th and 17th centuries.

Mid-Lent Sunday

The Fourth Sunday of Lent is also known as Refreshment Sunday, either from the Feeding of the Five Thousand, which used to be the Gospel of the day, or from the general air of relaxation from Lenten discipline, consonant with the other title Laetare Sunday (Lat. *laetare*, rejoice, the word with which the former Introit★ of the Mass began). Another name, Mothering Sunday, is said to derive either from the custom of visiting one's mother on this day or from the reference to the spiritual motherhood of Jerusalem in Gal. 4, which was read at Mass; and Simnel* Sunday, in some parts, from the simnel cake made for this day.

Milan, Edict of

This famous proclamation, neither an Edict nor issued at Milan, signified the agreement arrived at by Licinius and Constantine* in 313, the year after the latter achieved the position of senior ruler of the Roman Empire, whereby they granted freedom under the law to Christians and all others to practice their religions. In effect, it was the liberation of the Church and the beginning of its rapid and enormous expansion.

Militia of Jesus Christ

A military order founded in the 13th cent. to combat the Albigensians* and defend the Church; it merged later with an order of penance to form the Third Order* of St. Dominic.

Military Orders

An attempt, originating with the Crusades, to combine the monastic life with the military, the chief examples being the Knights Templars*, the Hospitallers* of St. John, the Knights of Alcantara*, the Teutonic* Knights and the Mercedarians*. The Knights took the vows of religion, were bound to the Office and their houses ranked as monasteries. The downfall of the movement, due to the impossibility of combining the true monastic life with the business of the world, was precipitated by the enormous power they obtained by the acquisition of so much property, albeit this was held in common. The title 'military order' is still used, however, of certain lay groupings, such as the Order of the Garter, the Order of the Golden Fleece, the Order of Christ*.

Mill Hill

A seminary in North London, for the training of missionaries of the Society of St. Joseph, founded by Cardinal Vaughan before he was made a bishop. Vaughan toured South America in 1863–65 to raise funds for the college, which was opened in 1866, the missionaries being at first intended for work among the coloured people of the U.S. More recently, other colleges have been opened and the missionaries' work is chiefly in Africa and the Pacific.

Minchen

An obsolete word for nun, surviving in some place-names, such as Minchinhampton—the Manor of Hampton in Gloucestershire was given by William the Conqueror to the community of the *Abbaye des Dames* in Normandy. Mincing *(Minchen)* Lane in the City had its name from a Benedictine convent in Bishopsgate.

Minims

A Mendicant Order, the Minim Hermits of St. Francesco di Paolo (the founder) originated in 1436, based on the Rule of St. Francis and called Minims to show their lowliness, *minimus* ranking lower even than *minor* of the Friars Minor. Their life is in contemplation, parish work, preaching and teaching and is very penitential, involving a fourth vow, of abstinence from flesh-meat.

Minorites

A former name for the Friars Minor; the nuns, being called correspondingly Minoresses, have left their name in the City: the Minories, a street in which they had a convent.

Miraculous Medal

The epithet here seems to apply rather to the supernatural circumstances which caused the medal to be struck than to any claims consequent upon its use. The design—an oval medal bearing on the obverse the Blessed Virgin standing on a globe of the world with rays of light coming from her hands and surrounded with the inscription, 'O Mary conceived without sin, pray for us who have recourse to thee!' and on the reverse, a cross, the letter M, and two hearts—is said to have been revealed to St. Catherine Labouré, who had three visions of Our Lady in 1830.

Missa de Angelis

(Lat., Mass of the Angels.) Besides its strict liturgical meaning—the votive Mass of the Angels— this is the title used popularly for Mass No. VIII in the *Liber Usualis*;* it has been very widely used, some say because it has so little of true Gregorian character and thus appeals easily to the 'modern' ear; the bulk of the music is of post-mediaeval origin, apart from the Sanctus.

Missa Papae Marcelli

(Lat., Mass of Pope Marcellus.) The most renowned of polyphonic Masses, which was composed for six voices by Palestrina (in 1565) and edited for four.

Missal

The liturgical book used for the celebration of Mass, containing Masses in all their variety, as well as directives, calendars, prayers and, in certain cases, blessings. The Roman Missal, revised after the Second Vatican Council, contains the General Calendar of the Roman Church, the Proper of the Saints, the Order of Mass, Masses of the Saints, Ritual Masses, Occasional Masses and Prayers, Votive Masses, Masses and Prayers for the Dead; all the Readings (greatly multiplied by being set now in a three-year cycle) have been transferred to another volume, the Lectionary*.

Mission, Congregation of Priests of the

See Lazarists.

Missions, Pious Society of

See Society of the Catholic Apostolate.

Mit Brennender Sorge

(Ger., with burning anxiety.) An Encyclical of Pius XI which, having been smuggled into Germany, was read from all Catholic pulpits on Palm Sunday (Mar. 21st) 1937. In it, the Pope denounced Adolf Hitler for breaking the Concordat* made with him in 1933—Pius had hoped for a bulwark against Communism—unequivocally proclaimed Nazism to be unchristian and attacked the theory of a German National Church, the omission of the Old Testament from educational programmes and other German-Christian* ideas which found favour with the Nazi regime.

Mitre

(Gk. μιτρα, turban.) The liturgical headgear of a bishop of the Latin rite; it originated in the East as a low loose cap of soft material and was later formalised into a structure of two stiff pieces irregularly pentagonal in shape bound at the base with a headband and with soft material attached at the top, so that the whole can be collapsed flat; at the back two fringed lappets *(infulae*)* hang down behind the wearer's ears. Other prelates besides bishops have been granted the right to wear the mitre: cardinals, certain abbots and protonotaries apostolic, and the canons of certain cathedrals.

Mixed Religion

The situation in which one of the two persons intending marriage is a Catholic and the other baptised but not Catholic; this prohibiting* impediment is frequently dispensed by the bishop, with proper safeguards.
See Difference of Worship.

Modernism

Some Catholic writers of the later 19th cent. published views about the Scriptures and about dogma expressing dissatisfaction with the current intellectual condition of religious thought; they were justifiably impatient with many Catholic Biblical scholars who still tried to explain away or 'harmonise' what are in fact human flaws in the sacred writers (in this, the Modernists, as they came to be called, drew encouragement from some rather unclear phrases in Leo X's encyclical on Biblical studies, *Providentissinus Deus);* they reacted against the 'intellectualism' of Scholastic philosophy, preferring a pragmatic and practical approach, so as to find the essence of Christianity in life rather than in creeds or formulae; and this led to their grand principle that what mattered was the teleology, the meaning of the historic process of religion as found in its historic process and fulfilment, rather than in its origins. Thus, they claimed, faith was not an intellectual assent to truths revealed by God but the experience of man's beliefs about God; the importance of the Church lay in its existence and its function in the world, not in its foundation by Jesus (they claimed, indeed, that once the eschatological Kingdom which was the pivot of his message failed to materialise, the disciples re-interpreted his message and themselves founded the Church, the value of this Church consisting in its world-wide influence in bringing men into touch with supernatural reality and saving their souls). Jesus likewise revealed no truths about God, but gave humanity religious symbols so powerful that they will inspire all future ages. His Resurrection, similarly, was not a physical event, but 'the divine personality of Jesus cannot die'—which is the true significance of 'Resurrection', and has had such an impact on man's intuitive sense of the divine that the Resurrection, though not accepted as fact, must henceforth be part of the religious man's equipment. In 1907, Pius X condemned the movement in the decree *Lamentabili* and the encyclical *Pascendi*, and in 1910, was persuaded to prescribe, in a *motu proprio* Sacrorum Antistitum,* that all seminary teachers and all clerics before ordination take an oath against Modernism (which had been called a 'compendium of all heresies') and in support of *Lamentabili* and *Pascendi.* There has been of recent years, a recrudescence of a certain 'modernist' mentality, with a fashion of denying the Resurrection of Christ as a historical, physical event and of speaking instead of the 'resurrection experience' of the Apostles, and a tendency to use terms like 'transignification' and 'transfinalisation' in place of *'Transubstantiation'* (see Real Presence).

Monastery

Strictly a house of men or women living the monastic life, the word is loosely used also to mean on the one hand, a house of men in monastic life and on the other a house of male religious, monastic or not. The Latin *monasterium* was also anglicised into the form 'minster', as in York Minster, Westminster, etc. See convent.

Moniales

(Lat., originally meaning *solitaries,* and derived from the Gk. root that gives us *monk* and *monastery).* This is the canonical word for nuns proper, viz those with solemn vows; according to Canon Law, other religious are properly known as 'sisters'.

Monita Secreta

(Lat., secret orders.) There was published, in 1612, a document of this title, containing instructions from Claudio Aquaviva, then General of the Jesuits, instructing all superiors of houses to use every possible means, honest and other, to increase the wealth and power of the Society of Jesus. No scholar careful of his reputation will now lend credence to this fantasy, as it turns out to be written by one Zahorowski, who had been dismissed from the Society.

Monk

Correctly used only of male religious whose way of life essentially includes 'stability', i.e. attachment to one community and its house, and whose occupation is basically prayer; as distinguished from other, usually later, foundations whose members can transfer from one community to another in pursuit of their preaching, pastoral or other apostolic work. There is, unfortunately, no equivalent in English for 'monk' to distinguish the woman religious of that type from her sister in the 'active' religious life, unless we fall back on the phrase 'enclosed nun'.

Monks of Union

A Benedictine community set up at the request of Pope Pius XI in 1924 to work for reunion with the Russian and other dissident Slavonic churches. Since 1939, there has been at Chevetogne, Belgium, a house with two groups, one of Latin rite, one of Byzantine; the monks are of several nationalities and have adapted the Rule of St. Benedict to their life and work.

Monogram, the Sacred

See I.H.S.

Monophysites

(Gk., believers in one nature.) Those heretics led by Eutyches (+454), who held that in Christ there is only one nature, the divine, thus denying the Incarnation in its orthodox understanding. Monophysitism was condemned by the Council of Chalcedon* (451) and such Eastern Churches as still retain the attribute of Monophysite appear to do so rather out of national or sectarian feeling than from theological conviction, since they all later repudiated the doctrines of Eutyches.

Monothelitism

This heresy, the teaching that in the person of Christ there is but one will, the divine, arose in the 7th cent., out of the efforts of the Emperor Heraclius to reconcile the Monophysites*. The monarch, anxious to reunite the heretics with the orthodox Christians for the defence of the eastern marches of the Empire against Persian and Muslim incursions, brought them to conferences in 624, which produced the formula, accepted by both parties, that in the Lord there were two natures but only one 'mode of activity (ενεργεια)'. The formula, once approved, was passed to Sergius, Patriarch of Constantinople, who, finding support for it in the writings of St. Cyril of Alexandria*, used it to reconcile the heretics, until he was challenged by Sophronius of Jerusalem. Receiving, on his appeal to Rome, Honorius'* use of the phrase 'one will', he got this widely published in the Eastern Church, which signified its acceptance in two Councils held at Constantinople in 638 and 639. However, the belief in the one will was vigorously condemned by Honorius' successors in the Papacy, by several lesser councils and finally by the Third Council of Constantinople* (680–681), which confirmed the decision of a Roman Synod of 679.

Monstrance

(Lat. *monstro,* I show.) A vessel of precious metal so constructed that the Host* placed within it is visible for the adoration of the faithful at Benediction* of the Blessed Sacrament and during processions; there is a centre, usually a metal cylinder lying horizontal, with glass at either end, into which the Sacrament can be inserted, the rest of the metal-work being frequently shaped in a design of rays from the centre, or as a Gothic facade; there is a broad foot on which the monstrance can be set to stand.

Montanism

A schism originating in the 2nd cent. with Montanus, who claimed the gift of prophecy and direct inspiration from the Holy Spirit. He proclaimed the Second Coming as imminent, forbade the faithful to flee from persecution and denied second marriages to the widowed. The dogmatic error into which Montanists fell was to deny the Church's power of forgiving sins. The sect endured for about 200 years, its only famous member being Tertullian, who was converted first to Christianity and then to Montanism.

Monte Cassino

The headquarters and most renowned house of the Benedictine Order. It stands between Rome and Naples and was founded by St Benedict in 529 or thereabouts. It houses the remains of the Saint and was declared a national monument by the Italian government in 1866. It has a tenacious history of re-building, after destruction by the Lombards c.585, by the Saracens in 884, by the Normans in 1046, and the Americans in 1944.

Montfort Fathers

(Company of Mary.) A congregation founded by St. Louis Grignion de Montfort in 1705 for retreats and missions overseas, now spread to Canada, U.S., England and elsewhere, with missions in Iceland and some African countries.

Morisco

The term used in Spain to describe a Moorish convert to the Faith. Many of the Moriscos later lapsed and suffered at the hands of the Inquisition.*

Morning Star

An epithet for the Blessed Virgin Mary, found in the Litany of Loreto; its first use is attributed both to St. Peter Damian (1007–72) and to St. Simon Stock (c. 1165–1265).

Morse

(Lat. *morsus,* bite, catch.) The clasp of a cope or the ornament, usually of metal and sometimes jewelled, attached thereto.

Mortalium Animos

An encyclical of Pius XI in 1928 on the subject of Christian reunion; the Pope warns therein those whom he considers may be contemplating rash or ill-considered methods of achieving this desired end, naming some organisations to which Catholics must not belong, and advocating mutual charity, prayer and understanding.

Mortification

The Church has traditionally stressed the place of the subduing of flesh and spirit, and has used, e.g. special seasons of the year and vigils of feast-days to encourage the faithful in these practices, the purpose of which is self-discipline in the service of virtue and the expiation of sins. Certain ascetical practices are likewise written into the rules of the religious orders.

Most Reverend

The title accorded to archbishops, and, in Ireland, to bishops. It forms part of the official address of a Cardinal* and of certain Roman prelates, and is used of some religious, e.g. the Abbot Primate of the Benedictines,* the Master General of the Dominicans*, the Custodian of the Holy Land, the Prior General of the Servites*.

Mother of God

The Blessed Virgin was thus described very early by the Greek Fathers* (see Theotokos), by Origen (185–254) and perhaps by St. Hippolytus (c.170–c.236). Its widespread and popular use was attacked in 429 by Nestorius* as inconsistent with the Christ's full humanity; the term 'Mother of Christ' was the most he would allow. The Council of Ephesus* two years later affirmed the title Theotokos, and this orthodoxy, confirmed by the Council of Chalcedon in 451, continued to be a mark of the Catholic sections of Christianity, the 16th-century Reformers shying away from the phrase.

Mothering Sunday

See Mid-Lent Sunday.

Mottoes

The Church of Rome almost from her beginning found herself in possession of that ideal instrument for mottoes, *marble's language, Latin, pure, discreet*, from which Popes, bishops, religious orders and other institutions and individuals have chosen words or phrases to identify themselves and their spirit or purpose; some of the more renowned of these are *Pax* (Peace—Order of St Benedict*), *Stat Crux dum volvitur Orbis* (The Cross stands fast in a changing world—Carthusians*), *Deus meus et omnia* (My God and my all—Franciscans) *Veritas* (Truth—Order of Preachers*), *Ad Majorem Dei Gloriam* (To the greater glory of God—Jesuits*).

Motu Proprio

(Lat., on his own initiative.) The official description of a letter or rescript sent out by a Pope when he wishes to emphasise his own part in deciding to write and in drawing up the document, which also bears his personal signature.

Mount Melleray

A Cistercian* abbey founded in 1832 at Cappoquin, Co Waterford, Ireland, from the abbey of Mellaraie, Brittany. Besides farming, the monks have a school for boys. There have been foundations from this abbey:– Mount St. Bernard* in Leicestershire, one at Roscrea and one in Iowa, U.S.A.

Mount St Bernard

A monastery of Cistercians established in Leicestershire in 1835, the first community consisting of monks from Melleraie in Brittany and Mount Melleray* in Ireland. It was made an abbey in 1848.

Mozzetta

(It., abbreviated.) The short cape, reaching to the elbow, buttoned in front and having a non-functional hood behind, which as a symbol of jurisdiction, is worn over the rochet by cardinals, by a bishop in his diocese, an abbot in his abbey and, as a privilege, by certain Roman prelates and others (e.g. canons in England). The Pope's mozzetta is red, as is the cardinal's, the bishop's or other prelate's is purple or coloured according to his religious habit.

Munificentissimus Deus

See Pius XII, Pope.

Mystical Interpretation

(of Scripture.) The method of interpreting Scripture which makes a person, event or thing represent, in God's intention, some later person, event or thing, e.g. Christ's use of Jonah (Mt.12:40–41), Paul's reference to Sarah and Hagar (Gal.4:22ff) and the author's use of Melchizedek (Heb.7:1–3); sometimes also known as the *Allegorical* interpretation, according to Paul's own words in Gal.4:24.

Mystical Rose

A title of Our Lady in the Litany of Loreto*, deriving presumably from the Biblical references to the rose (Sg.2:1, Is.35:1, Si.24:18, 39:17).

Mystici Corporis Christi

An encyclical* of Pope Pius XII issued in
1943; its theme is the Church as the
Mystical Body of Christ—as the title indicates—and the union of the faithful in
and with Our Lord as head and Saviour;
the document refutes certain contemporary errors, exhorts the Church's
members to love her as Christ does, and
appeals to non-Catholics and to political
rulers.

Mysticism

The knowledge of God can be obtained
immediately in this life by personal
religious experience which is not achieved
by effort but granted by His gift. There is
an enormous literature on the subject,
much of it dealing with non-Christian
mysticism; it is worth noting that Christian mystics differ on two main heads
from those of other faiths: in contrast to
the concepts of an impersonal, cosmic
Reality with its corollary of the soul's being absorbed into the All, Christians teach
that the underlying Reality transcends the
cosmos as it does the individual soul, and
that the mystical union—as likewise the
future Beatific vision—is an activity of
love and will in which the creature remains permanently distinct from the
Godhead, unabsorbed and unique. Of
late, there has been an efflorescence of so-
called Eastern cults and of others of native
Western origin, some identified with the
search for peace and love, some with
political affiliations, some with the setting
up of an 'alternative society', some plainly
sinister, some catering clearly for the less
intelligent, some dedicated to making
money, some with a seemingly hypnotic
influence over their members, some
demanding total and permanent obedience
to a *guru*; many of these are graced with
the name of 'mysticism'. It is necessary to
bear in mind that the result of true
mystical union, in the Christian soul or in
any other, will be an increase in charity,
humility and all the other expected virtues, and that mysticism is not given as a
therapy or a freak-out or a form of self-
aggrandisement, but for the glory of God.

Nails, the Holy

It was said that with the True Cross of Christ, St. Helena* also found the nails with which he had been crucified. Many relics are claimed for these, including those in the Iron Crown of Lombardy at Monza and at the church of Santa Croce in Rome, but there is no accepted authenticity.

Nantes, Edict of

The French Wars of Religion were concluded by an Edict of Henri* IV signed at Nantes in 1598, granting the Huguenots* freedom of religious practice, in private everywhere, in public in 200 towns (some fortified) of which they were given complete control, and in 3,000 domains belonging to the nobility; special departments were set up to try their cases in the courts, all public offices were open to them, and a State subsidy was instituted for the support of their clergy and their troops: in effect, there was established a state within the Catholic state. Later, however, less moderate counsels prevailed, and first Cardinal Richelieu and then Louis XIV, obsessed with national unity and using the hypocritical excuse of the persecution of Catholics in England, began to nibble away at the provisions of the Edict, until the King, in 1685, nagged by Mme de Maintenon and Père La Chaise, revoked it altogether. Profession of the Reformed Religion was now an offence against the law, and the law was enforced with violence and much cruelty, thousands of those who escaped it fleeing to England and Holland. The Pope, Innocent XI, protested to Louis, but in the prevailing atmosphere of Gallicanism* he was ignored.

Nativity

In some martyrologies and other such records, the word *nativity* is used to describe the day on which a saint died, i.e. the day on which he was born to the everlasting life with God.

Nazarene

The name, extended from its original application to Jesus in the N.T., was formerly used by some Jews and Moslems as a deogatory term for 'Christian'.

Nestorian Monument

(Sigan-Fu Stone.) A stone slab was discovered by Jesuit missionaries in 1625 at Sigan-Fu (or Hsi-ngan-fu, or Sian-Fu) in central China, which bears witness to the early existence of Christianity in that land. The monument, roughly two metres high and one in width, is dated 'the second year of the period of Kien-Chung', which is 781 A.D.; it describes a flourishing contemporary church and claims to have been set up by 'King-Tsing, priest of the Syrian* Church' in that year, to celebrate the arrival 146 years earlier of the 'Illustrious Religion', which it goes on to describe. The missionary of the year 635 is named as Olopan; he enjoyed the royal patronage and privileges (in the Tang dynasty), bearing the titles 'Guardian of the Empire' and 'Lord of the Great Law'. A further section of the stone gives a history of local Christianity from Olopan to the reign of Tih-Tsung (780–3). Besides these inscriptions in Chinese, there are some additions in Syriac. It goes almost without saying that the Jesuits were at first accused of inventing the stone or of forging the inscriptions, but it has long admitted to be a genuine testimony to the striking missionary activity of the Nestorian Church.

Nestorianism

The heretical teaching of Nestorius, Bishop of Constantinople (428–431) to the effect that in Christ there are two persons, one divine, one human; the latter, Jesus born of Mary, was only the dwelling-place of the Word; he, not the Word, was her son; he, not the Word, died on the cross. Nestorius came to prominence by attacking the use—already long established among Christians—of the term *theotokos**, which was vindicated by the Council of

Ephesus* (431). Those bishops who refused the Canons of the Council and adhered to the deposed and excommunicated Nestorius formed themselves into a separate church, based mainly in Persia, where the Christian community claimed direct continuity with the Apostles. The sect flourished, enduring several persecutions and sending missionaries into Arab countries, India and China. Their Patriarch-Catholicos holds hereditary office which passes from uncle to nephew; they suffered much in the early 20th cent. and dispersed to Syria (they are also known as *Syrians*), Iraq and the U.S. Some of them it is said, have abandoned their heretical stance as a result of the work of Anglicans among them.
See Assyrian Christians.

New Fire, Blessing of the

The first ceremony of the Easter Vigil Service, the blessing of the fire, takes place at the porch of the church, in which all lights have been put out. The fire, which has been kindled outside the building, is blessed by the celebrant and immediately the Paschal Candle is lit from it; the fire, like the Candle, is taken as a symbol of the glory of God lighting the world through his Son and of the purifying of minds.

Newman, John Henry Cardinal

(1801-1890.) The leading spirit of the Oxford* Movement, a thrust towards reform within the Church of England, he preached in the University church St. Mary's, of which he was vicar, a series of sermons whose influence, when published in the 1830's as *Parochial and Plain Sermons*, extended powerfully to the whole country. His deep and accurate scholarship—which was applied first to the study of the Fathers*—and his unrelenting search for truth, led him through the early stages of his anti-popery to the thesis of the *Via Media**, viz. that the Church of England occupied the place of the Fathers of old and was mid-way between the contemporary stances of Rome and of the Reformed Churches. Then, the publication of Tract* 90 (1841) in which he held that the Thirty-Nine Articles were to be interpreted as condemning, not the ancient Catholic doctrines of the Church but only the mediaeval Roman corruptions of them, roused a tempest of condemnation and caused him to put to silence by the Bishop of Oxford. In his subsequent retirement to semi-monastic life at Littlemore just outside the city, the doubts which had nagged him since 1839 brought him to the resignation of his living at St. Mary's in 1843, a few days before preaching the famous sermon at Littlemore on 'The Parting of Friends'. In 1845, he entered the Roman Catholic Church and published his *Essay on the Development* of Christian Doctrine*. Then, ordained in Rome, he returned and established the Oratorians* in Birmingham; an estrangement took place with Manning, who had followed him into the Church, Newman being blamed for a disparaging review of a book of Manning's in a Catholic review, *The Rambler*. In 1864, he recovered a great deal of his popularity with the English public with the *Apologia Pro Vita Sua**, his response to a peevish attack by Charles Kingsley; this was followed by the *Dream of Gerontius** and, in 1870, by the *Grammar of Assent,* a profound and original discussion of faith and religious certitude. His rectorship of the Catholic University of Dublin (1854-1858) was abandoned through lack of trust and support, though his *Idea of a University* (1852) is unsurpassed as an exposition of Catholic education. An invitation by Cardinal Wiseman to lead a team in the revision of the Bible was withdrawn for unworthy reasons; the Fellowship of Trinity, which he so ardently coveted on his merits in his earlier years, was offered as an honour to the revered sage of 78; and two years later, he was made cardinal, though his reaction to the offer of the red hat was so ambiguously presented—by Manning—as to puzzle the public. So much of his endeavour in and for the Catholic Church having come to nothing in his own day, Newman's genius has since been recognised both in and outside the Church, as that of one of the foremost of modern Christian thinkers, descended more directly from the Fathers than from the Scholastics, especially in matters of faith, and for his brilliant treatment of the concept of development.

Newport and Menevia

This See was erected in 1850, and in 1895 was divided into the diocese of Newport and the Vicariate apostolic* of Wales; the latter of these became, in 1898, the diocese of Menevia and the former was made the archdiocese of Cardiff in 1916. During its existence, the diocese of Newport had Belmont Priory* as its pro-Cathedral*, the chapter of canons being monks of that community.

New Style
Often simple N.S., to denote that a date is reckoned according to the Gregorian* Calendar.

Nicaea, First Council of
(First Oecumenical.) Summoned by Constantine the Great, who sought the unity of the Church in the Arian* controversy, the bishops, traditionally 318 in number, the only Western bishops among them being Hosius of Cordova, who presided, and those of Carthage, Milan, Dijon and two of unknown provenance, together with two priest-legates of the Pope, St. Sylvester I, met at Nicaea (Iznik near Ankara) in 325 A.D. They condemned Arianism, anathematizing 'those who say that there was a time when the Son was not, and that he was not before he was begotten, and that he was made out of nothing; or who assert that he is of other essence or substance than the Father or that he was created or that he is alterable or subject to change.' The Creed which grew out of their formulation contained the word Homoousion. They also fixed the reckoning of Easter.

Nicaea, Second Council of
(Seventh Oecumenical.) In 786, the Empress Irene summoned a Council, on the urging of the Patriarch Tarasius of Constantinople, who was anxious to clear up the controversy raging about Iconoclasm*. Pope Hadrian I agreed to send delegates on condition that an earlier Synod, of Iconoclast bishops, at Hiera should be condemned. The Council, assembling at Constantinople, was straight away broken up by Iconoclast troops and did not meet again until the following year, this time at Nicaea. The Fathers of the Council accepted the doctrine of the veneration of images set out by the Pope in his letter to Irene, and emphasised the distinction between latria*, the absolute honour to be given to God alone, and the relative respect afforded to images.

Nicene Creed
The first Creed to bear this name is the formula issued by the Council of Nicaea in 325, in defence of the orthodox faith against the Arians* and containing the word Homoousios. It is shorter than many subsequent creeds: it ends at the phrase 'and in the Holy Spirit', but there are then added four anathemas* against Arianism. More popularly, the title 'Nicene' is applied to the catalogue also referred to as the Niceno-Constantinopolitan Creed, a form of the previous document modified and expanded at the First Council of Constantinople* (Second Oecumenical) almost to its present form, which is in common use ever since all over the Western Church in the Mass, and in the Eastern as a profession of faith at Baptism. See Filioque.

Nicholas, St.
Bishop of Myra in Lycia, Nicholas has achieved the distinction of becoming one of the most popular saints in both Eastern and Western Churches without leaving any verifiable fact about his life and work apart from his ecclesiastical rank and his location. First definitely mentioned in the dedication of a church built by Justinian (who died in 565) to Ss. Priscus and Nicholas, he is said to have suffered imprisonment under Diocletian and, after his release, to have attended—most improbably—the Council of Nicaea*. His popularity in the West was a consequence of a claim by the people of Bari in S. Italy to have got possession of his body in 1087. His Symbols are three bags of gold, which he is supposed to have given to three girls to save their virtue, and three children standing in a tub, who have been explained in various ways; he is the patron of sailors, (with his churches built on coasts as landmarks), of Russia, and of children (now americanised into Santa Claus).

Nicodemus, Acts of
See Acts of Pilate

Nihil Obstat
(Lat. nihil obstat[quominus imprimatur] nothing hinders [it] from being printed.) The formula used by the Censor of Books—appointed by the Bishop—to say he finds nothing in the work contrary to faith or good morality.
See Imprimatur and Imprimi Potest

Nimbus

See Halo

Nine Choirs of Angels

See Angel

Nine Fridays

Part of the Devotion to the Sacred Heart*; one of the promises said to have been made by Jesus to St. Margaret Mary was that to those who received Holy Communion on the first Friday of nine consecutive months, he would grant 'the grace of full repentance', that 'they would not die under his displeasure' nor 'without receiving the sacraments.' The devotion was fostered as being a means of recommending more frequent Communion to those who contented themselves with the necessary single reception in the year; now its usefulness in this particular sphere has diminished since the habit of frequent reception of the Blessed Sacrament has become common.

Norbertines

The Premonstratensian* Canons, founded by St. Norbert.

Nullity

A marriage cannot be 'nullified' in spite of journalistic usage, all the Church can do is to examine a supposed marriage and, finding it good, declare so; finding there never was a true marriage, pronounce a null contract. The Church merely declares what she finds—as will civil law in similar circumstances: it is not the Church that makes a marriage null, but the lack of certain elements essential to the contract. Thus, the law of any civilised country will describe as null a 'marriage' contracted between two ten-year-old children. From the nature of marriage, it is evident that certain defects will render the contract invalid; e.g. the persons contracting must be physically able to perform the sexual act, thus impotence is an impediment; they must understand, at least in a general way, what they are doing in making this contract; they must be free, both in the sense of not being under compulsion ('Go through with the ceremony or you die!') and in the sense of not being under legal disability (a man who has a living wife may not, in English law any more than in Canon Law, contract marriage), and such an attempted marriage would be declared null (certain impediments can be dispensed, being not of their nature destructive of the essence of marriage—thus the Church will allow a Catholic, for good reasons, to marry a person of another Christian persuasion or a non-Christian). Another impediment can be the 'lack of form': both Church and State insist on a certain form for a valid marriage; and the Church's present legislation is that for valid matrimony, the contract must be attested by the couple before a properly appointed representative of the Church (usually a parish priest or assistant priest or deacon, but sometimes, with permission, a non-Catholic minister or a layperson). A mistake of one partner about the identity of the other invalidates the contract, but not a mistake about some quality or possession, unless this is explicitly laid down as a condition; one fears that Jacob's marriage to Leah (Gen.29:23) would not be upheld in Canon Law. Conditions regarding the future which are against the nature of marriage ('I will marry you for a year', 'I will marry you on the understanding that if things get too difficult we will divorce') invalidate the contract; others, e.g. 'I will marry you, provided you become a Catholic within six months of marrying', would suspend the marriage until the condition was fulfilled; whereas a definite condition barring normal sexual intercourse permantly in favour of continuous contraception could completely invalidate the marriage. A sacramental marriage (that is, a marriage between two baptised persons) which is consumated is not to be declared null nor dissolved, since it is taken by the Church to be 'What God has joined together' (Mt.19:6). On the other hand, in the case of non-sacramental marriage, besides the Pauline Privilege described in 1 Cor 7:12–17, there is a similar release, called the Petrine Privilege, whereby the Pope may, for sufficient reasons, dissolve a marriage contracted between a Catholic or other baptised person and unbaptised partner, the grounds of such dispensation being found, as in the Pauline privilege, 'in favour of the Faith.' One problem now exercising many theologians is the question of the evidently large number of persons who enter into matrimony without a true understanding of its nature, particularly in regard to permanence; such error or ignorance is, of course, very rarely declared, but it is held by many to be sufficient at least to bring into doubt the validity of the contract which it informs. Such ignorance and confusion are certainly deepened in the minds especially of the young by the effects of the worlds of entertainment and of advertising.

Number of the Beast

The number 666, or, in some MSS 616, of Rev.13:18. Since in both Gk. and Hebrew, each letter of the alphabet represents also a figure, mystical significances have from early times been read into digits and groups of digits. The most probable intended meaning of the figure in Rev. is *Nero,* as the sum in Hebrew letters adds up to 666 (using the form *Neron,* the Gk. spelling of the name) or to 616 (using *Nero*). It was considered additionally appropriate to read 666 for the 'man of sin' (II Thess.2:3—in the J.B., 'the Rebel'), as here each digit is one short of the perfect number seven. The next notable candidate was Mohammed; of recent centuries much ingenuity has been lavished on the interpretation of the number, with entertaining identifications such as Martin Luther, Napoleon and, recurrently, the Pope.

Nun

(Late Lat. *nonna,* f. of *nonnus,* old man.) Members of religious orders or congregations of women are, in Canon Law, either *moniales,* i.e. those in institutes of solemn vows, or *sorores* (sisters) in simple vows, the former being regarded as nuns in the strict canonical sense of the word.
See Contemplative Life, Active Life.

Nuncio

(Lat. *nuntius,* messenger.) A Papal or Apostolic Nuncio is an ambassador of the Holy See to a foreign court as permanent diplomatic representative of the Pope and accredited to the government of that foreign country—in which he also cares for the welfare of the Church.
See Delegate.

Nunnery

The term has dropped out of Catholic usage since the Reformation, having acquired a slightly derogatory flavour, and been replaced by *convent**.

O Salutaris (Hostia)

(Lat., O Saving Victim.) The final section, named from its opening words and consisting of two stanzas, of the hymn *Verbum Supernum*, written for Lauds of the Feast of *Corpus Christi** by St. Thomas Aquinas*. The *O Salutaris* became attached to the service of Benediction of the Blessed Sacrament, being traditionally sung as the tabernacle was opened.

Oates, Titus

One of the more colourful, if unsavoury, characters of 17th cent. England, Titus Oates, son of an Anabaptist preacher (with whom he conspired in false oaths against a vicar whose living he coveted), attained the distinction of a place in T. Seccombe's *Lives of Twelve Bad Men* (1894). His chief claim to celebrity was the Popish Plot, the offspring of his vindictive imagination, with his friend Tonge as obstetrician; the Catholics, he averred, were plotting to assassinate Charles II and replace him with the Papist Duke of York. In the public panic that ensued, there were executed, between Aug. 1678 and July 1681, 16 priests and laymen charged with complicity, and eight charged with priesthood; among the victims were Oliver Plunkett, Archbishop of Armagh, and Lord Stafford. It is a mark of the extremely jumpy anti-Catholic feeling of the times that Oates, expelled from both Caius and St. John's at Cambridge and from the English College at Valladolid—whither he went after joining the Navy to escape the consequences of blatant perjury—should find not only public credence but the encouragement of the Speaker of the House, who bade the traitorous witness, entangled in lies once more, 'Take heart, Master Oates, carry on and say boldly what remains: we are sitting here not merely to hear you but to believe you as well.' The only parallel to the man's lunatic wickedness is the short-sightedness of those who gave him Holy Orders in the Church of England and those who received him later into the Catholic Church. In his youth, Titus made the prophetic remark that 'poverty left him only the alternative of becoming a Jesuit or a Judas': he did not become a Jesuit. Convicted of perjury in 1685, he was sent to prison for a life sentence but released with a pardon from William III.

Obedientiary

A name, now very little used, for certain permanent administrators in a monastery, e.g. cellarer, bursar or procurator, novicemaster, guest-master, infirmarian, cantor or precentor, secretary, master of laybrothers, sacristan; these are appointed by the superior.

Oblate

i) a member of certain religious congregations, e.g. Oblates of St. Charles*, which so name themselves from the idea of the offering of the members.
ii) a lay person who, without taking vows, wishes to be associated with the work and merits of a religious order or congregation and for whom conditions are arranged for sharing in the life of prayer and works of the order; in some cases, such a person will live in a house of the Order.

Oblates of St. Charles

A society of diocesan priests who live in common without vows and put themselves at the disposal of their bishop for any work he may require; founded in 1578 by Don G.M. Martinelli in association with St. Charles Borromeo, to help raise the standard of the secular clergy; the English branch was established by Wiseman* and Manning*.

Obreption

(Lat. *obrepo*, I deceive.) In Canon Law, obtaining, or the attempt to obtain, a papal rescript or dispensation by telling a lie.

Occult

The term is used in Canon Law to describe facts or events for which evidence cannot be produced in legal process, and for which special arrangements are made.

Octave of Prayer for Christian Unity

From the Feast of St. Peter's Chair at Rome (Jan 18th) to the Conversion of St. Paul (Jan 25th) inclusive, prayer is offered by many, of Roman, Orthodox and most other Christian traditions, for the coming together of all Christians, and of all men, in the unity of Christ. The custom was initiated by Paul James Francis Watson of New York, an Anglican religious, who ended his days a Catholic priest.

Oecumenical

(Gk. 'οικουμενη, the inhabited world.) Belonging to, or representing the entire world, or the whole Church; used officially of a General Council.

Oecumenical Patriarch

This title assumed in the 6th cent. by the Patriarch of Constantinople, John the Faster, is still used by his successors. The title has never been clearly defined, but has been regarded in the West as a symbol of rejection of the central authority of Rome.
See Servus Servorum Dei.

Office, Divine

See Divine Office.

Oil of Catechumens

On Maundy Thursday, the bishop blesses olive oil, to be used in the consecration of altars, the coronation of sovereigns, the ordination of priests and of baptisms. The oil symbolises the royal and priestly power of Christ.

Oil of Chrism

See Chrism.

Oil of the Sick

This is olive oil blessed by the bishop on Maundy Thursday and used in the Sacrament of the Sick.
See also Holy Oils.

Old Brotherhood of the Secular Clergy

See Old Chapter.

Old Chapter

A chapter of 24 priests set up on the initiative of William Bishop, first Vicar Apostolic* of England, there being at that time (1623) no organised ecclesiastical government for the Church in this country. Its administration became redundant in 1688 with the establishment of four vicariates (later increased to eight: London, Western, Eastern, Central, Welsh, Lancashire, Yorkshire, Northern, themselves becoming obsolete on the restoration of the hierarchy in 1850); however, the Chapter remained, and remains. Its members, at their death or ordination to the episcopate, are replaced by careful choice and invitation. The chapter changed its name in 1850 to the *Old Brotherhood of the Secular Clergy* and continues as a living link with the Church's time of suffering in England, to commemorate which the members at their twice-yearly meeting pass round, after dinner, the snuff-box used by Cardinal Pole*. The Brotherhood, a philanthropic society, sturdily retains the administration of its own funds, which it distributes charitably, e.g. for bursaries and towards the upkeep of the English College in Rome.

Old Hall

St. Edmund's College, Old Hall Green, Ware, Herts, directly descended from the English College, Douay*: a boys' school founded by Challoner* in 1749 at Standon Lordship moved to Ware in 1769 and in 1793 amalgamated with certain students from Douay, and became the seminary of the Archdiocese of Westminster and a boys' school. The seminary has now moved to Chelsea and St Edmund's is now only a school.

Old Testament Saints

There is not in the Roman Rite anything so comprehensive as the Eastern Rite festival of the *Just Ones of the Old Testament;* but there are, besides the many feasts of Our Lady, commemorations of her parents, named by tradition Joachim and Anne, of St. John the Baptist, of Abraham, Moses, David, Jeremiah (the Carmelites add feast-days of Elijah and Elisha), of Abel, Melchizedek and some other male O.T. characters; and in the Nuptial Blessing, Rachel, Rebecca and Sarah are held up as models to the bride.

Ombrellino

The small canopy, unbrella-like in structure and usually of silk, carried by one person, and used in moving the Blessed Sacrament informally from place to place, i.e. not in procession.

Ontological Argument

The basis for this *a priori* argument for the existence of God, first used by St. Anselm*, is that the idea of God necessarily involves the actual existence of God; by the notion of God, said Anselm, we mean that than which nothing greater can be conceived—*id quo nihil majus cogitari possit*—then, by supposing He did not actually exist, we should fall into a contradiction because we could then immediately conceive of a greater Being, i.e. one to whom existence was added. The argument was criticised by Thomas Aquinas* and by Kant, on the ground that existence is not a predicate, but was defended by Descartes and some more recent thinkers.

Opus Anglicanum

The style of embroidery practised by English needlewomen in the Middle Ages, which became universally renowned and much sought after. As examples of this work, which in many cases took two or three generations to complete, there are copes, chasubles and other pieces in museums in various cities, including the famous Syon Cope in the South Kensington Museum, London.

Opus Dei

i) (Lat., the work of God.) St. Benedict's* name for the task of reciting the Divine Office, to which, he said in his Rule, his monks should prefer nothing in the world.

ii) The Sacerdotal Society of the Holy Cross (Opus Dei) or simply *Opus Dei*, is an association of laypeople and secular priests, each member being dedicated to the spreading of the doctrine of Christ, by word and example, in and through his or her own profession or job. The founder, Mgr. Josemaria Escrivá de Balaguer, set up two sections, the mens' in 1928 and the womens' two years later, each section remaining separate in government and specific apostolate, though retaining the same aims and spirit. First approved by the Holy See in 1943, *Opus Dei* is international and has a number of educational establishments, chiefly student residences and conference centres.

Orate Fratres

The invitation spoken by the priest, just after he washes his hands at Mass, named after the first words of the Latin original: Pray, brethren, that my sacrifice and yours may be acceptable to God the Father almighty. It may be of significance that in Scotland and Ireland, the translation used for *meum ac vestrum sacrificium* is 'our sacrifice', while the English text says 'my sacrifice and yours'.

Oratorian

Name for a priest who is a member of the Congregation of the Oratory*.

Oratorio

The musical composition so designated and cast in the form of a semi dramatic representation, a kind of opera without scenery, costume or action, and usually on a biblical theme, derives from the lively and popular form of evening service devised by St. Philip Neri* at his Oratory in Rome.

Oratory

(Lat. *oratorium*, a place for prayers.) In Canon Law, a building set aside for religious purposes for the use primarily of a distinct group, such as a school, family, community, and not for the general public. Such a building is ranked as a public oratory, a semi-public or a private oratory according as the faithful have a general right of access at least for liturgical services, have a limited right, or are excluded.

Oratory, Congregation of the

Founded by St. Philip Neri in 1564 and named after the oratory in the church of San Girolamo in Rome, the place of the first meetings, the Congregation consists of communities of secular priests under obedience but without the vows of religion, each man having independent means of support. Each Oratory pursues the apostolate of prayer, preaching and pastoral work. The Society has two

Oratories in England, where it was introduced by Newman: at Brompton in London, and in Birmingham, the latter having associated with it a boys' school at Reading. The Oratory is established in the United States also.

Order

The phrase 'religious order' is used in common parlance both for those foundations which Canon Law recognises as Orders (viz. those whose members take solemn vows*; in general, the older groupings of canons regular, monks, nuns strictly so called, i.e. *moniales**, and friars; to whom are added the Jesuits) and for religious in general, including such foundations as Canon Law terms religious institutes.

Order of Christ

The Supreme Order of Christ, a Portuguese military order founded in 1319 as some sort of replacement for the suppressed Order of Knights Templars*. From its decline in the 15th cent., it dwindled in dignity to being a mere title conferred by the kings of Portugal. In Rome, it lingers on as the highest pontifical order of knighthood, very rarely conferred.

Order of Penance (or Penitence)

In the early 13th cent., groups of lay people organised themselves to practise penance and to preach the Gospel. It is supposed that their origin was connected with the 12th cent. Waldensian movement; in any case, St. Francis in 1221 gave a rule to some of the members, who thus became the Third Order of St. Francis, while others, uniting with the Militia* of Jesus Christ, formed the Third Order of St. Dominic. The remaining sections of the Order of Penance as such seem to have disappeared.

Order of Pius

A pontifical order of knighthood founded by Pope Pius IV and refounded by Pius IX in 1847, as a distinction to be bestowed on deserving persons, not necessarily Catholics. Its ranks are Grand-Cross Knight, Knight Commander, Knight.

Order of Preachers

(Dominicans.) Known also as the Black Friars* (from wearing a black mantle over their white habit) and founded by St. Dominic*; the Order took definite shape at General Chapters in 1221 and 1222. Dedicated to preaching and study, the Friars were the first religious to abandon manual work. At first, the Order practised not only individual but corporate poverty, until in 1465, Pope Sixtus IV revoked the rule on this subject and allowed the Order property and permanent sources of income. Each priory with the obligation of enclosure and of the Office sends two members (the prior and one elected member) to the Provincial Chapter, where representatives are elected for the General Chapter, which legislates for the whole Order and elects the Master General. The Dominicans, being given to instruction and study, were chosen by various Popes to preach Crusades*, to collect finances, to carry out diplomatic missions, to staff the Inquisition* and to accompany many voyages of exploration. They were the *Domini canes* (Lat., hounds of the Lord), the watchdogs of orthodoxy, and their great names include those of such giants as Thomas Aquinas*, Albert the Great, Pius V* (from whose Dominican habit comes the Papal custom of the white cassock). Of recent years, members of Order have been notably active in the theological and liturgical revival in the Church. There is a Second Order of strictly enclosed nuns, while the Sisters of the Third Order live the active* life without strict enclosure; and, as with other Mendicant Orders, there are Tertiaries*.

Order of St. Augustine

See Hermits* of St. Augustine.

Order of St. Benedict

The Benedictine* monks and nuns.

Order of St. Gregory the Great

A Papal order of knighthood, with military and civil sections, with grand-cross knights first and second class, commanders and knights, commonly awarded in recognition for services to the Church. It was set up by Pope Gregory XVI in 1831.

Order of St. Sylvester

The oldest of the Papal orders of knighthood; its founding is no longer seriously attributed to St. Sylvester I (314–335). It was known as the Order—or Militia—of the Golden Spur* until it was reconstituted by Gregory XVI in 1841 (the title then later being revived for the other Order re-founded by Pius X); its highest rank is Grand-Cross Knight.

Order of the Golden Spur

An order of pontifical knighthood re-instated by Pope Pius X; the membership is limited to 100 and is conferred for notable work in any sphere, not being confined to Catholics or even to Christians.

Order of the Holy Sepulchre

A pontifical order of knighthood originating with the Crusades and renewed by Alexander VI in 1496. Its members hold the rank of Grand-Cross Knight, Commander, Knight or Dame, and clerics are admitted. Those who are accepted into the Order in Jerusalem (the Latin Patriarch of Jerusalem administers the Order for the Holy See) are invested with antique golden spurs and with the sword said to be that of Godfrey of Bouillon.*

Order of the Servants of Mary

See Servites.

Order, Religious

In Canon Law, the word 'order' is reserved for a religious institute whose members take solemn* vows, mainly the canons regular, the monks, such nuns* as are *moniales,* friars and the Society of Jesus. The term was first used in 1119 by St. Stephen Harding in the document 'Charter of Charity' which organised the Cistercians into an order, viz. a group of houses, each independent, but one of which was given pre-eminence and the right of visitation of the other houses. The Benedictines are recognised as the principal religious order: David Knowles called his history simply 'The Monastic Order'.

Ordinal

The form of prayers and ceremonial used in the conferring of Orders; that section of the Pontificale* Romanum which contains these.

Ordinary

A cleric with ordinary jurisdiction in the external forum over a given territory: the Pope has jurisdiction universally, a residential bishop in his diocese, an abbot*nullius, vicar general, administrator, vicar or prefect apostolic, vicar capitular, each in his allotted territory. Used without qualification, the term usually means the bishop of the diocese. The Ordinary of the Mass is that part of the Mass which remains unchanged throughout the year, the matrix as it were into which the Proper is cast; likewise the term is used of the unchangeable parts of the Breviary.*

Ordination

The conferring and receiving of Holy Orders*; the final step on the ladder of ordination—the making of a priest into a bishop—is usually referred to as consecration, although it is more properly termed 'episcopal ordination'.

Ordo

(Lat. *Ordo Divini Officii Recitandi Missaeque Celebrandae.* The Order of the Recitation of the Divine Office and of the Celebration of Mass). The booklet compiled annually for each diocese (many religious orders also publish their own *Ordo* or a supplement to the diocesan one) containing the calendar of feasts and instructions pertaining to the Office and the Mass, in accordance with local variants.

Orientation

The end of a church which contains the altar is described as the east end, the other, which usually has the main entrance, as the west end, whether or not these points correspond to the compass. The custom of building thus arose from the desire to set the altar, symbolic of Christ, towards that part of the world in which (from the point of view of Europe) he wrought our salvation; it is held that orientation was taken over from pagan practices of sun-worship, the Christians using the rising sun as a symbol of Christ (many Celtic churches are said to be built on the line of sunrise on the feast-day of the saint to whom the church is dedicated). The eastern placing of the altar, beginning with Byzantine churches, was consistently followed in England, Germany and Spain, and not so strictly in other countries; the earliest

Roman type, the 4th-cent. basilicas, had the altar in an apse at the west end so that the celebrant, facing his people, looked to the east. Orientation is no longer insisted on in churches, nor is the burial of the dead on the east-west line, the laity with their feet to the east, the clergy with their heads.

Origenism

Most of Origen's theological writings having perished, it is difficult in the extreme to distinguish how much of the great quantity of theory attributed to him or associated with his name is in fact his. His father, Leonidas, died in the persecution at Alexandria in 202, and the young Origen was prevented from rushing out to seek martyrdom by his mother, who hid his clothes; he became head of the renowned Catechetical School in his native city in succession to his master, St. Clement of Alexandria and, in his furious pursuit of asceticism, castrated himself, taking Mt. 19:12 literally. Until his death in 250, which is ascribed to the prolonged tortures he suffered for his faith under the Emperor Decius, he was a prolific and popular writer on Biblical studies, prayer, asceticism and apologetics. Later, there was much controversy over the philosophical and doctrinal views attributed to him, the Patriarch Theophilus in 402 naming him 'that Hydra of hersies'. There are lumped together under 'Origenism' ideas that the Son was not necessarily equal to the Father, that human souls existed before Adam, that matter was eternal, that spirits, being created equal, by their conduct earn transformation into angels or demons or human souls entrapped in bodies, and that after this long metempsychosis would come the *Apocatastasis*, when every creature, even the Devil, would be saved. Origen's preference for the allegorical sense of the Bible led him to distinguish Christians into the *perfect*, who could go to God through their understanding of the allegorical sense, and the *simple*, who had to be content with faith in the crucified Saviour.

Ornaments

In the question of the proper furnishing of church and altar, it should be remembered that, frequently in spite of appearances, the spirit—and often the law—of the Western Church demands a certain austerity. 'For the House of God is appropriate a sobriety, even a decent poverty'—thus the Pontifical Commission for Sacred Art as long ago as 1924—'Riches and pomp are never necessary'. The same document condemns 'useless ornaments', naming paper flowers, painted metal, aspidistras, and urges the elimination of 'those coloured plaster images and oleographs which are often exposed for the veneration of the faithful'. This was before the dawn of the day of plastics. There has been a change in the direction of simplicity, and thus of elegance, in the more recent styles of ecclesiastical vestments. It could perhaps be appropriately mentioned that in August 1978, a shortage of space in the Sistine* Chapel contributed to the cause of simplicity and lowliness, when the 112 Cardinals summoned to elect the Pope (who turned out to be John Paul I), had to do without the traditional canopied thrones, and be content with scarlet-covered armchairs.

Orphrey

(Lat. *auriphrygium*, ornament of Phrygian gold.) The broad band of embroidered ornament round the edges of a cope, or forming a pillar or cross on chasubles of the Renaissance style.

Oscott

St. Mary's College, founded (1793) as a lay and clerical school at Oscott, Gt. Barr, Staffs, had much to do with the Catholic revival in England. After being transferred to New Oscott near Sutton Coldfield, the college was the venue for the first three Synods of Westminster in 1852, 1855 and 1859 (the whole country was then the Province of Westminster). In 1889, the College was transformed into a seminary for the diocese of Birmingham*.

Our Lady

The traditional name among Catholics for the Mother of God, used apparently more frequently in England than in most other countries. (The Book of Common Prayer, in the *Lessons Proper for Holy-Days*, has 'Annunciation of Our Lady'*.) Its earliest recorded use, dating from Anglo-Saxon times, was for long 'Our Lady Saint

Mary', and the title is often joined with some descriptive phrase or with a place-name: Our Lady, Help of Christians, Our Lady of Pity—a frequent English phrase, translating *Beata Maria Virgo de Pietate* or *de Mercede*—Our Lady of Walsingham, etc.
See Mercedarians.

Our Lady in Harvest
A title formerly used for the Feast of the Assumption.

Our Lady in Lent
An ancient English term for the feast of the Annunciation.

Our Lady of Mount Carmel
Commemorated on July 16th, this feast originated with the Carmelites*, to celebrate the approbation of the Order by Rome and the vision of Our Lady granted to St. Simon* Stock, in which he received the Brown Scapular.*

Our Lady's Bands
(i.e. bonds.) A mediaeval term for pregnancy.

Oxford Movement
Several causes contributed to the rise of this reforming current in the Church of England (1833–45). It began in Oxford and drew its main strength from Oxford clerics; its causes were the decline of church life and the spread of 'Liberal' theology, a new interest in primitive and mediaeval Christianity, the apprehension that many would be converted to Rome in the wake of Catholic Emancipation*, the fears aroused by the Reform Bill of 1832, and the plan to abolish ten Irish bishoprics (which provoked Pusey's celebrated sermon on 'National Apostasy'). Dedicated to the defence of the Church of England as a divine institution, of the Apostolic Succession and of the Book of Common Prayer as a rule of faith, the Movement survived the loss of W. G. Ward, Faber, Newman, Manning, R. I. Wilberforce and others to Rome (to say nothing of the opposition of bishops, government and press) and exercised a deep and lasting influence on the Established Church, in the realm of liturgy and ceremonial, to which it gave a much larger scope than previously they had had, in the pastoral sphere—as witness the slum settlements—in the introduction of community life and monastic ideals, as with the Society of St. John the Evangelist ('Cowley Fathers') and the Community of the Resurrection at Mirfield; and, predictably, it made a solid contribution to scholarship: in 1836, Newman, Keble and Pusey began the editing of the *Library of the Fathers*.

Ozanam, Frederic (1813–53)
French intellectual and founder of the Society of St. Vincent de Paul.* At the age of 18, he wrote publicly against Saint-Simon, and at 20 founded the Society. On friendly terms with Châteaubriand, Montalambert and Lacordaire, he contributed to the Catholic revival in France. He was appointed professor of foreign literature at the Sorbonne, produced a masterly work on the philosophy of Dante, advanced the study of mediaeval spiritually through his researches into early Franciscan poets and, together with Lacordaire, disseminated new ideas on Catholic socialism. He spent his last years travelling to promote his Society.

Pachomius, St.

The founder of the Christian monastic community. The subject of a multitude of legends and of lives too late to be very reliable, he appears to have been a native of Upper Egypt, born about 290, to have been an unwilling conscript to military service, then, recently baptised, to have taken to the desert as a hermit. His reputation for holiness drew number of followers to his monastery on the right bank of the Nile, and he became their Abbot*, afterwards having under his authority nine monasteries of men and two of women, which became the model for other monastic foundations. He died in 346; his original Rule is no longer extant.

Pain of Loss

In Scholastic theology, the greatest pain of eternal punishment is the Pain of Loss. Thomas Aquinas writes: 'In every sin there is a turning away from the Unchangeable Good, which is infinite: whence sin itself is infinite; there is also a turning to changeable good things: whence sin is finite... to the first corresponds the pain of loss, which is itself infinite, since it means the loss of the Infinite Good—God...'

Pall

A square of stiff linen, or linen-covered board, used to cover the chalice during Mass, for the purpose of cleanliness; it developed in the 12th cent. from the use of folding over the corporal with this object, a practice still of the Carthusians*.

Pallium

(Lat., cloak) A narrow circle of white wool, to be worn over the shoulders, with strips hanging in front and behind, and adorned with crosses; signifying the fullness of the episcopal power, it is worn only by the Pope and by archbishops, who receive it from him. It is not only personal but territorial, so that an archbishop on being removed to another see must request another pallium; and it is not given to titular archbishops who are not residential prelates. The pallium, conferred only by the Pope, was always considered a mark of union with him; by some historic oversight it has not yet been removed from the coat of arms of Canterbury. Pallia are traditionally woven in Rome from the wool of lambs blessed each year in the Church of St. Agnes on that saint's feastday and are kept in the Confessio* of St. Peter after being blessed by the Pope on the feast of SS. Peter and Paul. The pallium is worn on the occasions prescribed in the Pontificale*.

Pallottine Fathers

See Society of the Catholic Apostolate.

Pallottine Sisters

A parallel congregation to the Pallottine Fathers, engaged chiefly in similar work to theirs and in teaching.
See Society of the Catholic Apostolate.

Palm

The foliage of palm trees is an ancient symbol of victory (the Gospel of John, recording Christ's triumphant entry into Jerusalem with palms, specifically quotes Zc. 9's greeting of the Messiah-King); the palm is frequently found in Christian art as an emblem of martyrdom, following the precedent of Rev. 7:9-15.

Palms, Procession of

(or Ceremony of Palms.) Part of the liturgy of Passion Sunday (Palm Sunday) is a procession in which the faithful, celebrant and assistants carry branches—or leaves—of palm or of some local tree, in memory of Our Lord's ride into Jerusalem (Mt. 21:1-11), and which marks the beginning of Holy Week*. The earlier, mediaeval, form of the ceremony was more elaborate and included blessing the palms with holy water and incense and distributing them to all present, and the ritual demand for readmission by knocking at the church door with the foot of the processional cross; it was simplified first by Pope Pius XII in 1956 and further in the wake of the Second Vatican Council*, so the present rite is closer to what was extant in the day of St. Bede the Venerable.

Panagia

The All-Holy (η παναγια Θεοτοκος, the all-holy Mother of God.) The term commonly used by Greek Christians in referring to Our Lady.

Pantokrator

(Gk., all-powerful.) The name given to Christ in the aspect of ruler of the world, judge of mankind, as represented in paintings and mosaics of the Byzantine tradition, frequently in the semi-domes of apses (cf. Mt. 25:30, 25:31, Mk. 14:62).

Papabile

The Italian word used, at the time of a Conclave*, of any cardinal who is considered to have a good chance of being elected Pope.

Papal aggression

The cry raised in England in 1850 on the restoration of the hierarchy by Pius IX's Brief Universalis Ecclesiae. The sudden burst of public indignation was sparked off by a letter of protest from Lord John Russell, then Prime Minister, to the Bishop of Durham, great exception being taken to the Brief's description of the Church of England as 'the Anglican schism'. Wiseman*, whose pastoral 'Out of the Flaminian Gate'* a week after the Brief, had aroused much hostility in the country, now applied himself to reconciliation with his 'Appeal to the English People'. This went some way to mollifying public anger, which was finally appeased by the passing of the Ecclesiastical Titles Act* the following year.

Papal choir

The choir of the Sistine* Chapel is sometimes thus described.

Papal states

See States of the Church.

Papist

(Lat. papa, Pope.) A contemptuous or hostile term for Catholics, its first known mention is in the writings of St. John Fisher, who quotes Luther as using it. Daniel O'Connell's disclaimer in 1814—'I am sincerely a Catholic but I am not a Papist, I deny the doctrine that the Pope has any temporal authority, directly or in-

directly, in Ireland'—illustrates the sinister implications the word originally had. It is now used hardly anywhere but among Orangemen, who tend to abbreviate it to 'Pape'.

Paralipomenon

The title (from the hybrid Latin-Greek expression in the Vulgate, Libri παραλειπομενων, the Books of Things Left Out) given in the subsequent Catholic translations as late as the Knox Version, for the Books of Chronicles.

Paray-le-Monial

A centre of pilgrimage in France (Département Saône-et-Loire). There in the Convent of the Visitation, is the chapel in which St. Margaret Mary had her revelations of the Sacred Heart, and in the same chapel, her body is now preserved.

Pardoner

The office of Pardoner, with licence to preach and raise money for specific objects, to which contributions was frequently attached an indulgence—and many an abuse (cf. Chaucer's Prologue, and the pardoner who made the parsoun and the people his apes)—survived until the Council of Trent*, being abolished in the 25th Session.

Parents

The Church has from the beginning stressed the responsibility that Christian parents' love for their children lays on them: they are to provide for them, protect them in body and spirit, show them Christian example, instruct them and provide education in the Christian truths. 'Every head of a household,' according to St. Augustine, 'should realise that he owes it a debt of fatherly love; for the sake of Christ and of everlasting life, he must teach, reprove and encourage those who belong to him... Thus will he perform towards them the duty of a pastor—you might say of a bishop—becoming so much a servant of Christ as to be with Christ for ever.' The Second Vatican Council says, '...with their parents leading the way by example and family prayer, children and indeed everyone gathered round the family hearth will find a readier path to human maturity, salvation and holiness. Graced with the dignity and duty of fatherhood and motherhood, parents will energetically aquit themselves of a duty which devolves primarily on them, namely education, and especially religious education' (Pastoral Constitution on the Church in the Modern World, Art. 48).

Parish

A division of the diocese*, having geographical boundaries and a church served by a priest who has the cure of souls. Usually parishes are the responsibility of the diocesan clergy, and such religious as serve them may be removed either by the bishop or by their own religious superiors. By reason of the vastly increased mobility of most modern populations, the parish is no longer the magnetic centre of the lives of the faithful, but it is still considered desirable that the Easter communion be made in one's own parish church, and that baptism, marriage and the funeral service should not be conducted elsewhere, except by arrangement with the parish priest.

Parkminster

St. Hugh's in Sussex, the largest Charterhouse* in the world, built to house 96 monks, was founded from the Grande Chartreuse* in 1873.

Parousia

The Greek word for 'presence', used frequently to mean a royal presence, a state visit, was used by the Christians to describe the return of Christ in glory, the Second Coming.

Particle

The term sometimes used of the small consecrated Host as usually distributed to the faithful.

Paschal Candle

A large candle which stands on a candlestick placed prominently on the sanctuary from the Vigil Service of Easter until Pentecost. The candle is solemnly blessed and lit from the new fire, after being inscribed with the sign of the cross, the Greek letters Alpha and Omega and the date of the current year; it has five grains of incense fixed in it to make a cross. It is carried into the darkened church by a deacon, who cries out three times, 'The light of Christ!' and is answered by the faithful, 'Thanks be to God!'; from it are lit candles held by the people, the altar candles and the sanctuary lamp*. It is set on its holder and venerated; the deacon then sings the Exsultet*, one of the finest sustained pieces of plainsong. The Paschal candle is lit for Sunday Masses and for the Mass of Whit Sunday, when it is extinguished. It is now usually kept in the sanctuary all the year and used at baptisms and funerals.

Paschal Precept

See Easter Duty.

Paschal Time

See Eastertide.

Passion Sunday

Previously the Fifth Sunday of Lent, on which day the pictures, statues and crucifixes in the churches were shrouded in purple until the Vigil of Easter, the following Sunday was designated the First Sunday of the Passion, the following Sunday, the Second Sunday of the Passion or Palm Sunday (Dominica Secunda Passionis seu in Palmis) being still known among the faithful as Palm Sunday; more recently the official change of names has been completed: the Fifth Sunday of Lent is now just the Fifth Sunday of Lent and the following Sunday is Passion Sunday or Palm Sunday (Dominica Passionis seu in Palmis).

Passionists

The Congregation of Barefooted Clerks of the Most Holy Cross and Passion of Our Lord Jesus Christ, founded in 1720 by St. Paul of the Cross, whose purpose was to keep before men's minds the sufferings and death of Our Lord on which subject the members take a fourth vow; this was to be accomplished by the preaching of missions and retreats. The Congregation also has parishes and foreign missions. A province was founded by Blessed Dominic Barberi* in 1842 in England, where the Fathers were the first religious to wear a habit in public since the Reformation. There are provinces also in Ireland, U.S.A. and Australia. The nuns, whose section of the Congregation St. Paul founded in 1771 together with Mother Mary Crucifixa, are contemplative.

Pastor Aeternus

The title (from its opening words) of the First Dogmatic Constitution on the Church of Christ issued at the fourth session of the First Vatican* Council, in July 1870. The Constitution defined the primacy and infallibility of the Pope.

Pastoral

In full, Pastoral Letter; the letter written by a bishop to all in his diocese (see *Ad Clerum*). These are sent as the bishop sees necessary, though it is traditional to write Pastorals regularly at the beginning of Advent and of Lent. A pastoral is published by being read from the pulpit, usually on a day appointed by the bishop.

Pastoral Staff

See Crosier.

Paten

(Lat. *patena*, dish.) The circular plate of thin metal which is used for the Host at Mass. If not itself of gold or silver, it must have at least a gilt upper surface; it is consecrated by a bishop before use.

Patriarch

Taken from the Biblical use, the word describes, in ecclesiastical organisation, a bishop of the highest rank in jurisdiction. The earliest large territorial units of the Church were based on Rome, Alexandria and Antioch, and by the 6th cent., there had been added Constantinople and Jerusalem: thus the five Great Patriarchates. The prelates who now hold these are designated major patriarchs, others—e.g. the Armenian Patriarch of Cilicia and the Chaldean Patriarch of Babylon—are minor patriarchs. There are also titular patriarchs of the Latin rite, either bishops resident in the Papal court but holding antique patriarchal titles (Constantinople, Antioch, Alexandria) or diocesan arch-bishops (Jerusalem, with that patriarchal title, Madrid, with the title Patriarch of the West Indies, Venice with that title, Lisbon with that title, Goa with the title Patriarch of the East Indies). A patriarch is independent of any authority save that of the Pope (who is also Patriarch of the West).

Patriarch of the West

One of the titles of the Pope, distinguishing him in his capacity of supreme bishop of the Western Church from his higher position as Supreme Pontiff of the whole Church and from his lower roles as Primate of Italy, Archbishop and Metropolitan of the Province of Rome and Sovereign of the State of Vatican City.

Patriarchal Basilicas

See the Four Basilicas.

Patrick, St.

The Apostle of Ireland and inspirer of so much of the tenacious and missionary zeal of the Irish Church appears to be the product of a certain tidying-up of historical loose ends. The Patrick of centuries of veneration, the noble, green-chasubled bishop driving the snakes into the sea and preaching the Trinity with the aid of the shamrock, tends to dissolve—or rather to multiply—under close scrutiny. The legend of the slave-boy from a foreign land who escaped home, got ordained and returned as bishop to convert his former captors, tends in the first place to underplay Palladius, sent by Pope St. Celestine I (422–432) as the 'first bishop of those of the Irish who believe in Christ'; it was to assist him that Patrick was commissioned to Ireland. The autobiographical *Confessions* also leave his episcopacy vague: having been refused consecration through the revelation of a youthful sin, he speaks of 'being a bishop in the eyes of God'. Again, the idiosyncratic and sometimes barbarous Latin of the *Confessions* accords ill with his reported 14 years as a priest at Auxere, which was a flourishing centre of culture. The snakes, the shamrock and the Vision of Purgatory are admitted to be late additions, but both Irish and Latin records contain the pre-800 hymn *Génair Pátraic*, in which there is clear indication of an existing tradition of two missionaries called Patrick, and the *Book of Armagh* tells us that Palladius was also named Patrick. The Irish scholar, O'Rahilly, in 1942, put forward the interpretation, using the work of Zimmer (1902), that Palladius-Patricius worked in the midlands and the East until he died in 461 and was succeeded by his assistant Patrick the Briton (the slave-boy) who, before his death in 492, had ministered in the North, in Connaught and Leinster; and that a couple of centuries later, the Acts of the two great missionaries were—by accident or design—amalgamated to produce a single, identifiable national hero, who would also facilitate the claim of Armagh to the primacy. A later theory (Esposito, 1956) reverses the order and sends Patrick the Briton to Ireland first; and in some of the later, less reliable mediaeval Latin *Lives,* there are three Patricks. Of whatever origin, whoever and however many-headed this *Patricius* or company of *Patricii* may have been, it is beyond question that the house of that faith was set most firmly on the rock, solid and able to weather the beating of the fierce and innumerable storms that were to waste their force upon it.

Patrimony of St. Cuthbert

The lands attached to the see of Durham were so called in the days when that see had its own prince-bishop.

Patrimony of St. Peter

Those lands and properties granted to the Church of Rome after the Edict of Constantine in 313. Though the Donation* of Constantine is a forgery, it does represent the fact that very large Imperial properties were made over to the Church from time to time, until the Pope was a prince ruling large territories, including what came to be, in the Middle Ages and until 1870, the Papal States* and, in earlier times, lands in Sicily, Illyira, Gaul, Corsica, Sardinia, N.Africa. The Emperors and kings concerned offered these areas as gifts 'to St. Peter' or 'to the Blessed Apostles, Peter and Paul'.

Patron Saints

One very evident aspect of the doctrine of the Communion of Saints* is the tradition in the Catholic Church of choosing Patron Saints for persons, communities, professions, states of life, places (especially churches); which doctrine is also the reason for the Church's insistence on the choice of a 'Christian' name for Baptism, since the patron should be the object of the Christian's devotion and his protector. Almost all human occupations and enter-

prises have their patrons, the connection in some cases being clear and logical, in some merely pious, in some eccentric. Our Lady is the patron of mothers and of families, St. Joseph of the universal Church and of builders and joiners, Peter of fishermen, Joseph of Arimathea of tinworkers (linking him with the West Country, as does the Glastonbury legend), Barbara of gunners (the story associates her martyrdom with lightning), Our Lady or Loreto* of airmen, Yves of lawyers

*(Sanctus Ivo erat Brito
Advocatus sed non latro—
Res miranda populo!*
There's Yves the Breton saint,
strange past belief:
For, though a lawyer,
never was he thief.),

the Archangel Gabriel of broadcasting and the communications industry; St. Jude is invoked by those whose case is considered hopeless, St. Anthony of Padua by those who have lost some possession or other, Dismas (such was the name traditionally put on the 'Good Thief') by criminals awaiting execution; St. Scholastica* protects against drought or excess of rain, St. Vitus against epilepsy, St. Maurice against gout, St. Bernard of Menthon against danger on mountains.

Paul of the Cross, St. (1604-1775)

Founder of the Passionists*, one of the most renowned preachers of his age, especially on the subject of the Passion of Our Lord; famous also as a spiritual director and a miracle-worker.

Paul VI, Pope

(1897-1978.) Giovanni Battista Montini, ordained in 1920, served in the Vatican Secretariate of State for 32 years, with a break of a few months in 1923 at the Apostolic Nunciature in Warsaw. Pius XII* consecrated him Archbishop of Milan in 1954, and in 1958, John XXIII created him cardinal and associated him with his work of preparing the Second Vatican Council, making clear his wish that Montini should succeed him as Pope. This happened in 1963, while the Council was still in progress. The following year, Paul VI made a pilgrimage to the Holy Land—in the course of which he met and embraced Athenagoras, Patriarch of Constantinople—and visited Bombay for an international Eucharistic Congress. His early encyclicals emphasised the traditional teaching on the Eucharist and the Real* Presence. In 1965, he.organised the Synod* of Bishops and re-shaped the Holy Office*, giving it the name of Sacred Congregation for the Teaching of the Faith*. In the subsequent year, in the spirit of Vatican II, he made some relaxations in the Church's laws on fasting and abstinence and those concerning the marriage of Catholics with non-Catholics; he distributed much power of dispensation from the Curia to local bishops, and in a motu proprio *Ecclesiae Sanctae,* he instituted a commission of 24 to exercise deliberative powers over foreign missions, to be subject only to papal veto and thus to take precedence of the Congregation for the Propagation of the Faith*; he directed bishops to set up diocesan councils of priests and ordered religious to adapt their Rules to the spirit of Vatican II. His encyclical *Populorum Progressio* (1967) dealt with aid to the developing countries. But the best-known document of his pontificate, both inside and out of the Church, was *Humanae Vitae,* which repeated the traditional ban on artificial contraceptives allowing the exception of oral contraceptives in case of disease, even at the cost of avoiding conception; the encyclical roused all the greater dismay and indignation because it totally ignored the majority report of an international commission Paul had set up to make preliminary inquiry into all these matters. The national hierarchies in many cases sought to alleviate the disturbance by explaining that, while the Pope spoke doctrinally, their task as bishops was pastoral, and thus they could counsel those of the faithful who found the Encyclical's teaching impossible not to refrain therefore from receiving the Sacraments; this was a new departure for bishops to intervene in mitigation of a papal pronouncement. The Pope's further travels took him to a Eucharistic Congress at Bogotá, Colombia, and to Geneva for the 50th anniversary of the International Labour Organisation, where he also visited the headquarters of the World Council of Churches and prayed with some of the leaders. He also went to Uganda and met President Obote and other African heads of state. He increased the number of the cardinals to 134 and gave orders for the simplification of the dress of the Sacred College and of other prelates.

Pauline Privilege

(C.I.C. 1120–27.) The concession accorded by St. Paul (I Cor.7:15) whereby a married person who becomes a Christian and finds that the non-Christian partner obstructs him or her from the practice of the faith, may have the marriage dissolved. The case must be examined by the bishop and the marriage is dissolved only by the contracting of a new marriage. The privilege seems not to have been widely used in the earliest times, but its use is affirmed by St John Chrysostom* and it was adopted into Canon Law* as time went on.

Paulists

The Missionary Society of St. Paul the Apostle was founded in New York by Fr. Hecker and four fellow-priests in 1858 to undertake the work of conversion to the Catholic faith by missions, writing and other means. The rule is based on that of the Redemptorists*, to which congregation the five founders originally belonged.

Pax

See Sign of Peace.

Pax Dei

(Lat., the peace of God.) Certain mediaeval synods in France laid down definitively the immunity of clerics, religious and all non-combatants from the effects of private wars, as also the sacred inviolability of churches, convents and monasteries and the prohibition of fighting on Sundays; they were supported in this by Pope John XIX in 1030, and besides the infliction of interdict for disobedience, there were set up armed leagues to prevent conflict, and tribunals for arbitration—foreshadowing the attempts of the League of Nations and of the United Nations Organisation.
See Truce of God.

Pax Romana

(Lat., the Peace of Rome.) An international association of university students formed for the advancement of mutual understanding and respect between nations.

Peace of the Church, the

The Edict of Milan promulgated by Constantine put an end to persecution and granted the Church safety and leisure to organise itself and present itself as a public body; there followed very quickly the granting of rights and privileges: recognition of ecclesiastical courts, the right to hold property and to release slaves, the exemption of the clergy from taxation and from compulsory public office. In this new atmosphere of peace and acceptance, the Church so flourished that in 380 Christianity was recognised as the official religion of the Empire.

Peculium

In accordance with the vow of poverty, a sum of money may be allowed by a religious superior to a subject, for a legitimate purpose, though the money remains in the power of the superior. This *peculium* is to be carefully accounted for, in view of the ideal of the perfect common life for a community.

Pelagianism

The theological system based on the proposition that man takes of himself the first steps towards his salvation, without the help of divine grace. Pelagius, its originator, was a monk, British or perhaps Irish, though not in holy orders, who arriving in Rome about 400 A.D., acquired a name for great learning and devotion, but took exception to St. Augustine's phrase about continence, *'Da quod jubes et jube quod vis,* Grant what thou commandest and command what thou wilt'. This, he said, undermined the moral law, since man would not be responsible for his good and evil actions. The main tenets of the doctrine which grew out of this assertion were that there is no Original Sin, as Adam's sin injured only himself, not his descendants, that death is due not to that event but to the laws of human nature, that children are born in the condition of Adam before his fall, that the human race neither dies because of Adam nor will rise again because of Christ's resurrection, that grace is not necessary apart from natural grace (i.e. any natural gift of God to which we have no actual claim, such as existence, our natural powers and talents, as opposed to anything supernatural). It

was when Pope Innocent I confirmed the condemnation of the Pelagian propositions by the Councils of Carthage and Milevis in 416 that Augustine coined the famous phrase *Causa finita est,* The case is settled; to which was later prefixed *Roma locuta est,* Rome has spoken. Pelagius appears to have died not long after the condemnation, but Pelagianism lingered in the West, particularly in Britain and Gaul, being again condemned as late as 529 at the Second Council of Orange and disappearing finally before the end of the 6th cent.

Pelagius

See Pelagianism.

Pelican

The ancient legend of the female pelican tearing her breast with her beak so as to feed her young with her blood gave rise to the symbolic use of this bird in Christian art and literature to represent Christ; the image is used in the sixth stanza of the *Adoro Te;* in carving and painting, one finds the pelican thus depicted, as in the quadrangle at Corpus Christi College, Oxford, and in some places the Blessed Sacrament was reserved in a hanging silver pelican (see Dove) as at Durham Cathedral. The heraldic description of the bird thus 'vulning' herself is the 'Pelican in her piety.'

Penal Times

The period (1559–1829) when Catholics in Great Britain and Ireland laboured under legal disadvantages (see Disabilities of Catholics)—the time up to 1700 being one of active, if intermittent, persecution, the remaining years an era of repression gradually and cautiously relaxed. The ecclesiastical authority for Catholics in England was from 1598 to 1621 an archpriest, while from 1623 to 1688, the Old Chapter* had jurisdiction; then a Vicar Apostolic was appointed until the creation of four Districts, London, Midland, Northern and Western, each with its Vicar Apostolic; these were titular bishops. In 1840, Rome set up eight Vicariates, and in 1850, restored the hierarchy. It was calculated in the year 1700 that the total Catholic population of England was 60,000 served by 30 chapels.

Penance

i) Penitence, repentance, the virtuous disposition to hate one's sin as displeasing to God and separating one from Him. This is a necessary and logical precondition for forgiveness.

ii) Until about the year 1000, the Church imposed public penance i.e. the public performance of painful, difficult or shaming tasks or sufferings, for public offences; an example of this is the whipping of King Henry II through the streets of Canterbury for his responsibility in the murder of the Archbishop. Such penance, often the next stage after excommunication for a notorious sinner, was imposed for a number of days or years or for life (the arithmetical value of indulgences was later based on such reckoning). Very often, penances excluded the sinner from Mass, or from the more important parts thereof.

iii) Canonical penance consists of prayers, good works, etc. laid on those who offend against Canon Law, as a means of release from ecclesiastical penalty or in place of it. Public penance may not, of course, be imposed for an occult* offence.

iv) Sacramental penance is the task imposed by the confessor* who gives absolution, usually of a very light nature, such as the recitation of certain prayers or the performance of some act of charity not too strenuous in nature. See i) above.

v) The Sacrament of Penance is in modern times coming increasingly to be called the Sacrament of Reconciliation, though the ordinary Catholic still talks of 'going to Confession'.

vi) Any act of prayer, mortification, self-denial undertaken with a spirit of reparation for sin; many of the faithful take on unobtrusive acts of penance during Lent.

Penitentiary, Canon

See Canon Penitentiary.

Penitentiary, the Grand

The Cardinal in charge of the Sacred Penitentiary*; during Holy Week*, he is present at St. Peter's*, St. John Lateran* and St. Mary Major* so that he and his assistants are available for such of the faithful as wish to make their confession. These kneel before him in turn and are tapped on the head with his *ferula*, acknowledging themselves sinners—a tradition sometimes connected with the Roman praetor's symbolic gesture in freeing a slave.

Penitentiary, the Sacred Apostolic

The tribunal in Rome for dealing with matters of the internal forum and the attendant absolution, decisions in cases of conscience, the practical application of indulgences; a court of mercy conducted in the strictest confidence and without fee. Any member of the faithful is able to apply to the Cardinal Penitentiary, in any language; the application is usualy made by the persons's confessor, using fictitious names, so that total secrecy is preserved.

Pentecost

(Gk. πεντηκοστη, fiftieth [day].) The Jewish feast of the first-fruits of the corn harvest, fifty days after Passover, was borrowed by the Christian Church for the descent of the Holy Spirit on the Apostles on the 50th day after the Resurrection of Jesus (Acts 2:1). In early times, the term was used for the whole 50-day period between Easter Day and the day of the Holy Spirit. It became the next feast in importance to Easter and its Vigil an alternative date for baptisms—hence 'Whit Sunday', a reference to the white robe then donned by the neophyte. The ancient reckoning of that part of the liturgical year as *Sundays after Pentecost* was dropped in the liturgical changes after the Second Vatican Council, those days now being numbered as *Ordinary Sundays* or *Sundays of the Year*.

Peregrinus

(Lat., a stranger.) In Canon Law, a person staying temporarily outside his place of domicile or quasi-domicile, who is for that time subject to the laws of the place he is in.

Perfection, Counsels of

The three principles traditionally associated with the quest for moral perfection, which are the bases of the vows of religion: voluntary poverty, perfect chastity (i.e. total sexual abstinence) and entire obedience. Also known as the Evangelical Counsels.

Perpetual Adoration

The unbroken worship of the Blessed Sacrament, usually exposed in the monstrance*; a custom which arose in France in the 17th cent. as a development of the Forty Hours* devotion, and which became attached to certain foundations of men and women as part of their rule.

Perpetual Succour, Our Lady of

One of the best-known paintings of the Madonna* is the 13th-cent. Byzantine work known by this name and kept in the Redemptorist* church in Rome. Some are uncomfortable about the awkwardness of the title in English, though no suitable alternative has been accepted. June 27th was chosen as the feast-day in 1876 and is still commemorated in the dioceses of Leeds and Middlesbrough, which have Our Lady of Perpetual Succour as patron.

Peter Damian, St.

A Doctor* of the Church, active as a reformer in the 11th cent. The child of poor parents, he tended swine, but, his talents being recognised, he was educated at Faenza and Parma, becoming a Benedictine at the age of 28. He was made Prior, reforming monasteries and founding new ones, preaching against the worldliness and simony rampant among the clergy; being made Cardinal Bishop of Ostia in 1057, he continued his work to reform. His writings recommend strict monastic discipline and severe mortification and treat of Purgatory, the Eucharist and the Sacraments. He died in 1072, his feast being celebrated on Feb. 21st.

Peter's Pence

A world-wide collection of offerings made by Catholics towards the expenses of the Holy See; so called because in the Middle Ages, it took the form of a tax of a penny levied on every household.

Philip Neri, St.

Known as the Apostle of Rome, St. Philip (1515-95) used his great gift for friendship—he was 'the merry saint'—to present the faith congenially especially to men and boys; having interested other priests in his work, he founded with them the Congregation of the Oratory (named probably from the place where they used to meet). Much sought after for his wise counsel, he averted serious conflict between the Papacy and France by persuading Clement VIII to absolve Henry IV of heresy.

Photius

Patriarch of Constantinople (+895). A man of great learning and blameless life, long regarded in the West as an ecclesiastical ogre and as responsible for tearing the Church in half by the Great Schism of the East; illegitimately elevated to the Patriarchate, excommunicated by Nicholas I, deposed by the 4th Council of Constantinople, reinstated as Patriarch by the Emperor Basil and approved by Rome, he then, says the legend, reopened schism and, excommunicated by Pope Formosus, retired from history. Modern research leads one to think that he was not nearly so obvious a leader of the Schism, that he was in all probability the rightful patriarch, that the 4th Council needs more examination, that Photius was not in fact excommunicated. The truth is obscured by a tangle of mutual hostility between Rome and Constantinople, political interference, Papal documents falsified, Papal legates exceeding their powers and being manipulated by the Emperor, parties in his own city working secretly against Photius, and the Court making unscrupulous use of the Church (Basil had in fact come to the throne by murdering his predecessor). However, the events of his career did deeply accentuate the growing rift between the two Patriarchates, which was really due to the incompatible claims, on the one hand, that Rome was the centre of Christianity and, on the other, that there should be five Patriarchs all with more or less equal status. The name of Photius had become, by the 13th cent., a rallying-cry for those opposed to reconciliation of the two great Churches.

Picpus Fathers

The popular name for the fathers of the Congregation of the Sacred Hearts of Jesus and Mary, whose headquarters were in the Rue de Picpus in Paris. Their work is foreign and home missions and perpetual* adoration, their most famous member being Fr Damien of Molokai.

Pilate, Acts of

See Acts of Pilate.

Pilgrimage

Civilised men have always had the desire to visit those places where it was believed the divine had manifested itself either by actual presence, or by some activity, or in the lives or characters of individuals; and, for the Christian, the most obvious such place was the Holy Land, to which pilgrims began to travel as soon as it was safe and convenient. Opportunities were vastly increased by the conversion of Constantine and the consequent Peace of the Church; an example was set by his mother Helena's visit to Jerusalem in 326, and by St. Jerome in the next century, who visited the Holy Places before settling at Bethlehem. The *Peregrinatio Etheriae*★ provides us with interesting details of the pilgrimages of those days. Soon also the tombs of the Apostles in Rome drew large numbers of pilgrims, especially from among the Anglo-Saxon nobility; another great pilgrimage arose to Santiago de Compostela in Spain, whither, according to tradition, the body of St. James the Greater had been translated. Many lands have many centres of pilgrimage, which have become more and more popular and more densely frequented as the means of transport have improved; nor is there any reason to think a mediaeval pilgrim ambling to Canterbury on a meditative mule any more devout than a modern traveller descending on Lourdes★ by airbus.

Pilgrimage of Grace

A rising in the North of England in 1536, led by Robert Aske of Aughton, demanding the restoration of the monasteries (the lesser houses had just been suppressed) and the deprivation of Thomas Cromwell and the heretical bishops. The banner carried by the insurgents, over 30,000 in number, bore the emblem of the Five Wounds★. Aske was offered safe-conduct and brought to London, to be promised that their grievances would be met, once his followers dispersed, but he was taken and tried for treason, to die with other gentry and four abbots. The immediate reaction of the King's men was the ruthless destruction of monasteries throughout the Diocese of York, a prelude to the Act for the Dissolution★ of the Greater Monasteries of 1539 (31 Henry VIII c.13).

Pillar of the Scourging, the

There is in the Church of the Holy Sepulchre★ in Jerusalem a three-foot length of porphyry, which is said to be a fragment of the pillar to which Christ was bound at his scourging (Mk 15:15). The Church of St. Praxedes in Rome possesses a similar relic. The Armenian Church in Jerusalem possesses a fragment of column on which it is claimed the Lord sat in the house of Caiaphas (Mt.26:57–68) and which also has been known since the 4th cent.

Pillar Saints

In Greece, Mesopotamia, Syria and Egypt, certain ascetics took to living on pillars, sometimes only a few feet high, sometimes in fact column-shaped huts. Most of the pillars had a platform on top and a rail or parapet against which the holy man would lean for his short sleep. Apart from extreme mortification and prayer for the corrupt and dis-ordered world they had left, the *stylites*★ occupied themselves with preaching, giving instruction, and theological discussion or controversy. The era in which they flourished was from the 4th to the 10th cent., in Syria until the 11th cent., and there have been isolated examples until comparatively modern times. The first and most famous of them was *Simeon Stylites* (c.390–459), whose sensational life-style attracted numerous pilgrims and disciples and who exercised a powerful influence on the contemporary world, counselling and teaching, converting pagans, reconciling enemies and lending significant support to the orthodox teaching of Chalcedon★ on the person of Christ.

Pio Nono

Pius IX was popularly known by this, the Italian version of his title, in countries other than his own.

Pisan Popes

The two claimants to the Papacy who were elected as a result of the Council of Pisa and its efforts to heal the Schism of the West, described since as Anti-Popes★: Alexander V (1409–10) and John XXIII (1410–15).

Pius V, Pope St.

(1594-1672.) A Dominican friar who was known for his austerity of life, Michele Ghislieri held high office in his Order and was appointed Commissar General of the Inquisition and then Inquisitor General of Christendom. Under Pius IV, he campaigned vigorously against the nepotism for which that pontiff was notorious. Elected Pope in 1566, he dedicated his energies to the reform of the Church, beginning with the Papal household; he made bishops and clergy accept the recommendations of the Council of Trent* and saw to the completion of the *Roman Catechism* in accordance with that Council's decree; he reformed the Breviary* and the Roman Missal, which he established as the centralised form of the Western Mass, and ordered a new edition of the works of Thomas Aquinas*. He made use of the Inquisition* in his continued fight against heresy. Had his zeal been matched with adequate information, he would probably not have issued against Elizabeth I the Bull *Regnans in Excelsis* for which he is chiefly remembered in the history of England. As it is, he remains an indefatigable champion of the embattled Church in those unforgiving days, and the stoutest promoter of the Counter-Reformation. It is perhaps symbolic that he should be the Pope who 'called the kings of Christendom for swords about the Cross', initiating what was to be called 'the last Crusade', when the Turkish thrust against Western civilisation was halted at Lepanto by the victory of the Papal, Venetian and Spanish fleets under the command of Don John of Austria, the engagement in which Cervantes received his wound. Feast, April 30th.

Pius IX, Pope

(1792-1878.) Succeeding in 1846 to Gregory XVI, who had antagonised the Italian people, Pio Nono* was welcomed as a liberal-minded pontiff. He declared an amnesty for political prisoners and exiles, and made known his support for the movement for Italian unification. But when, in 1848, he refused to lend his armies to help the northern Italian insurgents against their Austrian masters, the revolutionaries took Rome and drove him out, his return being made possible only by the French occupation of the city in the following year. Reinstated in 1850, and abandoning his liberal attitude, the Pope saw his temporal power and his influence in Italy steadily decrease. Cavour's Sardinian forces took the Romagna in 1859, and the Umbrian Marches in 1860. Deprived thus of the Papal States*, Pio Nono was left with the city of Rome until that also was taken in 1870 by the troops of the new King of Italy, Victor Emmanuel, and the following year saw the Law of Guarantees, which robbed him virtually of all temporal sovereignty, and which he vigorously repudiated. (See Prisoner of the Vatican.) However, in all these political disasters, the pontificate was a period of spiritual and ecclesiastical achievement: many new dioceses and missionary centres were set up, the hierarchy was restored to England in 1850, and to Holland in 1853, and many concordats were drawn up; Pio Nono defined, in 1854, the dogma of the Immaculate Conception, imparting new energy to Catholic devotion; he condemned heretical trends in contemporary philosophy; and the most important event of his time was the definition, by the First Vatican Council*, of the dogma of Papal Infallibility* (1870). Even the loss of the temporal power should be seen in a positive light as restoring at last to the Papacy its true status as a spiritual and moral force in the world, respected in all quarters and not only within the household of the faith.

Pius X, Pope St.

The latest of the Popes to be canonised, Pius, elected in 1903, declared his intention not to be a 'political' Pope, but the choice was not left to him. In 1905, the French government in separating Church and State, proposed the '*associations cultuelles*' to take possession of the remaining Church properties; the Pope took the bold step of issuing two encyclicals* in condemnation and thus, at the price of total material loss, assured the Church's independence in that country. In 1911, the Portuguese government followed the same course as the French. On the theological level, he dealt with Modernism* in the decree *Lamentabili* and encyclical* *Pascendi;* in social teaching, it fell to him to correct both the revolutionary tendencies embodied in the French movement *Le sillon* and the right-wing intransigence of *Action Française*, both of which he condemned. Pius also initiated difficult reforms: a new codification of Canon Law (finally delivered in 1917 under Benedict XV), administrative changes in the Roman Congregations*, the reform of the Breviary*, and an insistence on the primacy to be restored to the Gregorian Chant in the liturgy. He also preached convincingly the desirability of frequent reception of the Eucharist, recommending daily Communion, and thus presenting to the whole Church what had hitherto been the teaching and practice of a few bold spirits, among them St John Bosco*. Venerated as a saint in his lifetime, he was canonised in 1954.

Pius XI, Pope

(1857–1939.) A scholar who spent five years as Prefect of the Ambrosian Library in Milan and six as vice-prefect of the Vatican Library, Achille Ratti was elected in 1922, declaring as the aim of his pontificate the 'restoration of all things in Christ', as a symbol of which objective he instituted, in 1925, the Feast of Christ the King. His many and notable writings include the encyclical *Quadragesimo Anno**; the most important political event of his papacy was the Lateran Treaty*. He did much to foster the spiritual and devotional life of Catholics (on the occasion, e.g. of the Jubilee of 1925, and by his canonisation of St. Teresa of Lisieux*) and the apostolate of the laity. Pius XI's later years were troubled by his awareness of the increase of atheism and paganism, and by the state of Germany where he apprehended not only present persecution of the Church (see *Mit Brennender Sorge*) but a threat to the world.

Pius XII, Pope

(1876–1958.) Before his election in 1939, Eugenio Pacelli was a Vatican diplomat who had negotiated a concordat* with Bavaria in 1924, a less favourable one with Prussia in 1929 and later, in 1933 as Cardinal, a concordat with the National Socialist government of the Third Reich, which was rendered almost valueless by Adolf Hitler's repeated breaches of it. In 1930, the year of his reception of the red hat, he was also made Papal Secretary of State*, and thus came to the papacy by an unusual route. The pronouncements of his earlier years as Pope reflect his reactions to the Second World War: he appeals to the human race to restore to God his rightful place in the life of the world; he offers his Five Peace Points: recognition of every nation's right to life and independence; real disarmament, material and spiritual; institution of an international court to safeguard peace; recognition of the rights of minorities; establishment of a true Christian spirit among the nations. During the War and afterwards, he laboured especially for the welfare of prisoners, though severe criticism has been levelled at him on the ground that, through fear of the results to the Church, he earlier restrained his condemnation of the Nazis' excesses. Of his encyclicals, *Mystici Corporis Christi* (1943) dwells on the unity of the Church, *Mediator Dei* (1947) expresses sympathy for the movement for liturgical reform and for the use of the vernacular, while emphasising the need for caution, *Divino Afflante Spiritu* (1943) warns Catholic scholars to keep close to the literal meaning of Scripture where *possible. *Humani Generis* (Aug. 1950) denounces certain trends in contemporary theology, *Munificentissimus Deus* (Dec. 1950) defines the dogma of the Assumption of Our Lady. Pius also fostered relations with the Churches of the Eastern rite in the encyclicals *Orientalis Ecclesiae Decus* of 1944 and *Orientales Omnes Ecclesiae* (1945); he created thirty-two cardinals in 1946 and twenty-four in 1953, on both occasions including men from a wide variety of nations.

Plenary Indulgence

See Indulgences.

Pole, Reginald Cardinal

Born to eminence (his mother being a niece of Edward IV, his father a cousin of Henry VII), Pole frustrated certain early hopes entertained of him by choosing the scholar's life; tutored at Oxford by Linacre and Latimer, he studied at Padua and corresponded with More and Erasmus while living in the company of Italian humanists. He tried to avoid the question of Henry's divorce, but, having helped to persuade the University of Paris to accept it, and being then offered the See of York on condition of his personal acceptance, he violently rejected it and returned to Padua, joining a group of Catholic reformers which included Contarini and Carafa. Pursued by Henry for his answer, and still hoping to reconcile his king, he waited, observed from afar the deaths of More, Fisher and the Carthusians and in a year's time sent his matured reply, a full-sized book *Pro Eccesiae Unitatis Defensione* or *De Unitate,* a sharp attack on royal policy and defence of papal supremacy. This, meant for the King's eyes only, was published without Pole's consent. About this time, he was co-opted by Paul III to a committee for investigating the state of the Church and submitting proposals for reform; another move by the Pope, to use him as *legatus a latere** to take advantage, with help from the Emperor and the French king, of Henry's problems over the Pilgrimage of Grace*, put Pole's life in danger from Henry, who in fact executed the Cardinal's mother and eldest brother in 1541, on hearing of which Pole exclaimed, 'I am the son of a martyr!' A leading spirit of the Council of Trent and one of three legates* sent to open it, he just failed, on Paul III's death in 1549, to obtain the two-thirds majority which would have made him Pope; by this time, he had lost the trust of the powerful Cardinal Carafa. On Mary Tudor's accession, he was appointed legate to England, but his journey was impeded by the Emperor Charles V until his son Philip II was securely betrothed to Mary—Pole had frequently been mentioned as a possible husband and, being still only in deacon's orders, could have been dispensed. It was in Dec. 1555 that he reached England and proceeded to absolve and reconcile the realm, and to become Mary's adviser, though not in her policy of persecuting heretics. At the ensuing synod and later, the Cardinal laid down measures of reform for the English Church, particularly for priestly life, and demanded a translation of the N.T.; but most of these measures were lost because of the short duration of Mary's reign. In 1556, on the deposition of Cranmer, he was made Archbishop of Canterbury, being ordained priest two days earlier. Meanwhile, Carafa, who had become Pope Paul IV, went to war with Spain, thus making Mary an enemy, and

compounded his hostility by depriving Pole of his legation and bidding him to Rome to face charges of doctrinal unsoundness before the Inquisition. Mary delayed delivery of the summons, and Pole died at Lambeth in 1557, broken as much by ingratitude and distrust as by ill-health; he was buried at Canterbury, close to the tomb of St Thomas: a man in whom was found with the best of the humanist's civilised tolerance, a purity and austerity of life and an unambitious and undeviating loyalty to his faith.

Pontifex Maximus

(Lat., supreme pontiff.*) A title formerly much in vogue as a style of the Pope, now being allowed to fall into disuse, in view of its 'triumphalist' connotations and its origins as the title of the chief (pagan) priest of ancient Rome; having been adopted by the Emperors from Augustus onward as a hereditary title, it was surrendered by Gratian in 375 to the Bishop of Rome.

Pontiff

A title still used for a bishop; the popular derivation from the Latin *pons* and *facio* (he who builds a bridge) is less probable than that from the Oscan *puntis* and *facio* (he who offers sacrifice).

Pontificale Romanum

The liturgical book for the rites usually reserved to a bishop. It is in three parts, the first dealing with persons and containing blessings and consecrations for bishops, abbots and others, the second has blessings and prayers concerned with things (churches, altars, chalices, cemeteries, etc), the third part gives directions for visitation* of a parish, the blessing of the Holy Oils, the conduct of diocesan synods, the degradation of a cleric, the treatment of penitents, the reception of a legate* or a sovereign, the absolutions* for the dead.

Pontificals

The ceremonial equipment proper to a bishop includes the pectoral cross (recently in many cases not of such precious material or so richly ornamented as previously), the ring (formerly kissed by the faithful while genuflecting before the prelate), the mitre* and pastoral staff* when pontificating, the buskins, gloves, tunicle and dalmatic at pontifical Mass; the throne also comes under the heading of Pontificals.

Poor Clares

The Second Order of St. Francis, which he founded, together with St. Clare, in 1212, has two branches: the Colettines, strictly enclosed, and the Urbanists, who follow a modification (by Pope Urban IV in 1263) of the very severe Rule, and who undertake certain external works.

Pope

(Gk. παπας, Lat. *papa*—father; παπας, the title of a parish priest in the Orthodox Church, is still regularly, if confusingly, translated as 'pope')—the style used by the Bishop of Rome as chief bishop and father of the universal Church. Used earlier by any bishop, it was gradually restricted, so that, e.g. in 998 the Archbishop of Milan was rebuked in Synod for calling himself 'Pope', and finally, in 1073, Gregory VII* forbade its use by any but the Bishop of Rome.

Pope, Abdication of

A pope may resign his office without consent or consultation with the cardinals or anyone else.
See Celestine V.

Pope, Authority of

The Pope, being elected by the College of Cardinals, does not therefore hold his authority from them: it comes to him *jure divino* as successor of St. Peter, conferring infallibility* and full jurisdiction over the entire Church and over every individual Catholic.
See Conciliar Theory.

Pope, Deposition of

The only cause for which a Pope may be deposed is heresy, expressed or implied; his removal, which may be performed only by a General Council, is not strictly deposition, since by his heresy, he has already in fact surrendered the leadership of the Church. No Pope has been deposed; the deposition of an anti-pope is in fact the removal of one who has never been

Pope, and of the case of John XXIII who was compelled to resign, at the Council of Constance*, it has to be said that his election was in any case doubtful.

Pope, Election of

See Conclave.

Pope Joan

A piece of mediaeval folklore first recorded by the Dominican chronicler De Mailly in the 13th cent. to the effect that about the year 1100 (or on the death of St. Leo IV in 855) a woman called Joanna, after an impressive career as a scholar, rose, still undetected, to the throne of Peter; after two years as Pope, she gave birth to a child in the midst of a ceremonial procession and died on the spot. There have been times when the story was taken seriously, even by some scholars, though there is no shred of evidence for it.

Pope Pius IV, creed of

A profession of faith set down by this Pope in 1564, which after rehearsing the Nicene* Creed, goes on to elaborate the article on the 'one, holy, Catholic and apostolic Church' by listing such things as the Apostolic tradition, the seven sacraments, the sacrifice of the Mass, Purgatory, indulgences, the invocation of saints and the authority of the See of Peter.

Pope, Primacy of

This is not merely a primacy of honour,—which would be accorded by many non-Catholic Christians—but also of jurisdiction, which is universal, transmitted directly from Christ and independent equally of the bishops and of the civil authority. Hence the Pope stands as the centre of Catholic unity and orthodoxy, from whose authoritative pronouncements there is no appeal.
See Conciliar Theory.

Popery

The derogatory description of the system, practices and teachings of the Church of Rome, first found in the writings of Wm.Tyndale in 1534; recently little in fashion.

Popish

An offensive epithet for 'Catholic' (as in e.g. *Popish* Plot*) used particularly during the Penal* Times but not often since.

Popish Plot

Also known as the Titus Oates Plot. See Oates, Titus.

Popular Devotions

There are numerous devout exercises which have grown up alongside the liturgy (largely, it has been said, because this had become less and less intelligible) and, with encouragement from the clergy, have taken a strong grip on the laity as a whole. They include such practices as individual and collective devotions to the Blessed Sacrament and to the Sacred Heart of Jesus, the Stations of the Cross, novenas of various kinds (including the Perpetual Novena), devotions to the Mother of God and practices in honour of many saints, the wearing of medals and scapulars, rings and badges. Distrust of the excessively emotional appeal possible with such exercises was a factor in the rise and spread of the Liturgical Movement*.

Port Royal

A convent of French Cistercian nuns, settled in Paris in 1626; also a centre outside the city for priests and laymen which, besides maintaining schools, had a strong intellectual and religious influence on French thought of the time, traces of which linger in the modern *lycées*. Port Royal was deeply affected with Jansenism* and on this point withstood ecclesiastical authority for 50 years, its leaders being described as 'pure as angels and proud as devils'; it was suppressed in 1713 by Clement IX.

Portuguese Hymn, the

A name formerly used of the Christmas carol *Adeste Fideles*, which, being anonymous and not heard before the 18th cent., was first sung in England in the chapel of the Portuguese Embassy in London.

Porziuncula

(It., the small portion, *sc.* of land.) The name of the spot, and of the adjoining hamlet, in Umbria, where St. Francis* (of neighbouring Assisi) repaired the ruined chapel and founded his Order; there was built over it the imposing church of Santa Maria degli Angeli. From the 13th cent.—though not, apparently from Francis' own day—the faithful have been gaining there the Porziuncula Indulgence, also known as the Pardon of Assisi, for the benefit of the souls in Purgatory*. The Indulgence has been extended to other churches, not only of the Franciscans, but also of the Dominicans, Servites and some other religious.

Possession, diabolical

In accordance with her ancient teaching, the Church still acknowledges the possiblity of demonic possession, though the Order of *exorcist*, instituted of ancient times to deal with it, is now abrogated; only a priest authorised by his bishop is allowed to exorcise. Such possession is not taken by the Church as necessarily indicating sinfulness in the person possessed.

Postulate (the Pallium)

Whoever is made archbishop in the Latin rite must, within three months, request the Holy See for the *pallium**, the ritual postulation being triple in form made 'earnestly', 'more earnestly' and 'most earnestly'. Until his pallium has been granted and his oath of obedience accepted, the new archbishop's powers and privileges are in abeyance.

Postulator

The postulator, i.e. the official who urges the cause* of a candidate for canonisation or beatification before the Sacred Congregation for the Causes of the Saints*, must be a priest and must reside in Rome; he may appoint assistants, who are known as vice-postulators.

Poverty

Used in the religious sense, this term refers to 'holy poverty', the *evangelical counsel**, the renunciation of the right to or use of material goods in order the better to follow Christ (Mt.8:20, 10:8-10, 19:21:24). The vow of poverty is an essential part of the religious life, and its requirements vary among the orders and congregations, from the subjection to a superior's permission in the possession and use of worldly goods to total and permanent renunciation of ownership and disposal of them.

Power of the Keys

The expression, originating from Mt.16:19 and used for the complete authority of teaching, orders and jurisdiction granted by Our Lord to Peter and his successors and shared by the other members of the hierarchy according to their rank. The phrase has been used popularly since the time of the Fathers★ for the power of binding and loosing as exercised in the Sacrament of Penance★.

Powers

See Angel.

Praeconium Paschale

(Lat., Easter Proclamation.) See Exsultet.

Praemunire

The term is used indifferently for the statutes, the offence, the writ issued and the punishment: the several statutes, the first of them that of Edward III (1353) aimed at limiting or eliminating papal jurisdiction in England; from the prohibition of appeal to Rome, the statute of 1393 went further and laid down punishment for any who should promote a papal Bull or excommunication. In 1529, Wolsey, by submitting to a writ of Praemunire, became the first English prelate to accept the jurisdiction of a secular court. The penalties of Praemunire (outlawry, forfeiture of lands and other properties, arrest) were invoked in several of the post-Reformation penal laws against Catholics; James I used it to transfer power from ecclesiastical to civil courts; and a peer charged with Praemunire may not be tried by the House of Lords but must accept trial by jury.

Prayer Book

The term is used for a book containing a collection of prayers for private use, as opposed to any liturgical book. See, e.g. the Garden of the Soul. The Church has no equivalent to the Church of England's Book of Common Prayer.

Prayer for England

A prayer asking the intercession of the Mother of God for the return of the country to the Faith; it is usually recited at Benediction★ of the Blessed Sacrament. There is a longer prayer composed for the same purpose by Cardinal Wiseman★ in 1839 and seeking the intercession of many saints connected with the establishment, development or defence of the Church in England.
See Prayer for Wales.

Prayer for Wales

A prayer for the conversion of the people of Wales which is recited in either Welsh or English usually at Benediction★ of the Blessed Sacrament, in the dioceses of Cardiff and Menevia.

Prayer to the Saints

See Invocation of Saints.

Preacheresses

Nuns of the Order of Preachers★, formerly known as the nuns of the Second Order (though in fact they grew out of St Dominic's★ first foundation, an institute to protect woman from the Albigensian★ heresy, which pre-dated by eight or nine years his first community of men in 1214–15). Professing solemn vows, they are strictly enclosed and bound to the Office★. Their regimen includes manual labour and permanent abstinence from meat, their prayers and fasts being directed to the saving of souls and the support of the friars in their work. They have some convents in Ireland and one at Carisbrook, I.O.W. Other Dominican sisters are of the Third Order★ Regular.

Precious Blood

The appreciation of the redemptive value of the Blood of Christ, symbol and synonym for our salvation, from the Apostolic Age onward (e.g. Heb.9:12, 10:19, Eph.1:7, Rev.1:5, 7:14, 12:11) gave rise, naturally, to speculative and liturgical thought which manifested itself in such propositions as that the whole Christ is received entire under the form either of bread or of wine, in St. Thomas Aquinas' assertion that the Lord left no relic of the blood he actually shed in his Passion (see Holy Blood), and in the establishing of a Feast of the Precious Blood on July 1st (the naming of that month as the month of the Precious Blood is unofficial); the Precious Blood is likewise the dedication of Westminster Cathedral.

Preface

The solemn introduction to the Eucharistic Prayer in the liturgy of the Mass, spoken by the celebrant after the Offertory and its prayers are over; though it varies with seasons and festivals, the Preface always maintains the theme of praise and thanksgiving contained in the preceeding dialogue, *Let us give thanks to the Lord our God—It is right to give him thanks and praise.*

Prefect

i) The president of a Roman Congregation*, always a cardinal. Formerly some congregations traditionally had the Pope for their Prefect.
ii) Prefect Apostolic: see Prefecture Apostolic.

Prefecture Apostolic

In its first stage of ecclesiastical organisation (as Prefecture Apostolic), a territory is a missionary area and subject directly to the Holy See (the Sacred Congregation for the Evangelisation of Peoples*, otherwise known as *Propaganda**) and administered by a Prefect Apostolic, who, though not usually a bishop, is granted wide powers and a restricted use of Pontificals*

Prelate

(Lat. *praelatus*, set before.) The term for one who has external jurisdiction by right of his office; principally a bishop; also vicar* apostolic, prefect* apostolic, abbot* and other major religious superior, and higher official of the Roman Curia*. A prelate has the title Monsignor and in choir wears rochet* and mantelletta*. Many prelatures are conferred by Rome unconnected with office, duty or emolument, but in recognition of services to the Church.

Prelate, Domestic

A domestic prelature is conferred by the Pope on a priest in acknowledgement of merit, whereby he is counted a member of the papal household, regardless of where he lives. His official style of dress is similar to a bishop's, but with black biretta; he has no pontifical insignia and is addressed as 'The Right Rev. Mgr . . .'

Prelate Nullius

(sc. *diocesis*, without diocese.) One who has jurisdiction over a territory not subject to a diocesan bishop; he is usually a titular bishop, but in either case has the powers and duties of a bishop-in-ordinary*.

Premonstratensians

See Canons Regular of Prémontré.

Presbyter

(Gk. πρεσβυτερος, an elder.) The origin of the English 'priest'. At the time of the writing of the N.T. Letters and the Acts, the local Churches appear to have been administered by colleges of elders, perhaps on the model of the synagogue (Acts 11:30, 15:22. 14:23 indicates the appointment of elders by Paul and Barnabas to new churches). Some passages seem to equate *presbyter* with *overseer* ('επισκοπος, 'bishop'), as Acts 20:17ff, Phil 1:1, Tit.1:5,7; but from the 2nd cent., it is the president of the council of presbyters who is usually given the title 'bishop' and it is by him that the presbyters are delegated their authority.

Presbytery

Architecturally, the term is used either of the whole choir of a large church, or of the space between the choir-stalls and the altar-steps; in a Roman basilica* or Byzantine church, it is the space between the altar and the bishop's throne (which is in the apse). Domestically, it is the house of the priest or priests of a parish.

Presence of God, Practice of the

The awareness of God dwelling in the soul as powerful ally and inspirer has always been recognised by Christians as desirable, and the faithful, both clerical and lay, in the life of contemplation or the active life, have been admonished consistently to sustain this conscious realisation by ejaculatory prayer, by silence and solitude, by purity of intent in all actions and by the persistently renewed offering of oneself and one's thoughts, words and actions to God.

Presentation Brothers

A congregation founded in Waterford, Ireland, in 1802, by Edmund Rice, who took the name of Brother Ignatius; it evolved in 1822 into two separate institutes, the one becoming the Christian Brothers of Ireland who, under the leadership of the founder, adopted a new Rule as a centralised form of government, the Presentation Brothers maintaining their original foundation and having houses now in England and Canada. Both groups specialise in education.

Presentation Nuns

An enclosed Order with solemn vows, now in many countries; founded in Cork in 1777 by Nano Nagle to manage schools, orphanages and training-centres.

Presentation of Our Blessed Lady, Feast of the

November 21st is celebrated in honour of the presentation of the Blessed Virgin in the Temple at the age of three, a story found in the apocryphal *Protoevangelium of James**. The feast, established in the Eastern church, was accepted by the West in the late Middle Ages; Sixtus IV gave it liturgical status, Pius V removed it from the liturgical books and Sixtus V made its observance universal. The feast-day was often chosen by religious women for the ceremony of Clothing.

Presentation of Our Lord

Mary and Joseph brought the infant Jesus to Jerusalem, "to present him to the Lord, observing what stands written in the Law" (Lk 2:22–23); also called Candlemas, from the candles carried in procession and then held by the faithful during the Mass, this feast (Feb. 2nd) was formerly entitled the Purification of Our Lady, from the ritual purification mentioned in the same scripture passage.

Presentation of Our Lord, Feast of the

See Candlemas.

Prester John

Marco Polo, the Venetian, concurs, in his book of travels, with the fantastic story long current in Europe, Syria and Egypt, of a Tartar prince who was, according to local tradition, also a Christian priest with the title Presbyter John (in the Tartar language Ouan-Khan; Ouan could be derived from Joannes, to make Prince John), who was defeated and slain by his vassal Jengis Khan. The traveller goes on to claim that the contemporary ruler of one mainly Christian province, whose true name is George, holds the new hereditary title of Prester John, being the fourth in line of descent from the original Prester. Marco Polo mentions, in the previous chapter, a city that had three Nestorian churches in it; and it may be the existence of Nestorian* Christians to the south of Lake Baikal, their ruler's residence being at Karakorum, that gave rise to the legend. Later and wilder versions place Prester John in Abyssinia or other parts of Africa.

Preternatural

This word, used non-technically to mean exceptional or extraordinary or even supernatural, has its theological use: the preternatural gifts are those—such as integrity, immortality, impassibility—attributed to the first human pair and found in the humanity of Christ after his Resurrection, and described as gifts exceeding the capacity of every created nature.

Priestcraft

A word little used now, it had not the obvious signification (cf. Knox's "Whole *Art* of Chaplaincy") but was a polemicist's weapon: the Concise Oxford Dictionary gives "ambitious or wordly policy of priests".
See also Casuistry.

Primacy of Honour

The sort of precedence, accorded from reverence and courtesy, but without granting authority or jurisdiction, which is given by the Orthodox churches to the Patriarch of Constantinople and latterly to the Pope by leading prelates of the Church of England.

Primacy of Peter

The position of Peter as the chief man of the Church is clearly declared in the N.T.: the "Rock" passages (Mt. 16:15–19, Mk. 3:16, Jn. 1:42), those which single him out for prominence (Mk. 16:7, Jn. 21:15–17, Acts 2:14, 3:12, 4:8, I Cor. 15:5) or stress his authority (Acts 1:15ff, 2:14ff, 3:12 &

4:8, 15:7, Gal. 1:18—Paul's reporting of his contradiction of Peter's policy in Gal. 2:11ff conveys in its tone his acknowledgement of Peter's unique position); the miracles (it is Peter's shadow which heals the sick in Acts 5:15), the decisions (Peter is the one instructed by God in Acts 10 to admit Gentiles to the Church); a position assumed and confirmed by the attitudes of the early Church towards his successors in Rome.

Primate
A title, no longer recognised in Canon Law, of a bishop who, without being a patriarch*, has jurisdiction over all bishops and metropolitans of an area, being himself subject directly to the Holy See. Most primatial sees have had historical importance, such as those of Italy (Rome), Ireland (Dublin), All Ireland (Armagh), Africa (Carthage), Gaul and Germany (Sens), Bohemia (Prague) and others; they still retain the titles.

Prime
(Lat. *prima hora*, first hour.) One of the small hours of the Divine Office, intended as the first of the day hours. It was suppressed in the liturgical reforms introduced by the Second Vatican Council, and is now incorporated into Lauds (Morning Prayer).

Prince of the Apostles
A phrase to describe St. Peter as the chosen leader of the group of twelve; a direct translation of the Latin phrase *princeps apostolorum*, the word being used in its primitive, non-royal sense, as the Romans used it of Augustus before they began to think of him as Emperor.

Prince of the Church
Title used of cardinals, the "royalty" of the Church, historically recognised in many countries as taking precedence of all but princes of the blood.

Principalities
One of the ranks of celestial spirits (Eph. 1:21, Col, 1:16).
See Angel.

Prinknash
In Gloucestershire—where there is a strong tradition of pronouncing it "Prinnage"—a Benedictine abbey of the Cassinese Congregation of Primitive Observance, formerly a grange of the medieval abbey of St. Peter at Gloucester; well-known for its pottery.
See Caldey.

Prior
The title of the second-in-command of a monastery*, who will, when necessary, deputise for the Abbot*; though in some Orders (e.g. Carthusian, Carmelite, Dominican), there are no abbots and the superior of each house is a prior, the superior of the Order being Prior General.

Prior, Claustral
The second in authority of a community of monks or canons regular, sometimes called *dean*, who is appointed by the abbot and can have a sub-prior to assist him.

Prior, Conventual
The superior of a community of those orders which do not use the title of abbot (Carthusians, Dominicans, etc) or of an independent house, as of Benedictines and others, which has not yet been made an abbey. With the friars, this office usually has a term of years, with the canons and monks it is usually for life, with the notable exception of the Carthusian prior, who resigns after two years but may be reappointed by the Prior General.

Prioress
In general, the equivalent, in a religious house of women, to the prior in a male establishment; applied strictly speaking only in houses which have papal approbation and solemn vows.

Prior General
The superior general of certain orders of monks, friars (Augustinian, Calced Carmelite, Servite) and the Hospitallers of St. John, being elected to serve a set number of years.

Priory
A religious house whose superior is a Prior* or Prioress*.

Prisoner of the Vatican

The phrase was applied to several Popes, who, as an attitude of protest, spent their entire pontificates within the boundaries of what is now known as Vatican City, an independent State inside the city of Rome. Pius IX* in the *Risorgimento* was deprived of the Papal States* when Rome was taken by the forces of Victor Emmanuel in 1870; and the Law of Guarantees declared the Pope's territories forfeit to the new State of Italy. Rather than acknowledge himself a subject of the new kingdom, Pio Nono* chose never again to set foot outside the Vatican; subsequently other Popes took on this self-imposed "imprisonment" until Pius XI* in 1929 concluded the Lateran Treaty*. In this he renounced all claim to the Papal domains outside the Vatican and recognised the Italian State with Rome as its capital; in exchange, he obtained Italian acceptance of Papal sovereignty within Vatican City and in international affairs.It was his successor Pius XII* who resumed the Papal custom of travelling outside the Vatican; now the Popes again regularly spend some time at Castel Gandolfo, their summer villa about 15 miles from the city, in the Alban Hills; John XXIII* paid a historic visit to the Regina Coeli, the Roman gaol, and called often enough at seminaries, churches, hospitals and hostels throughout in his diocese ("After all, I am Bishop of Rome") to gain the affectionate nickname of "John-Without-The-Walls". His successor, Paul VI, visited Jerusalem, Istanbul, Bombay, Bogotá, Fatima*, Australia and the Far East; he also addressed the World Council of Churches at Geneva and made a historic speech to the United Nations General Assembly in New York.

Private Interpretation

The three chief principles of classical Protestantism are the acceptance of the Bible as the only source of revelation, justification by faith alone and the priesthood of all believers. The first of these, accepting no authority except the Bible, necessarily sets up every man as his own interpreter of the sacred writings, and, equally necessarily, this private interpretation leads to the fragmentation into so many and so varied sects which is typical of Protestantism.

Private Judgement

The Lutheran principle that each individual, by his own study of the Scriptures, obtains all the guidance he needs, and that the Church's claim to teach is an intrusion on the individual's rights.
See Private Interpretation.

Pro Armenis

The bull *Exultate Deo* (Eugene IV, 1439), addressed to the Armenians, contains a decree of some importance dealing with the seven sacraments.

Pro-Cathedral

A church used by a bishop as his cathedral until a suitable building can be erected for the purpose. In London, the "Old Pro" (Our Lady of Victories, Kensington), was used from 1867 until the newly-finished Cathedral was opened at Westminster in 1903. The first church used as a pro-Cathedral was St. Mary Moorfields, also in London.

Process

The "process" through which a (dead) person passes to be given the official title of Saint; the candidate for canonisation is first referred to as "Servant of God", then, when heroic virtue has been proved, the title "Venerable" is officially conferred, but public honour is not to be paid until the decree declaring him "Blessed" has been passed, the step before canonisation. There is, in the Roman Curia*, a Congregation for the Causes of the Saints*.
See also Canonisation.

Procession of the Holy Spirit

(i.e. the *proceeding*, Lat. *procedo*, I go forth.)
The Catholic doctrine of the Holy Spirit is that he takes his origin from the Father and the Son as from a single principle of *spiration*, this latter term conveying a mode of loving, exclusive of the idea of birth such as is attributed to the Son. The reason for the First Council of Constantinople*'s statement that the Spirit proceeds from the Father was the necessity to assert the divinity of the Holy Spirit against the denials of the Macedonian sect; later, this was interpreted as excluding procession from the Son, to correct which impression *Filioque** was inserted into the Nicene Creed.

Procopius Legend, the

The classic warning to hagiographer and historian alike: St. Procopius, executed in the first decade of the 4th cent., was described by a contemporary as the first victim in Palestine of the persecution of Diocletian, the "Great Persecution"; from this record, there grew legends which resulted in three martyrs of this name being venerated. There has been a similar conjecture, but in the reverse direction, about St. Patrick*, that the Saint now venerated is in fact a conflation of perhaps three missionaries of the same name and the same era.

Procurator

Each religious order has a representative resident in Rome, who is known as Procurator or Procurator General. In a religious house, the Procurator is that member of the community who has care of the feeding, clothing and general material welfare of the religious; the modern counterpart of the cellarer, of whom St. Benedict insisted that he be "temperate, not a great eater, not haughty or headstrong or arrogant, not slothful or wasteful, but a God-fearing man who may be like a father to the whole community. Let him . . . do nothing without leave of the abbot."

Profanation

This is the handing over of a church to some non-religious but proper purpose, and entails the removal of altars in a liturgical ceremony called *reduction*. (*Profane*, in its first sense, means that which is distinct from, though not necessarily hostile to, the sacred: Lat. *pro fanum*, in front of—i.e. outside—the temple).

Profession of Faith

It is required that anyone who takes part in a council or synod or is to be created cardinal* or made bishop, abbot or prelate nullius*, vicar or prefect apostolic, vicar capitular, dignitary or canon, vicar general, rector of parish, seminary professor or religious superior shall make—in person and not by proxy—to the relevant superior, a profession of faith: it usually takes the form of the Creed* of Pope Pius IV.

Profession, Religious

The contract whereby one binds oneself by vow to the religious life in a community approved by the Church. The vows thus made are either solemn (in what is strictly termed a religious order*, as distinct from a society or congregation) and for life, or simple (temporary or perpetual). The obligation thus assumed is that of striving for perfection by means of the three evangelical* counsels and the rule and spirit of the order. Contrary to popular misconception, profession is not made easy by orders eager for unsuspecting recruits: no permanent profession is allowed except after a period—three years—of temporary or preparatory vows (which may not begin under the age of 16) nor at less than 21 years of age. Dispensation from religious vows is reserved to the Holy See but a superior general can dispense from simple vows, provided the subject is not also in holy orders.

Prohibited Occupations

Canon Law* forbids clerics to engage in medicine, surgery, civil and military service, public political office, the practice of law in civil courts, trade and business; it also lists certain forbidden recreations, such as "clamorous hunting" (*venatio clamorosa*)—which would appear to include riding to hounds but not e.g. ferreting—theatre going, dancing, games of chance.

Prohibiting Impediment

See Impediments to Marriage.

Promoter of Justice

A cleric appointed by the bishop as judge in the diocesan court; he forms, with the bishop, a single court, so that there is no appeal from one to the other. He is very often the Vicar General*.

Promoter of the Faith

See Devil's Advocate.

Propaganda

The convenient abbreviation used for the Roman Congregation* called first the Sacred Congregation for the Spreading of the Faith, founded by Pope Clement VIII, on the model of two commissions of cardinals set up by Pius V and Gregory XIII;

having lapsed, this Congregation was re-established by Gregory XV in 1622. It was renamed in 1967 by Paul VI *Sacred Congregation for the Evangelising of the Nations* or *For the Spreading of the Faith*. The current use of the word *propaganda* reflects human hostility and historical prejudice: what I advance in support of my cause is truth, while the opponent's advocacy of his side is lies, or at best untrustworthy.

Prophecies, the

The word commonly used to describe the O.T. Readings, 12 in number, which were read or chanted at the Easter Vigil liturgy; in the reform of Pius XII, they were reduced to four, and the present number, established after the Second Vatican Council, is seven.

Prophecies of St. Malachy

A certain spurious document composed and discovered in Rome about 1590 contains a catalogue of descriptive mottoes, one for every Pope from Celestine II in the 12th cent. to Peter II, the Pope under whom the world comes to an end in a great persecution (*In persecutione extrema S.R. Ecclesiae sedebit Petrus II Romanus*, In the final persecution of Holy Church, the Pope will be Peter II, a Roman). While some of the mottoes would appear to be startingly accurate, e.g. Pius IX has *crux de cruce*, interpreted—a cross from the cross—as referring to Pio Nono's sufferings at the hands of the House of Savoy, whose flag bears a cross, they are of a conveniently elastic vagueness. Few of the ordinary run of Popes would be disqualified from the sobriquet Light in Heaven or Burning Fire or Angelic Father—and it would take more than ordinary ingenuity to fit Woodland Angel to Pius V or Rustic Animal to Benedict XIV. The saint to whom the forgeries are attributed was in fact one of the most prominent figures of the Irish Middle Ages, Maolmhaodhog, for years kept out of the See of Armagh (to which he had been nominated by Honorius II) by a stubborn anti-Roman faction; he was a close friend of St. Bernard of Clairvaux, in whose arms he died and who wrote his life (but with no mention of the Prophecies).

Protestant

In Catholic usage, the word has shrunk in its application: once, the world of these islands was divided into Catholics and Protestants; more recently the word has come to be used chiefly in such phrases as *Protestant thought, Protestant theology, Protestant tradition*, and, as an appellation of persons, (though the older practice still obtains to some extent in Northern Ireland only for such as explicitly claim it for themselves).

Protoevangelium of James

or the Gospel of the Infancy. The oldest of the extant apocryphal gospels, dating in part from the 2nd cent. and attributed to St. James the Less. Its chief importance is as testimony to early practices of devotion to the Mother of God.

Protonotary Apostolic

The College of Protonotaries Apostolic is part of the Pontifical Household (ecclesiastical section. See Curial Offices). The City Notaries were appointed, seven in number, in the 3rd or 4th cent. (legend attributes them to St. Clement, in the 1st) to be chroniclers of the Acts of the Martyrs and of ecclesiastical events, and, in the 5th, they formed a college. After many vicissitudes and multiplications, the members were reduced by Pope Paul VI to two classes: Protonotaries Apostolic *de numero participantium*—seven in number, still described as a college, and Protonotaries Apostolic Supernumerary. The chief work of the College is concerned with Causes for beatification and canonisation.

Province

The territory over which an archbishop exercises metropolitan jurisdiction, which will comprise his own diocese and at least one other. Also, a large district which is a unit of a religious order, frequently, though not necessarily or always, coincident with national boundaries.

Psalmi Idiotici

(Lat., psalms of private individuals.) Under this title were grouped a number of poetic compositions of the early centuries which, psalm-like in structure and execution but distinguished by this name from the "real" or Biblical psalms, were none the less used in liturgical worship. The only extant specimens are the *Gloria in Excelsis*, the *Te Deum* and the Greek hymn translated by Keble as *Hail, Gladdening Light* (A.&M. No. 18) and by Bridges as *O Gladsome Light, O Grace*, and still used in the Orthodox liturgy.

Pseudo-Dionysius

(Pseudo-Areopagite, Pseudo-Denis.) A collection of mystic writings of great influence during the Middle Ages, commonly attributed to Dionysius of Acts 17:34, reckoned now to be the work of an unknown writer about the year A.D. 500.

Pseudo-Matthew

An apocryphal work of the 5th cent., which claimed to be St. Jerome's Latin version of a Hebrew gospel by St. Matthew; it is the origin of popular tales of the Flight Into Egypt. There is another version entitled the Nativity of Mary, which ends with the birth of Christ.

Publican

(Lat., *publicanus*.) The translation in the older versions of the Bible for 'tax-collector' in the more recent (though the Jerusalem Bible prints the traditional title 'The Pharisee and the publican'—outside the text—in Lk.18.). Such officials were thoroughly hated by their fellow-Jews both because they often made extortionate profits for themselves and because they were collaborating with the enemy, hence the associations, "tax-collectors and sinners", "tax-collectors and prostitutes". In the States of the Church* just before the *Risorgimento** a great deal of anti-clerical opprobrium was heaped on the parish clergy, who were *ex officio* Papal tax collectors.

Pugin, Augustus Welby

A leader of the Gothic Revival, who passionately upheld that style as the only one suitable for a Christian church. Architect of the cathedrals of Birmingham, Nottingham and Southwark, monastic buildings at Mount St. Bernard, Ramsgate, Oulton and many churches.

Purgative Way, the

The beginner's stage of the spiritual life, a kind of infancy of the soul, in which mortification is important, together with meditation, particularly meditation on the four last things, and the determined renunciation of self. St. Thomas says of it that the principal effort is to turn from sin and oppose concupiscences, "which destroy charity; and this is proper to beginners, in whom charity is to be nourished and fostered, lest it be destroyed".

Purgatory

The state of existence in which the souls of those who have died in the grace of God expiate their unforgiven minor faults and work out the satisfaction still owing to Divine Justice for mortal sins forgiven in this world, by the pain of urgent longing for God—there so much more clearly perceived and more ardently desired—and, as is commonly taught, by some sensible pain, as of fire. The most commonly used O.T. passage in this connection is 2 Maccabees 12:39–45; in the N.T., our Lord's words in Mt. 12:32 imply the forgiveness of sins after death. As regards the Church in teaching and practice: Clement of Alexandria in the 2nd cent. maintains that those who die repentant but without time to do works of penance will be purified by fire beyond the grave; numerous inscriptions and the writings of such Eastern Doctors as Ss. John Chrysostom and Cyril of Jerusalem make it clear that there was already in the 4th cent. a custom of offering prayers and the Eucharist for the dead; St. Epiphanius (315–403) branded as heretical those who denied the usefulness of prayers for the departed—a neat retaliation, in advance, of Article XXII of the Thirty-Nine; in the West, there is a fairly clear indication of belief in Purgatory in the *Passion of Ss. Perpetua and Felicity*, a 2nd or 3rd cent. MS, and a definite teaching in St. Ambrose*; St. Augustine* elaborates the doctrine of the particular judgement of the soul at death with ensuing purifying pains, and Caesarius of Arles distinguishes between those sins which can be expiated either before or after death and those, capital, offences which lead straight to Hell. Through Gregory the Great*, who taught the privation of the Vision of God as one of the great pains of Purgatory, as did Bede the Venerable*, we come to the mediaeval writers, the Scholastics*, the

Council of Trent* confirming dogmatically, (the dissidents being Waldensians, Albigensians and the Reformation thinkers), and all subsequent theologians keeping pace with the Church's practice of offering Masses, prayers and indulgencies* for the repose of the souls in Purgatory, in the spirit of the modern Eucharistic Prayer II *Bring them and all the departed into the light of Your presence.* It is only more recently, from such theologians as St. Robert Bellarmine* and St. Alphonsus Liguori* that the practice has arisen of asking the intercession of the souls in Purgatory on our behalf.

Purification, Feast of the

The name previously used for the Feast of the Presentation of Our Lord (Lk.2:22).

Purificator

The small hand-towel of linen used by the celebrant at Mass to dry the chalice and his fingers after the Ablutions; similar to that used at the Lavabo*.

Puritanism

A religious mentality endowed with an exaggerated sense of the spiritual danger attaching to the things of this world and an indefatigable energy in controlling or denouncing their use; deriving naturally from Manicheism*, it induces intolerance in place of compassion, abolition instead of usage; where the scholastic philosopher, in company with the "average man" says, e.g., that drink, gambling and the appreciation of beauty are gifts to our humanity to be taken gratefully and with an awareness of possible excess, the Puritan is inclined to say, "Drink is the Devil's poison, gambling leads to Hell, beauty is a snare." Hence the jibe that the Puritan's commandment is "Thou shalt not enjoy thyself." Historically, the Puritans were extremists holding the view that the 16th cent. Reformation did not go nearly far enough and wishing to sweep away from worship all ritual and ornament and to destroy any connection between religion and festivity. Until that era, most holy days, besides having processions and other public rejoicings, were also associated with special recipes for food and drink, custard for Our Lady, simnel cake for Mid-Lent Sunday, pancakes for Shrove Tuesday, and also plum-porridge, cheese-cakes, mince-pies, geese-pie, etc. During that incredible interlude in which the Puritan power eventually and briefly ruled in England under Cromwell, Christmas was abolished and the vicar of Uggeshall in Suffolk, one Playters, was deprived "for eating custard after a scandalous manner". Perhaps the difference between the theocracy of the Jews and that of the Puritans goes back to the fact that the God of the Jews could smile.

Purple

(Lat.*purpureus*, scarlet.) To be "raised to the purple" (made a cardinal, an ecclesiastical "prince") or "born into purple" (i.e. of a royal family) are phrases deriving from the colour of the robes inherited by both Church and state from imperial Rome: only the Emperor and the statue of Jupiter were permitted the scarlet toga. The formula for the dye used in the cardinals' robes is said to be the secret of one Roman family. The colour we call purple (in the liturgy *violaceus*) is used for the vestments of Lent and Advent, votive Masses of the Passion and of Vigils, and an alternative for black in Masses for the dead; it is also the colour of the cassock of bishops and other prelates.

Puseyism

A name given by some contemporaries to the Oxford Movement*; from E. B. Pusey, prominent in the Movement.

Putative Marriage

A union which is invalid but contracted in good faith by at least one of the parties; such are still supposed to be marriages until nullity is established. Children of such a marriage are legitimate, and illegitimate children are legitimised by a putative marriage.

Pyx

(Gk. πυξίς, box-wood vessel.) Historically, any container for the reservation of the Host (C.I.C. can. 1270); currently, either the small, circular vessel usually hung round the priest's neck to bring Communion to the sick, or the larger, similar vessel with a base, kept inside the tabernacle for reservation of the large Host for Benediction* or Exposition*.

Quadragesimo Anno

(Lat., in the fortieth year.) In 1931, on the fortieth anniversary of the publication of Leo XIII's *Rerum Novarum**, Pope Pius XI put out an encyclical with the above name; its subject, the restructuring of society on the lines of the Gospel, and its clear condemnation of the evils of unrestrained capitalism, made it the most talked-of document to come from his pen. The encyclical analyses the contemporary industrial situation, speaking of the "economic despotism of the few", which it describes as a natural effect of "unbounded free competition"; it lays down the principle of the just wage and demands that the unpropertied wage-earner should be helped to "a certain moderate ownership". What the Pope wrote of his predecessor's encyclical, that it was "looked on with suspicion by some, even by Catholics", was certainly true of *Quadragesimo Anno*.

Quaestor

(Lat., one who seeks out.) Cf. Pardoner. A preacher appointed to "seek out" money for a specific purpose such as the building of a church, financing of a crusade, etc. Indulgences were frequently granted to the contributors, whereupon many grave abuses followed (cf. Luther's ringing protests against the sale of indulgences for the building of St. Peter's) and the system was abolished by the Council of Trent*.

Quarantine

(It. *quaranta*, forty.) Period of 40 days, once a description of an indulgence judged equivalent to 40 days of penance in the system of the early Church; a 'Lent' of penance.

Quarant'ore

(It., forty hours.) The name formerly in popular use for the Forty Hours'* Devotion.

Quarr

In the Isle of Wight, near Ryde, an abbey of the French Congregation of Benedic-

tine monks; a new foundation in the early 20th cent. as a relic of the community of Solesmes* who were then returning to France after seven years of exile at Appuldurcombe and about ten at Quarr. The abbey preserves the traditional excellence of liturgy and chant for which the mother house is justly famous.

Quasi-domicile

Temporary residence in a place (diocese, parish, vicariate* or prefecture*) brings some of the rights and obligations of domicile; it constitutes residence sufficient for marriage to be celebrated before e.g. the priest of the parish, and makes the resident subject to the laws of the place. Quasi-domicile consists of taking up residence with the intention of remaining more than six months, but not of living permanently, in a certain place.

Quartodeciman controversy

The first of the disputes about the date of Easter. The Quartodecimans were those who insisted that Easter Day should be kept on the Jewish Passover, the 14th (Quartodeciman from Lat. *quartus decimus*, fourteenth) of Nisan; the Council of Nicaea* ensured that it should always be a Sunday and never coincide with Passover.

Quicumque vult

(Lat., whoever desires.) A name for the Athanasian Creed, being the first words thereof in the Latin.

Quiñones Breviary

In an attempt to reform and "modernise" the Breviary from its cumbrous structure, Pope Clement VII in 1529 ordered Francisco Cardinal de Quiñones to simplify the Office; the Cardinal, who was at that time also engaged in the defence of the Queen of England against Henry VIII's claims, produced in 1535 a work which became very popular, running into a hundred editions. Sanctioned at first only for private recitation, the breviary, also known as the Breviary of the Holy Cross (from Cardinal

Quiñones' titular church in Rome), it was soon taken up into the community exercises of some religious, though in other quarters it was attacked as insufficiently traditional. Quiñones had brought down to a minimum the readings from the Lives of the Saints, reduced almost all feasts to one rank, cut out antiphons, responsories, versicles and hymns, besides arranging for the recitation of the complete Psalter in the course of the week and almost the entire Bible in a year. This move towards simplicity was reversed by the suppression of the Breviary by Pope Paul IV in 1558. Cranmer was much influenced by it, and the final shape of the Book of Common Prayer owes a good deal to Cardinal Quiñones.

Quinque Viae
See Five Ways.

Quire
Attempts have been made to secure "quire" for the architectural feature of a church as distinct from the musical "choir", but the public seems to have decided that the former is an archaic Tennysonianism and that "choir" will serve for both.

Ramsgate

The Abbey of St. Augustine at Ramsgate was the first foundation (1856) in England of the Benedictine Cassinese Congregation of the Primitive Observance. It was made an abbey in 1896, and the monks engage in parochial work.

Ransom, Guild of Our Lady of

(Catholic Church Extension Society, Ransomers.) The object of the Guild, founded in 1887 by Fr P. Fletcher and Mr L. Drummond, both converts, is to enlist Catholics to pray and work for the conversion of England and Wales. The Ransomers' activities have included processions (those of the 1880's were the first Catholic processions in public since the Reformation; and they still keep up the *Tyburn Walk*, a silent journey along the route by which the English Martyrs were taken from Newgate prison to the gallows at Tyburn), public speaking (the Catholic Evidence Guild arose as an off-shoot of the Ransomers' campaigns in Hyde Park), publications, preaching, pilgrimages (of devotion and of instruction) and financial support for poor rural parishes and the diocesan travelling missions. The Guild has the distinction, since 1975, of offering Mass annually, by invitation of the Dean, at the shrine of St. Edward the Confessor in Westminster Abbey. The founders took their inspiration from the Trinitarian* and Mercedarian* Orders.

Raphael

(Heb., God heals.) St. Raphael the Archangel* heals Tobit's blindness (Tobit 11:7-14) and in the apocryphal book of Enoch (10:7), heals the earth of its defilement by the sins of the fallen angels. Feast-day Sept 29th.
See also Angel.

Raphoe, Diocese of

Suffragan to Armagh and including almost the entire county of Donegal, it was vacant for long periods between 1610 and 1725. The cathedral and the bishop's residence are at Letterkenny; the patrons of the diocese are Ss. Eunan (Adamnan) and Colmcille (Columba).

Ratum non consummatum

(Lat., ratified, not consummated.) The canonists' phrase for marriage—*matrimonium*—between a baptised man and woman, validly and sacramentally contracted but not sexually completed; according to the Code*, this may be dissolved either by a pronouncement of the Holy See or by the solemn religious profession of one of the partners—this latter appearing an extremely unlikely eventuality, as such profession must be immediately preceded by the period of novitiate.

Real Presence, the

Against Zwinglian, Calvinistic and Lutheran errors, the Council of Trent* laid down that "in the Sacrament of the Eucharist, the body and blood of our Lord Jesus Christ, together with his soul and divinity, are contained truly, really and substantially, and not merely in sign, figure or virtue" (Session 13, can.1) In modern times, the Second Vatican* Council confirms the ancient dogma with such references as "that sacrament of faith where natural elements refined by man are changed into His glorified Body and Blood . . ." (Pastoral Constitution, *The Church in the Modern World*, Art 38) and "the most blessed Eucharist contains . . . Christ himself, our Passover and living bread. Through his very flesh, made vital and vitalising by the Holy Spirit, he offers life to men." (Decree, *The Ministry and Life of Priests*, Art 5). Other attempts at "reinterpretation" have been made, some of them carrying at least a whiff of Modernism*. Thus philosophical "perspectivism" (which denies the validity of discussing the nature of a thing, and places the thing's whole reality in its meaning for man, for me) produced among some Catholic thinkers the theory that the Real Presence is a reality only in so far as it is perceived by faith, ie the faith of the Christian community; Existen-

tialism suggested to some that, since the deepest meanings of things are in their human significance, their finality and their use as symbols of human relationships, this could be called their substance, and that, bread and wine having no meaning or purpose apart from humanity, then it can be said that Christ's use of them to express his self-giving, is in fact what Transubstantiation means and is. Another publication of 1955, from the pen of an ecumenically inclined Calvinist scholar was received in an ecumenical spirit by certain Catholics. Its burden was instrumentality: Christ's body being the instrument of his presence to the disciples at the Last Supper, his words "This is my body" brought it about that henceforth the Eucharistic bread and wine, while remaining unchanged themselves, should have that instrumentality transferred to them and be themselves the instruments of his presence to the believing Christian who ate in the response of faith. Thus, words like "transignification" and "transfinalization" were used in place of "transubstantiation". One surprising thing—evidence perhaps of the despairing shallowness of these new attempts—is that such Catholic thinkers offered in explanation to the incredulous laity the comparison of the effect of the words on the bread and wine to the change in a piece of cloth when it is adopted as a country's flag and, as a parallel to the manner of Christ's presence in the Eucharist, the way a hostess "puts herself", by her warmth and hospitality, into the food she offers her guests. After the Council, Paul VI* wrote the encyclical *Mysterium Fidei* (1965), with these errors in mind, and took the trouble to introduce phrases like "ontological reality" to emphasise that after the words are said, there underlies the species "something wholly other, and that not merely because the faith of the Church deems it to be such, but in objective reality since . . . nothing remains of the bread and wine save only the species".
See Transubstantiation.

Rebaptism
Baptism, of its nature, is such that, once validly received, it cannot be repeated; only in cases of genuine doubt may a person receive conditional baptism (viz. a rite whose wording contains a formula to the effect that this is being done only in case baptism has not previously been received). There was a great dispute in the 3rd cent. concerning the rebaptism of reconciled heretics, the practice being approved by St. Cyprian but finally anathematised by Pope St. Stephen I.

Rebellion
See Revolution.

Receptionism
The theory, held by some Lutherans, that Christ's presence in the Eucharist is brought about by—and at the moment of—devout reception.
See Real Presence.

Recollects
See Hermits of St. Augustine.

Recusant
(Lat. *recuso,* I refuse.) The refusal to attend service at the Church of England drew down many penalties over a long period of time from 1559 onward. Though all such nonconformers were liable, it was the most numerous, the Catholics, who were mainly contemplated, and, in several Acts, named; the Act of 1714, concerning the oath of allegiance and supremacy, threatened the penalties of "a popish recusant convict"—which had been fixed in 1593 as a fine of £20 a month together with various social and political disabilities; failure to pay meant leaving the realm and failure to leave meant death. In the rather uneven application of the law, there are nonetheless returns, made in Charles II's time, of 10,236 recusants convicted, mostly from the "lower orders" and mostly from the county of Lancashire.

Red
The liturgical colour for feasts of the Holy Spirit, of the Precious Blood, of martyrs and other specified feasts as indicated. Scarlet is also the colour for cardinals—it was adopted as the imperial colour by early emperors of Rome (only the Emperor and the statue of Jupiter Capitolinus were permitted a toga of complete scarlet) and in the early 6th cent., Pope John I accepted Justin I's offer of permission to use the imperial "purple"; the papal white cassock was introduced when Pius V*, the white-habited Dominican, became Pope.

Redemptoristines

The nuns of the Order of the Holy Redeemer, strictly enclosed and penitential in spirit, their prayer being devoted especially to the conversion of sinners and to the success of the work of the Redemptorist* Fathers; they received papal approval in 1750, and first came to England in 1843.

Redemptorists

The Fathers of the Congregation of the Most Holy Redeemer, founded in 1732 by St. Alphonsus* Liguori. Their work is the preaching of missions and retreats—and its modern extension, the use of the press—especially to the poor; when not thus engaged, they live strictly in community, with choral office where this is possible. There are provinces of the Congregation in England and Ireland and two in the U.S.

Red Mass

Traditionally, the Votive Mass of the Holy Spirit, from the red vestments then worn; in England, also the Mass of the Holy Spirit celebrated for the legal profession in Westminster Cathedral at the beginning of the law term every year.

Reductions of Paraguay

The mission lands administered in Paraguay by the Jesuits between 1607 and 1768 were perhaps the closest man has come to realizing the "Ideal Republic" of the philosophers. Voltaire wrote of the Jesuit period, in contrast to what followed, "(the Indians) . . . reached what is perhaps the highest point of civilised life to which is possible to bring a young nation . . . there was respect for law, a pure morality, men were bound by a happy brotherhood, the useful arts were cultivated and even some of the more pleasing sciences; everywhere there was abundance." The Fathers of the Society behaved as trustees responsible for the welfare of the Indians, respecting them and their culture, regarding them as children of God in need merely of instruction and guidance; the enemies, whose influence removed the missionaries, could bring no evidence of exploitation. Their removal was due to their resistance to Spanish imperialism, to the slavery prac-

tised by the colonists, and to the Inquisition. In 1767, Carlos III suppressed the Jesuits in the Spanish dominions, and in the following year the Fathers came home from Paraguay.

Refectory

In a monastic dining-room, meals are taken in silence, the midday and evening meals with readings. Carthusians usually eat in solitude, using the refectory only on Sundays and important feasts.

Reformed Orders

In the course of their history, most religious institutes (with the sole exception, among the Orders*, of the Carthusians) have found it necessary to tighten up discipline and revive primitive austerity, either by a reform of the whole order or be setting up a new, reformed, branch thereof; which is no descredit to the "unreformed" branches, e.g. the Calced Carmelites or Cistercians of Common Observance, who have papal approbation and whose rule is suitable to their state and work.

Refreshment Sunday

See Mid-Lent Sunday.

Regina Coeli

(Lat., O Queen of Heaven.) The Anthem of the Blessed Virgin used during Eastertide in place of the *Angelus*, and prescribed for that season in the Divine Office. It is named from its opening words. Its authorship is uncertain but the anthem has been used since the 12th cent.

Register, Parish

By Canon Law*, the parish priest is required to keep registers of baptisms, confirmations, marriages, deaths and the spiritual state of his parish. Confidential affairs such as marriages of conscience are set down in a separate private record; and later events such as confirmation, marriage, holy orders or religious profession are entered against the record of baptism and are reproduced on any subsequent baptismal certificate.

Regnans in Excelsis

The Bull by which Pius V* in 1570 excommunicated and deposed Elizabeth I, and which was issued under several misapprehensions, chiefly the idea that the Queen had support among only a small number of Protestants. Since the ban included all who obeyed the monarch and since the majority of the English at that time were not unduly dismayed at being cut off from the Bishop of Rome and his Church, the only real victims of the Bull were the hapless Catholic minority, already deprived by law. For their sake, the Bull was later suspended, but the damage was already done: the Tudor government's immediate reaction was the re-introduction of Article 29 (withdrawn since 1563) which denies the Real Presence*, the banning of the Mass and an intensified persecution of Catholics, including the insistence on oaths of loyalty and other tests, persisting until 1871 (the suspicion of Catholic loyalty aroused by this unfortunate document dies very hard: in a letter to the Times of July 6th 1978, a clergyman justified the continued exclusion from the British throne of a Catholic or anyone married to a Catholic by holding up for horrified contemplation "the inevitable risk that the ultimate secrets of state might possibly, through conscience, be made available to what is not only a Church but a foreign power and that the influence of this foreign power should be brought to bear, however indirectly, on United Kingdom affairs"). There has, in fact, been much controversy in the Church about the true meaning of the Bull and on the question whether it was ever canonically published and on its scope in any case—after cataloguing the Queen's activities against the Church, *Regnans in Excelsis* excommunicated her and all who adhered to her in these hostile acts; but it can be argued that such a ban is incurred only by active persecutors. The Bull contributed nothing to the welfare of the Pope's loyal subjects in the realm, or to the good name of the Papacy or to the reconciling of the English nation.

Regulars

The Regular clergy are, strictly speaking, those men who, being in holy orders, also live according to a rule (Lat. *regula*) in solemn vows, as distinct from secular priests, viz. those living in—and working for—the "world" (Lat. *saeculum*); com- monly the word is used to describe clergy of any religious institute as distinct from the diocesan clergy.

Reincarnation

(Metempsychosis, Transmigration of Souls.) Since its vogue among Indian philosophers and followers of Plato, this recurring theory was held by certain heretical sects e.g. Albigensians and Manichaeans, and seems to attract some modern Christians; it is quite irreconcilable with the doctrine of the Redemption. See Heb. 9:27 ". . . men only die once and after that comes judgement".

Relations, the Jesuit

From the letters written by early Jesuit* missionaries to their superiors and others in Europe, selections were published, under the title Relations, every year from 1581 to 1654. The North American Relations, circulated in book form for the general public between 1632 and 1673 are our chief source not only for the history of Christianity in the U.S. and Canada at that time, but also for our knowledge of the American Indians. The custom still survives in the annual letters written by missionaries trained at the Urban College in Rome to the Cardinal Prefect of the Sacred Congregation for the Evangelisation of Peoples.

Relationship

In Canon Law*, this is natural (arising from consanguinity, marriage or affinity), legal (from adoption) or spiritual, which is contracted at baptism between the baptised person and the baptiser on the one hand, and the godparents on the other, and, at confirmation, between the confirmed person and the sponsor. Spiritual relationship is a diriment impediment* to marriage, though it may be dispensed.

Relics

In accordance with the general human desire to treasure and honour relics of the great or famous (the bloodstained shirt of Lord Nelson, hair snipped from the head of a pop star), the Church has always encouraged the reverence to the bodies of the Saints which is represented by the keeping and honouring of relics, a relic being understood as the body of a saint or part thereof or part of his clothing or an object closely associated with the saint. The practice is certainly as old as the 2nd cent., one of its earliest manifestations being the custom of offering Mass on or near the tomb of a martyr (a building was called the Church of St. Peter or St. Agnes because the Saint was really present there, albeit dead), a custom later incorporated into the law requiring relics of a martyr to be sealed into an altar before its consecration. The Council of Trent laid it down that new relics should be authenticated by the bishop before being offered for veneration, but the Church will not guarantee the genuineness of any relic, this being a matter for verification by evidence, while the proving of a relic to be spurious (and the claims made for some are boldly imaginative, to say the least) can hardly nullify the worship of God and the homage to the saint already occasioned by it. Anyone who manufactures relics or knowlingly sells, displays or distributes false relics for veneration incurs excommunication; it is forbidden likewise to buy or sell actual relics (see Simony). It is a source of relief to some that the veneration of relics is not obligatory on Catholics.

Religion
One use of this word, technical and archaic, is as a synonym for monastic or religious life; of old, one spoke not of the Order of St. Benedict, for example, but of the *religion* of St. Benedict, and there remain the phrases "entering religion" and "religious life".

Religious
As a noun, the term for any person, male or female who belongs by vow to a religious institute, the first religious being those who constituted the first religion*.

Religious of the Sacred Heart
A congregation founded in St. Madeleine Sophie Barat and Père Joseph Varin S.J. in 1800 for the education of girls, particularly the daughters of the rich. The rule is based on that of St. Ignatius and the members have been referred to colloquially as "female Jesuits"; the congregation has spread to all parts of the world.

Reliquary
The casket, box or other container, of whatever shape or material, in which a relic* is kept. It is not permitted to offer a relic for public veneration except in a reliquary.

Remarriage
Remarriage is allowable in cases where one of the spouses has died or in which the "marriage" has been declared null by competent authority or in which the partners to a valid contract not yet consummated have been duly dispensed. (See *Ratum Non Consummatum*.)

Renewal of Baptismal Vows
The church encourages the faithful to renew their dedication to Christ in many ways including the repeating, on suitable occasions of the promises made at Baptism (not strictly speaking, vows*), e.g. when they come to the end of a period of spiritual exercises or assist at a baptism, such a renewal being also part of the liturgy of the Easter Vigil.

Renewal of consent
This is necessary, in Canon Law*, for the revalidation of a marriage. Where the marriage is invalid because of defect of form or public impediment, renewal of consent is made by the usual form of the sacrament; if the invalidity is due to an occult impediment, it is sufficient for the partner aware of the impediment to make renewal privately. A marriage invalid by defective consent is revalidated by the appropriate consent being given, viz. internal, private or public. In a marriage invalid for a reason other than lack of consent, the Holy See can dispense from renewal of consent by *sanatio in radice**, but validity will always be subject to the perseverance of the consent in the partner who gave it.

Rerum Novarum
The encyclical promulgated in 1891 by Leo XIII, who declared its subject to be *The State of the Workers*, which he proposed to ameliorate by the joint action of the Church, of the employers and the workers, and of the State. The solution, he says, is not in the transfer of ownership to the State; he vindicates the primacy of the individual and the family as against the State, he emphasises a man's natural right to private property, to reasonable comfort and a living wage; he accuses the rich of having enslaved the poor.

Rescript, Papal

A reply of the Holy See or of a Roman Congregation* to a question or request, usually applying only to the one to whom it is addressed, but having sometimes the force of a general law. Papal dispensations are granted by rescript.

Reservation (of the Blessed Sacrament)

The custom of keeping the Most Holy Body of Christ under the form of bread, to carry to those unable to attend Mass and receive the Eucharist thereat, dates from the early 2nd cent. Throughout the rise of eucharistic devotion, from the 11th cent. onward, the Church continued officially to hold to the original and permanent purpose of reservation and to regard devotion as incidental: "We adore because we reserve, we do not reserve in order to adore." By law, the Holy Sacrament is to be kept in a ciborium* within a tabernacle* (the key of which is to be held in a secure place) on one altar only of the church; recently, there was a change initiated against the very general, though non-liturgical, practice of reservation on the high altar, the significance of this being emphasised by the reversion to the primitive use of setting the altar for celebration between the people and the officiating minister, to which arrangement a tabernacle actually on the altar would be an obstacle. There is a corresponding return to the tabernacle built into the wall, as long used by certain High Anglicans, and dating from pre-Reformation times, when such a "wall tabernacle" was called a Sacrament House.

Reserved cases

Some sins or censures are reserved for absolution by a certain superior, e.g. the Holy See or the local ordinary. Reservation of sins lapses at Easter communion, at parish missions and in the case of a sick person unable to go out of doors; and in danger of death and certain critical situations, any confessor can absolve from any censure or sin, certain conditions being laid down for this in Canon Law*.

Residence

Clerics are obliged to live in their own diocese; cardinals in curia, diocesan bishops, religious superiors, canons, rectors of parishes and their assistants are bound to residence in their place of office.

Responsorial psalm

As part of the modern Liturgy of the Word at Mass, a psalm is chanted or read out with a response—usually part of that psalm—spoken or sung by the people after each section of it.

Restoration of the hierarchy

In 1850, by a letter *Universalis Ecclesiae*, Pius IX re-established in England a hierarchy of one metropolitan, at Westminster, and 12 suffragans, at Beverley, Birmingham, Clifton, Hexham, Liverpool, Northampton, Nottingham, Plymouth, Salford, Shrewsbury, Southwark and Newport-and-Menevia, a distribution much altered in the ensuing years. The restoration itself provoked much alarm in the country (See Papal Aggression). An episcopate was restored for Scotland in 1878, consisting of two archbishops and four bishops; the Irish hierarchy had never died out.

Resurrection of the body

It is of faith that all men will return to bodily life at the last day. The Church teaches the identity of the risen body (See Glorified Body) with the body we inhabit in this life, but without claiming, e.g. that it will be of the same actual particles of matter present at the moment of death: not surprisingly, in view of the scientific opinions on the continuing changes wrought in those particles even during life. According to St. Thomas ". . . human nature will be brought by the resurrection to its state of final perfection, at that age of youthfulness at which, the movement of growth having ceased, the movement of decay has not yet begun". (III lxxx) And Anscar Vonier O.S.B. writes, "Unstinted and complete restoration of all the sense life that makes us human beings is the true and primary meaning of the resurrection of the body."

Retraite Nuns, the

Les Dames de la Retraite du Sacré Coeur were established in 1678 at Quimper to provide retreats for women and education for girls; they are not enclosed, and recite the Little Office of Our Lady.

Revelation

(Lat. *revelo*, I unveil.) Supernatural revelation is the communicating to man of the hidden things of God (man's own discoveries of divine truths by reason alone is sometimes termed *natural revelation*); it may be immediate, i.e. directly to an individual by God himself or through an angel, as in Mt. 16:18, or, more usually, mediate, i.e. made through the instrumentality of men by Scripture and Tradition. The Christian faith is precisely that God has made such revelation of his truths first to a particular nation, the Jews, then to the whole race of men by Jesus Christ; the Church is the sole authentic interpreter of Revelation, and decided in the first place what was Revelation and what was not, by establishing the Canon* of Scripture.

Revelation, private

Whatever of a supernatural nature is communicated by God to a private individual, as is considered to be the case with e.g. St. Joan of Arc, St. Catherine of Siena, St. Bernadette, et al, is termed private revelation. Such phenomena are always treated by the Church with grave caution, in view of human fallibility and the possibility of wishful thinking or downright fraud; and the Church's approval, where it is obtained, means no more than that the "revelation" contains nothing opposed to faith or morals and that there is sufficient evidence for believing it. The Church will never impose belief in such revelations on any individual or on the faithful in general. Benedict XIV wrote, "Even though many cases of these revelations have been approved, we cannot and we must not give them the assent of divine faith, but only of human faith, according to the dictates of prudence, whenever these enable us to decide they are probable and worthy of credence."

Reverend

The ordinary title of a priest (it requires the Christian name or at least an initial before the surname, as the Reverend John Smith, or the Rev. J. Smith: the Rev. Smith is a solecism). In the case of a religious, *Father* is usually inserted after *Rev.* The title is extended also to deacons and frequently to nuns. The Carthusians*

reserve the title *Reverend Father* for their Prior General: others of the Order are *Venerable Father*. See Most Reverend, Right Reverend, Very Reverend.

Revolution

Theologians have allowed that it is lawful for the people to rise against their lawfully constituted government if that government has become gravely tyrannical and seeks private, selfish ends rather than the good of the people, or, tyranny apart, if it insists on remaining in power when its remaining only does harm to the country; but first, they say, peaceful means must be tried, there must be a reasonable hope of success, and there must be reason to believe that the uprising represents the aspiration of a substantial part of the population. Such considerations could be taken as relevant to contemporary "liberation" movements.

Rhythm of St. Bernard

The hymn *Jesu Dulcis Memoria*, used for the Office of the ancient Feast of the Holy Name of Jesus, and attributed to St. Bernard of Clairvaux, has, in one form, 50 stanzas, which were formerly used as a sort of rosary*, in five decades. The first English version is of the 24-stanza form found in the Office of the Eternal Wisdom compiled by Bl. Henry Suso and published at Douay in 1580 under the title "Certayne sweete prayers of the glorious name of Jesu, commonly called Jesus Mattens, with the howers thereto belonging", its first line being "O Jesu meeke, the sweetest thought." There have been later translations, the most commonly known being that of Fr E. Caswall, "Jesu, the very thought of thee."

Right Reverend

The style used for bishops (except in Ireland—see Most Reverend), abbots*, abbesses* (except Franciscan), vicars general*, protonotaries* apostolic, domestic prelates*.

Righteousness

(O.E. *rihtwisnisse*, goodness, virtuousness, uprightness.) This word, historically used for the perfection of God himself and for the state of man justified through the Redemption, went out of Catholic usage

almost altogether when the Douay*
translators used "justice" instead, but in
recent times, and in the Jerusalem Bible,
it is returning.

Rights of animals

If one is to speak correctly, animals have
no rights: the phrase above, often used,
but loosely, corresponds to stating, not
that an animal has rights as against the
human being, but that the human being
has a duty to treat the animal in a certain
way, a duty owed not to the animal but to
God. The animal in our charge lives the
life God wishes it to live by our behaving
as he wishes us to behave; '. . . in giving
man dominion over his creatures, he gave
it subject to the condition it should be used in conformity with his perfections,
which is his own law and therefore our
law' (Cardinal Manning).

Ring

A ring of gold, often with a gem, on the
third finger of the right hand, is part of the
insignia of a cardinal*, bishop* and abbot*; the custom of genuflecting to kiss
the prelate's ring is abating, as many
bishops no longer offer the ring, and in
some cases shake hands instead.

Ring of the Fisherman

A signet-ring of the pope, not usually
worn but used for sealing papal briefs,
made for each pope and broken at his
death. It has, as its device, St. Peter
fishing from a boat.

Rising of the North

In 1569, there was a revolt led by the Earl
of Northumberland on behalf of Mary
Queen of Scots as rightful heir to the
throne, declaring as its purposes 'to
restore the Crown, the nobility and the
worship of God to their former estate'.
The rebels occupied Durham and sang
Mass in the cathedral, as they did also in
the parishes of Bishop Auckland, Darl-
ington, Ripon and Staindrop. The movement quickly collapsed and ruthless
vengeance was executed on those involved.

Rising of the West

There was an insurrection of West Country men under Humphrey Arundel in
1549 in protest at the new English liturgy
being forced on them. Their demands included the restoration of at least two
monasteries in every county and a return
to the ancient worship: 'We will not
receive the new service, because it is but
like a Christmas game. We will have our
old service of Matins, Mass, Evensong
and Procession as it was before; and we,
the Cornish, whereof certain of us understand no English, do utterly refuse the new
service.' Ten thousand set off to march on
London and invested Exeter; but the siege
was raised, the rebels were defeated at
Callington Down and Bridgwater, and
4,000 men died either in battle or by execution.

Risorgimento

(It., resurrection.) The nationalist movement in 19th cent. Italy, resulting in the
unification of the many States under the
House of Savoy, which became the monarchy of the new country called Italy, in
1860 and concluding in 1870 with the
seizure of the remainder of the Papal
States*. Only the government of Ecuador
protested at this invasion and seizure.
See Prisoner of the Vatican and Lateran
Treaty.

Rite

(Lat. *ritus*, a manner or form in religious
observance.) The Church accepts and
fosters many rites for the offering of the
Eucharist and the performance of other
liturgical functions, all of which are of
local origin, some of them, by historical
circumstances, extended to very large
areas; beside the Roman (Latin or
Western) rite, there are the Byzantine, the
Coptic and the Ethiopic (both the latter of
Alexandrian origin), the Syrian and the
Maronite (both of Antiochene origin), the
Malabarese, the Armenian and the Chaldean (of Chaldean origin). All but the
Roman and Maronite are used also by
Christians who are not Catholic. The corresponding churches, which are
sometimes described as *rites* differ not only in actual rite and language but also in
having their own proper organisation,
canon law, customs, etc. There are also
smaller differences within these major
groups which do not involve language, but
which are also referred to as *rites*, e.g. the
Carthusian, a variant within the Latin rite,
the Ruthenian, within the Byzantine.

Rites (Sacred Congregation for)

See Roman Congregations.

Ritual Murder

The ancient slander against the Jews, of the killing of a Christian child in ritual re-enactment of the execution of our Lord, was repudiated by Rome twice in the 13th cent. and again in 1756 by Giovanni Cardinal Ganganelli, then Consultor to the Holy Office, later Pope Clement XIV. The young victims of Jewish violence who can be proved to have been deliberately murdered and whose cult the Church has approved, are to be considered as at most martyrs to private Jewish hatred of the faith, not as human sacrifices.

Rituale Romanum

(Lat., Roman Ritual.) The priest's handbook, containing the rubrics and words for his functions apart from the Mass and the Breviary; viz. Baptism, the Sacrament of Reconciliation, Matrimony, Anointing of the Sick, Eucharist outside Mass, the ministry to the dying, the burial of the dead, exorcisms, the ordering of processions, and blessings.

Robber Synod

(Robber Council.) The Latrocinium—Pope Leo I's phrase is non iudicium sed latrocinium, not a bench of judges but a band of brigands—was a council called at Ephesus in 449. Its purpose was the re-trial, on appeal, of Eutyches, a Greek monk condemned at Constantinople for heresy—his teachings make him the founder of Monophysitism.* In the threatening presence of the large corps of armed thugs attendant on the president, Dioscoros, Monophysite Patriarch of Alexandria, the Council reversed Eutyches' condemnation. Flavian, who had pronounced this condemnation, actually died of physical mauling and Leo's legates, bringing his tome*, were insulted. Consequent on Leo's protests, there was summoned the Council of Chalcedon* in 451, which overthrew the decisions of the Latrocinium.

Rochet

(cf. Ger. rock.) A narrow-sleeved linen garment, of knee-length, made of linen and usually with its lower part of lace. Part of the choir-dress of bishops, abbots and secular* prelates, it is worn under the mozzetta*; to wear it not covered by the mantelletta* is a mark of jurisdiction (but the uncovered rochet is part of the religious habit of canons and canonesses regular*). The right to wear the rochet (under the mozzetta) had been granted to many chapters of cathedral canons, e.g. in England.

Roman Catholic Relief Act

This title is given to five Acts whereby the Penal* Laws were removed; the parliamentary measures thus referred to were passed in 1778, 1791, 1793, 1829 and 1926.

See also Emancipation.

Roman Church, the Holy

In its strict, original sense, the 'Church that is in Rome' (cf. Paul's phrase 'the Church of God at Corinth'), i.e. the diocese of Rome; then, in an extended sense, the Latin rite, the Western Church, and further still, all Catholics who acknowledge the Bishop of Rome as head of the universal Church.

Roman Congregations

Those departments of the Roman Curia which deal with ecclesiastical affairs, particularly with legal and administrative matters. The first to be set up was that of the Inquisition, by Pope Paul III in 1542, but it was Sixtus V who, in 1588, organised the whole range of Congregations. They were originally 14 in number; at present there are nine, each consisting of cardinals (the number ranging from 17 to 40) and their assistants and officials, including a sprinkling of nuns and other non-clerical persons, male and female. Their titles are the Sacred Congregations For the Teaching of the Faith, For Bishops, For the Eastern Churches, For the Sacraments and the Divine Worship, For the Clergy, For Religious and for Secular Institutes, For the Evangelising of the Nations, For the Causes of the Saints, For Catholic Education. The decisions of a Roman Congregation, once they receive papal approval, are final as regards the person or persons concerned, but they have not the force of general law unless they are published with a special papal mandate.

Romanism

The Church and its system, faith and practice, have been thus described by its enemies since at latest 1674, the word *Romanist* being used as a term of offence in 1523 and its German equivalent earlier.

Roman Pontifical

See Pontificale Romanum.

Romish

A derogatory and clumsy word for 'Catholic' coined perhaps by Tyndale in 1531 and found in the Twenty-Second of the Thirty-Nine Articles—'The Romish Doctrine concerning Purgatory, Pardons . . .'

Rood

(A.S. *rod,* cross.) The large crucifix (the term came to include the standing figures of Our Lady and St. John) over the sanctuary of a church, usually between the sanctuary itself and the nave, either suspended or standing on a beam or on the wooden structure known as the rood-screen.

Rood of Boxley

There was a crucifix from the Abbey of Boxley in Kent put on show in London in 1538 as an example of fraud and profiteering on the part of the monks; it was 'made with divers devices to move the eyes and lips'. It appears to have been used as an ingenious, if bizarre, object of devotion, and there was no evidence brought to indicate any fraudulent use.

Rosary

(Lat. *rosarium,* chaplet.) The name given to the devotion and to the object used thereat: a method of meditating, with the help of spoken words, on the events of the life, death and resurrection of our Lord, as seen through the eyes of his Blessed Mother. Beads are fixed on to chain, rope, etc., to assist in counting and to concentrate the mind, each bead representing the Our Father or the Hail Mary. The contemplation of each of the events— 'mysteries'—occupies recitation of the *Our Father* once and the *Hail Mary* 10 times, the *Glory Be* being added, though not represented by a bead. The beads count five of these 'decades' and usually have a small crucifix hanging from them. See Joyful, Sorrowful and Glorious Mysteries. The devotion is of genuine antiquity and, though the 16th cent. attribution of it to St. Dominic⋆ is no longer accepted, it seems clear that it grew under Dominican and Cistercian influence.

Rosminians

See Institute of Charity.

Rota, the Sacred Roman

The principal tribunal for judging cases brought before the Holy See⋆; created in the 13th cent., and named, it appears, from the circular table used by its judges at Avignon, it experienced a shrinking of its power in the 18th cent. to civil cases, even these ceasing with the loss of the temporal power of the Papacy in 1870. The Rota was reconstituted by St. Pius X in 1908 and, after further modification by Paul VI in 1969, remains essentially a tribunal of appeal for ecclesiastical cases within the competence of the Roman Curia and not reserved to any other jurisdiction, and is also a court of appeal from the civil and criminal tribunals of Vatican City. The priest-judges, whose Dean is *primus inter pares,* form a college and are doctors of civil and canon law; and the Rota, unlike the Roman Congregations⋆, must give reasons for its decisions. It is best known as the court which deals with matrimonial cases.

Rotary Clubs

Membership of Rotary, formerly forbidden to Catholics on account of suspicion of secularism and religious indifferentism, is now permitted.

Rule

The daily life of a religious is governed by a rule, drawn up by the founder or foundress of the Order in question or by the early members thereof. St. Benedict, e.g., wrote his, the most famous of the Rules, but the Carthusians live by the *Consuetudines Carthusiae,* not written by St. Bruno but compiled after his death. According to their spirit and work, religious can be said to base their rule on one of the four great Rules: all eastern monks on the Rule of St. Basil (revised in the 9th cent.), canons regular⋆, Dominicans⋆, Augustinian⋆, friars⋆, Servites⋆ and some others on that of St. Augustine (his actual authorship is not certain, but probable), Benedictines*, Cistercians*, Vallombrosans and others on that of St. Benedict*, all Friars Minor*, Poor Clares* *et al.* on that of St. Francis. Carthusians*, Carmelites* and Jesuits* stand outside this classification, and other more recent foundations have shaped their rules to the spirit of their founder and their aims and work. Obedience to the Rule does not, of itself, bind under pain of sin, but deliberate and consistent disregard of it is a grave violation of the obedience to which the religious is vowed.

Russicum

The Pontifical Russian College of St. Theresa of the Child Jesus is of Byzantine Rite and was founded by Pope Pius XI in 1929 to train students, under the direction of the Jesuit Fathers, for work among Russian people but without being restricted to that nation.

Sacrament

(The Lat. *sacramentum* was an oath, especially the soldier's oath of allegiance, but its Christian meaning was decided through its use to render the Gk. word for *mystery*, e.g. in the Vulgate's Eph.5:32.) A sacrament is a perceptible sacred sign, of permanent institution by Christ, to signify sanctifying grace and to confer that grace on the person. St. Thomas'* brief form is *signum rei sacrae in quantum est sanctificans homines*, the sign of a sacred thing in so far as it sanctifies men. The Second Vatican Council speaks in similar terms: 'By his power, (Christ) is present in the Sacraments, so that when a man baptises it is really Christ himself who baptises' (Constitution on the Sacred Liturgy, 7); 'The purpose of the sacraments is to sanctify men, to build up the body of Christ and, finally, to give worship to God. Because they are signs they also instruct ... the very act of celebrating them disposes the faithful most effectively to receive this grace in a fruitful manner, to worship God duly and to practise charity.' (ib.59.) As sacraments confer grace, they must have been instituted by God, the source of grace, and it is Catholic teaching that they were, one and all, instituted by Christ our Lord. A sacrament has objective reality, and is not brought into being by, e.g. the wish or the belief on the part of any recipient; there are three necessities for any sacrament, the matter, the form, and the minister (i.e. the person who brings the sacrament into being doing and saying certain things with the intention of doing what the Church does).

Sacrament of the Sick

See Anointing of the Sick.

Sacramental

A sacramental is an action or thing so called from some resemblance, in its carrying out, to a sacrament; prayer is a sacramental, as are blessings, non-sacramental anointings, almsgiving, the sign of the cross, the use of holy water, etc. They resemble sacraments in their use of material things to signify spritual realities, but differ in that their effects are dependent entirely on the mercy of God in his regard for the prayers of the Church and the good dispositions of the persons involved.

Sacraments, the Seven

The lack of an early definition gave rise to many variants on the word *sacrament*, St. Augustine, e.g., calling a sacrament 'the visible form of an invisible grace' or 'the sign of a sacred thing' and applying it even to forms of words, such as the Creed and the Pater Noster. This wide usage of the word persisted into the Middle Ages, when Hugh of St. Victor (+1141) enumerated 30 sacraments. However, only a few years later, a turning-point was reached when Peter Lombard in his *Sententiarum Libri Quatuor* (1148-50) distinguished sacrament from sacramental and insisted that there were only seven sacraments. His list was followed by Alexander of Hales and St. Thomas Aquinas and confirmed by the Councils of Florence* and Trent*, the latter laying down as of faith that there are seven sacraments, Baptism, Confirmation, Holy Eucharist, Penance (the Sacrament of Reconcilation), Extreme Unction (the Anointing of the Sick), Holy Order, Matrimony, that these were all instituted by Christ (there is still discussion among theologians about the moment and the manner of his institution of e.g. Confirmation, Anointing, Matrimony), that, when worthily received, they confer grace, that three, Baptism, Confirmation and Order, impart an indelible character and may thus not be repeated, and that the sacraments are necessary to salvation, though not all for all persons. The Eastern Churches also accept seven sacraments. Luther abolished all sacraments but two, Baptism and Eucharist; in this, the Thirty-Nine Articles followed, 'those five commonly called Sacraments' being 'such as have grown partly of the corrupt following of the Apostles, partly are states of life allowed in the Scriptures; but yet have not the like nature of Sacraments with Baptism and the Lord's Supper, for that they have not any visible sign or ceremony ordained of God'; yet a good number of modern Anglican theologians have adopted a more positive attitude towards the five 'lesser sacraments' and approximate to Catholic thought.

Sacred Heart, the

The devotion to the Sacred Heart, very widely spread throughout the Catholic world, is the veneration of the human heart of Jesus as united to his divinity in the hypostatic* union, and as symbol of his love for the human race: not, therefore, the worship of the heart in detachment, as an anatomised unit, but as part of that body of flesh in which he suffered and died for us (images of the Heart alone are not permitted for public veneration). The cult dates from the preaching of the visions (1673-75) of St. Margaret Mary Alacoque; Bl. Claude de la Colombière preached thus in England in 1676, and it is worthy of note that a book written by Oliver Cromwell's Congregationalist chaplain, T. Goodwin, 'The Heart of Christ in Heaven Towards Sinners on Earth' bears strange resemblances to the French priest's message. The feast of the Sacred Heart was established as the Friday of the week following the feast of Corpus* Christi, the first request to the Holy See for the institution of such a feast coming from James II's consort, Queen Mary.

Sacred Heart Nuns

See Religious of the Sacred Heart.

Sacrifice of the Mass

The offering of the Body and Blood of Christ made present in the liturgy is a true representation and renewal of the sacrifice of Calvary: 'In this divine sacrifice,' says the Council of Trent, 'the same Christ is present and immolated in a bloodless manner, who offered himself in a bloody manner on the altar of the Cross . . . only the manner of offering is different' (Session xxii, 2). Deriving its merits from the death on the Cross as the one universal and absolute sacrifice, the Mass applies the fruits of that great Sacrifice, giving supreme honour and glory to God, thanking him for his benefits, obtaining pardon for sins

and procuring further blessings and graces. The Second Vatican Council says, in its Decree on the Ministry and Life of Priests, 'Through the hands of priests and in the name of the whole Church, the Lord's sacrifice is offered in the Eucharist in an unbloody and sacramental manner until he himself returns' (op. cit. 2).

Sacrilege

Insulting or irreverent behaviour towards, or treatment of sacred persons, places or things; it is personal (against a person in orders or a religious), local (such behaviour directed against a sacred building or performed in it) or real (abuse of the sacraments, theft or misuse of sacred objects, simony*).

Saint

The word is used in the N.T. in a wider sense than the later usage: the 'saints' there are the faithful, the members of a particular Church, as '. . . to all the saints in the whole of Achaia . . .' in II Cor.1:1. Saints have, from the earliest times, been held to have not merely an exemplary function but to be a living part of the Body of Christ in the Communion of Saints, in touch with the faithful on earth and willing to help them. Canonisation*, i.e. the formal declaration of heroic virtue, was firstly solemnly performed in 993 by Pope John XV for St. Ulrich of Augsburg. Since then the Church has declared the sanctity of individuals of the most varied sorts—'all human life is there'—including an ex-hangman among its canonised members, and makes sure of the unmentioned and uncanonised saints on the Feast of All Saints, November 1st. The mediaeval use of the word 'saint' as adjective, transliterating the Latin *sanctus*, lingers in certain names such as Saint Saviour's, Saint Cross; 'Saint Mary', in modern Catholic usage, refers to other persons, not to the Mother of God. The liturgy, for the most part, uses such words as 'blessed' instead of Saint, as in the Confession of Sins at Mass; and Welsh uses the designation 'Saint' only for three David, Brigid and Cynwyl; the others being spoken of with their title, if any, such as John the Baptist, Andrew the Apostle (the Mother of God being the Blessed Mary) and the rest by name simply, as members of the family.

St. Omer

Near Calais, where, in 1592, Fr Persons S. J. founded a college for the education of young English Catholics; it remained until the Jesuits were expelled in 1762, when it moved to Belgium under another name, and, at the Revolution, came to Stonyhurst* in Lancashire.

St. Patrick's Breastplate

A very ancient Irish hymn, known to be in use before the 9th cent., under the name *Canticum Scotticum*. It could, in fact, have been composed by Patrick:

May the strength of God pilot us,
May the power of God preserve us,
May the wisdom of God instruct us,
May the hand of God protect us,
May the shield of God defend us,
May the host of God guard us against
    the snares of evil and the temptations
    of the world,
May Christ be with us, Christ before us,
    Christ in us, Christ over us;
May thy salvation, O Lord, be always
    ours, this day and for evermore.

St. Patrick's Purgatory

A place on Station Island on Lough Derg, Co. Donegal, the centre of continuous pilgrimage since the 13th cent; the exercises there undergone by the faithful are peculiarly strenuous and last three days. The saint used this island for solitude and prayer, and legend has it that he was promised in a vision that whoever visited it in a spirit of true penance with unshaking confidence would have, besides a plenary indulgence, a sight of the joys of heaven and of the torments of the damned; be that as it may, the annual pilgrimages result in a remarkable number of marriages.

St. Peter's

The first church on the site of St. Peter's burial (in what had been the Circus of Nero) was a basilican* structure of the time of Constantine the Great, the present edifice being an initiative of Pope Nicholas V (1447–55), who decided to replace the ancient building with a cruciform church. Very little work was done by the time of his death, and the first stone of the new building was laid in 1506 by Julius II; work proceeded with various popes and a succession of architects, one major change of plan being the lengthening of the nave (Sixtus V, 1585–90) which made the basilica capable of holding a huge congregation and ruined the view of Michelangelo's dome. St. Peter's, consecrated in 1626, contains the remains of nearly 140 popes, and recent archaeological research has confirmed the antiquity, sometimes doubted, of the *confessio* * of St. Peter under the high altar. It is popularly regarded as the foremost church of the Christian world, though strictly speaking this title belongs to St. John Lateran*, the cathedral church of the See of Rome; the importance of St. Peter's grew during the period 1870–1929 (see Prisoner of the Vatican) and all papal functions of world-wide importance or interest take place there.

St. Peter's Chains

A feast on August 1st, now discontinued, commemorating the sending to Rome by the Empress Eudokia of a chain found in Jerusalem and reputed to be that which confined St. Peter in Herod's prison (Acts. 12) and the joining to it of another chain said to have held the Apostle in Rome before his execution under Nero.

St. Sophia

Sometimes erroneously taken as the patron of the former church in Istanbul, the greatest monument of the Eastern Church, this saint is found in the Roman Martyrology, a 2nd-century lady of admirable faith and courage but doubtful existence: according to the legend, her young daughters Faith, Hope and Charity having suffered under Hadrian, the devout mother soon after expired while praying at the tomb of the child-martyrs. She is sometimes, but rarely, referred to as St. Sapientia.

St. Vincent de Paul, Society of

The Society describes itself as an international Catholic organisation of lay people who, under the inspiration of St. Vincent, undertake to help, by personal service, those who are suffering, without distinction of wealth, position, race or creed; they seek, by their interior and exterior Christian lives, to bear witness to the love of Christ. The Society grew out of the first Conference of Charity held in Paris by Frédéric Ozanam* in 1833, the Rule being first written two years later. In 1973, the adapted Rule welcomed into membership women and non-Catholic Christians.

Sainte Union Nuns

A congregation founded in 1828 by the Abbé de Brabant at Douai: *Les Soeurs de la Sainte Union des Sacrés Coeurs* are engaged chiefly in education, and have a number of houses in England and Wales.

Saints, Intercession of

See Invocation of Saints.

Saints, Sacred Congregation for

See Roman Congregations.

Saints, Veneration of

The external honours paid to those who, after death, are credited with outstanding holiness, is carefully regulated by the Church: public veneration without limit of place is permitted only of persons canonised*, of the beatified* only where permitted by the Holy See. The canonised may be chosen as patrons for a nation, diocese, religious society, etc. with Rome's approval, but not the beatified. The theologians' name for the cult of the saints is *dulia**, of the Mother of God, *hyperdulia**. (see Latria).

Sale of Indulgences

See Indulgences.

Salesian Sisters

See Daughters of Our Lady Help of Christians.

Salesians of Don Bosco

Founded in 1854, in Turin, by St. John Bosco*, with the title of Society of St. Francis de Sales*, the Salesians have as their primary object, the spiritual and corporal works of mercy on behalf of the young and the poor. The priests, clerics and lay-brothers of the Society engage in education of many kinds and at all levels, and in missionary work, which has spread all over the world; there is one Province for England and one for Ireland.
See also Daughers of Our Lady Help of Christians.

Salt

Retaining its ancient symbolism for preservation, integrity and wisdom (Num.18:19, Mt.5:13, Col.4:6) salt is exorcised and blessed and may be placed on the tongue of one being baptised (cf. the antique Roman custom of putting a few grains of salt on the infant's tongue eight days after birth, to expel evil spirits), and is sprinkled in water about to be blessed into Holy Water.

Salvation outside the Church

St. Augustine has a phrase, *Salus extra Ecclesiam non est* (There is no salvation outside the Church), reputed to be his condensation of St. Cyprian's saying that a man cannot have God for his father if he has not the Church for his mother. Over the ages, thinkers rephrased the Augustinian dictum to *Extra Ecclesiam nulla salus*. This handy theological tag is to be interpreted as referring to deliberate refusal of membership by one who knows he ought to join. Pius IX*, in 1854, said, 'It is of faith that none can be saved outside the Apostolic Roman Church . . . it is nevertheless equally certain that those who are ignorant of the true religion and whose ignorance is invincible will not be held guilty . . .'. This is the age-old understanding of it by the Church, reiterated by the Second Vatican Council: '. . . Nor does Divine Providence deny the help necessary for salvation to those who, without blame on their part, have not yet arrived at an explicit knowledge of God, but who strive to live a good life, thanks to his grace. Whatever goodness or truth is found among them is looked upon by the Church as a preparation for the Gospel. She regards all such qualities as given by him who enlightens all men so that they may finally have life.' (Dogmatic Constitution on the Church, Art. 16). The most notorious misinterpreter of the tag *Extra Ecclesiam nulla salus* in recent times was an American Jesuit, Leonard Feeney, who was condemned by Rome in 1949.

Salvatorians

The Society of the Divine Saviour, a congregation founded in Rome by Rev. Francis Jordan in 1881, to undertake any work by which religion might be promoted; its priests work chiefly in education, foreign missions and social work.

Salve Regina
The title, and opening words, of the antiphon sung at the end of Compline, to close the day's Office, from Trinity Sunday to Advent: in other seasons, other antiphons are used (see *Alma Redemptoris Mater, Ave Regina Coelorum, Regina Coeli*). Outside the Office, where it was set to a very fine plainsong melody, the *Hail, Holy Queen* became a great favourite for public and private prayer and, among prayers in honour of Our Lady, is outdone in popularity only by the Hail Mary*. The earliest written evidence for it dates from the late 11th cent. and it is generally attributed to Hermann the Cripple, though there is a claim, not well supported, that the last invocation ('*O clemens . . .*') was added by St. Bernard.

Sampietrini
(It., Saint Peter's men, from *San Pietro*.) The permanent staff of craftsmen of the necessary trades and skills for the maintenance of the fabric and decoration of St. Peter's*.

Sanatio in Radice
(Lat., healing at the root, complete cure.) The rectification of a defective marriage in such a way that any impediment is dispensed, no renewal of consent is needed and the ordinary canonical effects are presumed to have been present in the marriage as if valid from the beginning. The granting of *sanatio* is in the power of the Holy See only, and it is brought into play only when ordinary forms of revalidation are impossible; in a marriage null for lack of consent, the *sanatio* can take effect only from the time of the giving of consent, and it cannot be granted for a marriage in which consent first given is then withdrawn; nor can it be granted for a marriage null by impediment of natural or divine law.

Sancta Sophia
The term still frequently used for Justinian's great church at Constantinople, the masterpiece and model of Byzantine building and ornament; at the conquest by the Turks, it was made into a mosque, which accounts for the minarets with which it is incongruously surrounded. It is now a museum. Perhaps it would be safer to use the modern Greek 'Ayia Sophia', to avoid confusing the title with Saint Sophia*; the meaning is *Holy Wisdom,* the church being dedicated not to the Third Person of the Trinity but to the Second, the eternal Wisdom of the Father, the Logos.

Sanctissimum
(Lat., the Most Holy Thing.) A term used of the Blessed Sacrament, especially with reference to reservation* or processions.

Sanctity of the Church
One of the Marks* of the Church is, appropriately enough, that, being a Church of sinners, she is nevertheless distinguished by the holiness of her teaching, her worship, the means to holiness she offers, and the eminent sanctity of so many of her members, as evidence of the working of the Spirit of God.

Sanctuary
That part of a church immediately round the high altar, usually enclosed within the altar-rails; because of the design of many modern buildings, the sanctuary need no longer present itself as a clerical enclosure excluding the laity.

Sanctuary Lamp
See Lamp.

Sanctuary, Right of
The ancient protection given by a sacred building (and its lands: cf. Broad Sanctuary by Westminster Abbey) was abrogated in England in the 16th cent., and has since disappeared everywhere else; however, according to Canon Law, one who takes refuge in a church must not, apart from cases of necessity, be taken out without leave of the rector or bishop.

Sanctus
That part of the Mass which forms the end and climax of the Preface*—also known as the Hymn of Victory and the Tersanctus ('thrice holy', not to be confused with Trisagion* which translates as the same)—consists of the words, 'Holy, holy, holy Lord, God of power and might; heaven and earth are full of your glory. Hosanna in the highest. Blessed is he who comes in the name of the Lord. Hosanna

in the highest.' The second part, 'Blessed . . .' used to be referred to as the *Benedictus*, and was sometimes, especially for musical purposes, treated separately. The Sanctus originates in the worship of the synagogue (Is.6:3, Ps.118:26), the use of the Benedictus in the Mass being first noted in Gaul in the 6th cent.

Sandals
See Discalced.

Sardica, Synod of
A council held at Sofia in 343; its chief claim to historical note is that it laid down that a bishop deposed by his fellow-bishops might appeal to Rome.

Sarum, Use of
(Lat. *Sarisburia*, Salisbury.) Perhaps established by St. Osmund in the 11th cent., but more probably by Richard Poore in the early 13th, this form of the Latin Rite overflowed the boundaries of the diocese and became the prevalent use in all England and Wales; it reached Ireland in the 12th cent. and Scotland in the 13th; it provided the main material for the First Book of Common Prayer, while for the Catholic recusants as for others of Latin rite, it was superseded under Pius V*, by the Roman Breviary in 1568 and the reformed Roman Missal in 1576.

Satisfaction
In the penitential sense, essentially a misnomer, for it means the attempt made by the sinner to give satisfaction to the infinite God for offences committed against him. The desire to make what satisfaction can be made and the willingness to accept the penance* imposed by the confessor are necessary dispositions for validity of absolution, and the effect of this 'token' attempt at satisfaction is to remove temporal punishment due.

Scala Sancta
(Lat., holy staircase.) There is, in the old Lateran* palace, a flight of 28 marble steps, now covered with wood, which are reputed by some to be the steps of Pilate's Praetorium, trodden by Jesus (Jn.18:28), and to have been brought to Rome by St. Helen. It is traditional for pilgrims to ascend the stairs on their knees as an exercise of penance and devotion; but the fact that e.g. Pio Nono* made that ascent, does not mean that he believed the story to be authentic.

Scapular
A diminution of the monastic scapular to two rectangles of cloth joined by strings and worn before and behind under the clothes, by members of various confraternities—most of them connected with a religious institute—about seventeen in number; there are indulgences* attached to the wearing of scapulars, of which the best-known is the Brown* Scapular.

Scapular Medal
A small medal, stamped with images of the Sacred Heart and Our Blessed Lady, which may be worn in place of any or all of the small scapulars, after it has been given the corresponding blessings.

Scarlet Woman
In the days of bitter religious polemic, the gorgeous harlot of Rev. 17 was taken by the more energetic Protestant writers and preachers as representing the Church of Rome: a symbolism no longer much in fashion.

Schism
(Gk. σχισμα, split.) A breaking away from the authority of the Church, the test for which has been the acceptance or refusal of the Pope as the central repository of the authority conferred by Christ; even in the aftermath of Avignon* and the Schism of the West* and the consequent weakening of respect for the See of Rome, St. Thomas More was able to write '. . . we shall find that, on the one hand, every enemy of the Christian faith makes war on that See, and on the other, no one has ever declared himself an enemy of that See who has not also shortly afterwards shown most evidently that he was the enemy of the Christian religion.'

Schism of the East
The separation from the Holy See of what is now known as the Orthodox Eastern Church took a great deal of time: after a number of lesser schisms, the first serious break, in the time of Photius*, was patched up, but hostility endured and, with the

violently anti-Latin Michael Caerularius as Patriarch of Constantinople, attempts at pacification failed; Rome issued a bull of excommunication in 1054 and Caerularius answered with anathemas*. The break was accomplished and became permanent in spite of brief periods of reconciliation (1274-82, after the Council of Lyons*, and 1439-72, after the Council of Florence*). On the taking of Constantinople by the Turks in 1453, it suited the conquerors' interests to reopen and deepen the rift with the powerful Church of the West, and they brought pressure to bear on the other Patriarchates—Alexandria, Antioch and Jerusalem, the Russian and Slav churches holding out longest. Among them all, Constantinople was the only one to make a formal and definite break, but with the passing of centuries, attitudes hardened, and the two great bodies remained apart. In the modern ecumenical movement of the Roman Church, and as a result of the Second Vatican Council, moves have been made, one outward sign of this being the historic meeting of Pope Paul VI with the Patriarch Athenagoras.

Schism of the West (Great Schism)

The name given, not accurately, to the events between 1378, when Urban VI was elected Pope, and 1417, when the Council of Constance* settled the matter with the election of Martin V: the opposing parties were not trying to throw off the authority of the Church but dividing the Church by each claiming to have the true Pope. In 1378, on the death of Gregory XI—who brought back the Papacy from Avignon* and who is still the last French pope—the conclave of sixteen cardinals, amidst a great and enthusiastic demand from the Roman populace for a native pope again, elected an Italian, Urban VI—in fact, 13 of them proceeded to a second election, confirming Urban, who was likewise crowned twice. The new pope turned abruptly indiscreet, extravagant and haughty, irritating the Sacred College by threatening to create a majority of Italian cardinals (later, in pursuance of a war against Naples, he was to have some of the cardinals tortured and five executed: some scholars have suspected intermittent mental derangement in him). In three months,

the electors were declaring that they had chosen Urban only as caretaker for a time, and that, in any case, their election of him was invalid because of their terror of the Roman mob, and they decamped in a body to Naples. Urban's reply was to confer the red* hat on twenty-eight of his supporters; the men at Naples elected one of their number, a Frenchman, as Clement VII, who took up residence at Avignon. This feud, originating in no theological or canonical grounds but in the overweening ambition of the French interest, divided the Church for forty years, offering political opportunity to princes, and honest perplexity to scholars, saints and undistinguished Christians. Urban kept the loyalty of Germany, the Scandinavian lands, England, Wales, Ireland, Portugal, Flanders and Hungary, while the rulers of Spain, Scotland, Provence and Naples followed Clement. Urban was succeeded by Boniface IX, Innocent VII and Gregory XII, Clement by Benedict XIII, who in his turn had rivals, Alexander V, put up by the unsuccessful attempt of the Council of Pisa to end the division, and his successor John XXIII. It was, ironically enough, this last claimant who summoned, at the urging of the Emperor Sigismund, the Council of Constance* in 1414, to set aside his two rivals and settle the Schism: the Council deposed John and Benedict XIII; Gregory XII resigned and Martin V was elected and accepted by all parties. Benedict, refusing to acknowledge his deposition, kept up papal state and, dying in 1423, was succeeded by disciples calling themselves Clement VIII and Benedict XIV; this line died out in 1430. Official papal chronicles count the succession from Urban VI as the rightful popes, and the title-numbers of the other claimants—antipopes—have all been taken by succeeding pontiffs, with the exception of Alexander: the next pope of that name, Rodrigo Borgia, is known as Alexander VI, of whom the footnote says 'ought to be V.'

Scholastic

A student or teacher of Scholasticism*. Also, a member of the Society* of Jesus who has taken simple perpetual vows is called a scholastic for the next period, of ten years or more, in which he studies or teaches in the Society, usually until he is ordained priest.

Scholastica, St.

Sister of St. Benedict*, who, having established a convent near his monastery of Monte Cassino*, used to visit her brother once a year to discuss spiritual matters. She is invoked against storms on the strength of the legend related by St. Gregory of her last visit: when evening came, she begged Benedict to let her stay; his refusal was frustrated by the breaking of such a storm as would permit neither to leave the guest-house. So they spent the night talking of the joys of heaven and when the sun rose in a clear sky, she departed; but three nights later, Benedict saw in a vision his sister's spirit ascending to heaven. He sent for her body to be buried in the tomb he had prepared for himself, so that, as Gregory recounts, 'these two, who in mind were always united in God, were not separated, even in the tomb.'

Scholasticism

(Lat. *scholasticus*, teacher, learned man.) The system of philosophy and theology prevalent in the Middle Ages and brought to its most highly wrought and organised form by St. Thomas Aquinas*; an effort at the better understanding of the Christian truths by philosophical and theological speculation, by applying such intellectual processes as analogy, definition, co-ordination, systematization. It has been described as a grand synthesis of the philosophy of the Fathers and one of its founders must be St. Augustine, who urged in *De Doctrina Christiana* the need for dialectical study of revealed doctrine and, in *De Praedestinatione Sanctorum* elaborated the idea that 'to believe is to ponder with assent' into *intellige ut credas, crede ut intelligas*, understand so as to believe, believe so as to understand. Another is Boethius, whose translations of and commentaries on Aristotle and Porphyry later put Greek logic into the hands of mediaeval thinkers; and it was one of Boethius' followers, Cassiodorus, who, in his *Programme of Divine and Human Letters*, a curriculum of studies for his monastery, established the *Seven Liberal Arts* (the Trivium: Grammar, Rhetoric, Dialectic, and the Quadrivium: Arithmetic, Geometry, Astronomy,

Music) as the basis of all learning, sacred and secular; this system also prepared the way for the Carolingian renaissance and for much of the philosophical and theological speculation of the Middle Ages. Masters such as Alcuin, Erigena, Lanfranc, Anselm (the teacher of the quest of faith for intellectual formulation, *fides quaerens intellectum*) were followed by Abélard and the University men with the method of the *disputatio*, and Peter Lombard's Sentences exercised a profound intellectual influence for centuries. It was in the 13th cent. that the writings of Aristotle —already translated into Latin in the previous century—and of his great Arabic commentators began to be noticed in the Schools. Two divergent trends resulted: a reactionary adherence to St. Augustine against all new ideas and an indiscriminate swallowing of the Arabic interpretation of Aristotle, even when it clashed with Catholic teaching. From the Dominican Order came the synthesis and reconciliation, indicated by St. Albert the Great and presented in masterly fashion by his pupil St. Thomas Aquinas* (who is said to have baptised Aristotle) in his *Summa Theologica*, considered to be the summation and crown of Scholastic thought. Under the vigorous attacks on Thomism by Duns Scotus and the aberrant conclusions of William of Occam (which later had a strong influence on certain Protestant thinkers) Scholasticism declined: *dunce* was a term of scorn for Duns Scotus as representative of Scholasticism. There was a revival when the Church felt the need of a corrective for wild 19th-century subjectivism and, under the urging of Leo XIII's encyclical *Aeterni Patris* (1879), Scholasticism began to spread further than the seminaries in which it had continued to be used. Among modern exponents of the system have been the French philosophers, Etienne Gilson, Jacques Maritain and Père Garrigou-Lagrange, O.P.

Schoolmen

The great masters of the Scholastic tradition, whose names would include Thomas Aquinas*, Albert the Great, Anselm, Alexander of Hales, Bonaventure, Abélard, Duns Scotus, Peter Lombard.

Scots Colleges
There were colleges founded abroad for the education of Scottish seminary students, in Rome in 1600, and later at Madrid (this transferred in 1771 to Valladolid), Paris and Douay; the latter two no longer exist but the French government compensates by the education of a number of Scots in various French seminaries.

Scripture
In Catholic teaching, the Bible 'is the Word of God inasmuch as this was committed to writing under the inspiration of the divine Spirit.' (Second Vatican Council, Dogmatic Constitution on Divine Revelation, *Dei Verbum*, 9); both Testaments, the Council of Trent says, 'the Church receives with piety and reverence, since the one God is the author of both.' (Session iv) Fundamentalism has always been far from the Catholic understanding of the Bible, which is in general that the sacred books are true in the sense intended by each individual writer; and the Church is the only authentic interpreter of Scripture.
See Canon, Inspiration, Interpretation.

Seal of Confession
The secrecy of what passes between priest and penitent in sacramental confession is so highly valued by the Church that excommunication ensues on the revelation by the priest or by any who may accidentally or otherwise have knowledge of such matters, and the priest is forbidden to make any use of his knowledge—even without revelation—if this would hurt or offend the penitent. In England, judges in court of law have in the past respected the seal, though the position of a priest who refuses to divulge is not actually protected by law; in many states of the US, information obtained in the confessional is regarded by the law as privileged.

Séance
Catholics are forbidden to attend, even as spectators, at séances assembled for the purpose of communicating with the dead.

Seat of Wisdom
A title of Our Lady in her Litany, first found in the writings of St. Anselm and St. Bernard.

Second Coming, the
The Church has always taken the same line as Paul in II Thess.2, discouraging speculation and jumpiness about the *Parousia*, repeating his exhortations and blessings (vv. 15–17), together with the Lord's own statement of the secret time of the event (Mk.13:32) and his reference to the General Judgement in Mt. 21.

Second Passion Sunday
See Passion Sunday.

Secretariat of State
Arising out of the need of Popes for rapid, reliable and sometimes secret correspondence, there were set up in the Roman Curia various suitable departments which crystallised in 1487 into a group of twenty-four called the Apostolic Secretariat, the chief of the number bearing the title of Domestic Secretary. Evolving over the centuries, the Secretariat now comprises over a hundred officials, men and women, ecclesiastics and laity, the Secretary himself being a Cardinal, who is also *ex officio* Prefect of the Council for the Public Affairs of the Church*. The Secretariat is the leading department of the Roman Curia.

Secular Arm
The civil power. In the days when the civil law was powerfully influenced by Canon Law and indeed enshrined many of its articles, a person condemned by an ecclesiastical court would be handed over to the civil power if he were judged worthy of a greater punishment than the church court was empowered to inflict, as in the cases of St. Joan of Arc and many persons condemned for heresy. The practice could easily be abused and was discontinued.

Secular Clergy
The 'ordinary' or parochial clergy; a secular priest is a diocesan priest, i.e. a man ordained by a bishop for work in that bishop's diocese. His life is one of ministering to the faithful of a parish to which the bishop appoints him, and in which he must live. He is not bound by rule or vow but by his promise of obedience to his bishop.
See Regular.

Secularisation

The process—involving papal indult—whereby a member of a religious order or congregation is separated from that body and released from the vows of religion. If such a person is in Holy Orders, he may not exercise these until accepted by a bishop. Readmission to the religious order needs a papal indult and another novitiate. Secularisation is also the term used to describe the action of a civil power in depriving the Church or any ecclesiastical institute of its possessions or of control over property, institutions such as schools, hospitals, etc. Where such seizure has taken place, the Church usually makes provision that property so held at present can be possessed in good conscience by those who hold it, e.g. the monastic properties of England taken in the 16th cent.

Sede Impedita

(Lat.) 'the See being obstructed' by the inability of the bishop, from whatever reason, to administer his diocese.

Sede Vacante

(Lat., 'while the See is unoccupied'). In which time, the affairs of the diocese are put into the hands of a Vicar Capitular*, appointed by the cathedral chapter within eight days of the occurrence of the vacancy. When the Holy See becomes vacant, the Cardinal Camerlengo* automatically becomes head of the Sacred College of Cardinals and takes charge of the administration of the Church.

Sedgley Park

Here, in Staffordshire, a school was opened under the direction of Bishop Challoner in 1763, the first Catholic school thus to defy the penal laws (see Disabilities of Catholics). It operates now at Cotton Hall, Oakamoor.

Sedia Gestatoria

(It., sedan chair.) An elaborate portable throne on which popes were carried e.g. in and out of St. Peter's* or the Sistine* Chapel on ceremonial occasions, on the shoulders of six scarlet-clad gentlemen of the Papal household, frequently escorted by Swiss guardsmen with drawn swords, Vatican officials and two huge ostrich-feather fans. The fans were the first piece of this accoutrement to be disposed of; the *sedia* itself, not much used by Paul VI, was put away by John Paul II who, some months after his election, encountering as he went on foot among the crowds a group of devotees calling out to him 'Sedia gestatoria! Sedia Gestatoria!', resolutely cried, 'No! No! No!' thus finally abandoning to history this splendid item of papal imperialism.

Sedilia

(Lat. *sedile*, seat.) The term is frequently used for the wooden seats provided on the sanctuary for the three ministers at a solemn ceremony, though purists might reserve it for such seats in ancient churches, highly wrought, carved and canopied, or even only for those cut into the stonework of the south wall.

Seminaries and Universities, Congregation for

Developing from foundations dating back to 1588 to oversee the Roman and other universities, this was established in 1915 by Benedict XV, for seminaries and universities; in 1967, Paul VI* named it the Sacred Congregation for Catholic Education, adding a third section for Catholic schools.
See Roman Congregations.

Separation

Though normally a married couple are bound to live together, there are causes which allow of separation, temporary or permanent, the bond of matrimony always remaining: adultery (unless condoned—or also committed—by the other party) is one such cause; likewise, if one party joins a non-Catholic sect or lives a criminal or infamous life or endangers the other in soul or body or makes life unbearable, the injured party will apply successfully to the Ordinary* for separation—or separate without his word if delay would be dangerous—until the cause is removed. Children in such cases are to be brought up with the injured party or, in a mixed marriage, with the Catholic party, according as the Ordinary judges best for them.

Septuagint

(Lat. *septuaginta*, seventy.) The first Greek version of the Hebrew Scriptures, made at Alexandria in the 3rd and 2nd centuries B.C., reputedly by seventy translators. Most of the N.T. quotations from the O.T. are taken from the Septuagint, not from the Hebrew. The chief differences between the Hebrew and the LXX (as it is usually abbreviated in print) are that the latter does not use the older division of the books into the Law, the Prophets and the Writings, and it includes works not found in the Hebrew and known to Catholic scholars as Deutero-Canonical, to others as the Apocrypha (Tobit, Judith, Wisdom, Ecclesiasticus, Baruch, the two Books of the Maccabees and certain parts of other books).

Septuagesima Sunday

The old term for the third Sunday before the beginning of Lent; the two following Sundays were Sexagesima and Quinquagesima. It is not known how these names arose (Septuagesima means seventieth, Sexagesima sixtieth and Quinquagesima fiftieth): perhaps by analogy with *Quadragesima* (fortieth), the word for Lent, all being now declared redundant.

Sequence

A kind of hymn, but not necessarily in regular metre, said or sung after the Alleluia Verse at Mass on certain great feasts. There were very many Sequences in use, but the Roman Missal now contains only five: for Easter Day (*Victimae Paschali*), Pentecost (*Veni Sancte Spiritus*), the Feast of the Body and Blood of Christ (*Lauda Sion*), Our Lady of Sorrows (*Stabat Mater*)—the latter two may now be abbreviated or omitted—and the fifth, the *Dies Irae*★ has been detached from the Requiem Mass and left to private devotion.

Seraphic

A description traditionally applied to St. Francis★ (see Stigmata) and those connected with him, e.g. the Seraphic Order—the Franciscans, the Seraphic Doctor—St. Bonaventure.

Seraphim

(Heb. *seraph*, to burn, be on fire.) A plural word, found most notably in Is.6:2–7 and associated etymologically with the 'fiery flying serpent' of chap.14:29 and the fiery serpents of Num.21:6ff—an indication that perhaps Christian thought and art have been too anthropomorphic. Each seraph in Isaiah's vision, standing above the throne of God, had six wings, two of which covered its eyes (lest it see God and die?), presumably also hands, since one of them took up a live coal with tongs, and a great voice which shook the doorposts of the Temple. Possibly we should compare the Chinese use of dragons in religious symbolism.

Servants of Mary

See Servites.

Server

One who assists the celebrant at liturgical functions, especially at Mass; the scope of the server has recently shrunken (except at solemn or pontifical ceremonies), from his previous tasks which included of old e.g. at Mass, making all the responses without the congregation, moving the missal from one side of the altar to the other. The server, a male with no upward or downward limit on age, is permitted to wear cassock and surplice, women being excluded, although they are nowadays to be found in some places.

Servites

Founded in Florence in 1233 by the Seven Holy Founders★, with the rule of St. Augustine; a mendicant Order whose work is in preaching, parish work, giving missions and the fostering of devotion to the Mother of God; they are bound to the recitation of the Office in choir. The Order did not exist in England before the Reformation. The second order, the Servite nuns, has existed in its present form since 1629; it is enclosed, contemplative, with Divine Office in choir and, in some houses, perpetual adoration.

Servus Servorum Dei

(Lat., Servant of the servants of God.) One of the traditional titles of the Popes. It is said to have been first used by Gregory the Great★ when in deacon's orders. Later, as Pope, he again styled himself 'servant of the servants of God' as a reproach to what he perceived as the overwhelming arrogance of John IV of Constantinople, who had publicly described himself as 'Universal Patriarch'. It was not until the

9th cent. that the title was consistently used by the Papacy. Civil rulers also were attracted by the title, such as Alphonsus II of Spain (9th cent.) and the Emperor Henry III (11th cent.); but since the 12th cent., it has been exclusively papal.

Seven Churches of Rome

The Basilicas* of St. John Lateran*, St. Peter*, St. Mary Major, St. Paul-outside-the-Walls, St. Lawrence-outside-the-Walls, St. Sebastian-outside-the-Walls, Holy Cross in Jerusalem. There are indulgences* attached to visits paid to these churches, which were traditionally visited by pilgrim penitents.

Seven Corporal Works of Mercy

These are traditionally: to feed the hungry, to give drink to the thirsty, to clothe the naked, to harbour the homeless, to care for the sick, to visit the imprisoned, to bury the dead (cf. Mt.25:35).
See Seven Spiritual Works of Mercy.

Seven Gifts of the Holy Spirit

The list of six from Is.11:2—Wisdom, Understanding, Counsel, Fortitude, Knowledge and Fear of the Lord was augmented in LXX and the Vulgate by Piety, inserted before Fear of the Lord, for which, the scholars say, it is a synonym.

Seven Heavens

The idea of a sevenfold series of heavens, or departments of heaven, rising one above the other, is a Hellenistic concept, which became popular among Christians, though it was never sanctioned by the Church. St. Paul's phrase about the *third heaven* in II Cor.12:2 is interpreted to mean 'the highest heaven'—St. Thomas Aquinas understands it as the vision of the truth and of the essence of God—while Dante constructs his *Paradiso* in 10 circles.

Seven Holy Founders

Seven Florentine gentlemen, as a result of a simultaneous vision of the Blessed Virgin, withdrew to Monte Senario to live as a community, from which grew the Order of Servites*. The Founders were Saints Bonfiglio Monaldi, Giovanni Buonagiunta, Benedetto Antella, Bartolommeo Amidei, Ricovero Uguccione, Gerardo Sostegni and Alessio Falconieri.

Seven Sacraments

See Sacraments.

Seven Sleepers of Ephesus

From the 6th cent., and perhaps earlier, there was a legend in both Eastern and Western churches that seven Christian youths, walled up in a cave in the persecution of Decius, woke again after two centuries. The Roman Martyrology commemorates them as martyrs on July 27th. Their cult and significance were probably connected with controversies over the Resurrection of the Dead, their reawakening being adduced as proof of this doctrine.

Seven Sorrows of Our Lady, the

The feast of this title, or of Our Lady of Sorrows, was first granted to the Servites in 1668 and extended to the universal Church by Pius VII in 1814, for September 15th; there was formerly also a commemoration on the Friday before Passion Sunday (Palm Sunday). The traditional list of the Sorrows names the sufferings of Our Lady at the prophecy of Simeon, during the Flight into Egypt, at the three-day loss of the Child, at meeting her Son on his way to crucifixion, while standing beneath the Cross, at his deposition, and at his burial.

Seven Spiritual Works of Mercy

These are traditionally: to convert the sinner, to instruct the ignorant, to counsel the waverer, to comfort the sorrowful, to bear ills patiently, to forgive injuries, to pray for the living and the dead.
See Seven Corporal Works of Mercy.

Seven Words

The seven sayings uttered by Jesus on the cross, collected from the Gospels and much used for meditation, prayer and sermons; a musical work of Haydn commissioned by the Cathedral of Cadiz and consisting of seven slow movements (1785) described as a 'fine work . . . unjustly neglected' (Alan Blyth in *The Musical Companion*, 1977 edition); the composer also gave this title—the Seven Words of the Redeemer on the Cross—to a set of seven string quartets.

Sext

(Lat. *sexta*, the sixth, sc. hour.) Formerly, one of the Little Hours of the Divine Office, meant to be recited at the sixth hour of the day, i.e. about noon; in practice, following the conventual Mass where the Office is recited in community. In the reformed Breviary, the Little Hours have been replaced by the 'Prayers during the Day'.

Shrewsbury, Diocese of

Suffragan to Birmingham and erected in 1850, this diocese comprises Shropshire and Cheshire, which had belonged respectively to the mediaeval dioceses of Hereford and Lichfield. The diocese was built around outposts like Acton Burnell and Plowden, where the faith had not died out, and missions set up in other parts, six of them in the 18th cent; its patrons are Our Lady, Help of Christians, and St. Winefride (whose shrine, from 1138 until the Reformation, was at Shrewsbury).

Shrine

(Lat. *scrinium,* box or cabinet for writing materials) is rarely used in its original meaning of a reliquary; its usual connotation is a place in which the tomb or relic of a saint is kept, or which is reserved for the practice of a particular devotion, usually with some image and the embellishment and symbolism of flowers, candles, lamps, etc., as at Lourdes*. There are very few shrines in modern England to compare with the numbers that proliferated before the Reformers took them in hand, but a few statues of our Blessed Lady are venerated as having survived that iconoclasm: at York, Buckfast*, Prinknash*, and some other places; and there has been of recent years a revival of pilgrimage* to Walsingham*. Other saints had shrines, some of which are still with us: there are relics of St. Thomas of Canterbury in the church of his name in that city, the great shrine in the Cathedral having been despoiled by King Henry's commissioners, St. Edward the Confessor's body is undisturbed in Westminster Abbey, the bones of St. Wite, an Anglo-Saxon lady martyred by Danes, and since latinised as Candida, sanctify the village church of Whitchurch Canonicorum in Dorset, where they were discovered in a lead coffin in 1900 (St. Wite's is said to be the only parish church in the country containing the body of its titular saint). A chapel in Westminster Cathedral is a shrine of St. John Southworth, whose body, discovered at Douai in 1927, now lies in London with silver mask and gauntlets; Drogheda has a Memorial Church of St. Oliver Plunkett where the martyr's skull has rested since 1722, transported from Rome whither it was taken in 1684.; one leg of the quartered body has been sent to Ireland by the monks of Downside Abbey, who retain the remainder of the cadaver.

Shroud, the Holy

There is in the keeping of the Archbishop of Turin what has been called 'possibly Christianity's holiest relic', the adverb being due to uncertainty as to whether there is a relic at all. The piece of cloth, about 14 ft. long by 3 ft. wide, known as the Holy Shroud, is of the size and cut used for burial in the Province of Judaea in the first cent. A.D., and is held by many, by reason of the marks it bears, to have been the winding-sheet in which the dead Christ was laid in the tomb. The marks represent the front and back view of a naked man 5 ft. 11 in. tall and with wounds such as would correspond with the descriptions given in the Gospels of the Lord's sufferings: lacerations all over the upper half of the skull, suggesting a helmet, rather than a crown of thorns, great wounds in the wrists, not in the palms, severe wounding across the torso, as of scourging, and smaller markings on the face consistent with blows. According to the chemists who have studied the Shroud, these marks are not painted nor are they the result of organic pigment such as blood; they do not show through on the other side of the fabric nor even penetrate below its surface, which has led to some recent speculation as to whether they could have been wrought by the exposure of the cloth for a minute period of time to very intense heat. The chief endeavour of the interested scientists is to establish the age of the cloth, since its history is not known before the 14th cent. and it has not been subjected to Carbon 14 testing, though learned opinion tends to pronounce it to be of Palestinian origin. It has, howewer, been well remarked that all the scientific testing could never prove more than that this was the shroud of a man of that time and place who had suffered similar physical torments to those of Jesus: it could lead to conjecture or probability, but never to proof, that this was the burial-cloth of the Lord himself. The Church, while permitting occasional public veneration, does not pronounce one way or the other.

Sign of Peace

At Mass, since the Second Vatican Council, the liturgy bids the priest invite his people to share a sign of the peace and love that should exist between those who are to share the Body of the Lord. In those places where the invitation is issued, the 'holy kiss' of I Cor.16:20 is interpreted as a handshake or embrace, according to the degree of acquaintance or embarrassment of the faithful. There is also the formal embrace of the ministers at concelebrated Mass, likewise of the newly-ordained bishop and of the cardinals offering homage to a new Pope.

Sign of the Cross, the

This is essentially a prayer, and part of all liturgical blessings. The practice of tracing a cross over some object, or on one's own or another's forehead, is mentioned by Tertullian in the 2nd cent., and by later writers; the 'sign of the Lord' was used as a reminder of the sufferings and death of Christ, to sanctify oneself on rising and going to bed, as a protection against temptation, and to make oneself known to other Christians in time of persecution; it was also part of the ritual of Baptism and Confirmation. Later, the faithful adopted also the current style of cross from head to breast and across the shoulders (the Eastern Churches moving the hand from right shoulder to left) and added the words 'In the name of the Father and of the Son and of the Holy Spirit', in blessing on some action being undertaken. The fury of the Reformers against signs has been watered down over the centuries to the opinion, held by many otherwise educated persons, that the Sign of the Cross is superstition.

Simnel Sunday

A name for Mid-Lent Sunday*, from simnel cake, a rich and ornamented confection eaten on that day, and, anciently, also at Easter and Christmas.

Simon Stock, St.

(c.1165–1265). The sobriquet derives possibly from the legend that in his youth he lived as a hermit with a tree-trunk for a cell. One of the first Englishmen to join the Carmelites* when they came to Britain, he became General of the Order in his old age; under his guidance the Order expanded rapidly, especially in England, and it was he who got papal permission for the modifications it underwent on leaving Palestine. He is known also as *Simon Anglus*.

Simony

(Simon; Acts 8:18–24.) The buying and selling of spiritual things or things with a spiritual value or content (as would be, e.g. a relic of a saint); it has a long and pervasive history: almost as soon as the age of persecution was over, the Council of Chalcedon (451) found it necessary to legislate about money changing hands for ordination, Gregory the Great* denounced it and the traffic in ecclesiastical preferment became shamefully common in the Middle Ages, its heinousness being described by St. Thomas* Aquinas and banned by many councils, and later, in particularly strong terms, by the Council of Trent*, men having bought their way into the papacy itself. In modern Canon Law, those who confer or receive ecclesiastical office simoniacally incur excommunication reserved to the Pope.

Simple Vows

The vows of religion (poverty, chastity, obedience) are either solemn or simple, the latter being such as render contrary acts unlawful but not invalid, e.g. those with simple vows may retain ownership of property, their marriage would be unlawful but not invalid. Simple vows are taken in religious societies ranked as *congregation*, as opposed to *order*, and religious women in simple vows are officially known as *sisters*.
See Order, Moniales, Solemn Vows.

Sins against the Holy Spirit

Six sins—despair, presumption, envy, obstinacy in sin, final impenitence, resistance to the known truth—have been classified as directly and explicitly frustrating the work of the Holy Spirit in the soul, thus rendering repentance unlikely.

Sisters of Charity

There are several congregations of Sisters with this title, e.g. i) Sisters of Charity of St. Vincent de Paul, founded by this saint and Bl. Marie Louise de Marillac in 1634, to be totally at the service of anyone in need. He wanted his ladies to be as unnunlike as possible: 'their chapel is the parish church, their cloister the city street and the hospital ward'—but Rome was not quite as radical as Vincent. From the mother house in Paris, the Sisters have spread to most parts of the world, and until recently were recognised and known affectionately as the 'butterfly nuns' from the vast white *cornette* they wore. ii) Sisters of Charity of St. Paul the Apostle: founded at Chartres, 1704, their chief work is in education, the English congregation being independent and having over 60 houses. iii) Irish Sisters of Charity, founded in Dublin, 1815, by Mary Aikenhead to care for the sick and poor; they now have schools, hospitals, refuges in Ireland, Great Britain and Australia.

Sisters of Mercy

Founded in Dublin (1827) for the practice of all and any of the works of mercy, this congregation, of which each convent is independent, has hostels, houses of rest, hospitals, refuges and schools in all the English-speaking countries. Sisters of Mercy accompanied Florence Nightingale in her work in the Crimea, together with nuns of the Society of the Faithful Virgin.

Sisters of Nazareth

The full title is the Poor Sisters of Nazareth; the congregation was founded in London (1851) by Mother St. Basil Lamenier. They have homes for aged poor, for those with incurable diseases and for children, for which work they collect alms; the congregation has spread to most English-speaking countries.

Sisters of Providence

The chief congregations using this title are i) the Sisters of Providence of the Institute of Charity, founded in 1762 by J. M. Maye but taking their title from the fact that their rule was re-written in 1833 by Rosmini (see Institute of Charity); their chief work has been in education: they were the first nuns in England to teach in elementary schools (1844); and ii) Sisters of Providence of the Immaculate Conception, founded in Belgium in 1833 for work in hospitals, schools and orphanages.

Sisters of the Cross and Passion

(not the same as the Daughters of the Cross and Passion★ or Passionist Nuns.) An unenclosed foundation established by Frs. Gaudentius and Ignatius, C.P., and Mother Mary Prout, in Manchester, 1850, with the objects of looking after working girls, teaching, caring for the sick and for lapsed Catholics; they have houses in Ireland and North America.

Sisters of the Holy Child Jesus

(to be distinguished from the Dames of St. Maur★.) Founded at Derby, in 1846, by Cornelia Connelly★, their work to be teaching. They were established in the U.S. in 1862.

Sisters of the Holy Faith

Rev. John Gowan and Margaret Aylward founded this congregation in Dublin (1857) to combat 'souperism'★ by caring for Catholic children who were orphaned or destitute.

Sisters of the Holy Ghost

Founded in Brittany, in 1706, for teaching and other charitable works, the Sisters have houses mainly in Belgium, Wales and the U.S. They are also known as the White Sisters.

Sisters of the Immaculate Conception

A section of the Association of the Holy Family★, whose chosen work is the education of all classes of children.

Sisters of the Sacred Hearts of Jesus and Mary

Several congregations bear this title, the best-known being the Picpus★ institute founded in 1797, founded for perpetual adoration and educational work. It has schools and hospitals in England.

Sisters of St. Joseph

Several congregations have this name; e.g. i) Sisters of St. Joseph of Le Puy, a foundation of 1650 by the Jesuit J. P. Medaille, for the undertaking of all works of mercy; from Lyons, where it was re-formed after the French Revolution, it spread to Great Britain, India, the Middle East and North America. ii) Sisters of St. Joseph of Peace, who were founded in 1883 by Bishop Bagshawe of Nottingham, originally to train girls in domestic work; houses were established in North America. iii) Missionary Sisters of St. Joseph, established by Cardinal Vaughan as an adjunct to the work of the priests of Mill Hill* in England and abroad. The sisters have the rule of the Third Order of St. Francis.

Sisters of the Temple
The Sisters of the Finding of Jesus in the Temple—Blue Nuns—are a congregation founded in London by Cardinal Wiseman and the Abbé Roullin in 1860, to be a nursing community. They later took houses in Belgium and France, with a celebrated hospital in Paris.

Sistine Chapel
The principal chapel of the Vatican Palace, named after Pope Sixtus IV, who began it in 1473. Apart from such public events as canonisations*, which take place at St. Peter's*, the Chapel is the scene of most papal observances: these, before the papal residence at Avignon*, were carried out in the various Roman basilicas*. It is best known as the 'polling station' of the cardinals in conclave*; in which also a newly-elected pope received their homage (adoratio), until John Paul I (1978) made this a public ceremony on the steps of St. Peter's.

Sistine Choir
The choir of the Sistine* Chapel, numbering 24 men and boys, sings always unaccompanied. It began as the papal schola cantorum in the Middle Ages, a college whose members lived in community; its present form came about during and after the paper sojourn at Avignon*.

Skull-Cap
Worn by cardinals, bishops and popes, in the appropriate colours, the skull-cap is a mediaeval derivative of the ancient tight-fitting cap (worn to protect the tonsured scalp), which also originally had ear-flaps.

Sloth
See Accidie.

Society of Jesus
First named the Company of Jesus by St. Ignatius Loyola when he founded it in Paris in 1534, the Society took as its twofold aim the support of the Pope and of Catholic truth against the heresies of that time, and the speading of the Faith among the heathen; it still holds itself explicitly at the command of the Pope and maintains many mission fields. It also engages, as from its earliest days, in education, and has contributed massively to Catholic thought and learning (see Bollandists, Gregorian University). The Jesuits are priests and laybrothers; of the former, a special number take solemn* vows at a second profession, and add a fourth vow, that of special obedience to the Holy See for missionary work anywhere in the world. The Society, besides producing an impressive list of canonised saints, and establishing itself all over the world, has been expelled from many countries, and, in 1773, it was suppressed by Pope Clement XIV, to be reinstated by Pius VII in 1814. In Great Britain, the Jesuits were martyred for the Catholic cause in the days of Elizabeth I and later, were reviled for such affairs as the Gunpowder Plot and at the time of the Vicars Apostolic, attracted the hostility of the secular clergy as having too much power. The Jesuit rule is not a secret document, despite such legends as that of the Monita Secreta*.

Society of the Catholic Apostolate
Founded by St. Vincent Pallotti in 1835 to spread and preserve the Faith and to carry out works of charity, the Society comprised priests (Pallottine Fathers) and laity, and was fortified in 1843 by the establishment of the Sisters of the Catholic Apostolate (Pallottine Sisters*). It had its name officially changed to Pious Society of Missions, and only of recent years has regained its original title. The Society engages in missionary and charitable works in numerous countries, the Fathers serving the Italian and German Churches in London and the English Church in Rome.

Society of the Faithful Virgin

Founded in Normandy in 1831, this congregation of women has as its principal object the education of the young and undertakes other works of charity as occasion arises. Members of the English Province of this society, together with some Sisters of Mercy, went to assist Florence Nightingale in the Crimea.

Socinianism

Two 16th cent. theologians of Siena, Lelio and Fausto Socino, produced a theory somewhat akin to that of modern Unitarians: Jesus Christ, they said, was not God but a man of miraculous birth who, being the secondary cause of our salvation as mediator of God, was deified and thus is to be worshipped; the Holy Spirit, moreover, is only an activity of God.

Solemn Vows

These are taken by members of an Order* properly so called; they render contrary acts not only illicit but invalid (see Simple Vows), and may not be taken by anyone under the age of 21. Religious women in solemn vows are, canonically speaking, nuns proper, *moniales**, those in simple vows being *sisters*.

Solesmes

The Abbey of St. Pierre in the département of Sarthe was founded in 1010 and refounded in 1833 as a priory of six monks, made in 1837 an abbey and mother-house of the French Congregation of Benedictines, being given all the privileges and honours of the extinct Congregations of Cluny, St. Vannes and St. Maur. This house is famous for scholarship and for its work in the revival, at the request of Pope Pius X, of the plainchant, its editions being accepted as the only authentic versions. There is an abbey of this congregation at Quarr in the Isle of Wight, which was the home of the Solesmes community for about 20 years when they were expelled from France by the anti-clerical legislation of 1903.

Solitary

The true solitary, viz. the person who chooses to live entirely alone and remote for the love of God, is now very rare, though the solitary life as regularised in certain monastic orders (e.g. Camaldolese, Carthusians*) flourishes as ever. The Church's attitude to the solitary life is discernible in Maritain—'. . . the contemplative solitude of a certain number of souls united to God who, in their turn, moved by love, intercede for the multitude. . .' and in Belloc's lines

'They that in dereliction grow perfected,
They that are silent, they that stand apart.
They that shall judge the world as God's elected,
They that have had the sword athwart the heart.'

Son of God

In Catholic doctrine, the Second Person of the Trinity is truly the Son, 'eternally begotten of the Father . . . begotten, not made, of one being with the Father. .' Jesus Christ, moreover, is this only Son of God, since the two natures, divine and human, inhere in the one Person, the eternal Word, consubstantial with the Father: cf. Jn.10:30; and, in Mt.16:18, Christ commends Peter's profession of faith as a revelation from the Father. Biblically, the phrase is used also of angels, as in Job 1:6, of the Jews as a race and of prophets in particular, and of Christians (Gal.4:5–7, 1Jn.2:29) as accepting the redemption of Christ; but none of these usages could be confused with the sense first described above.

Sorrowful Mysteries of the Rosary

The Sorrowful Mysteries are: the Agony of Our Lord in the Garden, the Scourging at the Pillar, the Crowning with Thorns, the Carrying of the Cross to Calvary, the Crucifixion and Death of Our Lord.

Sorrows of the Blessed Virgin Mary

See Seven Sorrows.

Souperism

A slang term coined in Ireland during the time of the Famine, when certain welfare workers offered help to the starving, on condition of renouncing the Catholic Faith and embracing the Established Church; this campaign to secure 'rice Protestants' is said to have been most intense in Connemara and Achill.

Southwark

The Metropolitan See of Southwark, erected in 1850, comprises the London Metropolitan Boroughs south of the Thames and the County of Kent; it has as suffragan sees Arundel and Brighton, Plymouth and Portsmouth. Patrons: Our Lady Conceived Without Sin, St. Thomas of Canterbury, St. Augustine, Apostle of England.

Spanish Chapel

The chapel of the Spanish Embassy in London which, by reason of immunity from the penal laws, was much frequented by Catholics of the capital in the 17th and 18th centuries. The chapel, taken over in 1791 from the ambassador, was replaced in 1890 by the present church of St. James, Spanish Place.

Species, Eucharistic

Also Sacred Species: the accidents* of bread and wine which endure after the consecration of the substances into the Body and Blood of the Lord.

Spiritual Direction

The guidance of the soul in its quest for sanctity has been recognised from the earliest ages as a task for which few are fitted (St. Francis de Sales says, 'fewer than can be imagined'). We read of the hermits of the ancient deserts and of the founders of orders acting as spiritual directors to their followers, using the Scriptures and their own rich spiritual experience in their task as instruments of the Holy Spirit. Many people have made use of the services of their confessor as a regular spiritual director.

Spiritual Exercises

A system of meditation on the fundamental truths of religion, together with prayer, temporary withdrawal from one's ordinary occupations, and the opportunity for advice and spiritual guidance, with the intention that there should be lasting effect on the understanding and the will and therefore on the future life of faith. Another name for such a period is Retreat. The term Spiritual Exercises used *tout court* refers to the book of that name composed by St. Ignatius of Loyola and used by the Society* of Jesus.

Spiritual Reading

Reading undertaken with the purpose of bringing the spirit into closer relation with God; after the Bible, such writers as Augustine, Teresa, John of the Cross, Francis de Sales, Thomas à Kempis and many English mystics have been much used, besides more recent authors such as Ronald Knox, Thomas Merton, and Teilhard de Chardin.

Spiritual Works of Mercy

See Seven Spiritual Works of Mercy.

Sponsor

One who presents a person for Baptism or Confirmation, undertaking thereby a certain responsibility for that person's practice of his faith and thus establishing a spiritual relationship; the chief condition of sponsorship is the readiness to undertake the religious education of the one baptised or confirmed, should it become necessary and in so far as he is able. The sponsor must be at least 13 years of age and a Catholic (to present anyone for Confirmation, he must himself be confirmed) and know the rudiments of the faith. In the case of Baptism, there may be one, of either sex, or two, one of each sex—who are referred to as 'godmother' and 'godfather'; in Confirmation, only one sponsor is allowed and must be of the same sex as the candidate.

Spy Wednesday

An ancient name, not yet out of use, for the Wednesday of Holy Week, which was understood as the day on which Judas struck his bargain with the chief priests (Matt.26:14–16).

Stabat Mater

The hymn (named from the first words of its first line *Stabat Mater Dolorosa*, There stood the Mother sorrowing), ascribed to Jacopone da Todi, a 13th cent. Franciscan, to St. Bonaventure (+1274) and to Pope Innocent III (+1216), which became the Sequence* for the Mass of the Seven Sorrows* of Our Lady and is still used, in the original Latin or in translation, at the Stations of the Cross*.

Stanbrook Abbey
A house of Benedictine nuns of the English congregation. The community was begun at Cambrai in 1625, and, being expelled from France in 1793, they eventually fixed their home at Stanbrook, near Worcester. Enclosed and contemplative, they come under the jurisdiction of the Abbot* President, not of the local ordinary.

States of the Church
The Papal posssessions, chiefly in central Italy, which accumulated round the original Patrimony* of St. Peter and were ruled by the Popes as temporal sovereigns. They were the source of a certain security of revenue and of continuous disputes; and, even for those popes (until about 1400) who reigned without directly governing, they were no help to the spiritual authority which is of the essence of that office. For those who did actively govern, they were a standing temptation to worldliness and ruthless political activity, which is symbolised for many in the image of Julius II riding in full armour at the head of his army against Perugia or Bologna. At their greatest spread, in the early 16th cent., the papal territories embraced the Romagna, Urbino, Spoleto and Castro, Parma, Piacenza, Modena, the provinces of Bologna, Perugia and Orvieto, and the Anconan Marches; in France, the Venaissin area round Avignon was Papal from 1273 until the Revolution. The Italian possessions, taken from Pio Nono between 1860 and 1870, were administered for the most part by lay officers of the Pope, but many a parish priest, being willy-nilly a papal tax-collector, became a focus of deep and abiding anti-clerical feeling.

Stations of the Cross
A devotion in honour of the Passion of the Lord, in which one moves in turn to fourteen crosses, each of which symbolises a stage in his journey to Calvary and the tomb. The crosses may be set up on the interior or exterior walls of a church or be free-standing in the open air, and are usually—though this is not required—accompanied by pictures or carvings representative of the successive events to be contemplated. It is an imaginative exercise of piety, and not all the events concerned in it are scriptural; those in current use in the Western Church are: Jesus' condemnation by Pilate, his acceptance of the cross, his first fall, his meeting with his Mother, the help given by Simon of Cyrene, the wiping of his face by Veronica, his second fall, his encounter with the women of Jerusalem, his third fall, his being stripped, his crucifixion, his death, the taking down of his body, his entombment. Over the ages, the Stations have varied in number and subject, and a modern style which has found favour in some quarters is the fifteenth station, the Resurrection.

Stephen Harding, St.
See Cistercians.

Stigmata
(Gk. στιγμα, prick, mark.) Wounds or scars which have appeared—or, in certain cases, been suffered without visible sign—in the hands, feet, head, breast and sometimes the shoulders and back of certain persons, in the presumed pattern of the wounds of Christ in his Passion. The phenomenon has been observed only since the 13th cent., the time of the growth of devotion to the suffering Christ. There have been over 300 stigmatists (the vast majority of them women) the best-known being St. Francis of Assisi, the most recent Padre Pio, an Italian Capuchin* (1887–1968). About fifty of the recorded cases are well attested, and some of these have been explained on natural grounds. The marks, usually associated with claims of miracles of healing, the reading of souls, conversion of sinners, bilocation and other wonders, have always been treated by the Church with the greatest caution, and never held to constitute cause for canonisation*.

Stonyhurst
A public school conducted by the Jesuits, near Blackburn: a school founded for Catholic boys in 1592 at St. Omer, about twenty miles from Calais, transferred to Belgium (Bruges in 1762, Liège in 1773) and settled in 1794 in Lancashire, where it still flourishes.

Stylite
(Gk. στυλος, pillar); one who lived on top of a pillar as a form of penitential retirement from the world.
See Pillar Saints.

Sudarium
(Lat., cloth for wiping sweat, handkerchief.) Sometimes used for the Veil* of Veronica, sometimes for the Holy Shroud* (as in the *Victimae Paschali*).

Suffering, the Church
See Church and Purgatory.

Suffragan
A bishop (or diocese) in relation to the archbishop* or metropolitan. The Roman Church has abandoned the usage of the word, dating from the 13th cent. in England, for a bishop appointed to assist the bishop of the diocese; a usage preserved in the Church of England.

Sunday Obligation
The obligation of attending Mass weekly has been broadened to an option of Sunday or Saturday by some bishops in certain countries of Europe, to accommodate those of the faithful who might be travelling on Sunday, or engaged in e.g. ski-ing in some remote part.

SVDP
See St. Vincent de Paul, Society of.

Syllabus of errors
Attached to the encyclical *Quanta Cura* of Pius IX in 1864 was a *syllabus*, i.e. list, of 80 propositions condemned in various earlier papal pronouncements. There are 10 headings: Pantheism, Naturalism and Absolute Rationalism; Moderate Rationalism; Indifferentism and Latitudinarianism; Socialism, Bible Societies and other matters; errors about the Church and her rights, about the Church and the State, about ethics, about Christian marriage, about the Pope's temporal power, and errors regarding Liberalism. The Syllabus raised furious protests from Gladstone and others; in France, its publication was banned for a time. Some understood the condemnations in the document to be issued infallibly on each heading, but this is by no means certain; and the several propositions are condemned only in the sense in which their respective authors intended them.

Synod of Bishops
Created in 1965 by Pope Paul VI in the motu proprio*, *Apostolica Sollicitudo*, the Synod, an international body of bishops representing the bishops of the world, met for the first time in 1967. It continues to meet under its *ex officio* President, the Pope, who decides when the Synod shall meet; there is a Council of the General Secretariat of the Synod of Bishops, consisting of 15 members, 12 elected by the Synod in assembly, three nominated by the Holy Father. The Synod, promised in the Second Vatican* Council's Decree on the Pastoral Office of Bishops in the Church (Chapter I), is recognised as an exercise in collegiality*.

Syrian Christians
(Syrian Church.) See Nestorianism.

Tabernacle

The Blessed Sacrament must be reserved in all churches whose rectors have the cure* of souls, such reservation of the Sacrament under the species of bread for the communion of the sick dating back to the 7th cent. or thereabouts. The mediaeval pyx* in which the hosts were kept was superseded in the 16th cent. by the Tabernacle (Lat. *tabernaculum*, tent), a cabinet which must, according to Canon Law, be strongly made of wood, stone or metal, and kept locked; it is usually ornamented as circumstances permit and has a veil* to cover the door. The tabernacle, which according to the mind of the Church, was meant to be kept on another altar (ideally in a Chapel of the Blessed Sacrament), was frequently set centrally on the high altar, a disposition which has become impossible now that the celebrant faces his people over the altar. In modern buildings, and in others in which it has not been left on the "old" high altar behind the one used for Mass, or placed on a separate altar, as above, the tabernacle is built securely into a side wall of the sanctuary.

Templars, Knights

The Poor Knights of the Temple were the first—and became the most powerful—of the Military Orders*. They were founded in 1118 for the defence of the Christian kingdom of Jerusalem, with headquarters near the site of the Temple, and took the Rule of St. Benedict. The Order became enormously wealthy and powerful, and by the 14th cent., it had fallen far enough from fervour to present an opportunity for Philip the Fair's desire to plunder its riches. At his insistence, Pope Clement V suppressed the Order on accusations denied, with vigour by Dante at the time and, after long controversy, by modern scholars. The English headquarters of the Templars was in London (now the Inner and Middle Temple) and their church there, dating from 1185, was shattered in the air raids of 1941.

Teresa of Avila, St. (1515-82)

The child who ran away from home to seek a romantic martydom at the hands of the Moors across the Straits of Gibraltar grew up to enter a Carmelite monastery in her native city in 1533. After leaving for a time on account of illness, she returned and lived a lax religious life until 1555, being then converted and beginning to have mystical experiences. Her desire for a stricter monastic life led her to found a new house in which the primitive Rule of the Order should be observed. Amid intense opposition from her fellow-religious and some ecclesiastical authorities, she established more and more houses of Discalced* Carmelites with the help of St.John of the Cross*. Concurrently with her years of unrelenting labour, her spiritual life deepened steadily into extraordinary mystical depths, and she wrote—in obedience to her confessors—masterpieces of spirituality, such as *The Foundations*, her *Life*, *The Interior Castle*, continuing the strain of her earlier work, *The Way of Perfection*. Her gifts to the Church are threefold: the Order of Discalced Carmelites, which still flourishes, her unsurpassed mystical writings, and the proof offered by this woman of unswerving will, merry disposition and shrewd business sense that the heights of contemplation can be combined with the most concrete achievements of practical life. Feast, Oct 15th.

Teresa (Thérèse) of Lisieux, St. (1873-97)

Observedly remarkable only for her impetuous desire for the religious life, she begged and obtained from Leo XIII in person permission to enter the Carmel of her native town in northern France. Having served as assistant novice-mistress, she died of tuberculosis, after seven years of profession. This unknown young nun whose desire to join her sister Carmelites in China was frustrated by illness, was later declared patroness of missions and is one of the most popular of saints. Her appeal rests largely on the simplicity and "ordinariness" of her type of sanctity, which speaks, particularly to lay people, of the holiness to be attained in the daily round, the unspectacular task, the practice of self-denial on a small scale. Her fame reached the world through the circulation to all Carmelite houses of a revised form of her autobiography *L'Histoire d'une âme*, written at the command of her superiors. Soon, reports of miracles attracted attention and Pius XI, dispensing with the fifty-year delay demanded by Canon* Law, canonised her in 1925, under the title St. Teresa of the Holy Child and of the Holy Face. In 1929, she was declared patroness of foreign missions, and in 1947, the French associated her name with that of Joan of Arc as patron of their country. Feast-day, October 1st.

Teresa of the Child Jesus, St.
See Teresa of Lisieux.

Tertiaries
A tertiary is a member of a Third Order*, and the word is usually taken to refer to a secular tertiary.

Test Act
The Act of 1673 (25 Car. II. c.2) requiring that all who held public office under the Crown, and some other positions, receive the Sacrament according to the use of the Church of England, take the Oaths of Supremacy and Allegiance and make the Declaration Against Transubstantiation*; the Act remained until 1829. See Disabilities of Catholics.

Theological Virtues
The infused supernatural gifts which have God as their object and which are imparted so as to enable man to reach his final destiny: *Faith*, by which we believe in God, *Hope*, by which we trust in the goodness of God, *Charity*, by which we love God.

Theotokos
(Gk. Θεοτοκος, giving birth to God.) The title given to Mary by the Greek Fathers* from the early 3rd cent. onward. In 429, it was challenged by Nestorius, who wanted to substitute Χριστοτοκος; however, the original title was championed by St.

Cyril* of Alexandria and confirmed by the Council of Ephesus*—the story is that the Fathers of the Council were afterwards escorted home with praises for the Lady Theotokos by the citizens, whose ancestors had stood two hours in the theatre praising the goddess Artemis (Acts 19:28ff)—and later at Chalcedon* in 451.

Third Order
a) *Secular*—a branch of a religious Order which consists of men and women (tertiaries*) living an "ordinary" life but provided with a rule, office and habit (worn on certain particular occasions, and usually for burial, replaced normally by a scapular worn under the clothing), and sharing in the fellowship of the first Order, whose spirit they are attempting to bring into their own particular world. Arising first in the 13th cent., there are Third Orders of Franciscans*, Augustinians*, Carmelites*, Dominicans*, Minims*, Premonstratensians*, Servites* and Trinitarians*.
b) *Regular*—such members of a Third Order as leave their life in the world and live in community with simple vows; these include the Third Order Regular of Carmelites, the Dominican Sisters, Franciscans (priests, brothers, sisters) and Third Order of Servites.

Thomas à Kempis
See Imitation of Christ.

Thomas Aquinas, St. (c. 1225-74)
Called *Angelic Doctor** and the *Universal Doctor*, Thomas was the son of a nobleman related to the Emperor and was intended by his parents to be Abbot of the neighbouring Benedictine house, Monte Cassino*. But, being drawn to the intellectual life, he joined the recently founded Dominican* Order, in spite of strong parental opposition. Sent to Paris, he came under the influence of Albert the Great, who introduced him to the works of Aristotle. He was soon lecturing at Cologne and at Paris again, where he wrote a treatise in defence of the Mendicant* Orders against some scholars of the University. After graduating as Master of Theology, he spent 10 years in Italy, then he was in Paris again for three years,

teaching until 1272, when he was despatched to Naples; summoned to attend the Council of Lyons*, he died *en route* at Fossanuova in 1274. There is indeed not much that is remarkable in the life of this busy student and lecturer, sent hither and thither by his superiors to teach and set up houses of studies, apart from the astonishing volume and quality of his writings, the volume all the more surprising in view of his style of Latin, which was terse and packed and wasted no word. From his earliest philosophical works, written under the influence of earlier Scholasticism*, he progresses to the *Quaetiones Disputatae De Veritate* and the *Commentaries* (chiefly on Aristotle's works and those of Dionysius the Areopagite and Boëthius). He puts much of his spirituality and theology into his biblical commentaries (on the Gospels, the Epistles and some O.T. books). His work reaches its climax in the *Summa Contra Gentiles* (a defence of natural theology against the Arab writers) and the *Summa Theologica*, (which ranks as the apex of mediaeval systematic theology and has stood since as the basis of Catholic theological thought and was not quite finished at the time of his death). Other, lesser writings, include the *Quaestiones Disputatae* and *Quaestiones Quodlibetales* which expand in greater detail certain points of one *Summa* or the other. His philosophy was wrought to its characteristic shape by the metaphysical works of Aristotle, then recently recovered by the West, and came timely to European thought, for it was evident not only to Thomas but to men like Abélard before him that much of the traditional Platonist thought had outlived its usefulness. Not that he considered himself bound by Aristotle: he still called on certain fundamental Platonist ideas filtered through e.g. St. Augustine. The Angelic Doctor held to the typical Scholastic doctrine of the distinctness of reason from faith and its powerful intervention as preparation and support for faith; his theory of knowledge is Aristotelian and, leading him to his aphorism *nihil in intellectu quod non prius fuerit in sensu*—no cognition without sense-perception—explains his approach to the discovery of arguments for the existence of God. Central to his thought is Aristotle's theory of potency and act (which makes the principle of

Causality fundamental for him: "nothing passes from the state of potency into act except by the intervention of something already in act") as is the Master's other antithesis, matter and form. In theology, he expended much interest on the Incarnation—maintaining, as against the Franciscan thinkers, that this would not have taken place had it not been for the Fall; and the Sacraments: all seven, he said, were of Christ's institution. Commissioned by Urban IV to compose the Mass and Office for the new Feast of Corpus Christi (1264), he produced a handful of works which are masterpieces of tautly concise doctrine, felicitous expression and metrical skill (*Lauda Sion*, *Pange Lingua*, *Verbum Supernum*).

Thomism

See Thomas Aquinas, St.

Thomistic philosophy

See Thomas Aquinas, St.

Throne

i) one of that rank of the celestial hierarchy so named (Col. 1:16).

ii) the throne is associated with the bishop, the chair being a sign of authority (see Cathedral and *ex cathedra*); in his cathedral or in a church he is visiting, the bishop's throne occupies a prominent place; for many centuries on the Gospel side of the sanctuary, so that he faced south, this seat in many modern churches is restored to its ancient position, the prelate facing his people across the altar.

iii) a long-standing custom in Rome dictated that the cardinals engaged in electing a pope should sit in the Sistine Chapel on thrones draped in purple, each with its movable canopy above, so that when the voting declared one of them pope, his canopy remained raised while the others were lowered in homage. However, at the election in August 1978 which chose John Paul I, there were found to be so many cardinals that there was not room for thrones, and they were given chairs and desks instead: a practice which will presumably remain indefinitely.

Tiara

A Gk. word describing the head-dress of the monarchs of ancient Persia. Tall, ornate head-dress of the Pope (worn from about the 8th cent. until 1978, when its use was abandoned by Pope John Paul I at his inauguration) for non-liturgical but solemn occasions. It began as a kind of Phrygian cap, its use being reserved to the Pope, and acquired, not later than the 11th cent., a coronet, and in the 13th, two lappets* at the back. In that century also, Boniface VIII* added a second coronet, possibly to signify the twofold power of the Church (see Two Swords), and a third appeared around 1304, the tiara being made taller to accommodate it. An anachronism since the loss of the Papal States, it was finally rejected as triumphalist and redolent of temporal power, surviving now only heraldically on Papal coats of arms, usually with the crossed keys.

Titular

a) *noun.* The person (divine or human), mystery or sacred object after which a church or altar is named; the titular of the main altar should be that of the church also.

b) *adj.* A titular bishop is one consecrated and given the title of one of those ancient cities, most of them Middle Eastern or African (some now mere ruins) which were once sees with bishops, but which are fallen away, many through the Muslim incursions of the 7th cent. A titular bishopric is generally bestowed on one who is to be auxiliary to a bishop-in-ordinary, or to be vicar apostolic, or it is granted as an honour, e.g. in recognition of the services of a bishop-in-ordinary, who resigns his see. There are well over 1,500 titular sees, including such resounding and evocative names as Antioch of Pisidia, Chalcedon, Caesarea, Ephesus, Iconium, Kells, Lindisfarne, Mitylene, Nazareth, Nicaea, Oxyrhynchus, Salamis, Tarsus, Three Taverns, Trebizond.

Tome of Leo, the

Also called *Epistola Dogmatica*, this was a letter addressed by Pope Leo I to Flavian (See Robber Synod), Patriarch of Constantinople, on June 13th, 449, to rebut the teachings of Eutyches the Monophysite*. An admirably clear, precise and vigorous resumé of the Western Church's doctrine of Christ, it is based on patristic writings, especially those of St. Augustine and Ter-

tullian: in it, Christ is one Person, the Word of God, with two natures, the divine and the human, permanently united in him, though not confused or mingled, and each exercising its own proper faculties within the unity of the Person; hence is deduced the *communicatio idiomatum* by which it can be truly said the Son of God was crucified, and that the Son of Man came down from heaven. The Tome was accepted by the Council of Chalcedon* as the definitive statement of Catholic Christological doctrine.

Tonsure

(Lat. *tonsura*, haircut). The cutting or shaving of all or part of the hair as a sign of the clerical or monastic state was used in Eastern monasteries as early as the 4th cent., and in the Western Church, as a sign of a cleric, in the 6th. The styles of tonsure varied: in the East, the whole head was shaven, the Celtic* tonsure was the shaving of the scalp in front of a line taken from ear to ear (and was associated with the Easter Controversy*), the Dominicans shaved the head above a line just over the ears, other Orders* leaving a unshaven fringe round the head (which has been interpreted as representing the Crown of Thorns), the secular priest's tonsure—though not worn in England or the U.S.A.—was a small circle cut clean on the crown of the head. The tonsure is not now kept by the diocesan clergy, and in place of the ancient ceremony called the Tonsure, by which a man was accepted as a cleric and accorded all the clerical privileges (and which was much abused in the Middle Ages by those who wanted the privileges without any idea of becoming priests), there is a ceremony of acceptance in which the bishop officially receives a man as a candidate for the priesthood.

Touriere

See Extern Sister.

Tract 90

The publications of the Oxford Movement*, named *Tracts for the Times*, beginning as brief leaflets, grew into learned treatises; and the series was brought to a sudden end by the storm roused in 1841 by Newman*'s Tract 90, *Remarks on Certain Passages in the Thirty-Nine Articles*, in which he ventured the theory that the Articles could and should be understood in a way not repugnant to the decrees of the Council of Trent*. The Tract marks one important stage in Newman's journey to the Church of Rome.

Tractarianism
The name given to the earlier stages of the Oxford* Movement and its principles, from the Tracts for the Times, the series of writings which carried the opinions and reforming suggestions of Newman*, Pusey, Keble, Percival, Bowden, Froude, Marriott, Williams and others, the first written being Newman's ("Thoughts on the Ministerial Commission Respectfully Addressed to the Clergy") and the last likewise his, Tract 90*, which was the occasion of the ending of the series. These writers, and the Movement's members generally, became known as the Tractarians.

Tradition
(Lat. *traditio*, a handing over, that which is handed over.) In its broad sense, the entire message of revelation, as in 2 Thess. 2:14, "the traditions that we taught you, whether by word of mouth or by letter". Later it became a technical term (Apostolic Tradition) for the sum of revealed doctrine not committed to writing in Scripture (though it may be found in other works) and transmitted through the *magisterium* from age to age. At the time of the Reformation, there was sharp controversy about the relationship of this unwritten store of doctrine to the Sacred Scriptures, and, against the Protestant assertion of the Bible as the sole source of truth, the Council of Trent* declared that Scripture and tradition were to be accepted as of equal authority (*pari pietatis affectu ac reverentia*, with the like loyal devotion and respect). Pius IX summed up the narrowest view of tradition as the possession of the Papacy in his saying, *Sono io la tradizione.*

Translate
Ecclesiastically, *translation* is used of the solemn transference of the relics of a saint from one shrine to another (usually thought more worthy), the days of such removals in some cases having been kept as feast days in the Calendar. The term is also used for the re-allocation of a feast-day to another date, and for the transfer of a bishop to another see.

Transmigration of souls
See Reincarnation.

Transubstantiation
A philosophic attempt to explain the *mode* of Christ's presence in the Eucharistic species. The word (meaning the change of the entire substance of bread and wine into the entire substance of the Body and Blood) was in large currency in the later 12th cent. and was described as *de fide* by the 4th Lateran Council* (12th Oecumenical) in 1215. Later in the 13th cent., after the acceptance by the Latin Church of the metaphysics of Aristotle, with the concepts of matter and form, the doctrine received its classical elaboration in St. Thomas' writings, both theological and liturgical (see e.g. *Lauda Sion*); it was reaffirmed at the Council of Trent in the simplest possible terminology: ". . . the wonderful and unique conversion of the whole substance of the bread into the Body of Christ and of the whole substance of the wine into the Blood, the species of bread and wine alone remaining" (Session 13, can. 2)—*species* meaning the sum of the accidents* which inhere in a substance. The Eastern Church has since the 13th cent., used the word μετουσιωσις, which means literally transubstantiation, approving the word and the doctrine at the Synod of Jerusalem in 1672.

Transubstantiation, Declaration against
The Declaration, imposed by the Test Act* of 1673 on all holders of civil or military office: "I, N.N., do declare that I do believe that there is not any transubstantiation in the Sacrament of the Lord's Supper, or in the elements of bread and wine, at or after the consecration thereof by any person whatsoever."

Trappist
See La Trappe.

Trappistines
A name used of the Cistercian nuns of the Strict Observance.
See La Trappe.

Trent, Council of

(19th Oecumenical.) The event which articulated and organised those aspirations towards reform within the Church which began long before Luther was heard of, but which had so little practical support from the central authority that by reason of the long delay thus created, they now bear the negative title of *Counter-Reformation*. In more modern times, a Catholic writer complained, 'Le tort du catholicisme fut d'arriver toujours tard, de manquer d'initiative et de laisser aux adversaires le temps d'occuper la place'. Urged first of all by the lower echelons of the clergy and a few in higher positions, and by the Emperor Charles V, until accepted by the Papacy, the Council was summoned by Paul III to meet at Mantua in 1537; the French opposing this and Charles failing to support another attempt at Vicenza the following year, the Pope proposed Trent in 1542, and succeeded in getting an assembly there in 1545: three papal legates (including Reginald Pole*), one cardinal, four archbishops, twenty-one bishops, five generals of Orders. From this small and hesitant beginning the Council took on stature and strength, and, consistently obstructed by the French monarchy and though interrupted from time to time (wars made travel impossible for the bishops, there was an epidemic, the princes of the Empire rose against Charles, no meeting could be held in the pontificate—1555–59—of Paul IV, who was so violently anti-Protestant), became one of the most important events in the history of modern Europe. In its various sessions, the Council dealt with Revelation, asserting the equality of Tradition* with Scripture and the Church's sole right to interpret the Bible, and the authority of the Vulgate*; with Original Sin, Merit and Justification, the Sacraments (special attention and separate decrees being allocated to the Eucharist and the affirmation of Transubstantiation*)—it was at this point that the Protestant theologians arrived under safe-conduct, demanding fresh discussion of all the subjects they had missed, the release of bishops from their oath of Papal allegiance, and the acknowledgment of the supremacy of a General Council over the Pope. A few sessions later and for various reasons, the Council was suspended for ten years; when it convened in 1562, Jesuit theologians took a prominent part but there was no longer any hope of reconciling the Protestants. The Council discussed Holy Communion (defending the presence of Christ under either species and denying the chalice to the laity), and the sacrificial nature of the Mass; the last few sessions were taken up with reform of the clergy, the sacraments of Matrimony and Order*, Purgatory, invocation of saints*, veneration of images and relics*, and Indulgences.

In its final stages, the Council was attended by four cardinal legates, two cardinals, three patriarchs, twenty-five archbishops, one hundred and sixty-seven bishops, seven abbots, seven generals of Order, nineteen proxies for absent prelates. From these islands, apart from Cardinal Pole, there had attended Pole's friend Bishop Goldwell* of St. Asaph, and three Irish prelates, O'Herlihy of Ross, McCongail of Raphoe and O'Hart of Achonry. Trent, though not comprehensive enough in its reforms to satisfy all Catholics nor flexible enough to please the Protestants, and though brought to a hasty conclusion, perhaps through weariness (it was the longest of General Councils, lasting almost twenty years) nonetheless set its deep and lasting mark on the Church. It laid a stout foundation for the renewal of spiritual life and discipline, provided a greatly enhanced and more clearly formulated system of dogma and imposed a mentality of embattled defence, which was no doubt necessary then but which has taken longer to discard than the times have warranted. By reason of the long delay beforehand, the hope of recovering the Protestants *en bloc* was a lost cause; it was perhaps inevitable in the circumstances that the Council's strenuous programme of reform did nothing to relax, indeed much to tightem, the total clericalisation of the Church that had taken place during the Middle Ages. A sign perhaps, of this clerical mentality was that proposals for the vernacular in the liturgy, put forward by those who had observed the powerful contribution of the German and English languages to the success of the Reformers, were dismissed as 'inopportune'.

Tridentine

The adjective to describe whatever is connected with or belonging to Trent.

Tridentinist
(from Tridentine*.) The name given to one who so thoroughly supports the work of the Council of Trent as to deny to any subsequent Council or pope the authority to change its liturgical decisions. See Latin Mass Society.

Trinitarians
The Order of the Holy Trinity, founded as Canons Regular* in 1198, by St. John of Matha and St. Felix of Valois, for the purpose of ransoming Christian captives from the Moors; they were given the status of Mendicant* Frairs in 1609, and now engage in teaching and nursing, in the US., Italy and Spain, but with no houses in England since the Reformation. The Trinitarian nuns, founded in 1685, for teaching, nursing and any works of mercy, have now no connection with the order of Friars.

Trinity, the Holy
The mystery of the Trinity is the centre and foundation of Christian theology; the word is not found in the Bible (being first used by Theophilus of Antioch, about 180 A.D. in its Greek form Τριας), but the concept is scriptural, implicitly and explicitly. Hints have been found by theologians in various groupings of three in the O.T.—the apparition of the three men to Abraham (Gen.18), the three-fold cry of 'Holy' from the seraphs in Is.6, the many mentions of God, his Wisdom and his Spirit. More explicit are e.g. the phrasing of the formula for baptism in Mt.28:19 ('in the name', not 'names'), the discourse in John's Last Supper story, especially 14:16 and 26, about Advocate and, clearest of all, the Letters: 2 Cor 13:14, which is considered to enshrine an already existing liturgical usage, and 1 Pet.1:2. The doctrine of Trinity was formulated in all the Creeds and doxologies, and presented in the decrees of Councils (Nicaea*, 1st Constantinople*). Eastern thinkers, occupied with the difference between the Persons, spoke of the Father as being ungenerated, the Son as generated by the Father, the Holy Spirit as proceeding from the Father through the Son, this last being changed at the time of Photius* to a procession from the Father only (see Filioque); while the West, dwelling more on the unity of substance, and thus on the co-equality of the Persons, attributed the procession of the Spirit equally to Father and Son. Among the Latin Fathers, St. Augustine propounded the comparison with the human activities of self-knowledge (the Son is the Knowledge, Logos, Wisdom, of the Father) and self-love (the Spirit is the substantial mutual love of Father and Son; the first half of this comparison he got from Tertullian). Subsequent thinkers, particularly the Scholastics*, took over Augustine's 'psychological theory' of the Trinity, which is now an accepted element of Western theology.

Trisagion
(Gk., thrice holy.) The invocation 'Holy God, holy strong one, holy immortal one, have mercy on us', borrowed from the Byzantine liturgies and used in the Roman Rite of Good Friday* during the Veneration of the Cross, chanted alternatively in Greek and Latin.

Triumphant, the Church
See Church.

Truce of God, the
An extension of the Pax Dei* by which private warfare was forbidden on certain days, beginning with Lent and Advent and Fridays, until the 'close season' covered three-quarters of the year, with excommunication as the penalty for noncompliance. The practice arose in France in the early 11th cent., and in the 12th, it had spread to Flanders, Germany and Italy and had confirmation from the first three Lateran* Councils; it began to decline as the rising power of monarchs enabled them to enforce local peace through their own courts.

Twelve Fruits of the Holy Spirit
The traditional list is: charity, joy, peace, patience, benignity, goodness, longanimity, mildness, faith, modesty, continency, chastity; the catalogue is based on Gal.5:22, in the Greek of which are to be

found the first six, the ninth, the eighth, the eleventh; some late MSS add the twelfth, and in the Vulgate appear two more, *longanimitas* and *modestia*, which could be reduplications. The A.V. gives as the 'fruit of the Spirit' nine, *love, joy, peace, longsuffering, gentleness, goodness, faith, meekness, temperance;* in the Jerusalem Bible, 'What the Spirit bring is . . . *love, joy, peace, patience, kindness, goodness, trustfulness, gentleness and self-control.*'

Two Swords
See Unam Sanctam.

Tyburn Nuns
The popular name of the Sisters Adorers of the Sacred Heart, from their convent and shrine to the English Martyrs very close to the site of the gallows at Tyburn (now Marble Arch), where many of those martyrs suffered; the nuns follow the Rule of St. Benedict and keep perpetual adoration.

Ubi Petrus Ibi Ecclesia

(Lat., Where Peter is, there is the Church.) A phrase dating from the very early ages of Christianity, at least to the days of the Fathers★, embodying the belief that the Church is to be identified in the last resort by its link with the authority granted by Christ to the Apostles as a group and to Peter as individual and as leader and chief of the group in Mt.16:17ff, Lk.22:32, Jn.21:15–17. The importance of this Apostolic Succession in the eyes of the early Church is attested by the readiness with which bishops recognised the primacy of the *See of Peter,* to which they would regularly appeal as to a referee in disputes, and no Council was considered General or Oecumenical unless it included the Bishop of Rome or his representative.

See Conciliar Theory and under Basle and Constance.

Unam Sanctam

A bull of 1302 named, in the usual fashion, from its opening phrase *Unam Sanctam (Catholicam et Apostolicam Ecclesiam)*—One, Holy (Catholic and Apostolic Church) issued by Boniface VIII in his struggle with Philip the Fair of France. If the text we have (from the Registers of Boniface VIII in the Vatican archives, the original not being extant) represents the tone and attitudes of the original, this bull must qualify as one of the most foolish public documents. Its main proposition is the unity of the Church and its necessity for salvation, so that, this unity being once established by Christ in the person of Peter and necessarily transmitted through Peter's successors, he who denies the authority of this Apostolic See is not of the flock of Christ. The Registers speak of the *Declaratio quod subesse Romano Pontifici est omni humanae creaturae de necessitate salutis*—a declaration that submission to the Roman Pontiff is necessary for salvation to every human being', which in fact was what the Church had taught for cen-

turies and was to go on teaching (it is reiterated in almost identical words by the 5th Lateran Council in 1516). Boniface, however, in *Unam Sanctam,* elaborated a far more inflated and ambitious scheme, chiefly with the use of the theory of the Two Swords★: by means of highly coloured symbolism and some very agile interpretation of Mt.26:52, Lk.22:38 (where he takes Christ's answer 'It is enough' to mean 'That is precisely the right number of weapons', when he was, in all probability, simply putting an end to the conversation), and I Cor.2:15, the Pope expounds the idea that Two Swords are in the control of the Church, the one wielded by the clergy, the other, in the secular hand, wielded under the direction of the clergy; one sword must be subordinate to the other, as the spiritual power has the right to establish and guide the secular power, and to judge it (cf. the history of the Power of Deposing★); this, he concludes, is a divine authority granted to Peter and his successors, 'subjection to whom we hereby declare, set forth, define and proclaim to be of absolute necessity for salvation to every human creature'. Then having thus crowned its naive and crude handling of the Scriptures with the solemn introduction of one about to announce himself *ex cathedra* master of the world in spirituals and temporals, this strange document

'that roars so loud and thunders in the index'

proceeds temperately to enounce the conventional, traditional doctrine: *nascetur ridiculus mus.* Indeed, within a few years, the next Pope but one, Clement V, was reassuring Francis that *Unam Sanctam* in no way restricted the political power of the Kings of France. It has been suggested in explanation that Boniface's ambition—or panic—led him to shape up as for an infallible definition of an absurdity, on the very brink of which the Holy Spirit stepped in and prevented him. In the event, *Unam Sanctam* marks a kind of watershed for papal temporal power, which afterwards began to decline;

Boniface, apart from his other illusions, had not noticed the extent of the growth of national feeling throughout Europe—one example of this is that in less than thirty years' time, the Electors were asserting that the Holy Roman Emperor held his rights by their sole choice of him without the need of any Papal confirmation of that choice.

Unigenitus

A bull issued by Pope Clement VI in 1343 setting forth the doctrine of the 'treasury of merits' on which the practice of Indulgences★ is based.

Unitive Way

The next stage following on the Illuminative Way; the highest condition of the spiritual life, characterised by the union with God epitomised in St. Paul's phrase, 'I live now, not with my own life, but with the life of Christ who lives in me' (Gal.2:20); the life of passive contemplation and of mystical union.
See also Purgative Way.

Universalis Ecclesiae

The title of three papal documents: the Letter Apostolic of Pius★ IX in Sept. 1850, by which the Restoration★ of the Hierarchy to England and Wales was effected; the Bull erecting the diocese of Brentwood in 1917, and the constitution establishing the diocese of Lancaster in 1924.

Upholland

St. Joseph's College at Upholland, near Wigan, was founded in 1880 as the seminary for the diocese of Liverpool; in the reorganisation of seminaries in the 1970's, the students removed to Ushaw★ and part of the building of St. Joseph's has now become the Northern Institute, established by the bishops of the northern dioceses for the training of clergy and laity.

Urbanist Popes

Those Popes who sat at Rome during the Schism of the West—Urban VI (1378-89), Boniface IX (1389-1404), Innocent VII (1404-06), Gregory XII (1406-15), who are regarded as being in the line of true Popes.

Urbi et orbi

(Lat., to the City and to the world.) A description of the solemn blessing which the Pope imparts on great occasions from the loggia of St. Peter's or, less frequently, from one of the other Roman basilicas★. The custom was discontinued after 1870, when the Pope became the 'Prisoner of the Vatican'★ and was revived in the pontificate of Pius XI★ (1922-39).

Ursulines

There are several congregations of this name, all engaged in the education of girls, the best-known being the Company of St. Ursula, founded by St. Angela Merici in 1537, the first teaching order of women to be authorised by the Church; they had solemn vows, enclosure and choir office until 1900, when very many convents of different countries joined to make the 'Roman Union' and to live in simple perpetual vows, the remaining houses continuing according to the original constitution.

Ushaw

Crook Hall near Durham, now St. Cuthbert's College, became the home of the northern students of the English College at Douay★ which was dissolved during the French Revolution. It is now the seminary for the northern dioceses of the country, having been joined by the former seminary of Upholland★. There is also a Junior Seminary (an amalgam of the Ushaw Junior Seminary and the junior institutes of the Dioceses of Liverpool and Lancaster) which also educated a few boys not seeking the priesthood.

Usual Conditions, the

The phrase is used of indulgences, which may be gained 'under the usual conditions': these conditions are usually understood as the reception of the Sacraments of Reconciliation and Eucharist, and prayer for the intentions of the Pope, these intentions being taken to include the general well-being of the universal Church, the spread of the Faith, the reconciliation of sinners, heretics and schismatics, and the peace of the world.

Valentine, St.

There appears to be no justification for connecting either of the two saints named Valentine (bishop and priest, both martyred in Roman times, whose martyrologies are legendary enough to allow of the possibility that they refer to the same person) with courtship and the custom of choosing a 'Valentine'. Perhaps the date of the feast (Feb. 14) suggested the season when 'a young man's fancy lightly turns to thoughts of love' or perhaps it got connected—or confused—with certain practices of the Roman festival of Lupercalia, held in early spring.

Valladolid

At Valladolid, a college was founded by William Allen* in 1589 to train priests for work in England (see also Venerable English College, Beda, Douay, Lisbon); a similar Scots* College was founded in 1627 at Madrid and transferred to Valladolid in 1771.

Vatican, the

The miniature city-state clustered round the traditional site of the burial-place of St. Peter (the tomb being beneath the high altar of St. Peter's Basilica*); residence of the Pope and headquarters of the Roman Catholic Church. It contains a remarkable collection of some of the most renowned art treasures of the world, particularly from the ancient, mediaeval and Renaisance periods, and one of the most famous libraries. The city occupies one of the Seven Hills of ancient Rome—*Mons Vaticanus*—and the site of Nero's Circus and his Golden House. A papal residence is said to have been erected near the church of St. Peter by Pope St. Symmachus (498–514), though very little, if anything, of the present building complex predates the 15th cent. On the Unification of Italy, Pius IX secured (1871) the Vatican's independence of the Italian State (and extra-territoriality for the Lateran Palace and Castel Gandolfo, the Papal country-house) and further concessions were obtained in the Lateran Treaty* of 1929. Vatican City is of roughly the same area as the City of London, a square mile.

Vatican, First Council of the

(1869–70, 20th Oecumenical.) Mooted first by the Pius IX (Pio Nono*) in face of the mounting influence of rationalism, pantheism, naturalism, and kindred errors, the prospect of a Council found an immediate welcome among Catholics everywhere, and no opposition among Protestant churches or states (though, in the event, the Russians prevented their Catholic bishops from attending.) However, alarm and despondency especially in France, Germany and England, spread wide, when it was realised that the intended Council would be expected to define papal infallibility*. The stance of the objectors was that it would be 'inopportune' to define and thus impose on the whole Church as of faith this doctrine which was accepted as part of God's revelation (although for a short time the name of Honorius* was thrown about by writers). Manning* became one of the leaders of the pro-definition party and Bishop Dupanloup of Orléans a prominent opponent. Newman* too was among the 'inopportunists' and opinion in Germany was so disturbed that 14 of the 22 bishops wrote to Pius expressing their fears of the results of definition. The Council met in 1869 at the Vatican, while the prospect of war loomed over Europe. Four permanent committees were appointed to prepare documents for discussion in full session, from the most important of which, the Committee on the Faith, the majority party, quite against the Pope's wishes, strove to exclude the 'inopportunists', many of whom were men of distinction and great learning and one of whom slipped in under their guard. Manning went so far, in defence of these tactics, as to say 'Heretics come to a Council to be heard and condemned, not to take part in formulating doctrine.'

The first decree (*Dei Filius*, against Rationalism) was passed after lively and sometimes violent debate and dealt chiefly with Faith and Reason and their relationship. The Council's programme had not provided for discussion of Infallibility, but keen canvassing, undertaken perhaps with an eye on the European political situation, persuaded 500 Fathers to petition for its introduction, 136 opposing. After a number of votes and various emendations to the text, the decree *Pastor Aeternus* was finally passed, on July 18th 1870, the day before the outbreak of the Franco-Prussian War; in this final vote of almost all the 774 Fathers (some had left in anticipation of the war), there were 533 for and only two against—one Italian, and Edward Fitzgerald of Little Rock, Arkansas. The decree, promulgated instantly by Pio Nono against a dramatic background of thunder and lightning, claims for the Pope primacy of jurisdiction and power over the whole Church and the right of free communication with the other pastors of the entire Church and with their flocks, adding that that primacy includes infallibility. The Fathers, after this session, left Rome, the Council being adjourned for a few months; but very soon, the city was occupied by the Piedmontese troops and, on October 10th, Pio Nono prorogued the Council indefinitely, with only a small fraction of its programme completed.

Vatican, Second Council of the

(1962–65, 21st Oecumenical.) According to Pope John XXIII*, whose summoning of it was totally unexpected and in some quarters dismaying, Vatican II was intended not only to restore the Church's energies and to seek out forms best adapted to her work in the modern world (this he symbolised by flinging wide a window in the Vatican), but also to invite the separated brethren of East and West to join in the search for reunion. He saw the Council as a 'new Pentecost', a spiritual renewal of the Church and a sign of her internal unity. At its convening, besides the Fathers of the Council themselves, 35 observers (without vote, but able to pass on their views through the Secretariate of Christian Unity) from 17 Eastern and Western denominations accepted the invitation issued, and at the last session there were 93, from 28 denominations. There were present also several Catholic laypeople—auditors—men and women who spoke in the Commissions. Pope John, in his opening address to the First Session, urged the Council not only to guard the deposit of faith but to take a step forward towards doctrinal penetration and the formation of conciences through the methods of research and literary forms of modern thought; not to condemn errors but to meet the needs of the present day by demonstrating the validity of the Church's teaching. In the event, the Council turned out to be pastoral, not speculative: emphasis was laid on the Bible as the source of faith and norm of conduct, on ecumenism, on the liturgy, on the laity's dignity, freedom and right to take initiatives. Members of the hierarchy were repeatedly reminded that their office existed as a service and not as a form of domination, and some decentralisation was achieved both at curial level and at diocesan, both during the Council itself and in the following few years. No dogma was defined; the sixteen official texts put out by the Council (in Latin) are as follows: a Dogmatic Constitution on the Church (*Lumen Gentium*), a Dogmatic Constitution on Divine Revelation (*Dei Verbum*), a Constitution on the Sacred Liturgy (*Sacrosanctum*), a Decree on the Instruments of Social Communication (*Inter Mirifica*), a Decree on Ecumenism (*Unitatis Redintegratio*), a Decree on the Eastern Churches (*Orientalium Ecclesiarum*), a Decree on the Bishops' Pastoral Office in the Church (*Christus Dominus*), a Decree on Priestly Formation (*Optatum Totius*), a Decree on the Appropriate Renewal of the Religious Life (*Perfectae Caritatis*), a Decree on the Apostolate of the Laity (*Apostolicam Actuositatem*), a Decree on the Ministry and Life of Priests (*Presbyterorum Ordinis*), a Decree on the Church's Missionary Activity (*Ad Gentes*), a Declaration on Christian Education (*Gravissimum Educationis*), a Decree on the Relationship of the Church to Non-Christian Religions (*Nostra Aetate*), a Declaration on Religious Freedom (*Dignitatis Humanae*).

Vaticanism

The slighting expression coined by Gladstone for what he considered the arrogant and erroneous claims of the Roman See in the proclamation of Papal Infallibility* in 1870.

Veil (1)

In the early centuries, a consecrated virgin received from the bishop a veil (the mark of the married woman in ancient Rome) to symbolise her mystical marriage with Christ. Hence the phrase 'to take the veil', traditionally used to describe entry into religion—though in modern times, many nuns have dispensed with the veil as an actual article of dress.

Veil (2)

Liturgical covering of varying size and shape, sometimes embroidered and otherwise decorated; a veil hangs before the door of the tabernacle*, the chalice is covered with a veil of the same liturgical colour as the vestments when it is being carried to and from the altar, the ciborium* is veiled, usually in white silk, when it contains the Sacred Species, the crosses and images in a church used to be veiled in violet during Lent.

Veil of Veronica.

See Veronica.

Veil of Our Lady

Many 'relics*' of the Mother of God are claimed in different places, usually pieces of material said to be part of her clothing, and described as Our Lady's Veil. One such is kept at Chartres in the cathedral and is the relic given by Charlemagne to Aix la Chapelle; another is the 'veil' or 'girdle' enshrined at Constantinople in 473, and it is believed that a similar relic is enclosed in the high point of the spire of Salisbury Cathedral.

Venerable

The title used of a person (deceased) whose cause* for canonisation has reached the stage at which, with papal signature, a decree has been published accepting proof of heroic virtue or martyrdom; but public veneration is not thereby permitted. The term is also used in Ireland and Australia as the style of an archdeacon (cf.

Reverend, Very Reverend, etc); it is also used of an ordained Carthusian* (Venerable Father). Uniquely among the Saints, it is the title of the chronicler of the English, St Bede* the Venerable.

Vernacular

See Liturgical Movement.

Veronica

An official Saint, who has attained permanence in the Stations of the Cross*, if not in Roman Martyrology*. The Acts of Pilate*—a 4th cent. work which some believe to be based on a 2nd-cent. original—says that the woman healed of an issue of blood in Mt.9:20–22 was called Veronica and that she later healed the Emperor Tiberius with a miraculous image of Christ. From this beginning, and from the not implausible idea that some woman in the crowd may have taken pity on Our Lord carrying his cross, came the legend of the woman who, having wiped the blood and sweat from his face with a veil or headcloth, found that he had left a picture of his face imprinted on it. Giraldus Cambrensis, the 12th-cent. historian, derives the name from the hybrid phrase *vera εικων*, true likeness. There was in existence from the 8th cent. such a portrait, which was believed to be the actual cloth and which was transferred by Boniface VIII* to St. Peter's in the 13th cent.; Milan and Jaen also claimed to have the original veil. Numbers of 'veronicas' were later produced by mediaeval artists, intended, presumably, not as fraudulent images but as objects of devotion like other sacred works of art.

Very Reverend

The title used for prefects* apostolic who are not bishops, archpriests, provosts, deans*, vicars forane*, cathedral canons*, rectors of seminaries and colleges, privy chamberlains, provincial, claustral and conventual priors and their equivalents, prioresses* and religious superiors below the rank of abbot* or abbess.*

Vespers

(Lat. *vesper*, evening.) The Evening Prayer of the Church (the mediaeval term *Evensong* having been abandoned to the

Reformers) and, with Lauds,* the most solemn of the Hours*; it is also the oldest of the day hours, but was originally part of the Night Office, and known as *lucernarium*, the office or time of lamplighting. The Magnificat* is a prominent feature of Vespers.

Via Dolorosa

(Lat., Way of Sorrows.) The route through Jerusalem which Jesus is supposed to have taken when carrying his cross from Pilate's praetorium to Calvary at the city gate. It is marked by Stations* of the Cross, and travelled by pilgrims as an act of devotion. The term is also used for the Stations of the Cross in the open air at a place of pilgrimage, as at Lourdes.

Via Media

The position of the Church of England as a safe middle way (Lat. *via media*) between the extremes of Roman Catholicism on the one hand and Dissent on the other. This concept, first used apparently by 17th cent. Anglican divines such as George Herbert and Simon Patrick, became more widely known through its adoption by John Henry Newman (until his conversion), and other Tractarians*.

Vicar Apostolic

A delegate of the Pope having authority as titular bishop and a see *in partibus* which brings him ordinary jurisdiction, but with no cathedral, chapter of canons or territorial diocese, though he has the delegated powers of a diocesan bishop and may vote at General Councils. England and Wales had Vicars Apostolic from 1623 to 1850 and Scotland from 1694 to 1878.

Vicar Capitular

On the vacation of a diocese, its temporary administration is entrusted to a cleric appointed by the chapter to be *vicar capitular;* he must be appointed within eight days from the beginning of the vacancy, and receives full episcopal jurisdiction with a mandate to administer the diocese without serious innovation *sede vacante**.

Vicar Forane

A priest appointed by the bishop to exercise limited jurisdiction over a certain part of the diocese, such as superintending clerical discipline, caring for sick clergy and church property and presiding over clergy conferences.
See Rural Dean*.

Vicar General

A bishop's deputy and assistant in the governing of his diocese (the mediaeval archdeacon) delegated with such episcopal jurisdiction as the law and the bishop permit; he takes precedence of all diocesan clergy and with the bishop, forms one tribunal, thus precluding appeal from one to the other. His office is concluded at the will of the bishop or on the latter's death or translation.

Vicar of Christ

The distinctive title of the Popes* from the 8th cent. onwards. From the earliest times, the Bishop of Rome would ordinarily call himself Vicar of St. Peter; Pope Gelasius I (8th cent.) styled himself Vicar of the Apostolic See, and Nicholas III, as late as the 13th cent., used the title of Vicar of God; but 'Vicar of Christ', having been used also by other bishops until the 9th cent., became then the exclusive designation of the Roman Pontiff.
See Servus Servorum Dei

Vicariate Apostolic

The territory governed by a Vicar Apostolic*

Viceregent of Rome

The chief assistant to the Cardinal Vicar in his task of administering the diocese ('Vicariate') of Rome, in which he is the Pope's Vicar General*; this assistant is a titular archbishop.

Vigil

In the early Church, it was common to hold night services of prayer, which would frequently conclude with the Eucharist; these are referred to by Pliny in his Letter to Trajan, and by the Lady Etheria*. Such a Vigil (Lat.*vigilia,* night-watch) would be associated with the greater days, and thus certainly with Easter, when it would last all night; for other feasts, e.g. Pentecost, the vigil would consist of a service about night-fall, which later gave us Vespers*, and one at dawn, which became Matins* and Lauds*. About the 5th cent., because of abuses, the public Vigils were arranged so as to finish before nightfall. By the 8th cent., the custom had crept in of anticipating the liturgy, and the Vigil service, with its accompanying Eucharist and fast, was shifted to the preceding afternoon, then to the morning, so that there was now a whole day of *profestum* or preparation for the feast. The surviving Vigils in the Roman Calendar are those of Easter, Pentecost, the Birthday of John the Baptist (June 24th), Peter and Paul (June 29th), the Assumption of Our Lady (Aug. 15th), and Christmas.

Vincent of Lerins, St. (+ c. 440)

A monk of Lérins*, known almost exclusively for his writings, particularly the Commonitorium (under the pseudonym *Peregrinus*), which contains the famous Vincentian Canon*. He held that the ultimate ground of truth was the Scriptures, of which the Church was the only rightful interpreter. However, he allowed for a Development of Doctrine*, claiming that as time went by, the truths contained in the Bible often admitted of clearer understanding and exposition.

Vincentian Canon

The epigrammatic principle laid down by St. Vincent of Lerins* as the test of orthodox belief: *quod ubique, quod semper, quod ab omnibus creditum est*—what has been accepted everywhere, from the beginning, by all (Christians), must be held to be true. Since the 19th cent., the phrase has often been misquoted by English writers, "*quod semper*" being placed first. The principle is acceptable, provided it be not taken as exclusive, in the sense of barring truths which have not always been explicitly held by Christians.

Vincentians

Also called Lazarists, from the College of St. Lazarus, where they were set up, being founded—as Priests of the Mission—by St. Vincent de Paul in 1625 for rural missions and for the education of the clergy; secular priests with the simple vows of religion and a vow of stability, and wearing ordinary clerical dress, they conduct missions, seminaries and colleges in many parts of the world, including De Paul University, Chicago and Niagara University in the State of New York.

Visit ad Limina Apostolorum
See *Ad Limina.*

Visitandine
A nun of the Order of the Visitation*.

Visitation of a parish

A bishop has the duty of visiting his parishes, to oversee pastoral and administrative matters; he will learn something of the spiritual state of a parish from examining the registers of baptisms and marriages and the records of the visitation of the sick (these he will sometimes visit himself). He will also inspect the financial accounts and all parish property. The bishop commonly delegates all or part of such visitation to his deans. There is provision in Canon Law* for a metropolitan to make visitation if a suffragan neglects his duty.

Visitation of convents

The bishop has the duty of visiting each convent within his territory at set periods; he—or his delegate—will concern himself with the well-being of the religious, granting an interview to each of them individually, to satisfy himself as to their spiritual observance, health and general contentment, and he will inspect the property and the financial conditions of the convent, as well as any precious objects it possesses.

Visitation of Our Lady

The feast which commemorates the visit of the Blessed Virgin to her cousin St. Elizabeth (Lk. 1:39–56) was first established in the Franciscan Order in 1263, at the instigation of St. Bonaventure. Urban VI decided to extend it to the universal Church, to help end the Great Schism. Boniface IX so prescribed in 1389, but only that part of the Church under his obedience accepted it. It was Pius V* who finally established the Feast for the universal Church. The date of its celebration has been transferred from July 2nd to May 31st.

Visitation of the sick

The solemn visiting of the sick, over and above the usual parochial rounds, is provided in the *Rituale Romanum*★ and includes psalms, prayers for health of body and soul, readings from the Gospels and a blessing.

Visitation, Order of the

Founded in 1610 by St. Francis de Sales★ and St. Jane Frances de Chantal, intended especially for widows and women in weak health; there are solemn vows, enclosure and the contemplative life (though some foundations maintain schools).

Visitation, Sisters of the

A teaching congregation founded in 1660, without enclosure, whose constitution was brought into line with that of the Visitation Order in 1826.

Volto Santo

(It., holy face.) Several images of the face of the suffering Christ, and some crucifixes, have been so known, particularly a renowned carving in cedarwood kept in the cathedral of Lucca, mentioned as early as 797 and widely venerated as the Cross of Lucca (Langland affirms *bi the Rode of Lukes!* in Piers Plowman, Passus VI); the Christ of Lucca wears a long velvet robe and a royal crown, which are removed on Good Friday.
See also Veronica.

Votive Mass

A Mass, not the Mass of the Day, which may be celebrated either at the choice of the priest on a day when no feast is prescribed which would take precedence and which is therefore decided by the devotion of the priest or of those who request the Mass; or at the request of the bishop for a particular and often pressing reason, e.g. the votive Mass for the election of a Pope, or for peace. The Missal contains a wide choice of votive Masses.

Votive Offerings

Any object offered in gratitude, homage or petition to God or the Blessed Virgin or a saint, usually in a public place such as a church; the candles set on the stand found in most Catholic churches are votive offerings, and the term includes historically a very wide range (model ships as at Boulogne, crutches as at Lourdes, wedding rings, jewellery and plate) and reflects an age-old instinct well represented in the temples of antiquity.

Votive Tablets

(See also Votive Offerings.) Tablets, bearing inscriptions in remembrance of favours received and placed on the wall of a shrine or church as an act of devotion and gratitude.

Vow

A vow is a solemn promise to God by which we undertake, freely and deliberately, to do some good work or to take to a more perfect state of life. (Thus, the "vow" of the Percy out of Northumberland, to hunt in Chevy Chace, was, in fact, no vow.) Private vows have their own conditions attached to them; public vows, the Vows of Religion, which are directed to the Evangelical★ Councils, are taken only after adequate preparation and testing of the candidate: thus, no religious may take final or perpetual vows immediately after novitiate, regardless of age, but only triennial (three-year) vows—except in those congregations which take only annual vows—and these may not be taken under the age of 16. The triennial vows may be renewed if the three-year period is not sufficient to bring the religious to the age of 21, under which age perpetual vows may not be taken. A diriment impediment★ to matrimony is constituted by the solemn vows of religion (as also, by privilege, by the simple vows of a Jesuit★); the simple vows of religion and private vows make a prohibitive impediment.

Vulgate

The Church's official Latin version of the Bible, declared by the Council of Trent★ the only authentic Latin text. The making of the Vulgate occupied St. Jerome★ for about 20 years, and was undertaken at the behest of Pope St. Damasus I, who was perturbed at the discrepancies found among the numerous Latin texts then extant. Beginning with the N.T., Jerome did much drastic work among the versions to dispel the confusion that had arisen from the assimilation of the Latin versions (chief of which was the *Itala Vetus*) to each other; he used, as a basis, a Greek text akin to the *Codex Sinaiticus*. For the O.T., he started by using the Septuagint* for two versions of, the Psalms, the second of which, the "Gallican Psalter" maintained its popularity over his still later "Hebrew Psalter", so that it is still the Gallican which is printed in modern editions of the Vulgate. With the help of Hebrew MSS, he totally revised the O.T.; of the Deutero-Canonical books, he seems not to have revised Wisdom, Ecclesiasticus or Maccabees, and he says he "passed over" Baruch. Once issued, the Vulgate had a very rough reception from traditionalists, and what with prejudice and the ease with which similar readings from the older versions could be unconsciously substituted for Jerome's words, and the usual crop of scribal errors, the whole enterprise almost foundered. One of those who laboured to re-establish the pure text was Alcuin, commissioned by Charlemagne; other mediaeval scholars followed, and the University of Paris issued its official, though defective, version in the 13th cent.; the first printed edition was the *Mazarin* or *Gutenberg* Bible. When Trent* made the declaration mentioned above, the text was still in need of much labour, but then, in 1590, Pope Sixtus V put out an edition which he labelled definitive, and forbade any alteration. One anomalous effect of this and later Papal prohibitions was that the best work published in this field was that of non-Catholic scholars (e.g. J. Wordsworth, Bishop of Salisbury from 1885 to 1911, H. J. White). In the interval, papal attitudes had been somewhat liberalised, and in 1908, Pius X appointed a Commission to produce a new edition of the Vulgate, which was substituted in 1933 by the Pontifical Abbey of St. Jerome for the Revision and Emendation of the Vulgate (Benedictines of the Solesmes* Congregation). Paul VI inaugurated, in 1965, the Pontifical Commission for the New Vulgate "to prepare a new Latin Bible, such as is demanded by the advances made in biblical studies and by the need to give the Church and the world a new and authoritative text of Sacred Scripture".

Walling-Up

There was current for a long time the legend, richly exploited—probably in inculpable and enthusiastic ignorance—e.g. by Scott in 'Marmion', E.B. Browning in 'The Lay of the Brown Rosary' and Rider Haggard in 'Montezuma's Daughter', that there was used in mediaeval convents the punishment of bricking up a wayward nun into a tiny cavity cut for the purpose into a wall, where she would soon die of suffocation, starvation or sheer terror. This could be a logical, if imaginitive, extension of the severity of many mediaeval penalties (cf. 'Little Ease' in the Tower of London) and perhaps a maliciously inventive transfer from the idea of the *inclusi**.

Walsingham, Our Lady of

Little Walsingham, Norfolk, became a place of pilgrimage in the 11th cent. The Lady Richeld, so the story goes, was told in a vision to build a replica of the Holy House* of Nazareth, and to this simple structure with its wooden statue of the Virgin and Child came pilgrims in large numbers, from all stations in society including Henry III and Edward I, and from many lands, so that Walsingham contributed a large share to the making of the phrase 'Dowry of Mary'*. The Augustinians and Franciscans set up houses there; at the Dissolution*, the shrine was destroyed together with the monastic buildings. The pilgrimage was revived in the last years of the 19th cent., new buildings have been erected, some built on to the remaining stones of the Augustinian priory church, and the place is now visited regularly under the auspices of both Catholic and Church of England authorities.

Ward, Mary

Foundress, in 1609, of the Institute* of (the Blessed Virgin) Mary, having spent three years as a Poor Clare. With houses already established at Vienna, Cologne, Liège and elsewhere, she went to Rome in 1629 for Papal approbation; but the un-orthodox nature of her foundation—she wanted something equivalent to the Jesuit establishment—startled the Curia, which informed her that Pius V had decreed that no congregation of women was to be set up without strict enclosure and solemn vows. Her Institute was suppressed in the same year and in the next she was imprisoned in the house of the Poor Clares at Munich; the Institute meanwhile was maintained secretly and against the Roman decree—without her consent—and when, on her release, she obtained approval from the Pope, Urban VIII, it was revived with some modifications. She spent her last years in England, dying in 1645.

Ware

St. Edmund's College, Old Hall Green, is, with Ushaw* one of the two direct descendants of the English College of Douay*. This latter, being at Rheims at the time of the Revolution, broke up into two parts to emigrate to England, one section coming to Ware, Herts, in 1793, to be housed with a boys' school first founded at Standon Lordship in 1749 under Bishop Challoner*. St. Edmund's is now the seminary of Westminster* and a boys' school.

Way of the Cross

See Stations of the Cross.

Wells of Grace

See Five Wounds.

Western Church

See Roman Church.

Western Patriarchate

A synonym for Roman Church*.

Westminster

The senior archiepiscopal see of England and Wales, consisting of the Greater London Boroughs north of the Thames and west of Waltham Forest, Newham, the boroughs of Staines and Sunbury-on-Thames, and the County of Hertfordshire; suffragans are Brentwood, Northampton, East Anglia, Nottingham, the Ukrainian Exarchate. Westminster, first made a diocese under Henry VIII in 1540 and suppressed ten years later, was chosen at the Restoration of the Hierarchy* as the one metropolitan, with twelve suffragan sees. Its archbishop is the successor, as ordinary, of Bonner, the last Roman bishop of London, who died in prison in 1569, and, as metropolitan, of Cardinal Pole, the last archbishop of Canterbury (+1558); he is also the representative of English Catholics in dealings with the civil power. Apart from the embassy* chapels in London, the main missions of any antiquity are at Isleworth (founded 1675), St. Mary Moorfields (1710), the Pro-Cathedral until 1867, that function then being transferred to Our Lady of Victories, Kensington (the 'old Pro' until 1903), Soho Square (1792), Somers Town (1798), St. Edmund's College, Ware* (1793). More ancient than any of such foundations is St. Etheldreda's, Ely Place (1297). The cathedral church of Westminister, in exotic 'early-Christian Byzantine' style, was begun in 1895 under Cardinal Vaughan and first used for his funeral in 1903. Dedicated to the Precious Blood of Our Lord, it is distinguished as the only cathedral with daily choral recitation of the entire Divine Office.

Whit, Whitsun, Whit Sunday (anciently also Whitsun Day)
(O.E. *Hwita Sunnandaeg*, White Sunday.) The popular Eng. term for Pentecost*, 'Whit' remaining a convenient adj., thus Whit Tuesday, Whit Week etc.

Whitby
The Danish name later given to Streaneshalch, where, in 659, St. Hilda founded a double monastery of men and women which rapidly became famous. Though the work of evangelising the Anglo-Saxons had gone on for the most part with success and was continuing, the chief obstacle now was dissension among the Christians: the Irish missionaries (see Celtic Church) and their Northumbrian church were in rivalry with the men from Canterbury (the Roman mission) for converts and ultimately for jurisdiction in England. In 663-4, King Oswy of Northumbria, wishing to end the disputes, called at St. Hilda's abbey a conference of the two sides, known to history as the Synod of Whitby. The King and the Abbess were of the Irish party, as were St. Colman, the Irish bishop of Lindisfarne, and St. Chad, a Northumbrian, later bishop of Lichfield; the chief proponent of the Roman view was St. Wilfrid, himself a Northumbrian, who, in having become dissatisfied with the Celtic religious life, had gone to Canterbury first and then to Rome. The chief concrete question in dispute at the Synod was the date of Easter, the Irishmen maintaining that their dating of the Pascal Feast was based on the custom of St. John, while Wilfrid prevailed, pleading the authority of St. Peter and quoting the decisions of Nicaea*. Hilda, Chad and Oswy accepted defeat equitably, Colman left Lindisfarne to spend the rest of his days in a monastry in Mayo. The importance of the Synod lay not in the settling of this difference but in the larger issue adumbrated in the symbolic arguments just referred to, the question whether the church in England was to be Roman or Celtic; the decision, which settled the Easter* Controversy for the remainder of the West, also fixed permanently the character of the English —and, ultimately, of the Irish— Church. From a personal point of view, Whitby can be regarded as part of the achievement of Wilfrid in bringing England into closer touch with Rome and Roman usages.

White Canons
The Canons Regular of Prémontré*, from their white habit.

Wilgefortis Legend, the
A mediaeval romance had for its heroine a beautiful and devout girl, Wilgefortis, who in order to avoid being married, grew a miraculous beard; unhappily married women would invoke her as St. Uncumber, (or Liberata or Livrade or Kümmernis).

Winifred, St.
(Also Winefride, Winefrid; Welsh *Gwenfrewi*.) Patron saint of N. Wales, who according to a not very trustworthy legend,

was a maiden of great virtue and beauty, slain (or perhaps only wounded) by Prince Caradog of Hawarden—who sought to marry her—when she rejected his attentions. A flow of water rose on the spot where the blow was struck, and where she was miraculously revived (or healed) at the intercession of her uncle, St. Beuno; this spring (see Holywell) is credited with similar cures to this day. The saint herself then established a convent, of which she was the first abbess; she died in 650 and in 1138 her relics were translated to Shrewsbury.

Wiseman, Nicholas Cardinal (1802–65)

An Orientalist with a position in the Vatican Library, Rector of the English College* in Rome from 1828 to 1840, Wiseman delivered in England, in 1835–6, a series of lectures on the Catholic faith which roused much interest; appointed in 1840 coadjutor to Bishop Walsh, Vicar Apostolic* of the Midland District, and, in 1847, himself Vicar Apostolic of the London District, he was chosen, on the Restoration* of the Hierarchy in 1850, to be the first Archbishop of Westminster and created cardinal. He tactfully allayed the fears and hostility which had been roused by his pastoral letter Out of the Flaminian Gate*, though he was blamed by the Catholics for introducing an Italianate spirit of devotion. His sympathy for the Oxford Movement* hardened somewhat under the influence of Manning*. His desire to see a Catholic culture in his country manifested itself in his early support of the Dublin Review and in his own widely read novel Fabiola. It was Wiseman's use, in one of his Dublin Review articles, of St Augustine's securus iudicat orbis terrarum, which sowed the first doubts in Newman's* mind about the Catholicity of the Church of England. Wiseman was taken to be the target of Browning's Bishop Blougram's Apology.

Wycliffe, John (1324–84.)

(Also Wiclif, Wyclif, Wyclyf.) Philosopher, diplomat, sometime Master of Balliol, translator of the Bible, country parish priest, condemned for heresy. He attacked certain doctrines of Duns Scotus*

and others, propounded the theory that 'lordship' or dominion i.e. authority, could not be found apart from the state of grace, and that, conversely, all Christians in a state of grace had true 'lordship'. The spectacle of the papal 'captivity' at Avignon and the Schism of the West* led him to distrust and then deny Papal authority as such, allowing in his De Potestate Papae (c.1379) no scriptural foundation for the papal claims. His anticlerical tone intensified as he later described the Pope and the hierarchy as Antichrist and their followers as the 'twelve daughters of the diabolical leech'; he belaboured the 'red and fat cheeks and great bellies' of the monks, his attacks lumping together indiscriminately pilgrimages, pluralities, reverence paid to saints, non-resident clerics, etc. Every humble and holy man, he said, should be able to read for himself the Bible, the sole criterion of faith and practice; so he undertook a translation, which he passed on, unfinished, to his followers Nicholas of Hereford and J. Purvey. In his De Eucharistia, he denied Transubstantiation*, asserting that the bread and wine remain, and that Christ becomes present in the Sacrament 'virtually' (vere et realiter, virtualiter et sacramentaliter, not substantialiter et corporaliter), as a king is present in every part of his kingdom. Wycliffe, who has been called the 'Morning Star of the Reformation', had a stronger following in Bohemia and Central Europe than anywhere else (see Lollards). He was condemned by Gregory XI in 1377 for eighteen specific errors, and again by the Blackfriars ('Earthquake') Council in London in 1382. After the posthumous condemnation by the Council of Constance, his writings were ordered to be burned, his body was dug up at Lutterworth, his last living, burned and thrown into the River Swift.

XYZ

Xaverian Brothers

A congregation of laymen in simple vows, founded by Francis Xavier Ryken at Bruges in 1839; their work is in secondary education.

York, the Use of

The version of the Roman liturgy used in the diocese and province of York before the Reformation.

Young Christian Workers

The YCW was begun in Belgium by Joseph (later Cardinal) Cardijn, the title *Jeunesse Ouvrière Chrétienne* being adopted in 1924, and spread rapidly into France, Austria, Yugoslavia, Gt. Britain, USA, Australia, Canada and many other countries. It is an effort 'to reclaim the worker for God', to revitalise the concept of work as dignity and apostolate by means of the working life itself, in the place and through the activities of work; it drew much of its inspiration from *Rerum Novarum*★ and from the experiences of the young Cardijn as seminarist and young priest, who also maintained that his work was partly motivated by discovering the strong religious character of early trade-unionism in England. The unit of the apostolate is the *section*, a small group formed in the parish or, preferably, in the place of work. In the USA, the name has been changed to Young Christian Movement.

Zucchetto

(It. *zucca*, gourd, head.) The small skull-cap worn by prelates; it dates from the 13th cent., and varies in colour according to rank: white for the Pope, scarlet for cardinals, purple for bishops, black for others.